FIRST IN
LAST OUT

The South African Artillery in Action
1975–1988

Clive
Wilsworth

30° South Publishers

Published in 2010 by 30° South Publishers (Pty) Ltd.
3 Ajax Place, 120 Caroline Street, Brixton
Johannesburg 2092, South Africa
www.30degreessouth.co.za
info@30degreessouth.co.za

Cover photo courtesy of Armscor: A G5 howitzer firing at full charge at a firing trial during the development phase. The line running from the breech to the right-hand side of the photo is the long firing lanyard used during the trials. The operational version was much shorter.

Design and origination by Melissa Schäfers

Printed and bound by Pinetown Printers, Durban

ISBN 978-1-920143-40-4

Contents

Foreword

South Africa has a rich and complex military history. Virtually all indigenous African peoples possessed armed forces of varying sizes, capabilities and traditions. The Zulu military tradition in the 19th century embodied organizational sophistication and strategic innovation that were to influence many aspects of subsequent defence doctrine. Similarly, the Boer commando tradition introduced new concepts of tactical flexibility.

These developments, as well as the role of South Africans from all backgrounds in World War I, World War II and Korea, have been well chronicled. It is only now that the history of the Border War and the freedom struggle is being told.

This book, *First in Last Out—The Story of the South African Artillery in Action 1975–1988,* provides great insight into operations such as Savannah, Protea, Daisy, Moduler, Hooper and Packer. It is not only an invaluable contribution to the recording of South Africa's military history and of the Cold War, but also provides a fascinating insight into the artillery tactics of the time. The development of the SANDF's artillery systems, which have received international recognition, is also clearly and informatively described.

At the risk of showing my bias as a fellow gunner, I believe that Clive Wilsworth deserves recognition for this well-researched and relevant book.

Major General R.C. Andersen SD SM MMM JCD
General of the Artillery

Message from the sponsor

Firstly, I would like to extend a sincere thank you to the author, Clive Wilsworth, for his energy, enthusiasm and initiative in acquiring all the available documents, personal accounts, various incidents, and for contacting all the relevant role-players who have recorded and contributed immensely towards the Southern African History and Archives.

The gunners: the South African Artillery Corps was, and is still today, a great combat unit and formation with excellent soldiers, which we are all proud to be part of and associated with—in the past, today and in the future. Friendships made then and now are forever bonded and must be cherished at all costs.

The integrated forces: all integrated South African forces worked very well with all the artillery units, and my personal experience with them all was the same. Their field disciplines were excellent, although navigation was mostly left to the artillery boys to give assistance and direction!

The conflicts of southern Africa and, more specifically, South Africa—from the Anglo-Boer War, the Battle of Blood River, the many internal tribal wars, to the full-scale conflict in southern Angola and the internal strife in South Africa—have led us to surely hope and pray that peace, harmony and joint effort from all sectors, cultures, religions and beliefs will prevail in making South Africa a nation of pride and a true example of unity to the rest of the world.

Let us not forget the past mistakes and lessons learned; to forgive and to forever remember the ones left behind on the battlefields, on both sides. May South Africa and her neighbouring countries build upon their histories and stand tall, united and unified. Let God be the point of departure in continually finding the remedy for southern Africa and the future.

Gunner Rob McGimpsey

Preface

It was a summer's afternoon in March 1999; a retired journalist and his wife walked into the Pheasant's Nest Restaurant to the east of Pretoria, needing something to quench their thirst. They had been researching the Anglo-Boer War Battle of Diamond Hill (June 1900) when they discovered the restaurant set on one of the British approaches to Diamond Hill.

I have always had a passing interest in military history, and this meeting became the trigger for more than just a passing interest—during the Anglo-Boer War, my grandfather, Willie Wilsworth, was serving with the 2nd Scottish Horse in the ubiquitous Benson's Column, which caused much mayhem in the (then) Eastern Transvaal. Willie had written a diary during this period, which I inherited and which consequently became the topic of conversation with our visiting retired journalist. Some weeks later, we had a meeting and Jan asked, 'Do you realize that your grandfather was a survivor of Bakenlaagte?' My negative answer prompted a research project as well as my membership of the Bakenlaagte centenary committee. It is strange what fate can achieve.

In 2003, after giving an illustrated talk on the Battle of Bakenlaagte to the South African Military Historical Society in Durban, I was asked by Ken Gillings (retired Regimental Sergeant-Major of Natal Field Artillery) if I would follow this up with another talk. My response was immediate, and the decision was made to present a talk on the South African Artillery's exploits in Angola.

It was a great idea at the time, but where was I to get the information I needed and how was I to compress all of it into a one-hour talk? Needless to say, I did collect a fair amount of information, some from the artillery's publication *Ultima Ratio Regum* (SADF, 1979); some from colleagues who were involved in the various battles; some from Willem Steenkamp, who was busy with the update of his book *Borderstrike*; and finally, some from my own experiences during that period. One of my biggest hurdles was the lack of war diaries—mainly attributable to the nature of the deployments, usually individual troops or independent batteries, and the short duration of operations. The other factor was the government's enthusiasm for secrecy—no cameras were allowed in the operational area and little was reported: we weren't there.

This work focuses wholly on the South African Artillery as it was during this specific period, and it does not pretend to compete with other publications and renowned military authors. It was written as a labour of love. It attempts to provide a complete history of the activities of the South African Artillery in operations from 1975 until they withdrew from operations in 1989. Included are technical issues for the die-hard gunners and for future gunners who may require reference material for their studies, as well as explanations and anecdotes throughout the text for the armchair military historian. This is not an attempt to justify being there or to make apologies for their actions. Neither does this book concern itself with who won or lost: this is purely military history.

The term 'artillery' in the South African Army refers to the surface-to-surface branch of the 'black art'. During the early 1970s, the anti-aircraft branch broke away and established a new corps, the South African Anti-Aircraft (SAAA); this is why little or no anti-aircraft activity is mentioned. The anti-tank capability was assigned to the SA Armoured Corps in the 1950s.

My thanks go out to my (then) colleagues and friends who have contributed to this work; their names are in the bibliography at the end of this book. And to Major General (Gunner) Roy Andersen, who not only encouraged me when others saw this exercise as a waste of time, but graciously and immediately agreed to write the foreword. However, there are others who helped make this work possible: Louise Jooste, Steve de Agrela and Gerald Prinsloo of the Department of Defence Archive for their professionalism and patience; my friend Rob Milne, the author of *Anecdotes of the Boer War* (Covos Day Books), who, after hearing one of my talks on the subject, prompted me to write this book; Chris Cocks, the publisher, who inspired me to finish this work; and, most importantly, Gunner Rob McGimpsey who, without any coercion, generously provided the sponsorship that greatly sped up its publication time. Part of the proceeds from this book are destined for the Gunners' Association, a charity close to our hearts.

Finally, I am truly blessed with the support of my family, especially my wife, Fio, who was left at home minding the children while I was away on operations, who never had communications with me apart from letters, was always there to support me, and sat through the numerous talks (by me), as well as helping in the archive. My eldest children, Cristina, Nikki and Adrian, who did not see much of their dad in those days. My son Stuart, who, although born on the day P and Q Batteries were attacked by the six MiGs during Moduler—too late for national service—was always available to listen to war stories and provide inputs. And, finally, my youngest daughter, Marzahn, who did sterling work with the editing—a precursor to her journalistic career.

Comments and criticisms are the views of all the contributors, mainly a product of the exact science called hindsight, but also from diaries and notes made during or just after operations. We all did a lot of growing up in those days and we did apply the lessons learned. Unfortunately, when we see what is happening in the South African Artillery of 2009, it seems that those lessons have been forgotten. One example: up until 1991, the batteries, no matter what equipment was used, had eight guns (or mortars or launchers). In an effort to cut costs the decision was made to reduce these to six guns. The question is: why? What sort of saving is this when the rest of the structure within the battery remains the same? One wonders if the 'poor bloody infantry' were asked for an opinion; if so, they would have asked for 12 guns in a battery! The quote from von Clausewitz springs to mind, 'In peace the cry is all mobility, in war, for weight of shell'. Because of the complications in providing logistic support to these small fire units (in particular, ammunition), the decision was made that nothing smaller than a regiment would be deployed on operations. The wheel has done a full 360° turn, and the South African Artillery is back to individual batteries.

Clive Wilsworth

Johannesburg, August 2010

South African Artillery Units

Listed in order of seniority, with HQ indicated in parentheses

School of Artillery (Potchefstroom)
Cape Field Artillery (Cape Town)
    1st (Amsterdam) Battery
    2nd (Imhoff) Battery
Natal Field Artillery (Durban)
    4th ('E' Force) Battery
    5th (Kings Cross) Battery
Transvaal Horse Artillery (Johannesburg)
    7th Battery
    8th Battery
    9th Battery
    10th Battery
4 Field Regiment (later 4 Artillery Regiment) (Potchefstroom)
    41 Battery
    42 Battery
    43 Battery (Walvis Bay)
    1 Medium Battery
    44 Battery
    4 Locating Battery
Transvaalse Staatsartillerie (Pretoria)
6 Field Regiment (Orange Free State Artillery Regiment) (Bloemfontein)
7 Medium Regiment (Benoni)
    71 Battery
Regiment Potchefstroom Universiteit (Potchefstroom)
14 Field Regiment (later 14 Artillery Regiment) (Potchefstroom)
    141 Battery
    142 Battery
    143 Battery
    2 Medium Battery
    144 Battery
    32 Locating Battery
17 Field Regiment (Pretoria)
18 Light Regiment (Pretoria)
    181 Battery

19 Rocket Regiment (Pretoria)
     A Troop, 191 Battery
24 Field Regiment (Durban)
25 Field Regiment (Cape Town)
26 Field Regiment (Pretoria)
27 Field Regiment (Bloemfontein)
1 Locating Regiment (Stellenbosch)
2 Locating Regiment (Johannesburg)
     22 Locating Battery
P Battery, 32 Battalion (Buffalo Base, South West Africa)
Q Battery, 4 SAI Battalion Group (Middelburg)
S Battery, 61 Mechanized Battalion Group (Omutiya, South West Africa)

Other South African Units

7 Infantry Division (Johannesburg)
8 Armoured Division (Pretoria)
10 SA Division (Oshakati—only for Operation Hilti)
Sector 10 (Oshakati)
Sector 20 (Rundu)
Sector 70 (13 Sub-Area) (Katima Mulilo)
32 Battalion (Rundu)
4 SAI Battalion Group (Middelburg)
61 Mechanized Battalion Group (Omutiya, South West Africa)
53 Battalion (South West Africa)
101 Battalion (South West Africa)
5 Signals Regiment (Pretoria)

FAPLA Brigades

7, 8, 11, 13, 14, 16, 19, 21, 25, 47, 59, 63, 66

Definitions

For those readers who are not familiar with the terminology or the battle handling of the artillery, the following are some explanations of how the gunners are organized and what some of the terms mean.

NATO symbols

After the end of World War II, NATO developed a number of standards, one of which was a set of symbols that were, and still are, used to indicate own forces (blue), allied forces (green) and the enemy (red) on maps and overlays. These symbols were adopted by the South African Defence Force (SADF) immediately and used throughout exercises and operations. The symbols that are used in this book are explained below.

Organization	Explanation	NATO map symbol	
Troop	Four guns controlled by a troop fire-control post and commanded by a troop commander.		Troop in a hide or not deployed
			Troop firing position
Battery	Two troops. This is supposed to be the smallest fire unit and is commanded by a battery commander (a major).		Battery in a hide or not deployed
			Battery firing position
Regiment	Three batteries and a support battery. The regimental commander is a lieutenant colonel.		Regimental HQ
Artillery Brigade	Really an ad hoc organization put together for a specific operation with its headquarters based on the HQ of the colonel artillery in a division.		

	Basic symbol for an artillery organization; the icon in the centre represents a cannon ball
	Infantry (motorized or light), the icon being crossed bandoliers
	Armour (tanks), the icon being a tank track
	Armour (armoured cars)
	Infantry (mechanized)

Organization sizes. The size of the organization is indicated by a set of symbols on top of its type symbol, thus:

▪ ▪ ▪	A sub-sub-unit (e.g. an artillery troop; infantry platoon; armoured-car troop)
I	A sub-unit (e.g. an artillery battery; infantry company; armoured-car squadron)
II	A unit (e.g. an artillery regiment; infantry battalion; armoured regiment)
X	A brigade

Equipment and deployment

	An artillery battery firing position; it is angled in the direction of fire, in this case, north.
	A field gun. The type of gun is shown at the bottom right of the symbol.
	A medium gun, in this case a 155mm G5
	A multiple rocket launcher (MRL)
	Mortars: left, a medium mortar (such as an 81mm); right, a heavy mortar (such as a 120mm)
	A bridge
	The defensive area of a battle group; the size symbol indicates the rear of the position

◇	armoured car
$^S\!\sqsubset\!\underset{G5}{\!\Vert\!}\!\sqsupset^{14}$	The firing position of S Bty, 14 Field Regt, equipped with G5s
⊔⊓⊔⌐	Trenches

Terms, acronyms and abbreviations

AA	anti-aircraft
Adjt	Adjutant, a captain, during operations responsible for the fire control of the regiment; call sign 0 (Zero)
BATES	British Artillery Target Engagement System
balsakke	canvas kitbags (Afrikaans)
BC	Battery Commander. The officer who commands and controls the fire and the movement of the entire battery. The official structure dictates that this officer is a major
Bde	Brigade
Bdr / L/Bdr	Bombardier / Lance Bombardier (artillery rank equivalent to corporal)
BK	Battery Captain. The officer responsible for the administration and logistics in the battery.
Bn	Battalion
BPO	Battery Position Officer
braai	barbecue (Afrikaans)
Brig	Brigadier
BSM / TSM	Battery Sergeant-Major / Troop Sergeant-Major. A posting in a battery, not a rank. Responsible for the physical replenishment of logistic support in the Bty / Tp. He organizes replenishment points to resupply ammunition, water, rations, fuel and other related items
Bty	Battery
Capt	Captain
CB	counter-bombardment

CF	Citizen Force
CFA	Cape Field Artillery
Cmdt	Commandant. South African rank equivalent to lieutenant colonel (changed to Lt-Col after 1994)
Col	Colonel
Cpl	Corporal
CSIR	Council for Scientific and Industrial Research
CTH	Cape Town Highlanders
DF	defensive fire
DLI	Durban Light Infantry
Div	Division
EFC	equivalent full charge
EW	electronic warfare
FAPA	Angolan Air Force (Força Aérea Popular de Angola)
FAPLA	armed wing of the MPLA (Forças Armadas Populares de Libertação de Angola)
FCP	fire-control post
Fd	Field. A classification of artillery ordnance—guns less than 120mm that are not air-droppable. However, the term is also generally used to differentiate between the three branches of artillery: field, locating and anti-aircraft. Later, some field units were renamed 'artillery' (e.g. 14 Artillery Regt)
FLOT	Ffront Line of Own Troops. The most forward positions of units in relation to the enemy
FOO	Forward Observation Officer
FNLA	National Front for the Liberation of Angola (Frente Nacional de Libertação de Angola)
FSCO	Fire Support Co-ordination Officer. This officer (a major) deploys in the Regt (and / or Arty Bde) tactical HQ at the sharp end and co-ordinates the fire and movement of the batteries under command. He is also responsible for safety of own troops, including own aircraft flying in the combat zone. He determines the rules regarding safety issues, such as no-fire areas; zones of fire; fire-support co-ordination lines (the line past which own aircraft may attack ground targets), etc.

Gen	General
Gnr	Gunner (equivalent to private / trooper / rifleman)
GOC	General Officer Commanding
GPO	Gun Position Officer. The officer in control of the fire of the ordnance at the blunt end. Reports to Troop Commander
GPS	global positioning system
Gunners	collective term used for members of the artillery irrespective of their rank
HAA	helicopter administrative area
HE	high explosive
HF	high frequency / harassing fire
ICV	infantry combat vehicle
IDF	Israel Defence Forces
L/Cpl	Lance Corporal
Loc	Locating
Log	logistics
Lt / 2/Lt	Lieutenant / Second Lieutenant
lt	a classification of artillery ordnance—guns of any calibre that are air-droppable
Lt-Col	Lieutenant-Colonel
LWT	Light Workshop Troop
Maj	Major
med	medium, classification of artillery ordnance—guns of 121mm to 160mm
met	meteorological
MPLA	ruling party in Angola (Movimento Popular de Libertação de Angola)
MPV	multi-purpose vehicle
MRL	multiple rocket launcher
NBC	nuclear, biological and chemical
NCO	Non-Commissioned Officer

NFA	Natal Field Artillery
NSM	national serviceman / men
OC	Officer Commanding
OP	observation post
OPA	Observation-Post Assistant (a trained artillery technical assistant, usually a bombardier)
OPO	Observation-Post Officer
ops	operations
ordnance	collective term for guns, mortars or rocket launchers
OT	observer-to-target distance
POW	prisoner of war
PF	Permanent Force
QF	quick-firing
ratpack	soldier's ration pack
Regt	Regiment
RV	rendezvous
Rfn	Rifleman
RGK	Regiment Groot Karoo
RHQ	Regimental Headquarters
RPG	rocket-propelled grenade
RPU	Regiment Potchefstroom Universiteit
RPV	remotely piloted vehicle
RSM	Regimental Sergeant-Major. The senior WO in the regiment, usually a WOI
SAA	South African Artillery
SAAF	South African Air Force
SADF	South African Defence Force
SAM	surface-to-air missile
Sgt / S/Sgt	Sergeant / Staff Sergeant
shona	open pan which becomes muddy in rainy season

sitrep	situation report, a daily report on the enemy and own forces' tactical situation.
SO / SO1	Staff Officer / Staff Officer Grade 1
SP	self-propelled
SWA	South West Africa (Namibia)
SWAPO	South West Africa People's Organization
SWATF	South West African Territory Force
TA	technical assistant
takkies	South African term for rubber-soled sports shoes
Tp	Troop
Tp Cmdr	Troop Commander. The officer who commands and controls the fire and the movement of an artillery troop. The official structure dictates that this officer is a captain
Tp Lr	Troop Leader. A subaltern responsible for the fire discipline and routine (such as camouflage, rest, meals, local defence, etc.) on the gun position. This officer would command the movement of the ordnance group of the troop during movement
THA	Transvaal Horse Artillery
TSA	Transvaalse Staatsartillerie
TSC	Technical Services Corps
TSM	Troop Sergeant-Major
UNITA	National Union for the Total Independence of Angola (União Nacional para a Independência Total de Angola), Jonas Savimbi's rebel movement
veld	open grassland (Afrikaans)
WO	Warrant Officer. The formal rank, the form of address being sergeant-major
WP	white phosphorus
2IC	Second in Command

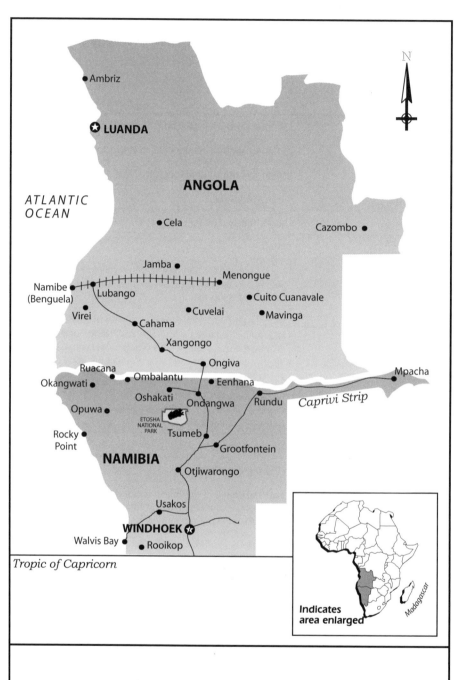

Northern South West Africa (Namibia)
and Angola

Chapter 1

A brief background to the build-up

Angola

Until 1974, Angola and Mozambique were Portuguese colonies. In Angola the war of liberation had been raging for over a decade; the main factions ranged against the Portuguese government were UNITA, FNLA and MPLA. These three forces were backed by the Soviets and the Chinese in one form or another.

During 1975, after a drastic change in government in Lisbon, the Portuguese, at almost no notice, pulled out of Angola and at the same time backed the MPLA as the de facto Angolan government. The date for independence was set at 11 November 1975: a date to remember as the first part of this story unfolds. At about that time, the three liberation organizations were deployed as follows:

- The MPLA in the central area, including Luanda, the capital
- The FNLA in the north
- UNITA in the central, south and east

South Africa, at that time, had the United Nations / League of Nations mandate to govern South West Africa (now Namibia) and that country was, therefore, *ipso facto* a province of South Africa. By implication, the state of affairs immediately to the north of South West Africa was a matter for concern, especially as the CIA had passed warnings on to Pretoria and had intimated that South Africa might need to get involved to chase out the communists. There is no clear picture as to which foreign armed forces entered Angola first, the Cubans or the South Africans, not that it matters for the purposes of this work: the fact is they were both there and both stayed there until 1988/89.

The South African Artillery (SAA) started with a thinned-out troop deploying two 5.5-inch guns and ended with a full artillery brigade in 1988.

Rhodesia

During the 1970s and up to 1980, Rhodesia was effectively in a state of war, the main proponents being the Smith government, ZANU and ZAPU, the former supported by South Africa and the latter two by the Chinese and Soviets respectively. South Africa provided limited military support, and economic and trade support. The military support came primarily from the South African Air Force (SAAF) in the form of Alouette helicopters along with their crews and support, and C-47 Dakotas on occasion. The SAA provided help in the form of training—Rhodesian Artillery Officers and NCOs attended courses at the School of Artillery in Potchefstroom with their South African counterparts. There was obviously also a free exchange of ideas and doctrine, an example being a visit by the senior members of the Natal Field Artillery to the Rhodesians in 1978.

From time to time, there were visits by the gunner Permanent Force officers and there were members seconded to the 'Rhodies' as advisers and liaison officers. Only in early 1980 did a battery mobilize for duty in support of the Rhodesian Army during the elections.

Geography

The border with Namibia varies in topography from the Cunene River in the west, running between steep gorges, to a river in the east, the Cubango (or Kavango), which lazily runs across flat country, finally to the man-made border between the two rivers, stretching 450 kilometres, which comprises two cutlines, or roads, 1 kilometre apart and a fence. From this border, for about 300 kilometres northwards, the country is flat with very few hills or even high ground. As we move farther northward, the vegetation changes from short grassland and palm trees to thick bush with trees averaging around 5 metres in height and thick undergrowth. The coastal belt is hilly, but interspersed with estuaries and mud flats. The central area is hilly (in fact mountainous) in parts and rich in vegetation—once known as 'Africa's breadbasket'—with plentiful water.

The eastern area where the bulk of operations took place is extremely flat with little high ground. However, the whole area is interspersed with rivers and streams and their characteristic, wide floodplains. The central area is covered with *shonas*, or open, dry pans (in winter) covered only in knee-high grass, and changing to muddy pans in summer. Roads are few and tarred roads even less so.

Place names

After independence, a number of place names changed from the Portuguese to their original or indigenous names. During the early operations, the South Africans used Portuguese names (as they were on the contemporary maps), but this changed as time went on. For clarity, the old and new names are set out below.

Portuguese name	Post-independence name
Ambrizette	N'Zeto
Cela	Waku Kungo
Luso	Luena
Nova Lisboa	Huambo
Nova Redondo	Sumbe
Pereira d'Eca	Ongiva
Robert Williams	Ca'ala
Sa da Bandeira	Lubango
Santa Comba	Waku Kungo
Serpa Pinto	Menongue
Silva Porto	Kuito
Teixeira da Sousa	Luau
Vila Roçades	Xangongo

South Africa's military

Despite the rumblings of the anti-apartheid movement and the rest of the world, the SADF at the time was not prepared for war, particularly one of a conventional nature.

Conventional warfare doctrine at that time was based on that of the British Army, and only some years later was the Israeli concept of combined arms warfare (invented by the Germans) inculcated into South African doctrine. It is true that the SADF was prepared for unconventional operations, but those operations are reliant on intelligence and infantry on the ground. The SAAF had just taken delivery of their new Mirage F1s, but the rest of the force lagged behind in technology and armament. The army was in the process of developing the Ratel Infantry Fighting Vehicle, but this would only be ready three years later.

It must be said, however, that the army was already reorganizing itself for conventional operations in that the concept of a corps (1 SA Corps) with two divisions (7 Infantry Division and 8 Armoured Division) and corps troops (maintenance units, signals units etc.) was in the process of being realized and the subordinate brigades were being formed. By 1975, 72 Brigade was the formation that was best prepared.

The Armoured Corps was equipped with Eland armoured cars (60 and 90mm) and tanks were virtually non-existent, as the old Centurion Mk Vs had been sold off years before. However, the purchase and upgrading of the Centurions was underway, albeit under difficult conditions, since the arms embargo was being enforced.

At that stage, the artillery was equipped as it had been at the end of the Second World War, the only difference being that batteries comprised eight guns rather than six. The units in the various brigades were field regiments, meaning that they were equipped with 25-pounder guns towed by Bedford gun tractors. Fire-control posts were still forward-drive Land Rovers ('gin palaces'), and the sharp-end teams drove around in Land Rovers or Jeep Gladiators. The divisional artillery units were medium regiments equipped with 140mm (5.5 inch) guns towed by Magirus Deutz gun tractors.

Target acquisition was done by artillery officers trained on maps and compass, and ballistic calculation was still driven by the artillery board, logarithmic tables and the slide rule. Life was not all log tables, however—a great deal of help came from the graphic instruments designed for the British guns. These included the displacement calculator, an aid that was used to determine the angle of sight to be applied to the guns when there was a difference in height between gun position and target. This instrument also calculated the 'displacement' of the guns that were deployed away from the battery centre should the guns be required to converge their fire, that is, each gun would be given its own individual bearing and range so that all guns would fire on the same spot on the ground. Normally, the guns are laid parallel to one another, thus the target covered would be the same as the width of the battery front.

Electronic calculators and computers were not available in those days, and meteorological data was calculated by the meteorological graph, a short name for a calculator set, correction of the moment. Readings from the radiosonde under a meteorological balloon were plotted onto the graphs— one graph for each charge—and the meteorological corrections read off from there. These graphic instruments were replaced in the late 1970s with Hewlett Packard 21C, 11C, and 29C electronic programmable calculators for ballistic calculation and the Texas Instruments Ti 59 for survey.

This book intentionally does not cover the history of the regiments of the South African Artillery, but an overview of the situation preceding hostilities is necessary here. Chapter 2 covers the main equipment of the time.

The role of the artillery was, and still is, to provide indirect fire support to the manoeuvre forces (infantry and armour) on the battlefield. This fire support, naturally, was not the exclusive right of those manoeuvre forces, and other arms also benefited from such fire support (engineers building a bridge, for example). In order to provide this fire support, targets needed to be identified and plotted on a map (fixed) and, therefore, the guns (field artillery) were supported by the locating artillery (often referred to by the nickname 'black-magic gunners').

In 1974, the South African Artillery comprised the following units, as shown overleaf (their home bases shown in parentheses):

- School of Artillery (Potchefstroom)
- Cape Field Artillery (Cape Town)
- Natal Field Artillery (Durban)
- Transvaal Horse Artillery (Johannesburg)
- 4 Field Regiment (Potchefstroom)
- Transvaalse Staatsartillerie (Pretoria)
- 6 Field Regiment (Orange Free State Field Artillery) (Bloemfontein)
- 7 Medium Regiment (Benoni)
- Potchefstroom University Regiment (Potchefstroom)
- 14 Field Regiment (Potchefstroom) (re-established in late 1974)
- 17 Field Regiment (Pretoria)
- 1 Locating Battery (Stellenbosch)
- 2 Locating Battery (Johannesburg)
- 3 Locating Battery (Potchefstroom)

The School of Artillery, 4 Field Regiment, 14 Field Regiment, and 3 Locating Battery were the only full-time units at that time and were responsible for the training of Permanent Force and national service personnel. The School of Artillery also had the responsibility of training Citizen Force (CF) officers and NCOs, as well as CF units when called up for training camps. During the reorganization of the army, the CF units were attached to the brigades. 7 Medium Regiment and Transvaalse Staatsartillerie were attached as divisional troops to 7 and 8 Divs respectively, and, therefore, were both medium regiments. The two locating batteries were upgraded to locating regiments, each assigned to a division (1 Locating Regiment to 8 Division and 2 Locating Regiment to 7 Division). As well as the old but serviceable equipment, the other determining factor was training. Training exercises for both Permanent and Citizen Force units were conducted in Potchefstroom because that was the only place where the gunners could train, as the General de la Rey firing range provided both sufficient range and tactical features to allow combat simulation, navigation and target acquisition practice. The Army Battle School was only established in 1978. The practice of the sharp-end teams (observation posts) deploying on top of hills with the comfort of 'chairs, officers', canvas, folding', and a supply of wet rations straight from the field kitchen was very well entrenched, and camouflage was nice, but tended to interfere with the day's shoot. The older CF regiments were more like old boys' clubs, and life centred on the mess during continuous and non-continuous training periods alike. Traditions abounded (and still do to this day) to the point that an outsider would be forgiven for thinking that he or she had been miraculously transported into a British establishment. These 'traditional' units scorned the newer units, which tended to take on a more realistic approach to training.

This attitude changed rather rapidly when war became a reality, and was not exclusive to the artillery, but was fairly general throughout the army. In their defence however, the traditions were carried over from the old colonial days and actively maintained by a cadre of officers and senior NCOs, who, through no fault of their own, had never seen active service and were serving in an army that had stagnated for more than 20 years since the cessation of hostilities in 1945. While all this was going on, the SADF was deploying small contingents on the South West African–Angolan border, and place names like Rundu and Ruacana were becoming better known.

Despite the fact that this book is intended to cover the operations of the South African Artillery deployed in its primary role, the story of the first casualties inflicted by enemy action is worth telling, as it helps to bring the war into context, and it happened during the period covered by this work.

In October 1975, 4 Field Regiment was deployed in the counter-insurgency role (as motorized infantry) in the eastern theatre in three bases around Katima Mulilo, then known as 13 Sub-Area. 42 Battery, under the command of Captain Carel Theron, was deployed as an infantry company and based at Kwando in the Caprivi Strip.

On 12 November, Lieutenant Brand's platoon was tasked to move out to set up an ambush on a known SWAPO infiltration route at a point some five to six hours' drive north of Luiana (23.00 E; 17.25 S). In order to reinforce the firepower of the platoon, Bombardier Duncan Mattushek volunteered to join this patrol. In addition, the splendidly named Second Lieutenant Christopher Robin, himself a platoon commander, volunteered to drive one of the vehicles back after dropping off the ambush party. The platoon was further reinforced by Rifleman Schonfeldt and his tracker dog, Rinty. The plan of action was to drive the ambush party to a point where they would debus and then continue on foot to the selected ambush site, the vehicles would retire to a safe area in order to collect the troops afterwards. The next day, the platoon departed Kwando base in two vehicles, a Hippo (an early mine-protected vehicle based on a Bedford chassis, nicknamed by one young outspoken gunner a year or two after this as 'an Apostolic Church on wheels', and a Unimog. The Unimog was driven by Gunner Huisamen, with Lieutenant Robin in the passenger seat on the right. (Almost all the Unimogs in South African service at that time were left-hand drive and none had any form of significant mine protection.) The Hippo was driven by Gunner Retief. The troops were distributed between the two vehicles with the mine-protected Hippo in the lead. Mattushek continues the story:

> All I can remember was a massive flash and then darkness. This was at about 17h00 on 13 November. I remember waking up and looking at my right hand with the full moon in the background and seeing all this skin hanging from it. I could not feel my left arm at all. Neither could I feel the rest of my body, [which] had been severely burnt as well.

All the troops on the Unimog were blown off the vehicle. Bombardier Mattushek, who was above the fuel tank, took the impact of the burning diesel. Gunner Hennie Bekker, himself blown off the stricken Unimog, with burnt hands, ran back to pull Bombardier Mattushek out of the inferno, thus probably saving the latter's life. Lieutenant Brand issued instructions for the care of the wounded and ran to move Lieutenant Robin, who, critically injured, was lying close to the burning Unimog. Despite this apparent chaos, Brand still issued orders for a perimeter defence and then tried to save Robin. By this time, the medical orderly had reported that the medical bag had been burnt and to make matters worse, the platoon radio had also been destroyed. Lieutenant Robin died of his injuries some 15 minutes after the mine explosion. Lieutenant Brand by this stage found himself sitting with the wounded and reading to them from Psalm 138. Because of the now total lack of radio communication back to base, Gunner Nel was dispatched with the Hippo to fetch help. In Mattushek's words:

Lieutenant Brand went to assess the firepower they had left and found that, of the 27 troops with rifles, they only managed to salvage seven rifles and some ammunition. Presuming that the helicopters would arrive shortly to casevac the dead and wounded, he then set about setting up a landing zone by marking it with weighed-down bundles of toilet paper. He also made piles of grass to light if the helicopters came in after sunset. Lieutenant Brand also had to chase away a herd of elephants that had wandered into the area later on. They waited all night for reinforcements to arrive.

At 07h00 the next morning, two helicopters arrived to evacuate the dead and wounded. Lieutenant Brand asked the aircrews for their rifles and to call for reinforcements. The wounded were undergoing surgery 23 hours later at 1 Military Hospital in Pretoria. Two hours after the helicopters left, a group of 70 SWAPO insurgents attacked the remnants of the platoon, their attack supported by RPG-7s and mortars. The gunners withdrew tactically as best they could under cover of fire from Brand, Gunner Retief and Rifleman Schonfeldt, with two of the withdrawing gunners being wounded in the process. Fortunately, on discovering the burnt-out Unimog, SWAPO pulled out; an awesome quiet followed. Brand found the bodies of Retief and Schonfeldt, both of whom had been shot, together with Rinty the tracker dog. It is notable that Retief and Schonfeldt were more than likely injured initially, but were killed by point-blank fire from the SWAPO group. Brand stayed with the dead through another night to protect the bodies from wild animals. Only the next morning did the helicopters collect the three men. During this period, the Hippo had duly arrived back in base. Gunner Nel reported to Captain Theron, who immediately packed rifles into the only available ambulance and set out to help Lieutenant Brand. En route, the ambulance suffered a blowout. Despite this, he continued, but by last light, realized that he would be in no condition to repel any form of attack and turned back for base. Bombardier Mattushek lost both arms, Gunner Nieuwenhuys was badly burnt, and two others were badly wounded. It is interesting to note that, despite Brand's leadership and actions under those conditions, he was never cited for any award or recognition—a shameful performance by the senior leader.

Chapter 2

Some explanations: adding a little colour

'The artillery adds a little colour to what would
otherwise be known as vulgar brawl.'
—Frederick the Great

Deployment

Because of the nature of its business, that is, providing indirect fire support, the artillery deploys both widely and deeply on the battlefield. It was not uncommon for batteries to be deployed upwards of 20 kilometres apart, with distances of more than 20 kilometres between observers and guns. The sketch below will provide some clarity.

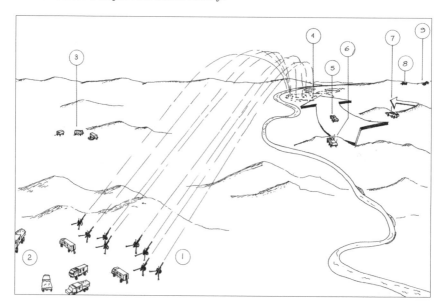

This sketch is intended to portray a simplified battery deployment, and shows the relationship between the so-called sharp end (the target area and the observers) and the blunt end (the ordnance and the rest of the battery). The battery commander (6) is usually located with the supported force (a battalion of infantry or an armoured regiment) commander. The troop commanders (7, 8) usually deploy in a relatively static position with the OPOs (5, 9), mobile and located with the attacking troops, their primary function to provide fire support and be constantly mindful of the safety of their own troops. When an OPO (observation-post officer) team is deployed with the assault troops it is usually referred to as the forward observation officer (FOO) team. These teams either 'leapfrog' one another or 'step up', rather like the movement of a caterpillar, and it can be understood how critical are communications between these teams. A communication failure may result in the catastrophic failure of a mission and the loss of one's own forces' lives by own fire (now known as 'blue on blue'). In a lot of operations the artillery deployed the static (or anchor) OPO in an aircraft, with the FOO on foot. It was also not uncommon for battery commanders to dismount and infiltrate between or behind enemy lines.

The range from guns (1) to target area (4) varies between 6,000 and 27,000 metres—this depends not only on the type of ordnance being used, but also the type of fire mission. Typically, a defensive fire plan and counter-bombardment fire is fired at maximum range; preparatory bombardment at medium ranges; and close fire support at medium to short ranges in order to achieve the best accuracy and, therefore, to minimize the possibility of a safety risk.

At the blunt end (2), we find the gun tractors, ammunition vehicles, and the A Echelon with the recovery vehicles, ambulance, battery sergeant-major and other support vehicles and equipment. All of these teams use radio to communicate with each other and, of course, their supported forces. A traditional (and still used) term for the area occupied by the gun tractors is the 'wagon lines'.

To give one an idea of the space occupied by a battery, the ordnance deploys approximately 50 metres apart, with the fire-control posts about

50 metres behind them where the blunt end occupies an area of approximately 450 metres wide by 600 metres deep. The three batteries in a regiment can deploy with spaces of 1 to 2 kilometres between them. The blunt end does not have to wait for the sharp end to deploy—usually they are given a grid square and time to be in action. A recce party (3) moves ahead of the ordnance (guns) group to find a suitable position and commence survey. The gun platforms (a steel marker) are laid out and the ordnance group is called to deploy, whereupon the centre of arc (the bearing from the battery to the centre of the target area) is given out and the guns orientated. Ammunition is unpacked and prepared, and the blunt end reports ready to the sharp end—a time-consuming activity often ignored by the supported commanders.

This sketch has been deliberately kept simple. For example, the attacking infantry and armour are not shown at all. Instead, the large arrow indicates the axis of attack and the smaller arrow the direct fire support base. In this scenario, one of the troop commanders (8) is deployed in readiness to fire on depth targets after the attack, and the other OPO (9) is deployed to observe enemy activities on the right flank, in preparation for any counter-attack.

Ordnance

The only ordnance in use by the South African Artillery at the commencement of hostilities in 1975 were the QF (quick-firing) 25-pounder gun howitzer and the BL (breech-loading) 5.5-inch medium gun / howitzer. The 25-pounder was first developed in the UK for the Royal Artillery in 1933 to replace the 18-pounder used in the First World War. Late in World War II, the 25-pounder was upgraded to a Mark II version by adding a muzzle brake and a turntable. It was this Mark II gun that served in the South African Artillery until 1990. During the 1980s, the nomenclature of this equipment in South African service was changed to QF 88mm GV1. The G1 was manned by a detachment (crew) of six, each member being known by their position in action, thus:

- The Number 1: The commander of the gun.
- The Number 2: The breech operator and responsible for ramming the projectile.

- The Number 3: The layer.
- The Number 4: An ammunition number responsible for loading both projectile and cartridge case.
- The Number 5: An ammunition number.
- The Number 6: An ammunition number and also responsible for setting time fuses when used. This number was also the *de jure* second in command of the gun.

Added to this six-man crew was the driver, who remained with his gun tractor at all times (except when required to help move ammunition forward).

The G1 had a maximum range of 13,000 yards (11,900 metres) and fired high explosive (HE) and screening smoke shells with a variety of fuses. Because it was a quick-firing (QF) gun, it made use of a brass cartridge case to seal the hot gas in the breech (obturation) when firing.

The bigger stable-mate was the BL 5.5-inch medium gun howitzer designed in the early 1940s in the UK and used in World War II. In South Africa this gun was later named BL 140mm GV2. The G2 weighed 7 tonnes and was served by a detachment of ten men.

The guns in South African service were a mixture of British and Canadian manufactures and were purchased from a number of countries, including Portugal, over time. This gun was arguably the most accurate and consistent medium gun in the world. It was ideally suited to point destruction shoots, where extreme, almost pinpoint, accuracy was required.

The HE shell weighed 80 pounds (36 kilograms), the smoke shell 100 pounds (45 kilograms). The G2 could fire these shells out to a maximum range of 18,000 yards (16,500 metres).

The G2 was termed a breech-loading gun, as its propellant gas sealing (obturation) was achieved by a seal, or obturating ring, in the interrupted screw breech, therefore the charge was contained in bags and not in a brass case.

Despite its vintage, the much-loved G2 served the South African gunners right through to the end of hostilities in 1988 when it was retired as more G5s came into service.

Ballistic calculation

Before the advent of computers, all prediction and calculation was done by the artillery board, range tables and either logarithmic tables or the slide rule. Added to this, were the displacement calculator and meteorological graphs, all of which were designed for use by both G1 and G2 guns and dated back to World War II. In these modern times, one wonders how much time was required for all this calculation and what accuracy could be expected. The fact is that it worked quickly and it worked well in all conditions, day and night. Technical assistants were thoroughly trained and every result was checked before sending fire orders to the guns.

Survey and deployment: a misunderstood activity

During the 1970s and up to the mid-1980s, there was no such thing as satellite navigation or GPS. Navigation was done by compass, map and protractor—which is fine when one is on a training exercise at Potchefstroom or at the Army Battle School at Lohatla. However, the bulk of the South African Artillery's operations were conducted in Namibia or southern Angola where the contour lines on 1:50,000 maps are indicated in 10-metre intervals (sub-contours). The trees in the forested areas were all the same height so it was futile to climb a tree in order to improve observation, as all one could see was another tree. At that time, artillery survey was done by trigonometry using the survey troop of a locating regiment equipped with theodolites and tellurometers (range finders), together with brightly coloured beacon banderols to mark the survey points. Although all troop commanders learned this science during their promotion course from lieutenant to captain, it was not applied during operations for the reasons above. However, the practice of 'battery survey' was exercised, the principle being the same, but the accuracy slightly diminished. Regimental survey would provide a 12-figure grid reference that was accurate to 1 centimetre, whereas battery survey would provide an eight-figure grid reference with an accuracy of 10 metres. The process of deployment into a firing position was as follows:

- The battery reconnaissance team would be given a grid square (1,000 x 1,000 metres) in which to find a suitable firing position. There were— and still are—certain additional factors to take into account before summarily selecting a piece of ground on which to deploy, including camouflage and concealment; communications; drainage (heavy equipment does get bogged down); and space to deploy.

- This team would travel by vehicle (at least three) to the deployment area, where they would dismount and prepare the position for the ordnance.

- The battery position officer (BPO) would indicate the two troop positions, the 'wagon lines' (the area, usually behind the guns, where the gun tractors and ammunition vehicles would deploy) and areas of responsibility for all-round defence.

- The two troop leaders, with their technical assistant sergeants, would set up their main theodolites and start the process of orientation.

- The gun theodolite is orientated by using its built-in compass; magnetic deflection is subtracted; the instrument is then laid in grid north (that is, the same north as shown on the map).

- During this process, the gun platform markers are laid out, indicating the position of each gun in the troop as well as the position of the fire-control post.

- The ordnance group (fire-control post and the guns) are instructed to occupy the position. The instruction can be either by radio or by sending the troop sergeant-major back to fetch them.

- Each gun is towed to its platform marker and comes into action, with the barrel facing in the approximate direction of the target area.

- The command 'aiming point theodolite' is given and the guns turn their sights onto the theodolite, whereupon they are given an angle on which to set their sights. Once the guns are laid on the theodolite they are all laid in the same direction (or bearing) and are parallel to one another.

- In the meantime, the gun position officer (later known as the fire-control officer) and his team prepare for receiving fire orders and calculating gun data. In those days, calculation was done by a hand-held programmable calculator, backed up by an artillery board.
- Simultaneously, the gun crews would unload ammunition, dig trenches or foxholes, camouflage and prepare for the fire mission.
- Once unloaded, the gun tractors would be led to their allocated positions in the wagon lines where they would camouflage, and prepare for a hasty getaway if so ordered.

This deployment drill was time-consuming and took anything from 30 minutes to two hours depending on the terrain and the time of day. Night occupations took longer because they were usually done without lights and often in radio silence.

The influence of meteorological conditions

A shell, or projectile fired from a gun over long ranges, is affected by the meteorological conditions as it travels through the air. For example, a headwind will cause the shell to fall short of the intended target; similarly, an increase in air pressure will slow that shell down, creating the same effect.

The firing tables prepared by the gun designers are based on conditions at sea level at a specific temperature—these are known as 'standard conditions'. As a result, the conditions at the firing position need to be measured and applied in order to increase the probability of first-round hits.

These factors are:

- Height above sea level
- Air temperature
- Air pressure
- Wind speed and direction.

To complicate matters even more, a rocket, while its motor is still burning, will 'weathercock' into the prevailing wind; consequently, rocket units need to measure what is known as 'active wind' in order to compensate for this phenomenon. All these actions need to be planned before deployment and taken into consideration when 'H' hour is to be determined.

Unfortunately, during the period of operations, the South African Artillery's meteorological support was not readily available—the main reason being that the balloon tracking equipment was not designed for the hot, dusty, rough conditions in the operational area.

The effect of this shortcoming was the practice of adjusting fire (also known as 'ranging') onto targets. This practice naturally warns the enemy in the target area and will cause him to take cover, thereby diminishing the effect required by one's fire.

Sound ranging

In 1972, the British Second World War vintage system was still in use by the SAA. This system comprised seven microphones deployed over a distance of 12 kilometres and connected by some 25 kilometres of twin-flex (Don 10) cable to a receiver in a command post. Each microphone had to be surveyed in to an accuracy of 2 metres, which involved a long, painstaking (by today's standards) survey process. The brains behind the system was the Azimtote board—a graphic representation of the incoming sound waves. This board took four hours to set up and about seven minutes to plot a hostile battery after the last microphone had registered the bang.

Plessey in the UK provided the new radio link Mk II system in 1974. This was essentially the same as the older model, but used a radio link instead of the Don 10 cable, thus making it marginally quicker to deploy.

Despite its accuracy and usefulness to the gunners, it was not popular with the cordite gunner community, who saw this long deployment time as a severe limitation.

Major Steve van Aswegen of the School of Artillery visited Germany in the early 1970s and brought back a training film showing how a cluster of three microphones, set out in a triangle, could determine the bearing to an enemy gun. This led to a semi-permanent test site being set up on the firing range in Potchefstroom. Here it was found that the existing receiver was too slow to collect accurate data. This prompted Captain Faan Bothma to replace the receiver with an oscilloscope obtained from the nearby signals unit and, hey presto, the system worked! Eventually, the Council for Scientific and Industrial Research (CSIR) was contracted to develop a local system that saw more action in (then) Rhodesia than in the South African Army. The Rhodesians mounted the microphones on poles in the Umtali area (eastern border), where they were connected by telephone line to the command post, and used in order to provide data to the helicopter gunships of the reaction force. This story is continued in Chapter 12.

Mortar-locating radar

Of all the locating systems in the artillery in the 1960s and 1970s, the most useful was probably the mortar-locating radar. Both the Green Archer and Cymbeline radar sets were manufactured in the UK and sold (then legally) to South Africa. Green Archer was never used on operations because it had become obsolete by then and had been replaced by Cymbeline in the early 1970s. Cymbeline was, at the time, a very advanced system. It was modular, lightweight and easy to move and deploy. Despite this, it still relied on survey for accurate fixation, but at least it could be surveyed in by battery survey to a 10-metre accuracy. Therefore, it could deploy as fast as the guns it was supporting. Its greatest disadvantage was that it was not designed for the rough and tough southern African theatre of operations; overheating was a constant problem. Cymbeline was wheeled and intended to be towed by a light vehicle such as a Land Rover. In the operational area, however, the rough roads precluded such activities, and the radar sets were generally porteed on the back of 10-tonne cargo vehicles.

Mortar-locating radar works on the principle that a mortar bomb, when in flight, has a parabolic trajectory. Therefore, the upward path of the bomb is exactly the same as the downward path. The radar picks up the bomb on its downward path and calculates where the offending mortar is. This data is given to the guns and counter-bombardment then follows.

The Cymbeline was deployed in most of the early operations and this is detailed in the relevant chapters.

Vehicles

During the 1970s, the gun tractor allocated to the medium batteries was the Magirus Deutz, an air-cooled diesel with a 6x6 drive. Later on, they were replaced by the Samil 100, a 10-tonne gun tractor based on the later Deutz and built in South Africa.

The shortage in equipment in those days lay in the command and control vehicles, specifically fire-control posts, reconnaissance vehicles and observation vehicles.

Fire-control posts in the operational areas in the 1970s were Unimog 416 vehicles, which, in standard configuration, were vulnerable to mines. This weakness was overcome by packing a sandwich of rubber conveyor belting between two layers of sandbags onto the cargo area, and replacing both the driver and passenger seats with sandbags. This arrangement provided a buffer against the blast of an anti-tank mine, as well as extra weight to reduce the possibility of the vehicle being lifted by the blast. The Unimog was not designed for such modifications, and, at that time, the SADF would not allow permanent modifications on vehicles despite the impracticalities of the original design. Inside the vehicle the gunners placed a 6-foot folding table on which the artillery technical equipment was set out. The A55 manpack / B56 vehicle radio was the medium for VHF communications, but, as no drilling of holes or welding was allowed, the fire-control officer had to be content with A55 radios in their carry harnesses strapped to the roof rails or sides of their vehicles. One must also bear in mind that these radios were battery-powered from disposable batteries and not equipped with amplifiers or antennae-tuning units, as were their vehicle-mounted siblings. The result: weak or non-existent communication between sharp end and blunt end.

Recce vehicles in the training bases were Land Rovers (109 inch), which, under those conditions, were adequate for the job. The operational area was a different situation and necessitated mine protection. The only vehicle available in sufficient numbers was the ubiquitous Buffel MPV, a Unimog chassis topped with a mine-protected hull and driver's compartment. Originally designed as an infantry-section carrier, it was fitted with ten outward-facing seats bolted onto a strong frame in the centre of the cargo area. Further protection was provided by a rollover bar above the occupants' heads and a water tank under the floor as blast protection (and for drinking water). The driver's cab was fully enclosed and separate from the crew at the rear, reducing the possibility of verbal communication between the vehicle commander and the driver. To make matters worse, the commander and crew faced outwards and not forward, as would be expected, and for good reason, they had to be strapped in with full harness seat belts. This vehicle would be expected to carry the troop recce party of four people plus their technical equipment, radios and personal kit. Thus was born a rough-and-ready form of transport unsuited for the intended use and one that was vulnerable—as the reader will see later in this work.

The sharp-end personnel were a little better off in that they were equipped with Eland 60mm armoured cars. The Eland was a locally upgraded version of the Panhard AML, having a four-cylinder, water-cooled GM petrol engine in place of the original French engine. The 60mm variant was equipped with a 60mm breech-loading mortar and a 7.62mm Browning machine gun fitted to a turret with a single, large hatch, making it better suited to observation than any other vehicle at the time. The drawback was that these vehicles were never issued to artillery units so familiarization was, at best, difficult, and at worst, non-existent. These armoured cars were the property of the South African Armoured Corps, which supplied the drivers as well, usually just before the start of the operation and definitely after marrying up and training was completed.

The result: a lack of understanding and cohesion between artillery crew and armour driver. Furthermore, the Elands were not fitted for radio in the configuration that the gunners required. As with the Unimog and Buffels, the additional radios were manpacks hung from the turret hatch or gun, or wherever one could find a suitable hook or place. Personal kit was either hung off the back of the turret or stowed behind the ditching plates in front of the driver's position.

Echelon vehicles were usually 10-tonne Magirus Deutz cargo trucks, which were quite suitable for the task.

Titles of fire units

Artillery batteries are not numbered, but instead have alphabetic titles or names:

- P Battery (phonetic 'Papa')
- Q Battery (Quebec)
- R Battery (Romeo)
- S battery (Sierra)

In some cases, an additional battery was added; this was referred to as T (Tango) Battery. Each troop has an alphabetic title starting with A through to J respectively.

Radio call signs

The artillery generally adhered to NATO conventional call signs, and only on occasional operations with 32 Battalion were other call signs used. The call signs below are not exhaustive, but they are an indication of those that were used:

- Artillery brigade commander / divisional fire support co-ordination centre: 0G (Zero Golf)
- Regimental commander: 9
- P Battery: all call signs start with 1 (i.e. battery commander: 19)
- Q Battery: all call signs start with 2 (i.e. battery post: 20)
- R Battery: all call signs start with 3 (i.e. senior troop commander: 35)
- S Battery: all call signs start with 4 (i.e. battery sergeant-major: 49F).

Each corps in the army had its own unique prefix to its call signs if it was operating with other corps, that is, in a battle group or brigade context, and only when called on the command net. The artillery's prefix was 'G' (golf). For example, the direct support battery commander of S Battery within 61 Mechanized Battalion Group was 'G 49' (Golf four niner).

Fire for effect

There are numerous tactics for engaging a target by artillery fire. These are some examples:

- By adjusting fire with one gun, and once on target, calling for fire for effect. This was the most popular method, but had the disadvantage of the loss of surprise. It was used whenever the target could not be accurately plotted and when there was insufficient meteorological data available.
- By predicted fire, where the target is plotted, variables are calculated and the fire mission starts immediately with fire for effect. Here the element of surprise plays a significant role. Generally, multiple rocket launcher (MRL) fire missions were predicted.

The number of rounds during fire for effect is usually given as the number of rounds fired *per gun*. For example, ten rounds fire for effect from a battery would deliver a total of 80 rounds on the target.

Guns versus howitzers

There are numerous differences between guns and howitzers. Guns fire a projectile at a high velocity in a flat trajectory from a fixed charge. Typically, tanks and armoured cars are equipped with guns. Howitzers fire a projectile at a lower velocity that will vary depending on the charge. Therefore, the charge can be selected. The trajectory is curved, and in some cases parabolic. Howitzers can fire in the upper trajectory or register, that is, above 45° elevation.

All the 'tube' artillery in the South African Artillery were gun-howitzers: they could fire on high charges with high or low muzzle velocities. For the sake of brevity, the term 'gun' is used throughout this book to describe guns and / or howitzers. In fact, during formal dinners the gunners drink a toast to 'the guns'.

General note

In the text, certain of the less-known, or even unknown, places have been referenced by indicating their position with geographic co-ordinates in brackets after the place name. For example, longitude 17-15-00 E; latitude 16-31-25 S.

An Israeli Soltam 155mm M68 gun mounted onto a Centurion tank chassis in the Negev Desert. At that time the South African Artillery was looking at numerous options to improve firepower. *Photo: H. van Niekerk*

Chapter 3

Operation Savannah:
the first shots

'D'you say that you sweat with the field-guns?
By God, you must lather with us – 'Tss! 'Tss!
For you all love the screw-guns.'
—Rudyard Kipling, from *Screw-Guns*

It was Wednesday, 5 November 1975 when the Officer Commanding 14 Field Regiment, Commandant Joffel van der Westhuizen received his first mobilization instructions from the general officer commanding (GOC) of North West Command, Brigadier Frans van den Berg. In short, he was ordered to prepare a field troop (25-pounders) for deployment 'over the border'. In order to set the scene, on the opposite page is the instruction, as written by Commandant van der Westhuizen:

Thu 6 Nov 75
1. **Move in with the following:** (received instructions on 5 Nov)
   a. Tp Fd—both ordnance and personnel—key personnel Permanent Force, 14 Fds ordnance.
   b. 2 x radar sets with 1 x crew
   c. Equipment—packed in crates and on vehicles
   d. 3 x Land Rovers, 1 x fire-control post, 2 x water trailers
   e. 3 x normal wet cell batteries (batteries dry for aircraft)
   f. Spares and technical equipment
   g. 75-man cooker
2. Phase 1 = by road to Waterkloof and by air to Rundu. Phase 2 = in (before 091500 Nov). Fly guns in.
3. Own chef (Rooie); long masts for A39s.
4. Operations = top secret. National servicemen only over the border voluntarily.
5. Tasks = counter-bombardment, fire plans supporting attacks and preparatory bombardment.
6. **D Signals will provide at airport:** 2 x chargers, 15KVA generator, signals electrician, 4 x A39s, 2 x C42, 2 x B47, radar technician.
7. Infantry will provide local defence.
8. Dry rations for two days per man—must keep until Rundu.
9. No SA uniforms—uniforms only until Rundu—get other uniforms there—can take 'bush civvies'—tags on baggage may not cross border. Minimum equipment, no radios, cameras, etc. No webbing, boots or anything with 'made in SA' on. ID cards and dog tags to be handed in at Rundu. Testaments and personnel cards ready. Wear label around neck with blood group.
10. Back in Potch. approx 14 Nov.
11. Exchange unserviceable signals equipment at 3 Electronic Workshop.
12. Col Cas le Roux = co-coordinating officer. I will go to Waterkloof to control and supervise.
13. List of all equipment and personnel to Ops (per mustering).
14. Vehicles—petrol tanks ½ to ¾ full.
15. D Log Services will provide accommodation and meals.
16. Follow up artillery ammo (for field troop) HE117 = 1,224, Smoke = 184, 213PM1 = 216, 221B = 240, Primers = 120, Charge N = 1,312, Charge S = 96.
17. **Personnel**

Tp commander	= Jack Bosch
OPO	= Chris B.
GPO	= Piet Uys
Troop leader	= Braam Coetzer
OPA	= Ray Hawkins
Troop comd assistant	= Leon le Roux
TA sergeant	= Bdr van Ryneveld
TA	= Bdr Olivier, Bdr Pretorius, Bdr Maasberg
TSM	= Dirk Kriek
Radar sec commander	= WOII Strydom
OPO driver operator	= Bdr Strydom
Troop commander driver	= Bdr Rimmer
Radar tiffy	= Sgt Truter
Sigs electrician	= Cpl Minnaar

18. Load as aircraft are available.

Savannah: The first two pages of Commandant van der Westhuizen's diary showing that memorable mobilization instruction. *Source: C.P. van der Westhuizen*

The first in

In August 1975, Lieutenant Herman van Niekerk was called in by Brigadier van den Berg and told to report to Brigadier Jannie Geldenhuys (Army Operations) in Pretoria. At that time, Lieutenant van Niekerk was one of the very few gunners with any form of qualification on the 120mm mortar, having been trained in Israel (see Chapter 12). All he was told was that 'they needed someone like you over there . . .' Only some days later, he learned that 'over there' was Angola. At Army Headquarters, in the old library building a group of some 40 men were given a very vague briefing on the situation in Angola and that training needed to be provided for UNITA and FNLA. They were to be known as American mercenaries who were employed by the CIA to provide this particular training.

'The States': This was the term used universally by all troops deployed in the South West African–Angolan operation to refer to South Africa, or home. The term originated from that first group of instructors in August 1975, probably from an abbreviated 'Orange Free State'.

The group was flown to Rundu, where they were briefed by a major with an oversized revolver on his hip. In Lieutenant van Niekerk's words, 'one of the poorest briefings in military history'. Shortly afterwards, van Niekerk arrived in Silva Porto with a few of the others to give 120mm training to the UNITA troops. On arrival in Angola only one 120mm mortar existed, a different type from the Israeli 120mm, and a very heavy piece at that. The group was told that the new equipment would be arriving shortly and, as promised, within days, the wooden crates were opened to reveal another surprise—not 120mm mortars, but surplus US 4.2-inch rifled mortars. The good news was that these mortars were brand new and included all the operating and maintenance manuals needed for training, operating and the limited maintenance required. Lieutenant van Niekerk was the only gunner in this group of instructors and, therefore, was saddled with the task of developing and presenting the training programme.

From Silva Porto the training moved to Capollo, 'a remote place in the bush where we stayed in a house and could do all the training right from the doorstep . . . a very nice place . . . except for the mosquitoes, of course . . . and from there we started with the war.' The group honed their skills in a number of contacts in a short time and soon all had had a taste of battle. Lieutenant van Niekerk said:

> The mortars, carried on an orange-coloured Scania vegetable transport truck with a 12-speed gearbox, proved to be very reliable and the gunners who manned them were diligent and skilled . . . they became a very dependable source of firepower to the armour . . . we did not have real infantry as front line . . . most of the time the artillery and armour were right next to one another on the front line . . . it sounds crazy, but it was like that and everyone was quite content with it.

At about 20h00 on Friday 7 November 1975, the battery commander of 2 Medium Battery, Captain Jacob van Heerden, returned home from having a few drinks in the unit canteen. Commandant van der Westhuizen, having received his orders at 19h15 that same night, dropped in at van Heerden's house, where he gave him an order to prepare a troop of medium guns (3 guns) to move that same night to the operational area. Information about the mission was completely vague, and, as will later be seen, the gunners had to literally and figuratively prepare in the dark. The first problem was that the battery's personnel had been sent home on weekend pass and, therefore, none were available, with the exception of Captain van Heerden, WOII Hennie Pretorius, S/Sgt Klaas Ackerman, Sgt 'Wessie' van der Westhuizen (the gun tiffy, or, more correctly, the Technical Services Corps' ordnance fitter), and some junior leaders scraped together from 14 Field and the School of Artillery. They eventually succeeded in mobilizing 17 members by 23h00 when they left Potchefstroom. The second problem was that 14 Field had no electric lights, and it was a challenge to collect technical equipment for the guns in the dark. Time was so limited that, while they were struggling to prepare at the unit, at home the wives had to pack their husbands' personal kit. A nightmare: wives don't really know what one needs in the operational area.

On arrival at Waterkloof in the early hours of the morning (8 November) it was dead quiet and the only soul in the departures hall was a sleeping Colonel Coetzee from Chief of Staff Logistics dressed in dress no. 2 (tunic etc.) On waking, he informed Captain van Heerden that the guns they were supposed to take with them were already parked on the apron and that they could send theirs (14 Field's) back to Potch. WOI Dirk Venter, the RSM of 14 Field, was in command of the drivers and left immediately back for Potch with the guns they had so thoroughly prepared. Thankfully, they kept the technical equipment to take along. The guns they were issued with were from the mobilization stores, painted in Walvis Bay Yellow, each with their breech mechanisms dismantled, preserved and packed in wooden charge boxes. This would cause them problems later in Ambriz because they could only get two out of the three guns operationally ready—a result of incomplete breech mechanisms. On enquiring about vehicles, Colonel Coetzee informed them these were already in Angola. They helped the SAAF personnel load the guns into two C-130s together with a limited amount of ammunition. At 07h00 they left for Grootfontein, totally unaware of the task ahead of them. On arrival at Grootfontein, Commandant 'Tinky' Jones (the C-130 SAAF pilot) suggested that Captain van Heerden go into the base and find out what was going on. All was quiet in Grootfontein that Saturday, as they had had their Christmas / year-end function the previous evening and were all sleeping it off. The only person Captain van Heerden could find was a colleague whom he addressed over a shut toilet door. He suggested that they might as well fly on to Rundu, as not much was happening in Grootfontein.

At Rundu they came to realize that something big was happening. General Viljoen (at that time, a major general and GOC of the SWA Territory Force) met them and attached Major Jack Bosch as troop commander, and gave him orders, the content of which the rest of the troop did not know; in those days orders were a rather closed affair. Dr Abel Steyn was attached as the medical officer, equipped with an open wooden Pimlico box (a term used by the 'logies'—logistics personnel—for clothing) full of medical equipment and medication. They were given green uniforms and takkies (canvas sneakers), rations and odds and ends. With this, they departed at 15h00 for Ambriz.

At this stage they still did not know what awaited them and what they would be doing. Their enquiries about the vehicles that were needed produced the same answer: 'in Angola'. In fact, at that time they did not even know where they were going. Flying time from Rundu to Ambriz was three hours; they arrived there at 19h00 local time and were met by Holden Roberto and Brigadier Ben de Wet Roos. (Brigadier Roos was deployed as liaison officer to Roberto and later became GOC of 8 Armoured Division.) The order given was clear: 'Hide yourselves.' This time, the enquiry into the gun tractors produced a result—Roberto summarily commandeered three 2x6 trucks that had arrived to load salt. These vehicles were not too successful in that the roads were narrow and rough; much time was spent recovering a truck (now gun tractor) that had slipped off the road. They occupied a hide under the mango trees that are prolific in that area and awaited further orders.

A hide is a place where a fire unit (battery or troop) occupies to rest, perform maintenance and, if necessary, prepare for the next firing position. It is usually situated in a safe area out of enemy observation and out of enemy range, but radio communication is essential. The Armoured Corps use the term 'leaguer area'.

At mid-morning the next day (Sunday, 9 November), they received orders to move to the front to take part in the impending attack on the MPLA–FAPLA positions by the FNLA and Zairian forces. It was quite a frightening experience to cross the Dondo River on a makeshift pont—this because the bridge had been destroyed. As they were driving over this flimsy affair, underneath them an FNLA engineer was welding up the damage after the guns had crossed. They arrived at the front in the afternoon; on arrival, Major Bosch decided to deploy them in an excavation below a survey beacon. This position was in direct observation of the enemy deployments approximately 11 kilometres away across the swamp upon which the 'road of death' was built. While they were occupying the firing position, the FNLA and Zairian troops swarmed like bees to stare at this performance. Later that afternoon they observed the enemy deploying and immediately decided to engage them. However, while they were busy with target acquisition, a tropical storm broke, which restricted vision and effectively stopped the engagement.

Captain van Heerden at the time believed that had they engaged the MPLA, the counter-bombardment would have destroyed the South African gunners there and then. At 05h00 on Monday, 10 November, the SAAF Canberras bombed the MPLA positions unsuccessfully, to be followed by the FNLA attack, which did not go according to plan. Just after the bombing, in accordance with the plan, the troop fired the preparatory bombardment at 05h40 with two G2s on charge super: the first rounds in anger since World War II. Chaos reigned in the FNLA–Zairian ranks, and the attack was delayed for a number of hours. Eventually, the attack went in, with the troops walking in 'Indian file' on the same 'road of death'. They hit strong resistance and immediately turned tail and chaotically retreated. A rout is probably a better way of describing this rearward move.

Then the gun position came under fire, the rockets falling within metres of the guns and their vehicles. Mercifully, the ground was soft and the fragmentation of the rockets generally ineffective. However, the blasts from the explosions were enough to shred the canvas on the vehicles. Thankfully, only one South African gunner was injured from a fragment in his heel; he was evacuated back to South Africa.

This disorganized rout of the FNLA and Zairian troops left the front completely open, the result being that the South African guns were effectively the front line own troops (FLOT). This would not be the only time that this happened, as will be seen later in this book.

When the MPLA broke out, Brigadier Roos gave the order to cease firing and evacuate the gun position to prevent the possible loss of the guns. The instruction was for the troop to withdraw and redeploy near Caxito to protect the withdrawal. Here the reality dawned: the vehicles that had towed the guns in had joined the retreat when the counter-bombardment started. The gunners effectively commandeered two blood-stained troop carriers to tow the guns back, only to be left in the bush on the side of the road when the vehicles were required for some other task. A point of concern, of course, was the state of the crossing of the Dondo River: one of the reasons why Brigadier Roos wanted the troop back on the northern bank, is it was safer. For the gunners, the rest of the battle consisted of

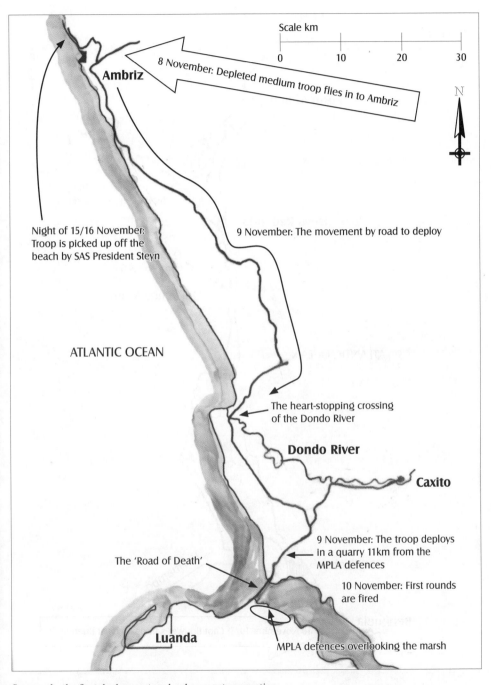

Savannah: the first deployment and subsequent evacuation.

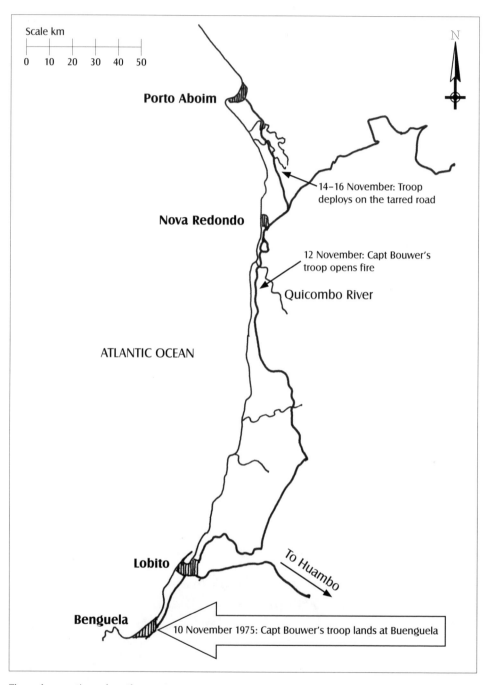

The early operations along the coast.

protecting the retreat by day and withdrawing by night, a move which did not go down too well with the allies, as they considered the guns a terrific morale booster, to the point where they set up roadblocks (typically African: two fuel drums and a tree trunk) to stop both the rout and the withdrawal of the guns.

Brigadier Roos and two members of the Bureau of State Security (BOSS, an unpopular South African version of the CIA at that time) were quartered in a servant's room at the back of the house in Ambriz occupied by Holden Roberto; by now the troop had occupied a hide approximately 5 kilometres out of Ambriz under the ubiquitous mango trees. It appears as though the gunners were subjected to the time-honoured 'mushroom principle' (keep them in the dark and feed them with sh-t); of military principles and drills there was no evidence and it could be said that the limited success was due to the old SADF flexibility and ability to 'make a plan' under any conditions. More about this later.

The early battles along the coast

At the beginning of 1975, Captain Piet Uys was an officer-instructor at the Regimental Training Wing of the School of Artillery in Potchefstroom. In April that year, he was transferred to the Gunnery Wing to act as the Chief Instructor Gunnery and take charge of the gunnery courses for the rest of the year. The first course that Captain Uys presented at the Gunnery Wing was a Citizen Force battery commander's course. On 8 November 1975, Captain Uys, together with Bombardier Willem van Ryneveld, was summoned to the office of the second in command (2IC) of the School of Artillery. To their great surprise, the 2IC, Commandant Peet Booysen, instructed them to report to 14 Field Regiment HQ within two hours. They were informed that they were to take part in an operation in Angola.

At 14 Field, they were briefed on the foreseen activities and allocated to a 25-pounder troop under the command of Captain Chris 'Smokey' Bouwer with Uys as the gun position officer, and Bombardier van Ryneveld as his technical assistant. The troop of four guns with their officers, NCOs and gun crews travelled to Waterkloof air base, Pretoria, that same afternoon and

The School of Artillery was organized into three main training wings: Gunnery Wing, Locating Wing and Regimental Training Wing. Gunnery Wing trained candidate officers in technical subjects such as fire control, observation and blunt-end deployment (battery survey and reconnaissance); it provided promotion courses for both Permanent Force and Citizen Force officers and NCOs from 2/Lt to major, and bombardier to WO respectively. These courses ranged from observation of fire through to battery commanders (the battery commander course qualified an officer to become a regimental commander). Likewise, the NCOs' courses ranged from gun numbers 1 on the various types of ordnance, to echelon systems and logistics in the field. Locating Wing trained the 'black magic' gunners throughout the rank groups in the locating subjects, such as regimental survey, mortar-locating radar, artillery intelligence, sound ranging, meteorology, and observation. Regimental Training Wing focused specifically on the junior NCOs (national servicemen), who learned how to drill, take inspections, instruct on basic training subjects and, together with Gunnery Wing, were trained in gunnery subjects (ordnance commanders, technical assistants, etc.).

Smokey

For years, during gunnery training on 140mm (5.5 inch) G2s the tradition was that if someone forgot a drill or safety check, or even the correct sequence of fire orders, that person would be ordered by the senior instructor to run to the OP post with a 100-pound (48 kilogram) 140mm smoke shell (known as a 'smokey'), and report his misdemeanour. On the way, he would have time to consider his actions, especially while repeating what he should have done over and over, out loud, to himself. This practice worked particularly well, not only for national servicemen, but also for young officers and NCOs, and no one was ever injured or mentally affected by it. Capt Bouwer, however, only received his nickname in 1977 during his year at the army staff course after his room burnt down.

left for Rundu at about 22h00 that evening. (By C-130 Hercules, Rundu was approximately two and a half hours' flying time from Waterkloof.)

When they arrived at the Rundu airfield, they were received by Lieutenant Tobie Vermaak (a gunner officer), who helped them obtain accommodation for the night. The next day was spent in preparation for an airlift to an unknown destination. During that period, Captain Bouwer had come across some air photos covering the area between the Quicombe River and Nova Redondo. With these, he and the infantry commander plotted the enemy gun and machine-gun positions. During these preparations it became clear that the operation facing them would require a lot of improvisation because it was apparent that, not only were they forced to use Unimog vehicles as gun tractors, but that they would have to 'liberate' vehicles to be used to transport the ammunition. Furthermore, the gunners would not be allowed to take their shooting pro formas along, as these were printed in Afrikaans and, therefore, posed a security risk.

On 10 November 1975, the whole troop was airlifted to Benguela airport in Angola, where they were met by Captain Gert Grobler of the South African Infantry. He was in charge of a group of UNITA soldiers, who started offloading the guns. The gunners were immediately instructed to hide their guns because the presence of artillery in Angola apparently was to be kept a secret. Meanwhile, the ammunition needed by the troop was flown in from Rundu to Benguela by SAAF C-130s.

Captain Bouwer's troop now joined up with an organization known as Task Force Zulu under the command of Colonel 'Proppies' van Heerden, who had advanced towards Benguela to dislodge the MPLA forces in that area. This task force comprised some Portuguese bitter-enders, a collection of Angolans who we assume were UNITA sympathizers, and a few armoured cars (ex-Portuguese Panhard 90mm). This force, with no artillery support, had managed to roll the MPLA up to Benguela in short shrift; Colonel van Heerden, therefore, became known as 'Rommel' because of the speed of the advance. The force had come under MPLA artillery fire, which stopped them in their tracks and for which they had no reply.

The next day, the gunners were told that the airport was expecting a planeload of foreign journalists and reporters, and that the guns and Unimogs had to be hidden from view. (It is interesting to note that foreign journalists were welcome: one wonders what the outcome would have been had the South African media been allowed in.) Captain Uys ordered the guns to be parked in an open shed together with their Unimogs. To camouflage the presence of the guns, the most convenient source of camouflage material Captain Uys could find was a pile of onions, which had been dumped virtually on the runway, presumably en route to somewhere else. There and then, he ordered the troops to stack the onions in the shed in such a way that they would conceal the artillery equipment. Shortly after this task had been completed, the journalists arrived, but were fortunately escorted away from the airport soon after landing, with the gunners having to hide in another hangar behind closed doors. That same afternoon, the troop was ordered to deploy on the perimeters of the airfield owing to rumours of enemy tanks in the town of Benguela.

On 11 November, Captain Bouwer's first meeting with Colonel van Heerden was somewhat unusual, in that, on arrival, Captain Bouwer was heartily welcomed by the commander and Commandant Pale Kotze (also a gunner), when almost immediately, van Heerden was called to the radio. Upon returning to the group, van Heerden's words to Captain Bouwer were: 'You must get going.' On asking about his new destination, Captain Bouwer received the reply, 'To Nova Redondo. Lindford's battle group is in trouble!' This battle group (Alpha) was deployed to the south of Nova Redondo, where it was pushing the MPLA forces back. Captain Bouwer led his troop, which consisted of the four guns drawn by Unimogs, one Land Rover fire-control vehicle and a number of Unic tipper trucks transporting the artillery ammunition. These trucks had been 'liberated' at the harbour of the small town of Lobito, just north of Benguela. The troop travelled the rest of the day without finding the UNITA force that they had to join. They continued into the night and stopped frequently to try to establish radio communication with the South Africans who were fighting with the UNITA forces. (The South African officer assisting UNITA was Commandant Delville Lindford, a well-known artillery officer.) The 25-pounder troop of Captain Bouwer met the South African (Eland) armoured cars that evening at the bridge over the Quicombe River south of Nova Redondo; the armoured cars were transporting wounded soldiers under the cover of night to a medical-aid post for assistance.

After consultation with Commandant Lindford, Captain Bouwer gave orders for the deployment of the 25-pounder troop. The reconnaissance of the gun position was done in darkness and the guns were deployed in dead ground, out of enemy observation, immediately after the position was laid out. The guns were prepared to be ready to provide fire support from first light the next day. The next day, 12 November 1975, shortly after sunrise, Captain Bouwer, acting as forward observation officer, ordered the first fire mission. Under control of Captain Uys, the fire support started and lasted for the whole day. It is interesting to note that a large amount of airburst shells were used, not something the gunners were used to. The firing was so intense that, after a short lull in the engagement, the GPO had to report 'Gun loaded, gun hot!' to the FOO, who replied with the order, 'Cartridge only, unload!' That night, the guns were moved forward and deployed near a plantation of palm trees adjacent to the main road.

The next day, the guns remained in position to cover the advance of the UNITA forces, but their fire was only needed to help a busload of MPLA troops evacuate the town a little more quickly. It was clear that the MPLA forces had withdrawn and that the town of Nova Redondo could be occupied. The troop was then moved into a waiting area in Nova Redondo.

A few days after their first battle, the troop was ordered to support a UNITA force that intended to advance along the coastline to occupy a town by the name of Porto Amboim, a place of strategic importance to FAPLA, as its harbour could handle sizeable ships and was connected to Quibala by rail. The troop, now in support of Battle Group Bravo (Commandant Jan Breytenbach), advanced along a narrow tarred road towards Porto Amboim, but was soon ordered into action by Captain Bouwer, who, at that stage, was accompanying Commandant Breytenbach and Major Frank Bestbier (one of the infantry company commanders). The advancing forces arrived at a bridge crossing the Queve River 15 kilometres south of the town, but were prevented crossing the bridge by heavy infantry and rocket fire.

The guns were deployed on the tarred road because any movement off the tarred surface would result in veheicles getting stuck in the mud. A very intensive firefight now ensued and it became necessary for Captain Uys to split the troop's fire by using two guns on one target and the other two guns on another. The expert assistance of Bombardier van Ryneveld made it possible to engage two targets simultaneously. (Willem van Ryneveld was one of the best technical assistants at that time and would be for some time. He reached the rank of lieutenant-colonel, and was tragically killed, together with Major Mark Brown, in a road accident in Pretoria in 1993.) The guns were then given fire orders to cover the withdrawal of the UNITA force. While doing so, the MPLA forces identified the 25-pounder troop on the tarred road and started adjusting (ranging) with rockets onto the gun position. In Captain Uys's words:

> The [only] advantage of being under rocket fire was that you could actually determine whether the rocket is aiming directly for you or not, by observing the smoke trail emitted by the rocket. The first rocket fell behind the guns, followed by the second, which fell 100 metres in front of the guns. Captain Bouwer then gave orders for the guns to withdraw, which they did in a hurry, the other rockets falling without any effect on the now vacant gun position.

The lesson learned by the South African gunners on that day was that they were hopelessly outranged by the 122mm BM21 rockets, and some deep tactical thinking would have to take place. After this excursion, it was decided not to capture Porto Amboim, and, in effect, that was the end of the battles along the coast for a while. A short rest before the move on 21 November to redeploy to the central front gave the gunners a chance to do some maintenance on their guns. Only one small problem though: no cleaning material. Unduanted by such minor details, the resourceful gunners tore the sleeves off their shirts to use as pull-throughs.

The South African Navy steps in:
the story of the troop north of Luanda

This troop had in effect become isolated from the rest of the South African forces, which all deployed relatively well farther south. Captain Jacob van Heerden takes up the story:

> We drove to Ambrizette by truck. The trip was rather slow owing to the appalling condition of the roads in the rainy season as well as having to face a number of 'Africa roadblocks' and not create the impression that we were evacuating. The FNLA was also on the run and these roadblocks were specifically there to prevent this.

The order was that we were to be picked up by a ship somewhere in the vicinity at 03h00. Details were not very clear. We signalled the SAS *President Steyn* by flashing the headlights of the truck from the beach out to sea, which was then answered by the *Steyn*. Radio contact was not possible as they were under electronic silence. Brigadier Roos had, however, tried to make contact by radio, but without success. When contact eventually was made, the ship dispatched two or three (cannot remember exactly) rubber ducks under command of Lieutenant Rowan Erleigh [SAN]. When Captain Davis [the ship's commander] discovered that there was no immediate danger, a helicopter was dispatched to pick up Brigadier Roos. I accompanied him by helicopter, and, if I remember correctly, the evacuation was completed by 05h00 when we then set sail to Walvis Bay, docking on the Sunday night at 23h00. The following day, we were sent by road to Grootfontein to join the rest of the gunners. There we laid up for a number of weeks and we did not deploy as a battery again. Individuals were deployed with batteries operating in Angola.

The three guns remained at Ambriz, and Roberto undertook to tow them by road to Kinshasa. We also left one or two Unimogs, which were sent in by air during the last days of our deployment.

Operations on the central front

Captain Bouwer's troop was ordered to join Battle Group Foxbat at Santa Comba, in the central part of Angola. Initially, the troop occupied a hide at Cela airport from where they moved to Santa Comba together with the rest of the UNITA forces and a squadron of South African armoured cars (Eland 60mm and 90mm). Arriving in Santa Comba on a Sunday afternoon, the gunners heard the far-off rumble of artillery fire. What they did not know was that the battle of Ebo was taking place. That evening, Captain Uys and his guns were deployed to cover the withdrawal of the UNITA–South African forces from the very same Ebo.

The Battle of Ebo

Ebo (11-01-32 S; 14-41-44 E) was thrust into the limelight due to its geographical location and its terrain. Because of the rapid advance northwards by Foxbat in early November, the Angolans became concerned for the safety of Luanda, as the distance between the city and the approaching forces was becoming shorter by the day. It was here that the first sizeable Cuban force deployed to put a stop to the South African advance. This Cuban force of 70 men comprised Special Forces elements, advisers to FAPLA and artillery made up of anti-aircraft (AA) guns and BM21s. This small force at Ebo had selected their delaying positions carefully and were the cause of the decision by the South African commander, Commandant Eddie Webb, to bypass this position on the way to Catofe and Quibala. Despite this, on 15 November, one of the combat teams, having crossed a makeshift bridge (i.e. made by them) at Hengo, reached the town of Ebo to find the place deserted, but signs 'there were aplenty, fresh tyre tracks, stoves with the omnipresent pots of *mieliepap* (maize meal) still cooking on them . . . open boxes of ammunition in the streets, but the population seemed to have disappeared into thin air'.

By 16 November, the third troop to go into action was an 88mm G1 (25-pounder) fire unit under Major Chris Venter with Lieutenant Jakes Jacobs (the adjutant of 14 Field Regiment) as the OP (observation post) officer, assisted by Lieutenant Snyman, a national service officer. The gun position officer was WOII Sampie Claassen, and the troop sergeant-major, WOII 'Penkop' van Dyk. Attached to this troop was a Cymbeline mortar-locating radar section under the command of WOII Willie Strydom.

Ebo

Three days later, after appreciating all the factors, the only option for the approach to Conde was via Ebo because of the state of the rivers and crossings. The state of the Tunga crossing made it the choice of the new commander, Commandant George Kruys. In this vicinity and around 12 kilometres from Foxbat's HQ, the road forked and almost immediately became known to all as the 'Y'. Here the first contact took place between the South African armour and FAPLA in the battle for Ebo. There were a number of factors leading to

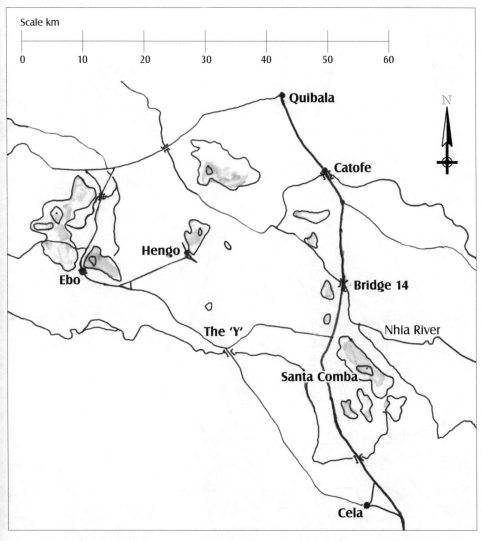

A general view of the central front.

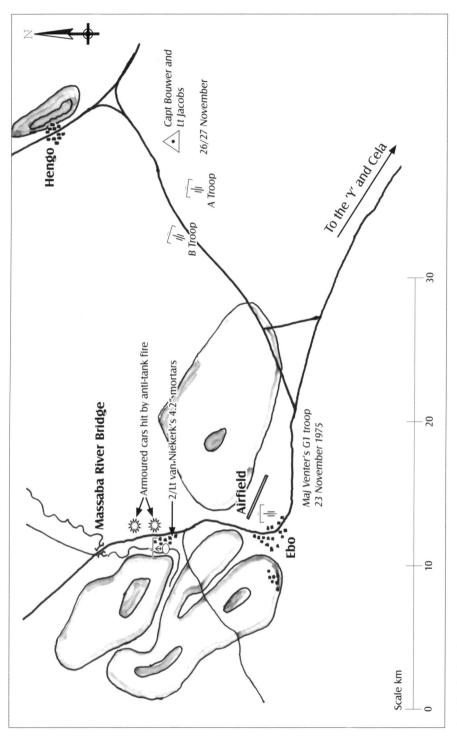

Activities in the Ebo–Hengo area.

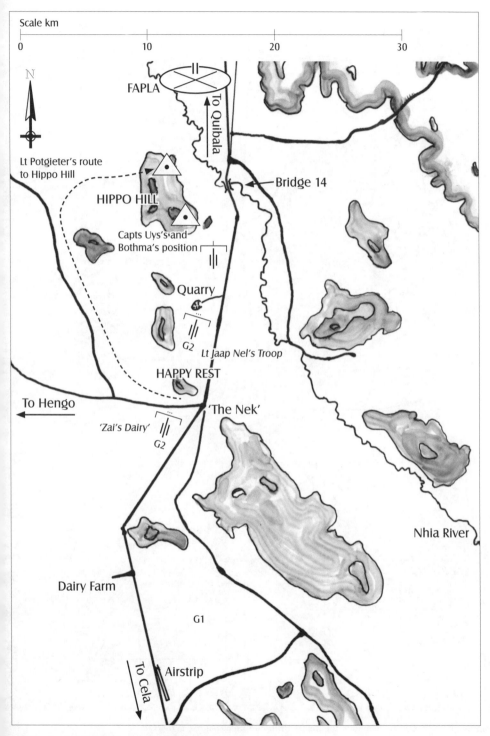

Savannah: the deployments in the central front.

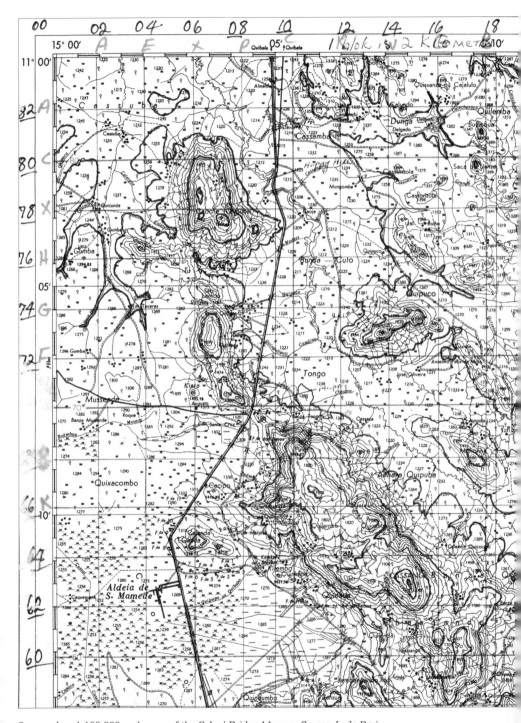

Savannah: a 1:100,000 scale map of the Cela / Bridge 14 area. *Source: L. de Bruin*

the decision to attempt the Ebo route, the most important of which was that the bridge over the Nhia River (Bridge 14) was destroyed and would take a long time to repair. The second was that the higher HQ (not yet deployed anywhere near the combat zone) made the decision, which had to be carried out by Kruys who continues:

I recommended that we abandon the Ebo route due to the enemy aircraft reconnaissance and information we received from Portuguese freedom fighters that the route beyond Ebo was very rugged and full of suitable delaying positions. Nevertheless, higher HQ ordered us to continue the advance via Ebo [the first of many such decisions taken by an HQ from the safety of the far rear areas]. We advanced in single file because our vehicles could not move off the road. The roads were bad enough, but going off the road for an Eland or a vegetable truck was impossible. We did have a newly arrived battery of 25-pounders, so our firepower had improved, but we still had no trained South African infantry. The force mix was poor and only suitable for a type of bush war . . . I decided to attack them head-on and use the guns as firepower to dislodge them. The armoured cars had difficulty moving and got stuck in the mud, and the guns could get no strike indication from the air because the shells simply vanished in the mud. If we had delayed [delay-action] fuses or other ammunition indicating where we were firing, the whole sequence of events may have been different. The artillery was ranging up and down, but with no result.

By Sunday 23 November, the sappers had performed miracles and prepared the bridge for the crossing, the lead elements of the battle group arriving in the deserted town of Ebo at 08h00. An hour later, contact was made at the next river bridge 16 kilometres to the north of Ebo and the first armoured car was lost to 75mm anti-tank fire. This loss was followed by another three, and within moments the FAPLA artillery bombardment started. The battle now focused on extracting the rest of the armoured cars (eight) from this defensive fire target. It is noteworthy to mention here that the FAPLA fire was disciplined and caught the South African force by surprise. Although expecting fire from FAPLA, which would normally have been sporadic and ineffective, they were surprised by the accuracy and intensity of the fire delivered by an obviously Cuban-led and -manned force (the Cuban force was, in fact, only 70-strong). The field troop had deployed on an old runway just to the north of Ebo and commenced a counter-bombardment under the direction of the Air OP, Lieutenant Williamson, of the SAAF in a Cessna 185. Another surprise for the gunners: Williamson's target grid references were cast in doubt and the counter-battery fire was initially ineffective, the rounds passing way over the enemy. The Cubans had deployed as close as 2,500 metres behind their front lines and not well behind, as was their custom.

The armoured car squadron commander, Captain Johan Holm, had somehow liberated a small, blue Honda 4x4 and made this his rover vehicle. The driver of this runabout was Lieutenant Herman van Niekerk from 14 Field Regiment, who was the troop commander of a 4.2-inch mortar section (these rifled mortars were probably supplied by the USA to UNITA). This section was manned by UNITA soldiers and had been supporting Battle Group Foxbat since early November. Shortly before the contact, Captain Holm was instructed to use an armoured car for his own safety, a fateful decision as will be seen. Van Niekerk's 4.2-inch mortar troop deployed on the high ground to the west of the road in full view of the FAPLA force. This deployment was out of necessity, as the troop did not have the technical expertise nor the communications to fire indirectly and, therefore, were forced to deploy where the mortars could see the target area. During the counter-bombardment by the Cubans, the Honda, parked close to Holm's Eland armoured car, was hit by a 122mm rocket, killing Holm and wounding Lieutenant van Niekerk and two others. Van Niekerk, his back and legs now full of shell fragments, under fire, carried a wounded armour officer to a safer place. For this he was awarded the Honoris Crux silver medal. Some time later, the Honda was captured by the Cubans and FAPLA, who attempted to spread propaganda by announcing that the vehicle had been found to contain women's underwear. To make matters worse, South African Intelligence interrogated Lieutenant van Niekerk and refused to believe his story. This tale was further accepted by an author in 1976 who published the story as fact. Despite this, Lieutenant van Niekerk had a very successful career in the South African Artillery and later in Special Forces, where he eventually retired as a colonel.

This battle finally ended late in the afternoon, the UNITA infantry having run away and the armour losing four men. The end result was the decision to approach Quibala from farther east by Bridge 14.

On the same Sunday (16 November) that Major Venter was deploying his battery in the Ebo area, Captain Koos Laubscher found himself in Pretoria clearing out of the Army College after the entire staff course had been terminated two days earlier. The next morning, the staff course held a brief farewell function and were addressed by, amongst others, Major-General van Deventer, who had very recently returned from Ambriz. Captain Laubscher spent the rest of the day researching the capabilities of the Soviet artillery equipment as preparation for his next deployment. At 19h00 on Monday 17 November, Captain Laubscher was instructed to report to 14 Field Regiment for operations, where, arriving the next day, he was appointed as 2IC (the actual 2IC, Major Chris Venter, was already in the process of deploying). Within two days, Commandant van der Westhuizen, Captain Laubscher and the RSM, WOI Dirk Venter, found themselves in Grootfontein, where preparations were being made for the deployment of the gunner reinforcements mobilizing in Potchefstroom (14 Field Regiment), Walvis Bay (43 Battery) and in Katima Mulilo (4 Field Regiment).

That same day (20 November) saw Lieutenant Bernard Pols and a number of troops arrive by air from Mpacha (the air base serving Katima Mulilo), and a group from Walvis Bay comprising Major Wyllis Blaauw, Lieutenant Sarel Myburgh, WOII Schoonwinkel, S/Sgt Jim van Zyl, and Sgt Mill, who arrived by train.

So this build-up continued. Captain Laubscher accompanied van der Westhuizen on a recce of the Grootfontein commando training area to determine if this facility could be used as a temporary artillery firing range. Unfortunately, it was too limited, as the terrain was so flat that observation would have had to be done from Grootfontein's control tower or by air.

At 09h10 on 22 November, the first trainload of reinforcements (Major Brown, Captain Rheeder et al) and ammunition arrived in Grootfontein. That same day the next train, with WOII Jenkins and more guns and vehicles, arrived from Pretoria. This was also the day that the first field gun and tractor were spray-painted in a 'do it yourself' camouflage scheme to everyone's interest and amusement. On Sunday 23 November, the pace picked up and things began to get organized. Major Brown was instructed to form a field battery to be ready to fly out to Silva Porto to support Battle Group X-ray in the east by 25 November; a 'light' RHQ (a tactical HQ) under Commandant van der Westhuizen with Captain Laubscher as the 2IC, and the RSM and Sergeant Boet Homan making up the balance, was to be ready to move by road later that week; Captains Chris Human and Carel Theron, as well as Lieutenant Johan Potgieter were arriving with their batteries from Mpacha; and another train was arriving with G1 ammunition.

The intention was to establish a regiment that would look like this:

- P Battery (medium)   Major Chris Bouwer (already deployed)
- Q Battery (field)   Major Jack Bosch (in the area, having been rescued from Ambriz)
- R Battery (medium)   Captain Louis Rheeder
- S Battery (field)   Captain Chris Human
- T Battery (field)   Major Thinus Brown
- U Battery (medium)   Major Willys Blaauw

However, personnel problems typical of any army (promotions, transfers in the new year, and ability to do the job, among others) were to change the configuration of this ad hoc regiment. There was to be one HQ with *two* 2ICs (Major Hurter and Captain Laubscher) and the batteries would be grouped into the three sectors (west, central and east). The eventual deployment and allocation of personnel would change within days, as will be seen as this story unfolds. The first change was in T Battery, where Captain Laubscher was posted as the troop commander of I (India) Troop, his place in the RHQ being taken later by Major Blaauw. The second change that week was the transfer of Captain Rheeder from his post as battery commander to that of troop commander in U Battery under Major Blaauw. On 25 November, after numerous false alarms I Troop's GPO, André Brand, together with his recce vehicle, one G1 gun and its Bedford tractor, an ammunition vehicle (Bedford) a water bowser and 20 troops moved to the Grootfontein airfield where they were to spend the night in readiness to depart early next morning. At 22h00 that night the Cela reinforcement force started their move to Cela.

Battle Group Beaver

This organization was created in Grootfontein during late November 1975 to act as the reserve. By 10 December, this reserve had deployed at Lobito, with instructions to cover the roads to Silva Porto, Benguela and Sa da Bandeira. However, its artillery support was the first to leave to reinforce other formations deployed farther north.

By 19 November, the bulk of Task Force Zulu was in the process of moving to the central front and taking their artillery with them. This left Battle Group Alpha in Nova Redondo without artillery support. The gap was filled on 10 December by a 140mm troop from 4 Field Regiment under the command of Captain Louis Rheeder with Lieutenant Sarel Myburgh as his OP officer. This troop deployed initially just to the south of the town.

After some disconcerting enemy actions from both air and sea, the battle group was reinforced by an 88mm G1 battery commanded by Major Felix Hurter, a gunner officer at the Army College, who was initially appointed as one of the two 2ICs of the regiment, which detached from Battle Group Beaver. This addition provided the battle group with the ability to cover a somewhat wider front, particularly its right flank which was vulnerable.

It should be noted that the road infrastructure had suffered from neglect for years. It was the rainy season and one can imagine trying to move medium artillery on those slippery, muddy tracks. In one instance, a gun tractor, negotiating a steep pass, slid off the road and rolled with its gun over the embankment. Fortunately, no one was injured and the gun was eventually brought back into service. After the Ebo battle, the planners went back to their maps—happily, FAPLA had bequeathed a huge pile of maps by deserting one of their cargo vehicles in a contact with the armoured cars just before the Ebo battle—and considered their options. The result of this 'appreciation' was the decision by Colonel 'Blackie' Swart (the newly appointed OC of the restructured Task Force Zulu) to approach Conde via Hengo (10-59-37 S; 14-47-14 E). An armoured recce revealed that FAPLA were rebuilding the bridge in that area. The armoured cars and FNLA infantry attacked this bridge-building team, whereupon FAPLA withdrew, leaving the bridge open for the South African sappers to complete.

Major Venter's troop withdrew to a hide at a T-junction 5 kilometres south of the village of Ebo. There, Major Venter was posted to the Task Force Zulu HQ to reinforce the staff component, and was replaced by Major Jack Bosch. The latter instructed Lieutenant Jacobs to accompany an armoured car troop under the command of 'Vennie' van Vuuren, who was later awarded the Honoris Crux for bravery at Bridge 14. The troop was tasked to recce a road to the east in order to bypass Ebo. This road led to a bridge across the river just southwest of a place called Hengo. During the recce, Lieutenant Jacobs looked for firing positions for two troops south of the river as well as likely OP positions to cover a possible bridgehead and beyond. On successful completion of the recce, Jacobs reported back at the hide at Cela airport, where his troop and that of Major Bouwer would be regrouped into a battery. The new battery was now under the command of Major Jack Bosch with his senior personnel being:

- Troop commander, A Troop: Captain Chris Bouwer
- Gun position officer, A Troop: Captain Piet Uys
- Troop commander, B Troop: Lieutenant Jakes Jacobs
- Gun position officer, B Troop: WOII Sampie Claassen

A day or two later, the newly formed battery deployed to Hengo, A Troop to the east of the road behind high ground and B Troop behind a plantation to give them cover from observation from the north. The sharp-end teams, with a paratrooper section for protection, deployed in an observation post on a high, bouldered hill east of the road and just south of the river. (Jacobs likened the hill to the Matopos in Zimbabwe.) Lt Connie van Wyk (Special Forces), together with an FNLA company established the bridgehead. The only vehicle to cross the log-and-gravel bridge was Lt van Wyk's Sabre (a Land Rover mounted with a .50 Browning machine gun). The bridgehead was established without incident; the gunners could not detect any movement from Hengo on the far side of the river. Lieutenant Jacobs describes what happened next:

> . . . it suddenly started raining, and did it rain. I have never experienced rain like that again; even the footpaths between the huts in Hengo became torrents. After the boulders on the OP were struck by lightning, we decided to descend a very slippery and dangerous route; the rain had washed the gravel off the boulders.

Wisely, Captain Bouwer and his paratrooper protection element moved down the hill to a safer spot. On reaching their new position, he observed a vehicle moving into the village of Balabaia close by. The visibility was poor and Captain Bouwer had to wait to find out what this activity entailed. Once visibility improved, he discovered that it was a FAPLA element laying a minefield and immediately called for a fire mission. The first adjusting round landed about 80 metres from the vehicle. The FAPLA party hastily mounted and sped off, but not fast enough for the next artillery round: two FAPLA soldiers were seen to fall off the back, then the truck careered off into a grove of trees. The bridge was completed on 28 November and the bulk of Foxbat deployed near the 'Y' close to a deserted coffee plantation. The gunners deployed close by and kept the rest awake through the night by firing harassing fire tasks. One wonders who was actually harassed that night. After the rain had subsided, the bridge was inspected; as a result of the volume of water the gravel had been washed away, revealing a number of anti-tank mines. The bridge now only constituted a log structure, which would have to be repaired.

The next morning, Major Bosch called an order group at B Troop's position. While awaiting the arrival of A Troop's officers, the position came under heavy fire from the direction of Ebo. Although this position was out of observation from the north it was open from the high ground north of Ebo—a distance of 8 to 10 kilometres away. On the run, Major Bosch gave the order to cease fire, and in the process almost 'took out' WOII Claassen.

Cease fire!
A command given to the blunt end to come out of action and be ready to move.

Alternative positions had not been prepared and the battery moved quickly to a hide at the road junction to the south. Once there, some order was established and on Friday 5 December 1975, the battery occupied another hide at the *Melk Plaas* (milk farm / dairy), where they met up with Commandant van der Westhuizen, who had recently arrived with the advance party of 14 Field Regiment. Lieutenant Jacobs completes this story:

> Part of the advance party was Lieutenant Jaap Nel with a wedding invitation for me—to my own wedding! As my wife-to-be wrote in the card, 'your presence will be appreciated' and, as there were eight days to go, it was my cue to start my journey back to South Africa. I managed to get to Potchefstroom late Tuesday night and was married on the Saturday [13 December].

Despite the bombardment and the dangerous conditions, there were no casualties to this battery.

The build-up continues

Just before the battle of Ebo started, Captain Faan Bothma, the battery commander of 4 Locating Battery, was appointed as acting OC of 4 Field Regiment in Potchefstroom; the RHQ and the other batteries of 4 Field had been deployed around Katima Mulilo in their secondary role: that of infantry to perform counter-insurgency operations. Captain Bothma received a call from Brigadier van den Berg, instructing him to report to 14 Field Regiment's HQ 'to provide Commandant van der Westhuizen support in whatever he needs'. At that stage the requirement was for one radar section to be attached to a field troop 'for a special task' and WOII Willie Strydom of the Locating Wing of the School of Artillery the designated section commander.

Not a week later, Captain Bothma found himself appointed as train commander and ready to depart from Safarcamp Station in Potchefstroom with four radar sets, field and medium guns, associated vehicles, personnel, which included Major Thinus Brown, Captains Louis Rheeder, Koos Laubscher and Carel Theron, and a number of wagons of ammunition routed from the Lenz (west of Johannesburg) ammunition depot. On arrival in Grootfontein, Captain Bothma joined up with the Cela reinforcement force as radar troop commander.

A second train had been scheduled and arrived at Safarcamp Station a few days later. This train was commanded by Lieutenant Danie de Villiers, who, just before this move, had been on the GPO course at the School of Artillery; he was ordered to withdraw from the course and report to 14 Field Regiment for deployment to the 'operational area on the border', as the foray into Angola was euphemistically termed at that stage.

The loading of this second train was entrusted to the transport officer of 14 Field Regiment, a captain who, it was rumoured, enjoyed not only a bottle or two, but, in his part-time job as an elder in the church, also the occasional lonely wife. At this point, the story of the secrecy surrounding the train and its loading is told by Lieutenant de Villiers:

> . . . the captain refused to tell the stationmaster where the train was headed: very security-conscious this officer was. The joke was that the South African Railways and Harbours were probably more secure than the army was, as they operated according to the 'war book', which meant that train movement data was sent in encrypted form between stations. The captain was having none of this, 'If I tell you then I may as well announce this on the f---ing TV!' The stationmaster quietly seethed. Come the Monday morning, the troops and I arrive at Safarcamp siding. I take command of the train, load the troops, six to a compartment, and note that the engine is still standing on a separate siding. At this point, the stationmaster walks

up to the captain and again asks him where the train is heading. Standard reply from the captain, with the addendum: 'F--k me, man, I've been telling you the whole f--king week! Why do you keep f--king bothering me with this f--king sh-t? What the f--k has it to do with you?' Says the stationmaster: 'Sir, just tell me on which end of the f--king train should I hook the engine: this end or that end?'

This was only the start of a long and painful journey—all the result of one individual's arrogance and lack of comprehension of the bigger picture. The train was stopped at Klerksdorp (some 60 kilometres from Safarcamp–Potchefstroom) because it lacked a load manifest; and once again because the canopies of the trucks on board had not been lowered and there was a danger of them fouling the high-tension power cables above the track; and still later again on the same trip as Lieutenant de Villiers describes:

At some stage, some of the guns broke loose due to the swaying on the track somewhere around De Aar. It gave me great pleasure to order the captain to collect a party of senior NCOs to re-secure them while on the move. This was carried out without mishap despite the fact that the captain had been steadily pissing it up with a couple of the WOs, who had smuggled hard tack onto the train.

The equipment and some of the personnel from this consignment formed the battery under Major Hurter, with Captain Chris Human and Lieutenant de Villiers as the two OP officers.

The reinforcement in the centre

By late November 1975, the fighting had escalated and more South African forces were deploying. On 25 November, van der Westhuizen found himself at Grootfontein and appointed as the commander of what was called the Cela reinforcement force, an organization put together for the purposes of movement control until arriving in Cela. Between 28 and 30 November, the next two trainloads (one mentioned above) containing two 140mm G2 batteries arrived in Grootfontein. They were P Battery, temporarily under the command of Lieutenant 'Whitey' du Toit, including Lieutenant Danie 'Div' de Villiers and WOII Johan Stapelberg with a full complement of personnel and heavy equipment; the full complement of personnel for a 140mm battery, together with additional vehicles and four G1 guns; Captain Flip du Plessis, Captain André Steyn (the quartermaster of 14 Field) and 16 national servicemen with additional vehicles.

Just before this, Lieutenant Johan Potgieter, the battery commander of 1 Medium Battery, 4 Field Regiment, found himself and his battery on their secondary task: infantry patrols in the Caprivi. Based at Kwando, they were responsible for border protection and had just been ordered to prepare for an operation in the Luiana River area where Commandant Delville Lindford's Alpha Battalion had run into a 130-man-strong SWAPO ambush. For five weeks, this company patrolled the area and quite suddenly, seemingly from out of the blue, came a message that it should return to Kwando as a matter of urgency. The gunners could not understand why, as their job had not yet been completed. On arrival at base, Potgieter was informed by telex that they were to report to Grootfontein a.s.a.p., as 'someone is in big sh-t and was galloping to a place called Ebo somewhere deep in Angola. They are outgunned and are in serious need of medium artillery'. They already knew that there was fighting in Angola, but were blissfully unaware (as was the South African public) of the scale of operations and exactly who the enemy was.

The group flew to Grootfontein in a C-130 at low level and on arrival began to grasp the magnitude of the impending operation. Here they met Commandant van der Westhuizen and nearly every gunner from Potchefstroom, whom they hadn't set eyes on for the last three months. The hangars were full of new equipment: guns, crates and brand-new diesel Land Rovers, not unlike Christmas morning back home. There were, of course, shortages: the guns were not accompanied by their history books, and they varied in age and barrel wear, from one gun that was used by the Royal Artillery in Aden in the late 1940s to others that were almost new and unused. The battery was ready within two days, but, unfortunately was split—as an operational necessity— into two troops. H Troop was assigned to Battle Group X-ray in the Nova

Redondo area on the coast and G Troop was grouped with a troop from 14 Field Regiment to form a battery under the command of Major Wyllis Blaauw. The two troop commanders were Lieutenants Potgieter and J.P. Nel (not to be confused with Lieutenant Jaap Nel), with Bernie Pols as the OP officer.

By this time, the artillery component comprised members and equipment from all three permanent units: School of Artillery, 4 Field Regiment and 14 Field Regiment; batteries were mixed and matched as the operation demanded.

Another battery commander from 4 Field Regiment was Captain Carel Theron, who was also appointed as a troop commander together with Captain Koos Laubscher in a battery under the command of Major Thinus Brown. This battery was to drive to Silva Porto, where they would join up with Battle Group X-ray and be loaded onto a train to travel to Luso in the east, where they would support the effort to keep the Benguela railway line open. During their preparation, they realized that the roofs of the gun tractors would be too high to fit into either C-130s or C-160s. This led to the hasty removal of the crew compartment roofs from the gun tractors—by cutting them off.

H Troop, with Lieutenant Sarel Myburgh as troop commander and Lieutenant Hennie Nel as GPO, prepared to move to join up with Major Hurter's field battery to operate along the coast as far as Nova Redondo.

The Cela reinforcement force

The Cela reinforcement force travelled by road, leaving Grootfontein on 25 November at 21h50 in order to cross the border before first light so as to maintain secrecy, particularly about the presence of the guns, refuelling at Pereira da Eca (Ongiva). While on the move, a medium gun unhooked itself, taking out a wire fence and several telegraph poles. Undamaged, the gun was hooked up and the convoy continued. The force crossed the border into Angola at 05h50 on 26 November, arriving at Pereira da Eca at 08h00. Later that day, a radio message from Rundu instructed the force to move immediately and not wait for the AA battery that was supposed to join them. This resulted in the convoy leaving Pereira da Eca at 18h30 and, with difficulty, halting at the outskirts of Rocades for much-needed sleep. The next day, after a successful seven-hour run, the force arrived in Sa da Bandeira, where they were told to wait for an aircraft loaded with equipment.

It is interesting to note the mix of vehicles and equipment at this point. The convoy comprised the following:

- Artillery: 11 Land Rovers, 3 fire-control posts, 8 5.5-inch guns, 8 Magirus gun tractors, 2 Unimogs, 3 water trailers, 2 MAN trucks, 2 radar sets
- Infantry: 1 Bedford
- Armour: 3 Eland armoured cars, 1 Bedford
- Engineers: 4 Unimogs
- Maintenance: 4 Magirus Deutz cargo
- Technical services: 2 Land Rovers, 1 Bedford bin truck, 1 Mercedes Benz recovery
- RHQ: 3 Land Rovers, 2 Unimogs, 1 ambulance
- Total personnel: 22 officers, 232 other ranks.

A high point at this juncture: the force received 100 cases of free beer and fresh meat and bread; the only proviso was that the empty bottles had to be sent back. Needless to say, a traditional South African braai (barbecue) was spontaneously started. Included in Commandant van der Westhuizen's orders for that day was that the town was out of bounds for all because of loose women and enemy.

At 08h00 on 28 November, the convoy left Sa da Bandeira after being joined by a platoon of freedom fighters (UNITA and FNLA), arriving in Robert Williams at 17h00 so as to sneak through Nova Lisboa early the next morning. Unfortunately, the freedom fighters' excitement, and the fact that they were at loggerheads with one another caused the deaths of two FNLA troops by UNITA. This incident was followed by S/Sgt van den Berg being wounded in his side the same day by an accidental discharge of a Bren machine gun—it would seem by one of the senior gunner NCOs. To quote Commandant van der Westhuizen's notes, *'Amper vir Jenkins gedonner.'* (I almost punched Jenkins). S/Sergeant van den Berg was evacuated back to Sa da Bandeira.

Having passed through Nova Lisboa (and the Cuca Brewery) by 03h45, the convoy arrived at Cela at 12h00 after an armoured car under tow fell over a culvert, becoming a complete wreck (fortunately, the crew were only lightly injured); the freedom fighters suffered four dead with three seriously wounded after one of them blew himself up with a grenade and a rocket. Almost immediately, Major Blaauw's battery deployed in an open field next to the field hospital where testing of equipment continued and Lieutenant Potgieter managed to find 1:100,000 scale maps in a church in Cela. In the distance, the newly arrived gunners could hear the rumble of gunfire from Captain Bouwer's battery, motivating them to prepare properly for the forthcoming battles. Early the next morning, the battery shattered the tranquillity of Cela by opening fire on a target so as to calibrate the guns.

Gun calibration

During firing, gun barrels wear and their bore increases. The higher the charge, the more they wear. This wear causes a drop in projectile speed or, more correctly, muzzle velocity. Therefore, under the same conditions, a new gun will fire farther than an older, more worn gun. Gun calibration is the science of adjusting the sights of a gun so that it will fire the same distance, or range, as required by the map and at the same range as the other guns in the fire unit. Normally, this exercise takes a week of firing, measuring and calculating on a surveyed firing range. Under operational conditions, such facilities do not exist and the gunners have to make other arrangements.

On opening firing, the military doctor, Colonel (Dr) Tony Dippenaar, came rushing out of the hospital, scalpel in hand, asking, 'What is going on? Must I sew up or can I carry on?' The gunners apologized for the inconvenience and completed the fire mission.

At this time, Captain Uys was moved to the post of troop commander of the 25-pounder troop (Captain Bouwer), which meant that he would be employed as observation-post officer.

As this was the rainy season in Angola, the gunners often had to suffer the effect of the abundant rain. Dirt roads turned into mudbaths, and trenches filled up to the brim with water in minutes. At this stage, there were three captured BM21 MRLs and 60 rounds of ammunition in the theatre, for which plans were being made to put them into use to increase the firepower of the artillery effort. The headquarters of Task Force Zulu in the central sector realized that they were wasting their time on the dirt roads to the left and right of the main tarred road to Quibala. The approach towards, and through, Ebo would also not contribute much to the general advance of the South African troops and it was decided to advance along the tarred road towards the town of Quibala and then on to Luanda. On the night of 29 November 1975, the task force commander, Colonel Blackie Swart, gave orders to Battle Group Foxbat (under command of Commandant Frank Bestbier, SA Infantry) to capture the 14- and 16-kilometre bridges over the Nhia River, to enable the force to advance northwards; the artillery was to provide priority fire support to this force. The 14km bridge eventually became known as Bridge 14.

At this time, the main force (Task Force Zulu) apprehended the danger of their unprotected right (east) flank and were concerned about the possibility of being threatened from Melange to the northeast. Battle Group Orange was formed for just this purpose and deployed with the support of the recently arrived medium battery (140mm G2) under the command of Captain Philip du Plessis. Orange made short work of moving the 200 kilometres from Silva Porto to the Cuanza River, where they were halted by the demolished bridge at Ponte Salazar on 14 December.

At this time, the South African gunners knew very little about their opponents and some important questions were asked:

- Did the enemy have sound-ranging equipment? The one way to test this was to set an explosion in a dummy gun position and wait for counter-bombardment.
- Given that they were out-ranged why not use captured guns against their former owners?
- Where were they deployed? In the absence of own sound ranging and survey, each and every member was tasked to provide what information they could.

Under the cover of night, an infantry company took the hill overlooking the river and bridge, enabling the rest of the force to advance to, and deploy immediately south of, the bridge. The bridge, however, was destroyed, and had to be repaired by the South African Engineers. The sappers started to construct a crossing over the remains of the demolished bridge by laying long steel beams, each shaped like an oversized angle iron. They also had to make use of front end loaders to clear the approach to the bridge and to make a proper crossing. The unfortunate element in this whole task was that they were frequently subjected to enemy fire—mainly 122mm rockets from a BM21 multiple rocket launcher. During this period, one sapper was killed and Captain Douw Steyn (SA Infantry) was awarded the Honoris Crux.

Captains Uys and Bothma and Lieutenant Potgieter were deployed around the clock as observation-post officers. Their main task was to cover the bridge-building activities with artillery fire and to prevent the enemy from approaching the bridge. The main enemy culprit was a lone multiple rocket launcher that kept bombarding South African positions at regular intervals. Fortunately, it was fairly easy to judge where the rockets were aimed at, as their fire and smoke emissions clearly indicated the direction in which they were travelling. The launcher would fire one or two adjusting rockets, which were then followed by a salvo of ten to eleven. These rockets earned themselves the nickname of *rooi oog* (red eye) from the South African forces, as a bright-red flame could be seen emitting from the rocket's tail as it travelled through the air. The OPOs warned all the gun positions and the rest of the force when they saw the rockets being fired. As the rocket launcher was firing from about 19 kilometres away, it took approximately 12 seconds for the rocket to reach its target.

The OPOs could not understand why the 140mm (G2) guns could not put the rocket launcher out of action. Their fire was accurate, and it was clear that the rounds were falling very close to the rocket launcher, but it still kept on firing. They decided to send Lieutenant Bernard Pols to a hill west of the tarred road, from which he should try to observe their rounds from a flank. This could help solve their problem. When Lieutenant Pols reached the hill he reported that the rocket launcher was deployed at the back of a steep hill and that all the South African rounds were either falling in front of the hill, or travelled over the crest to fall far behind the launcher. He quickly provided adjustments, and the OP Officers waited for the rocket launcher to fire again. When this happened, they could clearly see the smoke and fire trails. Just one shell from a 140mm gun was enough to silence the rocket launcher. (This particular ordnance is today exhibited at the National Museum of Military History in Johannesburg.)

With the main threat of the rocket launcher now eliminated, crossing Bridge 14 and continuing the advance could take place. This was done after careful planning, and the OP Officers had a busy day engaging all the relevant targets. The 25-pounder troop concentrated on a kraal (a cattle pen or enclosure) overlooking Bridge 14; more than one of the 76mm anti-tank guns that were deployed in this enclosure were put out of action. The 25-pounders also succeeded in destroying one recoilless anti-tank gun. The OP officers and their guns played a major role in the success of the fighting at Bridge 14. They could also observe the retreat of the enemy forces and urgently persuaded their own headquarters to pursue with vigour.

On 1 December, the intelligence picture indicated that the FAPLA forces were struggling with logistics problems in the east, but not the same could be said for the force at Porto Amboim, as they were in the process of handing out 2,600 rifles, of which 400 were earmarked for their artillery battalion. On their southern front, bridges were under construction in preparation for an advance and the force at Mussende intended withdrawing, demolishing the bridges behind them.

A regiment is established

By 5 December, the gunners were reorganized into a single unit under the command of van der Westhuizen. At the same time, Louis Rheeder was tasked to move his medium troop to join up with Commandant Delville Lindford's force at Nova Redondo, where an attack was expected. Own forces saw Task Force Delta (Battle Groups Alpha and Beaver) at Nova Redondo supported by Major Louis Rheeder's 140mm troop; Task Force Zulu, comprising Battle Groups Foxbat and Bravo, was supported by Majors Bouwer, Bosch and

Blaauw's batteries; Task Force X-ray at Manengo had been pushed back to Cangumbo; and Battle Group Orange was supported by a 140mm battery in the Silva Porto area.

Bridge 14

The South African forces then cleared the valley alongside the tarred road to Quibala. The OPs and the guns were redeployed northwards; Captains Uys and Bothma were deployed on a hill with the nickname 'the Nek' (neck) that 'overlooked a river with a bridge, but, fortunately, this bridge was not demolished' (Bridge 14). Soon enough, the South African forces were subjected to rocket fire from an enemy MRL. This time, the launcher was deployed out of the reach of the 140mm guns and Commandant van der Westhuizen ordered one gun to be deployed directly behind the OP's position. According to Captain Uys:

> The gunners deployed after darkness in order to surprise the enemy; when the MRL fired again the next morning, they were truly surprised to experience the effect of a 140mm shell exploding behind their gun position! They immediately packed up and retired to the rear and did not fire at South African forces again in this sector of the campaign.

The focus of Task Force Zulu was Bridge 14 and this resulted in observers being tasked to occupy the high ground of Carubal (nicknamed Happy Rest) hill and register defensive fire (DF) targets on and around the bridge. The focus also included the attachment of a 25-pounder troop each to the battle groups in direct support and the deployment of the 140mm battery to within range of Dunga. Lt Michael Prins had occupied an OP in the Battle Group Bravo area with an outstanding command of the enemy positions in preparation to support an offensive against Bridge 14. At this point, Lieutenant Potgieter, with his troop of G2 guns, and Bernie Pols as OPO arrived in the Cela area to join up with the rest of the artillery regiment. Potgieter continues:

As I worked my way up to the front, I met a lot of people that I [had] not seen for a while. The bulk of Combat Group Foxbat at the time was made up of units from 2 SAI Battalion Group in Walvis Bay (I served there a few years). Seeing Lieutenant Jan Lusse in his Eland 90 was a sight. He smiled from ear to ear and offered me two eggs from his chicken basket attached to the back of the turret. The desert vehicle, unmistakably light Kalahari sand, was further camouflaged with pink paint: 'It was all we could find.' They were on their way out since they had started the war at Calueque some weeks before. He reckoned that the fun was over and he didn't feel like heavy fighting any more: 'The Cubans are here now and they shoot back.' At Foxbat HQ I was met by Captain Fritz Thirrion, the adjutant for Foxbat, outside his VW Kombi (with blacked-out windows). He nearly kissed me, but gave me a better idea of the problem targets and almost begged me to go and sort them out.

Two guns of Lieutenant Potgieter's 140mm troop were moved forward to cover the 'neck' and the bridges; there was only sufficient space in this area for two guns to deploy. The other troop was still in Cela awaiting transport. This was overcome the next morning by 'finding' five vegetable trucks to do the job. What was becoming an ad hoc allocation of fire units was resolved by Commandant van der Westhuizen the next day when he reorganized the regiment between Cela and the front.

By this time, the situation was becoming vague and Commandant van der Westhuizen was considering calling for a sound-ranging troop and a survey troop to help fixate the enemy artillery. The local population showed signs of moving, giving indications of an impending attack. C Troop (25-pounder), deployed at Hengo, and fired three harassing fire tasks before withdrawing to the fork.

During the afternoon of 3 December, the task force came under fire from 120mm mortars, 122mm guns and 122mm MRLs, but the erratic fire caused no damage at all. The gunners immediately returned fire on three Angolan gun positions and on some infantry who were in the open. One of the G2 troops fired 125 rounds and destroyed a gun position, silencing all enemy fire for the rest of the day. According to Lieutenant Potgieter:

Lieb and I occupied an observation post next to the neck in the mountain range overlooking the Nhia River and Bridge 14. There they were—three targets on a platter and well within our range. Four enemy 75mm M1942 field guns in a stone-enclosed kraal covered the neck next to us and bombarded anything that attempted to come through. We fired two adjusting rounds and opened with five rounds fire for effect. A South African armoured car troop was ready to pass through the neck and occupy the high ground on this side of the bridge [the eastern slope of Hippo Hill]. As they moved through the neck, the enemy guns opened fire once again and scared the living daylights out of the troopers. I had a sense of humour failure and spent the rest of the afternoon destroying those gun positions. Hence the saying about firing medium guns: 'Stick to the rules, be bold and don't piss on the target!' Something that amused me (even today), was the sight of those armoured cars reversing out of the neck with maximum revs, while under fire—at three kilometres per hour. Why? That was the fastest those little Noddys could go, backwards.

The observer to target (OT) distance was some 6,500 metres and with my 8 x 60 naval binoculars, point destruction was a bit of a rumour [that is, the OT distance was too far to observe the detail required to control the accurate fire of a single gun required by a point destruction shoot]. However, the targets were temporarily neutralized. I had to get much closer to the targets beyond Bridge 14 to make any difference.

With the enemy guns out of the picture, Commandant George Kruys could advance Combat Group Foxbat through the neck and occupy the terrain on the high ground south of the Nhia River. The heavy downpour and regular rain caused the Nhia to rise and burst its banks in the flatter areas. The river had to be crossed farther upstream to the east to establish a foothold. A team of recces

[Special Forces] under Captain Hannes Venter were ordered to make a crossing and neutralize the targets on the other side. At nightfall, the heavens opened their sluices once again and then all hell broke loose. The recces ran into heavy resistance, Sergeant Wannenburg being badly wounded and Hannes picking up a wound in his hand. The command radio net became congested with shouting and pleas for help. I felt angry for not being able to have the guns retaliate, as it was pitch dark and the rain came down in king-sized buckets. Adjusting fall of shot was virtually impossible. The recces and the support on our side of the river were too close to the target and firing meant endangering them even further.

At this stage, the war was, in effect, an artillery duel: there was no activity from any of the other arms involved. However, the South African gunners were still losing on range, and this had to be compensated for by movement, concealment, well-planned fire missions and good observers constantly searching for enemy artillery positions: in the words of Commandant van der Westhuizen:

Added to this was the unimpressive performance of our own infantry [although primarily allied forces], the difficulty of using earthmoving equipment to prepare gun positions—they were under enemy observation constantly—and the lack of suitable firing positions generally. This led to the deployment of guns in pairs rather than troops.

In the morning of 4 December, Lieutenant Potgieter was briefed by van der Westhuizen before leaving to set up an OP on Hippo Hill (the hill overlooking Bridge 14) and the targets beyond so as to support the crossing of the Nhia River. By now, Potgieter's troop had occupied a new position on a farm where the farmhouse became the HQ and kitchen. The GPO, 2/Lt Enslin Beetge, was ordered by Potgieter to 'stack 500 rounds per gun and at all costs to keep those numbers up—40 per cent charge supers and charge four for the rest'.

The stables and other outbuildings served as shelter against the rain, and with typical ingenuity the TA sergeant had cut holes in the walls so that the gun director (a type of theodolite) could see each gun and the TA sergeant could stay dry. The troop leader, Lieutenant Zai van den Heever, came from a farm in the Zeerust area and in no time had the dairy up and running where he would exchange milk for anything edible. The first cow was named Zai and was painted with UNITA-green letters on both flanks. Unfortunately, she was too late to move out of the way of number two gun during a shoot and became stone deaf; it seems that subsequent firing bothered her little. Number three gun removed the tiles from the farmhouse roof, which then had to be covered with a tarpaulin. The farm tractor was repaired by van den Heever, who then pressed it into service as an ammunition mover, thus saving an enormous amount of labour.

Lieutenant Potgieter takes up the story of his move to Hippo Hill:

An eager stick of paratrooper volunteers were ready in no time to escort me and Lieb [the OP assistant] on this 14-day outing. Our backpacks were heavy and each patrol member had to carry two additional radio batteries. In comparison with today's batteries these weighed a ton and lasted only a couple of hours. Claymores, flares and lots of grenades made up the rest of the dead weight. I was impressed by the logies that organized me a telescope that arrived just in time. The 16-odd kilometres we had to cover took us through marshes and thick bush—and the worst was the mountain. The heavy rain made the slopes so slippery that it became virtually impossible to make any progress. Two steps forward and five slides back. Somehow I felt more secure under the cover of the downpour. Halfway up the mountain I heard a cough and the squalls of a radio up ahead. We froze for a while and slid back some 200 metres and approached the mountain directly from the north. We were exhausted, the heavy backpacks and mud sapping our energy. Lieb was struggling as he also had to carry the heavy radio and antennas. I told him to hand me the radio and his protest came immediately in no uncertain terms in a deep whisper, 'Lieutenant, you carry the responsibility and I will carry the radio, OK?' I giggled and as we set off, I thought about Lieb. Mark Liebenberg was one of a kind. He had some sort of growth deficiency and when he started his national service was just more than four feet tall. I remember his gutsy performance during a boxing tournament in basic training when he would not budge against a former South African champion. He was awarded the boxer of the tournament trophy there. He was also a Springbok scout. The growth-hormone treatment given to him by the medics since then helped him to grow some six inches during that year. He earned the respect of the whole battery and was worthy as my signaller and closest friend for the last five months.

During their climb to the summit of Hippo Hill, the OP party were confronted with the problem of thick mist. Opening their maps in that rain and mist would have effectively destroyed these paper documents, so Lieutenant Potgieter had to trust his original navigation plan plotted out at the farm and rely on his prismatic compass. By first light they were very close to the top of the hill. Here they found that a steep cliff protected the eastern side, and massive natural piles of boulders gave them cover against the rain as well as observation from every direction. Furthermore, the height and position of this spot gave the party clear observation over the deployed FAPLA forces. That first morning in the thick mist gave them enough time to study the detail on the map and they analyzed every potential crevice, nook and cranny in the observation zone ahead of them. Lieutenant Pogieter:

When the fog eventually disappeared, we were semi-dry and ready. We could see for miles. Bridge 14 was about 900 metres below us. A FAPLA infantry company was deployed and dug into a defensive position on the other side of the river covering Bridge 14. The FAPLA troops were strolling around their trenches with their shirts off. Some of them were playing a game of sorts with sticks and stones. Troops are the same all over, I thought. A BRDM armoured car with a 23mm mounted gun was parked next to the road and camouflaged with branches. Two 82mm mortars were deployed, and I could hear the laughter of the mortar crews as they sat on ammo boxes probably drinking coffee. Two of the recces' Sabre jeeps were bogged down across the river from FAPLA with 7.62 Browning machine guns still intact—evidence of the unfortunate attempt to cross the river a few nights before. I spent the rest of that afternoon recording targets in the [FAPLA] defensive positions. Late in the afternoon, the sun swept under the trees and exposed more than the Cubans would have wanted. I identified at least an infantry battalion in classic Soviet echelon defensive deployment. I started drawing a panoramic sketch of the whole area and plotted some 200 targets. But something bothered me the whole time: where were the armour and artillery deployments?

By 10h00 the next morning, the mist lifted and the sun broke through. There, laid out in front of the OP team was a gunner observer's dream—a deployed battalion, a bridge that needed rebuilding and a FAPLA party attempting to capture the two South African Special Forces' Sabres that were bogged down. (A Sabre was a Land Rover 109 inch converted by the addition of machine-gun mountings, smoke grenade launchers and the like.) Two Soviet Ladas were parked at the blown bridge and four Cuban officers were walking through the forward company position, waving arms and shouting instructions that resulted in the FAPLA troops quickly dressing and manning their firing positions. At this point, the branches covering the BRDM were thrown off and it was moved down to the river opposite the two bogged-down Sabres on the opposite bank. With the Cuban officers shouting instructions, the winch of the BRDM was let out and two FAPLA troops struggled to get the winch-cable across the fast-flowing river. After attaching a thinner rope to the cable, they eventually managed to get it across and hooked this up to one of the Sabres. Lieutenant Potgieter continues:

I ordered a troop fire mission, applied a 'drop 200' correction, ordered five rounds fire for effect, airburst at my command and waited for the right moment. When the BRDM started retracting the cable, the troops were ordered to help and they grabbed the cable, assisting the struggling BRDM winch to pull the Sabre across the river. I ordered fire, and some 50 seconds later all hell broke loose. Black smoke puffs and the bright detonations of the proximity fuses covered the whole target. The troops at the Sabres were sliced down. I gave an 'add 50' correction and ordered 20 rounds fire for effect. One of the Ladas started burning. The driver in the BRDM panicked. He tried to reverse, but skidded around like a Jack Russell playing with a rag. Somehow, the cable snapped and the BRDM started to move out onto the road. I ordered a fire mission on number one gun (Gas Liebenberg's gun crew were the fastest and most accurate) and applied a small correction to intercept the vehicle on the road some 200 metres ahead. The gun reacted remarkably quickly, considering the range of approximately 9,000 metres. The first round landed just in front of the vehicle, forcing it to stop. The next round fell slightly short, but thanks to the driver's hesitation, the third round landed right on top of the BRDM. The detonation wave virtually lifted the rear of the vehicle up and plunged it into a sand embankment. We only found out later that the officer in the Lada was Raul Diaz Arguelles, commander of the internationalist operation in Angola, a hero of the anti-Batista struggle and an extremely popular figure in Cuba, who died on the spot.

This fire mission was to cause a full day's counter-bombardment. The Cubans opened fire with their 120mm mortars on Major Luther de Bruin's company, which was in a defensive position some 1,000 metres south of the bridge. A few stray shots landed near Commandant Kruys's HQ (the VW Kombi), causing Major Willys Blaauw to complain profusely about the discomfort. Having given their positions away by opening fire, the FAPLA mortars now became the targets for the medium gunners. Six mortar positions were identified and four were engaged simultaneously (one gun per target). It took some concentration and fancy footwork to control four fire missions at the same time. The rain started again and brought the darkness earlier than usual. The day ended with the guns having fired an average of 500 rounds each.

At the same time, an instruction was given to move a 25-pounder troop forward to a position close to Danger Bay—a high hill where one of the gunner OPs was deployed—in order to provide covering fire to a patrol operating in the Quipuco area. Later in the day, a plan was made to bring in a captured BM21 and 12 rounds of ammunition, to be fired in the general direction of the enemy the next morning.

The next day brought mixed news, firstly that the Angolan forces were once again moving on the green route and helicopter activity was on the increase; added to this, the enemy was infiltrating around the South African positions. Secondly, the news from the BBC was that the Angolans were evacuating hundreds of casualties after a 'heavy artillery bombardment'; and there was a report from Special Forces that the enemy artillery had been destroyed, some equipment by direct hits, resulting in troops withdrawing over the Nhia River (which was in flood) and leaving their equipment behind.

There were those gunners who, for various reasons, did not have any faith in the locating branch of the corps. The Cymbeline radar deployed in the area detected two blips on its display screen. Seeing this, WOII Strydom, an experienced radar instructor, advised Captain Bothma that there were enemy helicopters flying around. Bothma, in turn, warned the RHQ, who replied with the message: 'You are talking sh-t, stay off the air.' This warning was reinforced by an OPO on Hippo Hill who had visual contact with the helicopters. In hindsight, had this warning been accepted it may have reduced the risk of a bombardment to Lieutenant Jaap Nel's troop, which was deployed in a quarry to the east of Hippo Hill. A similar situation occurred shortly afterwards when the radar section offered to help navigate a helicopter one dark night.

On Saturday 6 December, the commander of Task Force Zulu gave the order to capture and establish a bridgehead at Bridge 14 on Monday, 8 December.

Battle Group Foxbat would attack, supported by the fire of the artillery, the guns moving into position at first light on Monday morning. A critical task for the gunners was to keep the enemy artillery quiet while the sappers cleared the mines off the bridge.

Preparations began in earnest on Sunday when the gunners provided covering fire with one medium troop and two 25-pounder troops for the Special Forces, who were airlifted in by helicopter. The results of the day's shooting were:

- the destruction of an infantry platoon and one of two vehicles;
- the destruction of an armoured car and its crew; and
- the successful cover for the Special Forces' insertion.

The anticlimax on Monday 8 December was a bitter disappointment: the artillery OPs spent all day ready to fire their defensive fire plan; not a round was fired. Battle Group Foxbat advanced as ordered and met no enemy fire at all. However, an enemy infantry company was seen to be active on the blue route in the Hengo area and the Special Forces made contact.

That night, the task force's mission was confirmed: secure Bridge 14 and advance to Quibala; secure both the blue and red routes. The green and blue approach routes were to be covered by a field troop each, and the medium battery was to cover both routes. During the night, Foxbat drew mortar and small arms fire from the east, but this was quickly silenced by the gunners. At 06h00 one field troop deployed under cover of mist to provide support to Battle Group Foxbat on the green route and the forwardmost medium troop engaged the enemy approaching Bridge 15 where they were driven back. At 13h00 a field troop once again silenced enemy mortar fire on the blue route, and at 17h00 one of the medium troops destroyed a convoy of five vehicles on the green route.

The ammunition consumption—or, more correctly, the resupply—was becoming a serious point of concern for the regimental commander, and here the traditional logistic lines of supply were very quickly reorganized. An arrangement was made that, instead of artillery ammunition being moved by road from Grootfontein, it would now be flown directly from Waterkloof by C-130 and delivered to the echelon at Cela airport some 30 kilometres behind the combat zone. As time went on, the ammunition was eventually delivered directly from the factory to Waterkloof Air Force Base.

Finally, on Wednesday 26 November, the first part of I Troop left Grootfontein by air for Silva Porto. This group had been strengthened by the addition of one gun and Lieutenant du Preez, the troop leader. The next morning at 10h45, Captain Laubscher left Grootfontein by air, together with 25 men and two guns, for Silva Porto. Their arrival is described by Captain Laubscher:

> On setting foot on the airfield my hat blew off and was picked up by a UNITA soldier, my first introduction. UNITA guard the airfield, the buildings covered with slogans. We moved by Unimog to a monastery about 6 kilometres west of the town. A beautiful country. The rest of the troops (and the rest of the force) under the cypress trees. Gardens are full of fruit and vegetables—the troops eat! The monastery was left with most of its contents, beautiful kiaat rafters, etc.

The troop (or, at least, the part that was in Silva Porto by that stage) was told that it would move the next morning (28 November) by road to a point east of General Machado where they were to protect a bridge, as the eastern front was crumbling rapidly and FAPLA was already at Cangumbe with approximately 1,600 infantry, five armoured cars and a 122mm BM21. Captain Laubscher was introduced to Dr Jonas Savimbi, the UNITA leader, by Commandant Willie Kotze, the battle group commander. The introduction was, 'this is my artillery commander'. The troop carried on with sight tests and gun director drills. The troop slept in a classroom that night.

X-ray had been formed specifically to protect the Benguela railway line from Silva Porto to at least Luso in the east. The commander of this battle group was Commandant Willie Kotze, an experienced gunner officer, who is mentioned on numerous occasions in this work. This formation was unique in that it was no longer a 'vegetable truck' organization, but was (at last) equipped with South African military vehicles and equipment.

At 09h00 on Friday 28 November, the vanguard of Battle Group X-ray left Silva Porto by road, arriving at General Machado at 12h00. This forward element comprised an infantry company, nine armoured cars (South African), I Troop, an engineer element (less than a troop) and a doctor with an ambulance. The battle group's matériel and troops (together with a collection of pigs for UNITA) were loaded onto a train in Silva Porto bound for General Machado where they would meet the vanguard that had travelled by road. Here the whole battle group was loaded onto two trains and after leaving the next day at 05h00, arrived at Munhango 100 kilometres farther east. This 'armoured train' must have resembled something from the Anglo–Boer War as the guns were actually deployed on the railway trucks, the rearmost gun facing back, the middle two guns facing the flanks and the front gun covering the front of the train. The OPO was deployed on the locomotive.

The train wound its way eastward through rolling grasslands and thickets interspersed with marshes and meandering rivers. At Munhango, the troops disembarked earlier than expected; it was reported that the enemy had already occupied Cangumbe, 60 kilometres farther east, where they were originally to stop. The road from here was nothing more than a pair of deep tracks winding through the bush. Giving orders to advance, Commandant Kotze instructed the UNITA company to deploy as the vanguard. However, this was unacceptable to UNITA as they could not understand why the artillery was behind them, so a live-firing demonstration was set up, with the OP deployed in front of the assembly where they could hear the radio orders being passed through to the guns. Only once the identified target was engaged did the UNITA troops begin to understand the concept of the artillery's ability to fire on a target without the guns being able to 'see' the target. Satisfied, UNITA accordingly deployed in the vanguard and the advance continued. This move was completed without any enemy contact.

On unloading the train, I Troop deployed in a plantation to the east of the town. This was carried out in pouring rain, causing everyone and everything to become drenched. Here the gunners received a taste of the refugee problem, as these unfortunates were moving west on foot, by train and in trucks. Later that day, the gunners redeployed three kilometres farther east for the night.

The next morning, the vanguard commenced its move to Cangonga where UNITA had an HQ under the command of a general. Here the artillery troop deployed to the west of the town, and Captain Laubscher deployed with three troops of armoured cars in an observation line to the east. As yet, the gunners had not fired a round; the troop commander was concerned that he didn't even know if the four guns could 'fire together'; that is, if the rounds would land on the ground in the same pattern in which the guns were deployed. Laubscher ordered a fire mission for the purpose and to attempt to get a round within his field of view. The first round in the eastern theatre was fired at 10h55 on 30 November 1975. This was followed by another HE round and then by a smoke round in order to see the fall of shot. However, the battle group commander put a stop to the use of smoke because he was worried about the element of surprise. At 16h00, after hours of heat and boredom, a smoke signal was seen in the distance, and 30 minutes later a FAPLA armoured car and a swarm of infantry appeared over the whole front. The South African armour joined the fight and destroyed the enemy armoured car after four rounds. This fight was to cause much difficulty for Laubscher in that he couldn't see the fall of shot in among all the other firing—bear in mind that the detonation of a 90mm HE round from an armoured car and that of a G1 gun is almost identical. It must also be borne in mind that this was Laubscher's first contact with an enemy. He continues:

Problem to control artillery fire—bad communications. My ears deafened from the fire around us. I ran dodging between armoured cars and bushes. Lay down next to a mortar fire controller and his signaller and aimed my rifle at the enemy on the left flank. Battled to identify fire between other rounds. Fired proximity fuse. Brought one gun forward for direct fire. Chaos reigned and everyone was shooting. I ended up in the back blast from a 106mm recoilless gun and Terblans, my signaller, thought that he was wounded after some ricocheting rocks hit him. A shell splinter from an airburst round hit him on the head. We received a message that the enemy was flanking us from the left flank; I withdrew the gun.

After dark, the shooting eventually stopped and the force withdrew to Simonge, where they spent the night. There were no South African casualties and a few lightly wounded within the UNITA ranks.

Over the next two days, the force moved steadily eastwards, with the two artillery troops switching between supporting the vanguard and deploying with the main guard. Thus the two troop commanders could also take a break. On 2 December, Captain Theron fired 18 rounds fire for effect with I Troop in a demonstration shoot for UNITA. The next day, the two troops closed up on one another to engage (under the control of Captain Theron) a target in the town of Cangumbe. They fired 15 rounds, but there was no sign of any enemy activity in the town. Continuing the advance, the gunners registered a target on a bend in the road just to the east of the town of Cachipoque with a smoke round. An HE round after that suddenly created a stir among the FAPLA troops, who hastily fled from their cover onto the road. The following day, 4 December, was a great day for the gunners: they received cooldrinks, cigarettes, beer and dubbin (a gel for softening boot leather). J Troop took over the direct support of the vanguard on 5 December again, with Captain Theron in an Eland 60 to control their fire. The forward armoured cars almost drove straight into a truck full of MPLA troops, but because of the height of the road above the surrounding countryside, the forwardmost Eland 90 could not bring its gun to bear. Captain Laubscher's view is:

> What an opportunity! The enemy jumped off and came under fire from the Eland 60, where Cala [Captain Theron] attacked with his machine gun and mortar, causing casualties. Cala and the others came under accurate mortar fire at a bend in the road, where Cala and Lieutenant Frans Rocher dismounted. My troop deployed and we met Cala in a donga next to the road. My men and I moved on foot through the bush on the northern side of the road in an attempt to get observation over the enemy or [the town of] Chicala.

It was here that the sharp-end gunners experienced the sound and feeling of bullets flying past, this while trying to concentrate on the job of controlling artillery fire. They fired both HE and smoke rounds again, with no success in observing the fall of shot until one round fire for effect eventually came up 500 metres in front of them. Because of the density of the bush (and the lack of maps) the gunners had to virtually guess where Chicala was in order to move the fire to the eastern side and to physically move to maintain what limited observation they could.

After moving once more, Captain Laubscher and his team found themselves on the northern side of the town, the armoured cars and Captain Theron's team having arrived before them. On arrival at the first huts, the I Troop observation party was greeted by three rounds of HE fire from the battery some 100 metres from them, these rounds intended for the eastern edge of the town. Having informed Captain Theron that he was firing close to own forces, the party continued their trek on foot behind the forward armoured cars in order to register a defensive fire target in the close vicinity. After last light, the force withdrew and held a debriefing where the gunners, once again, highlighted their problems, these being observation in flat terrain covered in thick bush; and the deployment of one troop commander in the main guard, from where he would have to move forward—a distance of some 5 kilometres on foot. The issue here was the waste of time that this walk took, especially if there was a firefight at the same time.

That day the MPLA forces fired their BM21, another new experience for the South African battery, the two rounds passing over their heads and landing harmlessly in the bush. It seems as if the artillery's complaints were listened to because, on 6 December, Captain Laubscher 'dug' himself into an Eland 60 in readiness for the continuation of the UNITA-led advance to Luso. At 13h30, the advance finally commenced and the gunners fired a few rounds on either side of the road on the approach to Luena in order to register targets for later. In this process an HE round burst just in front of the forwardmost UNITA troops, one of the fragments causing a head injury.

The plan for the next day was for the artillery to recce a new gun position north of the road to Luso. Lieutenant Brand and du Preez were tasked to do this and would be accompanied by two infantry platoons to a point some 7 kilometres west of Luso. J Troop spent the day in the main guard. On

7 December, I Troop deployed 15 kilometres east of Chicala in support of the recce patrol: a good move because a short time later, the patrol on the south side of the road reported enemy in the process of preparing an ambush, and immediately the guns opened fire, the corrections being given by using the patrol's position as a reference point. The result was that MPLA vehicles were heard moving towards the rear, giving the impression that they were withdrawing. This was not to be, as the patrol then reported that the enemy had moved forward to a position some 150 metres in front of them. The patrol withdrew, and the gunners fired HE airburst on that spot. Confusion abounded, as it was discovered later that the 'enemy' was in fact allied forces setting up an ambush without authority. Later that day, Captain Laubscher received an air photo of Luso, which he duly enhanced by drawing a set of superimposed grid lines. The gunners planned to use air observation for this next phase (the attack on Luso) and allocated priorities to targets, the first priority being the airfield (the MPLA were using a Cessna for air observation, based at Luso) and the second being the governor's house, which accommodated the local commander and a BM21 deployed close by. At midnight, the battery formed up for the advance to Luso.

The night move towards Luso was painstakingly slow, with vehicles travelling with only their convoy lights on, to be switched off as they moved closer to the objective. Captain Laubscher couldn't find the guide that was supposed to meet them at the turn-off to the gun position and eventually dismounted, called a gun detachment forward and continued on foot using occasional torchlight, and found the infantry section (guides) some 500 metres ahead. After a difficult occupation because of the thick, wet ferns and bush, the battery was in action by 03h30. At 05h00, Captain Laubscher prepared to move back to meet the SAAF Cessna at 06h00: an exercise in futility, as his Land Rover would, once again, not start. He ended up being towed to the arranged rendezvous only to find out that the expected aircraft was going to be late because of bad weather. On hearing this, he planned to move forward using an armoured car, however, the Cessna arrived in time to participate in the attack. Accompanied by the infantry mortar observer, they took off immediately, attempting to find the gun position, initially to no avail. It turned out that the guns had deployed farther back than was planned. The first fire mission was not a success because the observers could not see the fall of shot, even when firing smoke. To add to the misery, once the rounds were observed, the aircraft's fuel was running low and the team had to turn back to refuel. In Captain Laubscher's words, 'We landed, vomited, refuelled and took off again.' Once they were over the target area, the airfield was registered together with a possible road ambush site and a bluegum plantation in the town. On landing again, Captain Laubscher reported to the commander (Commandant Moller) and almost immediately took off again, this time to attempt to engage the barracks to the south of Luso—it turned out that the fire was accurate this time.

The first attempt at attacking Luso was, in the artillery's eyes, a failure because the assault force did not make contact with the defending MPLA forces, the armoured cars ran low on ammunition and, to crown it all, the artillery troop commander could not make communication with the guns and the battle group commander had to direct fire from the air. Luso was taken finally on Wednesday 10 December by an assault from the west screened by a smoke shoot from the battery, the fire being controlled by the battery commander from the air. The airfield was occupied without much effort and very little supporting fire. By 16h00, the force was ordered to move into the town of Luso. At this time, the MPLA launched a counter-attack in the pouring rain.

Once again, Captain Laubscher couldn't get radio communications with his guns and had to resort to using the 60mm mortar on his Eland in the direct role. To make matters worse, the Browning machine gun had stopped. The radio problem turned out to be the result of a faulty antenna—at that time, the Eland 60 was not equipped with sufficient radios for artillery command and control, and observers had to use a manpack radio somehow strapped inside the turret, the antenna poking through the hatch. Therefore, the hatch could not be closed and the occupants felt the full effect of the persistent rain and, worse still, the antenna would make contact with the steel turret and, therefore, not function.

The NFA during their trip to Rhodesia in April 1978. From left: Capt Eric Evans (Rhod Arty), Capt John Johnstone-Webber (NFA), WOI Jan Wessels (NFA), Maj Richard Lovell-Greene (NFA), WOII Ken Gillings (NFA), an acquaintance, Maj Frank Vincent (NFA) and Cmdt Don Guthrie NFA. *Photo: K. Gillings*

Rhodesia 1968: A group of South African Artillery officers at an OP position during a training exercise. From left: Lt Joffel van der Westhuizen, Capt Pale Kotzé and Lt Jaap du Rand. Note the Rhodesian uniforms. *Photo: C.P. van der Westhuizen*

2Lt André Brand and Rinty. *Photo: D Mattushek*

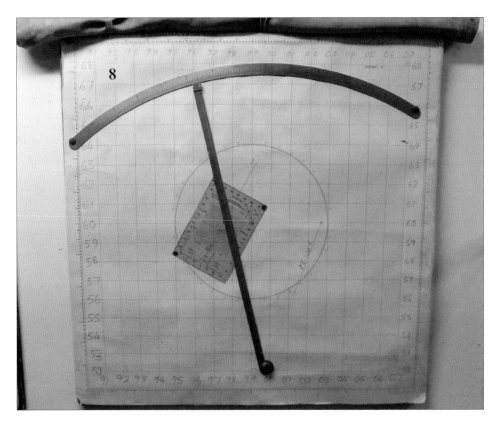

An artillery board fitted with its 1:25,000 scale, bearing arc and range arm. In the centre is the target template for applying the corrections given by the observer. *Photo: Author, TSA Museum*

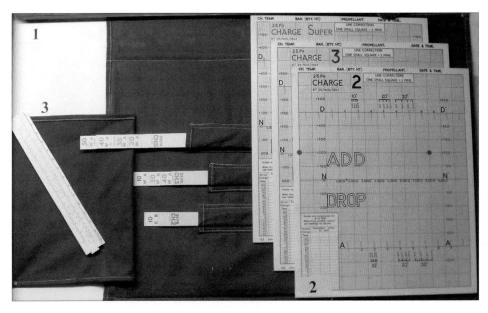

A met graph. On the left is an artillery slide rule. The large numbers in these photos are TSA Museum's reference numbers and not part of the equipment. *Photo: Author, TSA Museum*

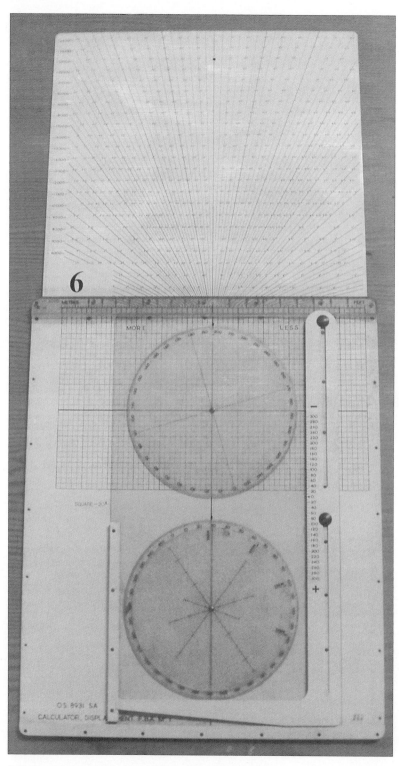

A displacement calculator used to calculate the angle of sight as well as the convergence, should this be required for a shoot. *Photo: Author, TSA Museum*

A radar, Field Artillery no. 15 Mk I, also known as Cymbeline.
Photo: SANDF Archive

Eland 60 armoured cars in Angola, circa 1975. Note the headgear worn by the crew; the helmet-fitted intercom only arrived later. *Photo: SANDF Archive*

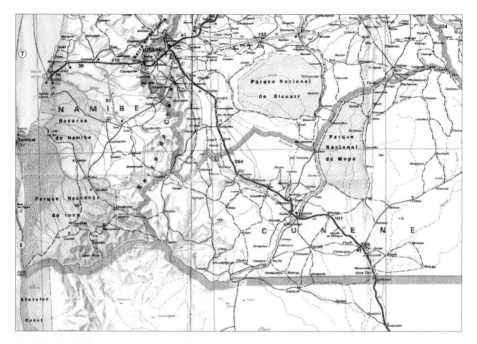

The western theatre of operations. Towns and rivers in this theatre are referred to in almost all operations during the period covered by this book. *Map: Cartographia Kft*

Savannah: 2Lt H. van Niekerk receiving his Honoris Crux Silver from Minister of Defence P.W. Botha, on 29 November 1976. *Photo: 14 Field Regt*

Savannah: 2Lt M.J. Prins receiving his Honoris Crux from Minister of Defence P.W. Botha, on 29 November 1976. *Photo: 14 Field Regt*

(1)

Don 6 Nov 75

1. Bew die volg in: (3 meters op 5 Nov oorlewer)

   a. Tp × Od – Beste gekled en peos – skiddspers 5 mag
      14 Od se gekled

   b. 2 × Rds Stelle met 1 × bemanning

   c. Uiti – opgele in kiel en in orle

   d. 3 × L/R'a, 1 × V8, 2 × Waterbos

   e. 3 × Normale Nabel Blry behoefte (Blry droog op it)

   f. Opdele + Teg Uiti

   g. 75 man kokers

   h. Opdele + Tegn Uiti

   ↗ RV

2. Fase 1 = Per pt na Waterkloof in pos bg na kunla
   Fase 2 = In (voor 091500 Nov)   Olieg N° in

3. Lie Sif (Rooi), dang met uit R39'a

4. Opo = Uiters Geheim. Alles, NDP'a slegs onywillyelik
   oor grens

5. Take = TB, Remstore + Voorbomb

6. D Sein set op Lugtawe verskaf:
   2 × Leaiers, 15 KVA Gen, Sein Elkes, 4 × 39'a, 2 × C42,
   2 × B47, Rds Tegni kus

7. Inf set plaaslike Bakm verskaf

8. Rats per man uit 2 dae (Droog) – Moet hou tot op kunla

9. Nie SA Uniforms – Slegs Uniform tot op kunla – kry daar
   ander uniforms – Kan Boskiewis saamneem – Tag ean
   bagasie wat nie oor grens gaan. Nian Uiti, geen
   radios, kameras ens. Geen web/stuwels of enige iets
   met "Made in SA" daarop nie. 90 kaarte +
   Dogtag word op kunla ingee. Testamente +
   Pers Kaarte reg. Dra etikel met Bloedgp om sak.

10. Terug in Potch @ ± 14 Nov (Die!)

11. Kuil orduisbare cements by 3 Elkta Eenh om

(2)

12. Kol Cas le Roux = Koord off. Ek gaan self na
Waterkloof vir behe & beveg.

13. Naamlys v alle Uits + pers aan Ops. (Per Verbindeling)

14. Orte - Petroltenks ½ - ¾ vol

15. DNS sal akkom + Etes verskaf.

16. Vlieg Volg Art ammu op (Sit Vd Tp)
    Bris 117 = 1224 , Rook = 184 , 213 PMi = 216 , 221 B = 240
    Primers = 120 , Charges N = 1312 , Charges S = 96

17. Pers   Bekke Jans (30 Nov)
        Ogek Bosch = Tp Bev   Vd BB
        Chris B = OPO   C Tp Bev
        Piet Uys = KPO   C Tp KPO
        Tp Lt = Braam Coetzee   L Bty Kapt
        OPA = Ray Hawkins   L OPA
        Tp Bev asist = Leon le Roux   Bty Lug OTO
        TA Sers = Bdr v Reynevald   C TA Sers
        TA = Bdr Olivier   C TA
        TA = Bdr Pretorius   C TA
        = Bdr Maarberg   L Bk Klerk
        TSM = Dirk Smik   M Grootf - Suk
        Bdr Sel Bev = Strydom (402)   C TSM
    OTG Dwr B Bdrs = Bdr Strydom   C OPO Sers
    Tp Bev " " " = Bdr Rivervies   O BB Dwr B Bdrs
        Bdr Tiffie = Sers Trautes
        Sein Elekes = Kpl Mutrai

18. Lewe soos wat bereikbaar is

_____

7 Nov 75

                              ↗ 24h00
1. Jakof v Heerden vertrek vanaf Potch po pad na Grootf - verlaat
   po vt in - orders om 19h15 vanaf Brig vgk Berg
   ontvang. Uits neem. Adv uits + geluit kom vanaf Vlot stor
   hy vte in opo gebied. Ammu word ingevlieg

Savannah: Maj J.H. Potgieter HC. This picture was taken some time after the awards were presented.
Photo: SANDF Archive

Savannah: A G1 gun of P Bty Cape Field Artillery in Catuiti after a night of rain. *Photo: Cape Field Artillery*

Savannah: The hospital at Cela. *Photo: J.P. Nel*

Savannah: A panoramic view of the main road leading to Bridge 14 and Quibala. The 'nek' is clearly visible, as is Hippo Hill on the left. *Photo: C.P. van der Westhuizen*

Savannah: The errant BM21 captured by South African forces. This launcher is now on display at the National Museum of Military History, Johannesburg. *Photo: J.P. Nel*

Savannah: Lt Potgieter's troop deployed in the farmyard. Note how the roof tiles have been blown off by the muzzle blast from the guns. *Photo: SANDF Archive*

Savannah: A FAPLA 122 mm BM21 multiple rocket launcher in action. *Photo: J.H. Potgieter*

Savannah: Lt Nel's 140 mm G2 troop in the Santa Comba area. *Photo: J.P. Nel*

Savannah: Lt Nel's troop in action during the fight for Bridge 14. *Photo: J.P. Nel*

Savannah: Lt Jaap Nel's troop in action in the quarry. In the background is the high ground around Santa Comba. The chickens were adopted by the gunners and eventually used to supplement the rations. *Photo: J.P. Nel*

Budgie: NFA and DLI boasted a large number of Old Hiltonians in their strengths. This photo was taken during the deployment in 1976. Standing from left: Sgt Ed Fyvie, Lt Rod Tweedie, Maj Mike Adrain, Capt Mike Heenan, Capt Bruce Warner, Capt John Johnston-Webber (NFA), Sgt Mike Phillip (NFA), L/Cpl Fred Grant and 2Lt Dave Krige (NFA). Front: WOII Tim de Gersigny (NFA), Lt John Havemann, Cpl Campbell Peter, Lt Liege Hopkins, Sgt Kim Fraser (NFA) and Sgt Allen Sherrard. Capt Richard Lovell-Greene (NFA) was absent for the photo, as he was on duty at the OP at the time. *Photo: The Hiltonian*

Savannah: The gun that sank in the Nhia River and her crew. Back row from left: Gnrs Adam Dewar, Peter Barnes, Glen Hawkins, Barry van Wyk, Roland Hunter, Nic Strimer and Gert Meyer. Front row: Gnrs Gary Isherwood, Paul Haak, Tony Carter (the No. 1), Martin McKeen, Bdr Rick Davies and Gnr Tony Liss. *Photo: C.P. van der Westhuizen*

Savannah: The soft, muddy conditions in the central front often limited deployment to the roads. Note how close the guns are deployed to each other. *Photo: 14 Field Regt*

Savannah: Cmdt van der Westhuizen standing on the recently repaired Bridge 14. *Photo: C.P. van der Westhuizen*

Savannah: Looking weary are Maj Bosch, Lt Potgieter and WOII Stapelberg at P Batteryy, Battle Group Orange. *Photo: J.H. Potgieter*

Savannah: FAPLA 122 mm D30 guns in action.
Photo: J.H. Potgieter

Bruilof: Landing a Cessna 185 at the Oshivello airstrip after a practice air OP mission.
Photo: Author

Seiljag: G Troop moving out of Grootfontein. Note the DIY camouflage on the front gun tractor—a relic of Operation Savannah. *Photo: Author*

Seiljag: G Troop returning to Grootfontein.
Photo: Author

Seiljag: G Troop on the road from Rundu to 32 Battalion's base at Omaune. *Photo: Author*

Reindeer: Airborne in an SAAF Kudu over Oshivello training area. In the background, Etosha Pan; in the foreground, the main road from Tsumeb to the operational area. *Photo: Author*

Reindeer: G Troop engaging Dombondola. This picture was taken by Capt Mike Cowley, the FOO. The sharp-end officers on the ground travelled in Eland 60 armoured cars. *Photo: M.G. Cowley*

Reindeer: Late afternoon of D-Day; the two combat teams about to occupy a leaguer area. Note the close spacing of the vehicles. At that stage, the Angolan Air Force (FAPA) was not a threat and had just lost a MiG to a SAAF Mirage above Cassinga. *Photo: M.G. Cowley*

Reindeer: The next morning (D+1). POWs about to be moved south. *Photo: M.G. Cowley*

Seiljag: A Buffel fire control post on the road to 32 Battalion's HQ. The 'poncho' was rigged on the vehicle to keep the passengers dry. It was unsuccessful. *Photo: Author*

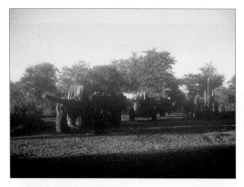

Reindeer: Guns forming up prior to movement from Oshivello to the deployment area. The gun on the right is 'Mona Ambriz', one of the two guns used in the first fire mission near Luanda in November 1975. *Photo: Author*

The South West African–Angolan border post at Ruacana in 1977. *Photo: Author*

That same day, the attackers were confronted with an apparition that appeared out of the surrounding bush—this 'thing' worked its way slowly towards the armoured cars whence it was engaged by machine gun fire. Thinking that it was a tank, the gunners could not understand why the 90mms did not attempt to engage. When they eventually did, five rounds could not stop this vehicle, but finally it and its smaller stablemate, stopped of their own accord. The gunners fired three rounds fire for effect into the plantation whence the 'thing' had appeared and to where the enemy was withdrawing. By now, the firing had stopped and the South Africans could dismount to inspect these two strange vehicles. The larger of the two turned out to be a red bulldozer complete with dozer blade and covered with steel plating and painted in a green camouflage. Its crew had been killed by the machine gun fire and the 'Luso monster' (as it became known) had continued moving on its own! The smaller of the two was a similarly converted Land Rover, and each was equipped with an 82mm recoilless gun and a machine gun. Both vehicles were full of Portuguese ration packs, which were subsequently liberated and enjoyed by all.

Later that evening, the blunt end of the battery arrived at the airfield while the armoured cars attacked the MPLA headquarters, destroyed the BM21 nearby and captured the MPLA leader element.

The next morning, the gunners were up early and by 05h00 had formed a defensive locality, which they occupied until first light. The day was quiet, the MPLA having evacuated Luso leaving the airport buildings in a disgraceful state. Despite the fact that they had eaten and slept in those buildings there was human waste, cooking fires and rubbish spread throughout. The place stank of fish, maize meal, smoke and olive oil. The rest of the force arrived later in the morning.

I Troop deployed on the concrete hardstand at the airfield after a rumour that the MPLA were about to attack the airfield from the southeast; on arrival, J Troop deployed a short distance away. All to no avail, as the rumour proved to be just that: a rumour.

The gunners came out of action on 12 December and spent the day performing equipment and vehicle maintenance. A Dakota flew in with ammunition, and the Cessna landed with news that a train of 12 coaches / wagons was on the move from Texeira da Sousa collecting groups of people from the sidings along the way. To counter the possibility of an attack, Combat Team Barron was formed of two armoured-car troops, I Troop, an infantry mortar group (81mm), engineer and medical elements, complemented by a UNITA component. This combat team was tasked to repel a potential attack from this trainload. The team deployed near a place called Camitenga in a position where they could cover the railway line, the guns deploying within 200 metres of the line so that they could be used in the direct fire role. After waiting through the moonlit night during which no train appeared, the combat team came out of action and moved towards Leua thus continuing the advance eastwards; the town was reached without any interference. On arrival, the gunners went into action deploying to cover the bridges over the road to Henrique de Carvalho as well as the railway line to Texeira da Sousa.

On Saturday 13 December, just after lunch, Captain Laubscher moved out to do a silent registration of the targets. Despite the intention to register the targets without fire, it was decided to fire at least a single round to confirm the accuracy of the target plots. However, on closer inspection, it was found that there were concentrations of local population in, or very close to the targets, so confirmatory rounds were totally out of the question. The opportunity was used by the gunners to have a wash, the first in a long while; hardly had they finished when the order came through from battle group HQ for Barron to withdraw to Luso without delay. This move was completed by 19h00, whereupon the washing ritual was eventually completed.

On that same day, Captain Theron was instructed to join up with Combat Team Carrot to provide direct support in a move that would take them northwards some 40 kilometres towards Henrique de Carvalho. Their first action was to drive the MPLA forces out of a place called Buçaco, where J Troop fired nearly 150 rounds, resulting in some 25 MPLA killed. For I Troop in Luso it was a long, boring day.

At first light on 12 December 1975, the guns in the central front reported ready on the fire plan to support the assault and crossing of the Nhia River at

Bridge 14. On cue, the preparatory bombardment came down on the FAPLA and Cuban positions, systematically bombarding their infantry positions, HQs and echelons. An ammunition dump behind the forward defensive positions received a direct hit, another hitting some vehicles carrying ammunition. Potgieter's words again, from his vantage point on Hippo Hill:

> The air was filled with an orange mushroom cloud followed by the loudest explosion I have ever heard. The barrage rolled onto the second defensive position consisting of 75mm guns, anti-aircraft guns and 120mm mortars, and suddenly the enemy cracked. The few remaining vehicles started moving towards the tarred road leading through Catofe to Quibala. After a few minutes, at least 50 vehicles of all sorts were on the road trying their best to overtake the one in front. I ordered two guns to fire continuous fire (i.e. until I told them to stop) on a point about 1,000 metres ahead of these vehicles where a rocky outcrop covered in thick bush stretched across the tarred road. The embankments on either side of the road were very steep and all vehicles had to pass through this point. The front five vehicles drove into the fire and were destroyed. I ordered the other two guns onto single gun-fire missions on the same road and gradually bunched the whole convoy in by firing at the rear of the convoy. As the fall of shot was adjusted, more and more vehicles were destroyed; eventually 12 wrecked vehicles were connected like a train. The enemy soldiers jumped out and scrambled into the bush and some of them started running towards the point where the other two guns were firing at. I stopped the engagement. They were neutralized anyway and we could do with a few vehicles.

Under the cover of the artillery fire the armoured car squadron and the infantry company, strengthened by UNITA support, crossed Bridge 14 and advanced slowly. By this time, there was very little resistance. The enemy fled and could have been stopped 5 kilometres farther on if only the armoured cars could have moved faster. Chaos ensued and the withdrawal became a rout, with the last few vehicles disappearing over a hill close to Bamba Catofe. The armoured cars worked their way through the objectives and cleared up what resistance remained. They engaged the fleeing enemy until they ran out of ammunition.

At about that moment, two BM21s appeared again and fired off a 40-rocket (per launcher) bombardment, this time, firing from a position much closer to the South Africans than previously and, happily for the gunners, within charge super range. This time, the medium gunners were ready. (The FAPLA and Cuban rocket gunners had developed a routine so the South Africans knew that after firing they would return to their echelon, reload and come back to the same firing position.)

By this time, the BM21 gunners assumed that they were out of range and had become complacent. By the time the two BM21s arrived back at their firing position, five rounds fire for effect were already committed. After two corrections, one BM21 took an almost direct hit and exploded. The other was immobilized without firing a shot. Commandant van der Westhuizen sent a tiffy recovery party in to collect the launcher.

Potgieter stated: 'Apart from the heavy casualties reported by the Cubans that night, they also reported that we had guns that could fire up to a distance of 30 kilometres. Lieutenant Xavier, the BM21 MRL platoon leader, was not impressed and fumed when we sent him a message declaring it a fair fight.'

15 December saw a little flurry of excitement for the troops in Luso as they were warned to prepare to move to reinforce J Troop. They had only just formed up ready to move when the news came through that the MPLA had demolished the bridge north of Buçaco, so the next order was 'stand down'. The day was not all boredom however, as a SAAF Dakota arrived carrying post—the first since T Battery had been deployed.

16 December is a South African public holiday (then the Day of the Covenant). War, however, does not always provide for such occasions and this day in 1975 was no exception. The gunners received their first warning order to be ready to move any time from 08h00; this was soon changed to 10h00, which came and went without incident, giving the troops time to attend a church service in one of the hangars, a service conducted by

the delightfully named Padré Goodenough, a ubiquitous man of the cloth who spent many years in the operational area and who was liked by all. Finally, at 14h00, the newly formed Combat Team Derrick (formerly Barron, but renamed for deception purposes) moved out of Luso heading for a point some 30 kilometres south of Luso, on the tarred road to Gago Coutinho. At the 30-kilometre point, the combat team occupied a leaguer area (hide) and settled down for the night. Here the gunners heard what they thought were human voices and vehicle movement, which led to a patrol being dispatched to find the source of this concern. It turned out to be a troop of monkeys.

At 06h00 on 17 December, Combat Team Derrick recommenced their move southwards and, on entry to the village of Lucusse, discovered a cheese mine (an anti-tank mine that resembled a loaf of gouda cheese—without the red wax) and came under fire from the village. I Troop went into action immediately and engaged a number of buildings in the settlement in support of the armoured cars. The firefight ended very quickly, the MPLA leaving a large amount of equipment and ammunition behind.

On the move again, the combat team drew fire from the flank very close to the village of Maria Amelia. Once again, the artillery fired back—this time only one round fire for effect, but good enough to drive out the enemy. UNITA forces moved into the settlement; the gunners remained approximately 2 kilometres back, where they spent the night, moving back to a better position later the next morning where they could perform maintenance tasks on men and equipment. I Troop not only rested and recuperated, but also had the privilege of a donated cow, which, without any delay, was slaughtered and turned into a traditional South African braai.

The days that followed saw the combat team moving farther south, but delays were experienced by the enemy burning the small wooden bridges over the rivers. Eventually, Major Fred Rindel, the combat team commander, decided to turn around and head west to the town of Cassamba, where, it was reported, the enemy were so isolated that they had only heard of the fall of Luso on 19 December.

On 20 December, I Troop went into action again to engage a mortar position in Cassamba that was firing on own forces. That day the gunners did not do as well as they should have, and Captain Laubscher had a constant battle to bring down accurate fire, as there were persistent line (azimuth) errors at the guns. The MPLA defenders did not remain in the town long enough to criticize the artillery's performance, however, and by 18h00 the whole combat team was back at the Luso airfield. One positive aspect of the capture of Cassamba was a number of maps that were found in the deserted headquarters—at last some maps of military value.

The own forces' situation changed at this point in that 2 SAI embarked for home, to be replaced by 5 SAI and Commandant Moller was relieved by Commandant Joop Joubert. Commandant Joubert's order groups were far more formal; his HQ was bigger; he moved out ahead of the advance; and the days of informal, anything-goes clothing changed when the new commander instructed that steel helmets were to be indented for.

On 23 December, the force moved out once again in the direction of Lumeje, which they reached and the gunners duly engaged, unfortunately causing the first serious damage to a gun during this operation. It appears that a branch may have been in the way of the gun's trajectory as an HE proximity shell prematurely burst, damaging the gun's barrel and muzzle brake and putting this equipment out of action for the duration.

Christmas Day found T Battery in pouring rain on the move back to the town of Cassai Gare because the rivers ahead were impassable. Once again, X-ray had to change their axis of advance as a result of the burnt wooden bridges. The new route was to be through the Parque Nacional de Camela, which they tackled after they had been delayed waiting for a ration resupply by the maintenance unit.

The rigid thinking of the motorized infantry was demonstrated on 26 December when the gunners were told that a leaguer area was always occupied by the vehicles moving in clockwise; furthemore, the vehicles were always on the inside of the leaguer with the weapons and ordnance on the outside. Major Brown did not agree with this and proved his point when it was found that the battery's guns had to fire over the tops of their vehicles! J Troop then raced off to the Luacano area to help an armoured car troop that had apparently been encircled. Here the gunners also engaged the long-awaited armoured train.

The next three days were spent back in Luso where the troops finally heard when they would be withdrawing. Stories abounded, some true and others rumours—by-products of boredom and inactivity. The euphoria did not last long as I Troop were put on 30-minute standby to support the battle group reserve (Major Rindel's combat team, now called Pink Panther), and J Troop moved out to support the demolition of a bridge north of Cangumbe.

At 14h00 on 30 December, I Troop moved out with the reserve and by 17h40 the artillery were deployed and firing at targets in depth over the Luxai River. In the meantime, J Troop had withdrawn to Silva Porto after the charges had been prepared for the demolition of the bridge north of Cangumbe.

Back in Luso once again to observe UNITA firing in all directions; it seems the peach wine might have contributed to this one-sided firefight. During the last days of 1975, everyone in X-ray was confused as to the next move. Were they going home? Were they to advance again? Lieutenant Lubbe of J Troop arrived by air from Silva Porto with the news that a signal had been received to the effect that the operation would 'carry on as normal', whatever that meant.

To keep busy, Captain Laubscher (having just heard that his promotion to major would take effect on 1 January) set about designing a 'transportable' bridge, having witnessed first hand the frustration of not being able to cross relatively narrow rivers throughout the Luso area.

He picks up the story:

> Became possessed with the idea of designing a transportable bridge. Propose to first use the steel roof trusses in the hangars. Find out that there are similar assemblies on a rubbish heap in town; went to look. Unsuitable, but there are loose beams available. Got a new idea from demountable columns—the problem is to fix them to the side trusses. Moved material to airfield and put heads together. Sunset.

The first morning of 1976 started with a church parade immediately followed by the newly promoted Major Laubscher measuring and fitting steel trusses. The story continues:

> Went to have a look in JAEA [Public Works] for a large drilling machine and welding equipment, bolts, nuts, hacksaws, drill bits, etc. Found everything. Liaised with UNITA's Major Chata in town for the removal of the equipment from town to the airfield—no electrical power at JAEA premises. Found out that the airfield's plugs are also dead and that the gas cylinders are empty. Rummaged around town; did not find any gas. Came across Major Vittorio [UNITA] at the HQ, who appointed a guide to show us where to find gas; landed at a house—30-pound Handigas! [Handigas is a trade name for a brand of liquid petroleum gas.] Point out some welding on a children's swing and explain by means of a 'sss' sound that we need a welding cylinder [oxyacetylene]. Ta, Major Vittorio's servant, understood perfectly and into the house he went, returning with a can of aerosol spray!

They returned to Major Vittorio and then moved on to the railway station workshops to find that the adjacent power station was equipped with a wood-burning steam generator. This archaic machine's operation was demonstrated to the gunners, whereupon Major Laubscher decided to continue with his invention at the aforementioned workshops, as there was everything he needed there to perform heavy engineering.

The idle time was a cause for concern for the senior members and the order was given to the battle group to start a daily routine. I Troop spent their time washing bodies and clothes alike while the troop commander and his assistants continued with their engineering work. Just before starting the bridge design, Major Laubscher had manufactured a bath for himself out of a 200-litre (44 gallon) petrol drum, the resultant sharp edges being covered with garden hose duly split along its length. That day the bath was commissioned.

On 2 January, at long last, the instruction for the withdrawal finally arrived. Major Laubscher flew to Lumeje to pass on the message to Captain Theron, whose troop was still on the move in that area. By now, the excitement could be felt and vehicle maintenance was fully underway. The instruction stated that X-ray was to move south to Nkurukuru, a village on the South West Africa-Angolan border, but was countermanded later that day to read, Caiundo, a place to the south of Serpa Pinto. At this stage, the battle group's mission was changed and they were now to act as the Task Force (Zulu) reserve—with a possibility of supporting Battle Group Orange in their efforts to make a clean break. X-ray was to deploy at Caiundo as a containment force until everyone was out.

Next morning, X-ray departed from Luso in pouring rain bound for their first stop at Cuemba. In the meantime, the name X-ray had been changed to Boxer for deception purposes. By 4 January, Boxer had reached Silva Porto, which had become a massive mudbath, having been churned up by the vehicles of the maintenance unit.

Maintenance unit

A logistics unit, normally part of a brigade, that provides all the supplies necessary for the combat force. Supplies include rations, water, ammunition, fuel, oil, etc. The maintenance unit does not maintain vehicles: this is the task of the field workshop unit.

At Silva Porto the battery was reunited after a dew days' separation and here the gunners learned that they had caused some 400 casualties during the attack on Luso in December.

On 5 and 6 January, J Troop, plus one gun from I Troop, moved out of Silva Porto northwards, eventually turning off the tarred road in a northwesterly direction to engage a Cuban company equipped with 60mm mortars and 75mm recoilless guns, which was infiltrating behind battle group Orange. Major Laubscher was appointed as battery commander to replace Major Brown, who left for SWA and home.

The battle group stopped at Caureau ou Cotile and deployed on the high ground in defensive positions. Here, the gunners silently registered twelve targets in preparation for a possible defensive fight; at night, an FOO was deployed, together with an infantry listening post, at a position some 1,000 metres in front of the guns. Whilst in this position the gunners heard the story of Captain Johan Potgieter's stand at Calucinga and the South Africans that were captured and paraded in Luanda; however, no one was really sure whether or not Captain Potgieter had been taken prisoner. The situation was tense and the artillery were ordered not to open fire without the battle group HQ's authorization, and the armoured cars deployed some 3,000 metres in front of the main force in an observation (and defensive) line. Everyone dug in, but the gunners stopped at 500mm depth, as the gun pits were filling up with water.

The period between 9 and 11 January was spent on reconnaissance for future gun positions in the likelihood of tactical withdrawal, listening to the sounds of Captain Potgieter's battery in action to the northeast, and Major Laubscher being informed that he was to move out immediately to report to the School of Artillery, his place to be taken by Captain Jacob van Heerden. Movement ebbed and flowed for the next two days, with very little progress to show, but on Wednesday, 10 December, things changed dramatically. Commandant van der Westhuizen's diary indicates that it was 'the worst day thus far'. A single medium gun (Gunner Tony Carter's) was sent out on the blue route towards Hengo under the protection of a troop of armoured cars, where, within 3 kilometres of Hengo, it went into action in the only available place—the road.

The gun tractor, now in front of the gun, attempted to turn around to be ready to hook in and move when required. Here the heavy rains took their toll.

The Magirus Deutz became bogged down to its axles as it left the road. The effort to recover this gun tractor required some hours as Gunner Martin McKeen relates:

This is where we battled for a few hours to get out and eventually a Unimog attached to a Bedford managed to pull us out. At this time, we came under fire for the first time [from 122mm guns] and followed Captain Bouwer's example by eating dirt.

A damaged Land Rover with two seriously wounded South African officers arrived on the scene where they were given Captain Bouwer's vehicle to continue on to the echelon for medical treatment. They were later evacuated by helicopter. The gun crew hastily replaced the damaged Land Rover's flat front wheel and shortly after were given the order to cease fire and hook in. Gunner McKeen continues:

> We got the gun out of action without firing and hooked up while still coming under fire. In our haste, one of the spades [trail spades] was not secured properly and after racing down the road, it fell off. We stopped to recover it and immediately a mortar round landed about 10 metres to our left. We raced out of there and only stopped when we were safely out of range.

Gunner Carter's medium gun was thus hastily withdrawn to a point some 16 kilometres from Hengo. The enemy fire could still reach the fork so the guns were moved another 2 kilometres back to safety. By now, Commandant van der Westhuizen had been informed of the missing trail spade and immediately put Gunner Carter to work to drive back and recover the errant, and vitally important, item. The green route came under fire where four sappers were wounded and evacuated; the gunners fired continuously through the day even while under counter-bombardment with rockets falling between the guns. To make matters worse, van der Westhuizen's Land Rover detonated an anti-personnel mine on the blue route near Hengo, luckily without any serious damage. Finally, a gunner sergeant-major, having been tasked to oversee the collection of ammunition, was found to have been in Cela for some eleven hours, having left his troops, and ignoring the ammunition.

It was fortuitous that Gunner Carter's crew did not have to fire there that day because, during the move forward the previous night without lights, the gun had been towed through a narrow culvert, stripping a number of teeth off the elevation gear. This could have resulted in an unstable barrel during firing, with catastrophic consequences. The gun was taken back to the echelon where it was replaced by a new gun flown in from Pretoria.

The tide turns

The next two days saw a marked increase in enemy artillery fire, the rounds landing on both the gunners' and the infantry's positions and once again, being silenced by 196 rounds of medium gun fire. Support was provided to the Special Forces who evacuated an infantry patrol over the river. This continuous action over the last week was beginning to affect the serviceability of the guns, and it was found that the packings in their breech mechanisms were wearing out fast.

Lieutenant Jaap Nel from 4 Field Regiment was the GPO of the troop deployed close to Bridge 14:

There are three days that I will probably never forget, namely 10–12 December 1975—the *real* battle of Bridge 14. My troop—five guns, with a sixth out of action for some reason—was fired upon by a BM21 early in the morning of 10 December, and this went on for three days. We just could not get them. Piet Uys, Bernie Pols and Pottie took turns to engage targets with my guns, since we were at that time deployed the furthest forward—probably not more than 100 metres from the makeshift Bridge 14—so that we could reach most targets. Fortunately for us, the BM21 withdrew at night; they were probably scared of our Special Forces, or else it would have been even worse. On the third day, i.e. 12 December, Bernie saw the BM21 take up its deployment position, and mmediately ordered, 'Fire mission troop!' The BM21 managed to release one salvo before we got it. From then on, we really had a ball and took out numerous other targets, including 120mm mortar positions, infantry and vehicles fleeing through the bush and on the road. The 88mm battery joined in the fun then, since targets popped up as close as 4 kilometres from our position. At one stage, we ran out of ammunition and had only super charge left, which we had to use to engage mortar positions some 4 kilometres from us. It looked like we were firing direct, since the guns were depressed to almost horizontal. What fascinated me was that, after the three days, all the lights and reflectors on my vehicles were shattered from BM21 splinters. I would not call them shrapnel, since they were flimsy compared with what our guns delivered. We had to hide the vehicles in a quarry in front of the gun position, since the terrain did not allow us to move them further and there was a risk of enemy forces finding them if we moved them too far away.

Despite all this, on Friday 12 December Foxbat finally occupied the high ground 10 kilometres north of Bridge 14 without loss or damage. The gunners had successfully destroyed the enemy, who by now were fleeing from the fire and abandoning their equipment. Some of the captured equipment included 76 and 57mm guns, 120mm mortars, gun theodolites and range tables. All this was fine, but Bridge 14 was structurally too weak to carry the guns and would have to be reinforced before the gunners could even consider crossing the river.

On both the blue and red routes the armoured cars, supported by an artillery FOO formed an observation line and came under mortar fire; there were no losses and the gunners returned fire with one medium gun putting paid to the irritation.

The battlefield was quiet for the next three days, during which the regiment continued with movement to new firing positions and subsequent fire missions, this being interspersed with administration matters—the high point of which was the delivery of beer, cooldrinks, cigarettes and fresh uniforms!

The medium battery supporting Battle Group Orange, which was occupying the area around the Salazar bridge over the Cuanza River, north of Mussende, required a replacement battery commander; Major Bosch was instructed to take over that task.

Generally, gunners are flexible in their approach to the conduct of war and often find themselves in double appointments and filling in for others. A case in point was Commandant Paul Lombard (a gunner officer who was attached to UNITA for a time), who found himself that December in the role of mayor of Silva Porto!.

With the movement of Bosch (who was acting as the regimental second in command) to Orange, WOII Ben Jenkins was temporarily appointed as RSM to perform limited 2IC tasks, and WOII Strydom was appointed as BSM of the medium battery.

By 15 December, Battle Group Orange had withdrawn from the Cuanza River and had moved southwest to a position 30 kilometres east of Quibala where they were stopped by yet another demolished bridge over the Pombuige River at Cariango. It was here that Orange made contact with the Cubans and remained under fire and infiltration almost continuously for 12 days.

On Wednesday 17 December, the gunners, after some six weeks of operations, lost their first man, Gunner B. Neethling, who died as a result of an accident on a 106mm recoilless gun. Orders were given for the forces on the green route to dig in, to prepare defensive positions.

Lieutenant Herman van Niekerk arrived back in theatre after having partially recovered from his wounds sustained at Ebo, and was immediately posted to Captain Bouwer's battery as a troop commander. At this time, the artillery RHQ was deployed at the experimental farm and was moved forward the next day.

On 20 December, the artillery was deployed in Angola as follows:

- At Nova Redondo: one medium troop (Major Louis Rheeder)
- At Bridge 14 / Cela: Task Force Zulu
- At RHQ / Artillery HQ (Cmdt Joffel van der Westhuizen); one medium battery (Major W. Blaauw); one field battery (Captain Chris Bouwer)
- With Battle Group Orange: one medium battery in the Cariango area (Captain Philip du Plessis)
- With Battle Group X-ray: one field battery in the Luso area (Major Thinus Brown).

There was also another medium troop in transit at Grootfontein, which was earmarked for Task Force Zulu. To add to the regimental commander's worries, the acting RSM vanished for about seven hours; his abandoned vehicle was eventually found between the Task Force HQ and Cela. Captain Bouwer's battery, reinforced by two medium guns, found themselves at the pont on the Nhia River. In the process of driving the fully loaded gun tractor and gun onto the pont, the restraining cables gave way, the pont drifted forward and the gun slipped off and into the river. Some quick actions by the crew separated the tractor from the gun, which then disappeared into the swollen waters of the Nhia, a loss that could be ill afforded. One wise young officer commented that it would be possible to recover this gun provided he was given a pair of flippers and a snorkel. With help from the Special Forces team deployed nearby, this gun was eventually recovered after a 14-hour struggle—without a snorkel. Gunner Martin McKeen estimated that the river at that point was probably some four metres deep. To make matters worse, the air effort was reduced by 50 per cent: this would affect both air observation over the immediate front and the vital logistic support from Pretoria. At 23h00 on 20 December, the group that had been rescued from Ambriz, as well as Captain Flip du Plessis (from the battery supporting Orange) reported for duty at Cela—an event that caused much merriment and a good reason for a party. The Ambriz group included:

- Captain van Heerden
- WOII Pretorius
- Staff Sergeant Ackerman
- Sergeant van der Westhuizen
- Bombardiers van der Westhuizen, Botha, Loubscher and Davis
- Second Lieutenants Malan, Vincent and Summers

That same day, Orange reported that they were being threatened by a large force approaching Mussende (i.e. behind them). In effect, this meant that Orange was pinned down by the river and under fire from their front (west).

After a visit to Nova Redondo with the new Task Force Commander Brigadier J.D. Potgieter (Brigadier Potgieter was, in the late 1960s, the OC of the School of Artillery), Commandant van der Westhuizen decided to make more changes in the artillery organization. Briefly, these were as follows:

- Move Lt Potgieter and S/Sergeant Ackerman to the Orange battery.
- Send Captain van Heerden, WOII Pretorius and 2/Lt John Malan to Grootfontein to prepare and move that troop up to Task Force Zulu .
- 2/Lt Summers would take over from Lieutenant Potgieter as troop commander.
- 2/Lt Vincent and the remaining bombardiers would reinforce the two fire units in action until the new troop arrived from Grootfontein.
- Withdraw Captain du Plessis from Orange and immediately appoint him as adjutant.

During this time, the gunners had an opportunity to review their situation, in particular their employment. They were bearing the brunt of the fighting, being available at all times and with no relief; the artillery was even being used to make up for the inefficiency of the infantry. This included placing a battery commander in command of a flank guard while still having to provide fire support.

By now, the South African involvement was no longer a secret and the troops were issued with their R1 rifles again—these in exchange for their AK-47s and PPShs, which they had carried for the last two months.

An attack was planned on the Catofe area for 23 December; this area had been occupied by artillery observers until a short time before. Furthermore, a warning was issued that snipers were active; this warning became reality on 21 December when, at 16h00, Lieutenant Prins's OP party on the Quisobi high ground was shot at and two men were wounded. A helicopter was called in to evacuate the wounded and was fired on, resulting in this aircraft withdrawing to cover.

Another helicopter brought in 2/Lt Hawkins as a replacement, but could not pick up 2/Lt Prins, as one of his men was missing. This helicopter flew north and was shot down by ground fire. Fortunately, the four men aboard walked

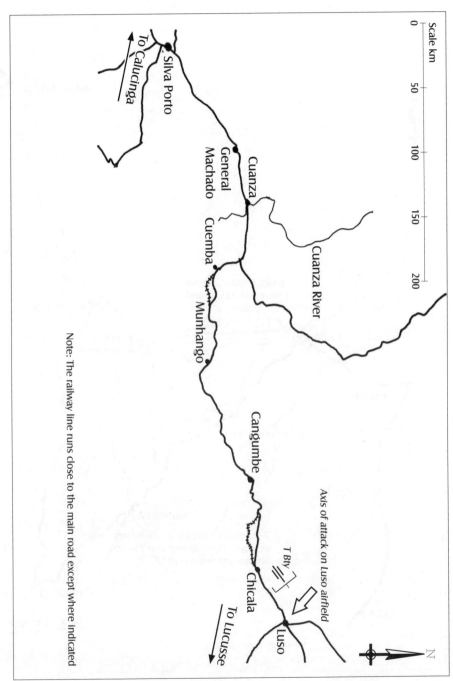

The activities in the east.

Note: The railway line runs close to the main road except where indicated

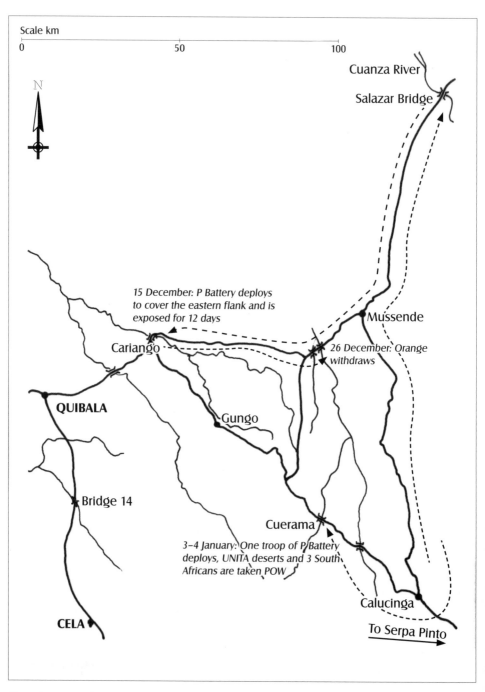

Orange's movements.

back to safety the next day, exhausted, but relieved, and were subsequently evacuated from Q Battery's position. The OP party was later rescued by a Special Forces team on foot.

On arrival at the medium battery (P Battery) supporting Battle Group Orange, Lieutenant Potgieter was disheartened to find a fire unit where there was no, or very little, ammunition. What was there was left lying around the gun position unprotected against the sun and rain. Gun tractors were parked between the guns making for a 'juicy' target; no trenches or foxholes existed; and the survey was out by at least 2,000 metres. The centre of arc was out by 15° and the guns were not parallel to each other. What's more, he also found that rations were in short supply, the gun position was untidy and disorganized and, most importantly, the troops' morale was extremely low. All of this could be ascribed to a battery commander and battery sergeant-major who, although qualified, were unsuited to the job and had not bothered to carry on training these only partially trained troops. By the time Lieutenant Potgieter arrived, the battery commander was already redeployed within the regiment. Now Potgieter not only had to familiarize himself with the general situation, but also had to act fast to replenish ammunition and build morale. It is strange, though, how a seemingly simple act like a change of commander can change morale—in this case for the better. The other factor influencing the morale was discipline: within a short time the battery position was cleaned up; the men cleaned themselves and their equipment, and almost immediately morale was lifted. It should be mentioned that the use of a toggle rope on the behinds of a few stubborn gunners also helped. After a quiet Christmas, P Battery was rudely awakened on 26 December to find that the observers were being encircled and A Troop was under fire from three sides. It should be appreciated here that the terrain favoured the FAPLA–Cuban force, in that the high ground was predominantly on their side of the river, giving them good command of the battlefield. During another contact, one of the OP teams was rocketed by a jet fighter aircraft. All of this was happening within 40 kilometres of Foxbat's forward elements and Captain Bothma could observe the BM21s firing their rockets from his post, left to right, at the P Battery gunners. Orange was instructed to withdraw to Mussende in early January 1976.

Once again, the fire units were on the move. Q Battery's medium troop deployed 10 kilometres west of the main tarred road and the two troops of U Battery to a point north at Cungo. At 05h30 on the morning of 23 December, Q battery fired two harassing fire tasks at the enemy deployed in the west. Once again, the gunners found themselves forming the front line own troops (FLOT), the infantry having moved away and left their 81mm mortars in the vicinity. This situation was worsened by the fact that enemy snipers, armed with silenced rifles, were now moving in closer to the guns.

This sorry group of men was desperately in need of training, and the decision was made to train them during actual fire missions. Lieutenant Potgieter moved to an OP position 8 kilometres away overlooking the river, where a hive of FAPLA–Cuban activity was observed. A fire mission was ordered and after some hours of adjusting and widely dispersed fire for effect, they could fire three slow, but acceptable, fire missions just before sunset. The next day (24 December) training continued until the blunt end reported that their ammunition was low, or in some cases, zero; they were not yet used to firing large amounts of ammunition and replenishment was not being done. The question is, where was the battery sergeant-major during all this time? During this replenishment, a company of six BM21s opened fire on the gun position. The crews, busy with unloading ammunition from the vehicles, could not reach their own trenches in time and dived into any available trench, piling on top of each other.

It was here that Gunners Theunnissen and Muller were killed and five others wounded, including Staff Sergeant Gert Engelbrecht. By the next morning, the battery had moved to a new position and the BM21s fired another salvo into their old position.

Beaver: the west flank

In the first half of December, Major Hurter's field battery (this was, in fact, 41 Battery, having been redeployed from a three-month infantry task in Katima Mulilo) arrived in the Lobito area to reinforce Battle Group Beaver. By this time, the G2 troop of Major Rheeder was already in action as a counter to the

BM21s operating north of the Queve River. Major Rheeder was withdrawn in the early part of December, and his place as troop commander was taken by Lieutenant Sarel Myburgh. During the preparation phase in Grootfontein one of the weaknesses in the logistics support system was felt by the troops on the ground: the optical equipment for the guns (sights and clinometers), although issued in protective cases, were accounted for separately. This accounting system resulted in this sensitive equipment being shipped to Grootfontein in bulk in crates, separately from their cases. To make matters worse, they were mixed up with spanners and other heavier, more robust gun stores. The end result was a large number of damaged or unserviceable lenses and vials (levelling bubbles). The South Africans had levelling bubbles, but the main supply route was becoming too long and too vulnerable, so the port of Lobito in Angola could provide a solution to this problem. Lieutenant de Villiers, while still preparing with his battery in Grootfontein, was tasked to command a protection element for the logistics personnel to reconnoitre Lobito harbour. After a day or two in Rundu, this group arrived at Lobito airfield fully prepared to leave immediately, as they were not sure who was in control of Lobito at that time. Fortunately, UNITA–FNLA was, and the group duly commenced their business. Lieutenant de Villiers's other task was to recce possible deployment positions for the incoming regiment (provision was being made for more than one battery's deployment). A week later, the battle group arrived. Lieutenant de Villiers describes the scene:

> . . . it was like a Roman triumph. The streets were lined with ululating masses. I remember standing with Commandante Renato [UNITA] and him saying over and over, 'Man, this is a real army' as the convoy moved past. The battle group was billeted in town while the battery deployed on the golf course outside the town on the coastal plateau. We lay here for a few days.

The gunners went into action within a short time, firing on a suspected FAPLA base and then revising their technical work and gun drills, as this battery had not touched a gun for the last three months. This short period of seeming inactivity was soon interrupted by the battery being tasked to support Battle Group A at Nova Redondo, where they met up with Lieutenant Myburgh's medium troop and deployed at a cotton mill to the north of the town. Major Hurter deployed his OP teams to watch the floodplain and bridge. They had barely arrived in their position when they were attacked by a small element of FAPLA infantry that had infiltrated the position. The guns, having not yet deployed, could not provide any support so the OP teams had to resort to their personal weapons to drive the attackers off. There were no casualties from this fight.

As an aside here, WOI Schoonwinkel, the RSM of 4 Field Regiment, was tasked as the battle group sergeant-major. The gunner OPs made their acquaintance with the FAPLA BM21s at this point, but once again, the fire was desultory and inaccurate. Nevertheless, Captain Human immediately put everyone to work in the construction of a massive bunker—the precursor to a facility in Katima Mulilo that would later be known as Fort Human.

Enemy forces were observed moving near the river bridge, and the order was given for the artillery to engage. For better observation Myburgh was assigned the task of air OP for this mission. However, the mission was not as successful as expected because the weaving, bucking Cessna caused Myburgh to become airsick. This officer was not the first or the last to suffer from the discomfort of airsickness, and only later did the artillery begin classifying observers for flying fitness. De Villiers continues his story:

> I was given a lesson on how to engage a moving target by the master himself. Felix Hurter engaged a convoy that was moving on a road parallel to the river on the far side. I had been watching it for a few days, but when he came to visit, the action started . . . some vehicles were left stationary, but not burning, while most managed to get away.

On 24 December, the battle group was tasked to attempt to force a crossing over the Queve River at a place called Vila Nova de Celes to the northeast of their positions. In order to reach this place the route traversed a series of mountain passes that were slippery and muddy from the rains. This combination was the cause of a number of vehicles rolling, including the Land Rover of the battery commander, the BSM, a gun tractor and numerous other vehicles. Luckily, all these vehicles were travelling slowly and there was no serious damage or injury.

Christmas Day 1975

In the west, the battle for the crossing of the Queve River became an anticlimax, as it was found that the bridge had already been blown and some sporadic firing was forthcoming from the FAPLA side of that demolished structure. Unfortunately, mines were everywhere and Lieutenant Dave Wessels of the SA Engineer Corps lost a leg to these while recovering abandoned trucks. The gunner OPs of Major Hurter's battery had a close call that morning when they moved out to occupy their observation positions ahead of their FNLA protection element (who were late) and, to save time, took a short cut across country to avoid a loop in the road.

On their return, Captain Human and Lieutenant de Villiers discovered that the loop had been strewn with anti-personnel mines. From their OP they could observe nothing and so returned to the blunt end.

In the centre, firing continued throughout the day from both sides. The enemy fired from behind Catofe hill and a rocket launcher was silenced by the gunners after some inaccurate fire. The day was marked by three sorties of enemy aircraft over the firing positions, creating a certain amount of confusion; no one was sure whose aircraft they were; should they fire at them or not? As it was, no rounds were fired from either side. Later that night and into the morning, the enemy fired harassing fire tasks, which kept both the RHQ and Q Battery awake until 05h00.

Captain Uys, Captain Bothma and Lieutenant Bernard Pols spent Christmas 1975 on Catofe hill, from where many targets were engaged. Shortly after 25 December, they received orders to withdraw and redeploy behind the Nhia River. The withdrawal took place in a very orderly fashion, and Captain Uys stayed in the OP until the sappers were ready to blow the bridge.

When done, Captain Uys also left the area to join the guns in their new gun position.

The general situation was worsening, with the Angolan forces threatening on all fronts and advancing on both Luso and the logistic base at Silva Porto. On the central front, the gunners fired a single gun mission on Quisobi with a 140mm gun, killing nine Cubans.

By now, the rainy season had started in earnest and the problem of observation and off-road movement was beginning to rear its head.

The national servicemen of the January 1974 intake should, by this time, not only have been relieved, but demobilized and back home. The situation was such that there were simply not enough replacements with sufficient training and, as a result, that particular group's service was extended to 6 February 1976.

Despite the attempts by the gunners to dislodge the predominantly Cuban force, the rest of Battle Group Orange, the infantry in particular, made no move to make contact and remained, almost frozen, on the riverbank. Any thoughts of attempting to establish a bridgehead, building a bridge without bridging equipment and then crossing the river with a horde of untrained, undisciplined, leaderless UNITA soldiers would create a catastrophe. With the artillery ammunition running low and a lack of action within the battle group, the inevitable happened. On 26 December, Orange's rear echelon and future artillery observation posts were attacked by a Cuban force that had infiltrated the previous night, finally creating a situation where the battle group was authorized to withdraw to safer terrain closer to Mussende. Contact was broken and the battle group made good speed to their new position—an unfavourable, undefendable piece of ground where they waited for another enemy advance.

Just after Christmas, the enemy in the west was noted as becoming more active. This action caused Battle Group A's commander to split the battery, with Captain Human's troop remaining at Nova Redondo, and Lieutenant de Villiers's troop, together with the battery HQ, moving to Vila Nova de Celes to counter any threat of a FAPLA outflanking movement. Here, this troop prepared defensive positions. Lieutenant de Villiers provides some insight:

'Don't ever consider blasting gun pits to save spade labour. We spent hours dusting off the shrubs to remove the telltale brown circles in the green veld.'

The situation was gradually worsening, but on 28 December the gunners received some good news in the form of feedback from intelligence that two BM21 MRLs had been destroyed; all the 120mm mortars were either destroyed or captured, and 61 Cubans had been killed during the battles for Bridge 14.

Furthermore, a captured Cuban officer told his interrogators that the MPLA troops were petrified of the medium artillery and believed that the South African medium guns could fire at a range of 27 kilometres.

Battle Group Orange was in the area around Mussende by 29 December and instructed to hold that position.

On the morning of New Year's Eve, a message came through that a patrol in the Catofe area, accompanied by a forward observation officer from one of the field troops (call sign 21), had drawn enemy fire and that Second Lieutenant Zai van den Heever was missing. An armoured car troop was hastily organized to look for him; they found him later that day, seriously wounded. The rain and mist masked the helicopter that evacuated him to the medical post. Eight pints of blood and some skilful surgery saved the young officer's life; he returned to 4 Field Regiment on 21 January 1976. A little light relief that same night: a promotion and combined New Year's party was held at the task force HQ. The next morning, the gunners' morale was lifted by the delivery of parcels and a visit from the chaplain, who conducted services for both batteries in their firing positions. Morale was even further lifted by a New Year lunch.

While the rest of the regiment was celebrating New Year, Commandant van der Westhuizen and Major Bouwer undertook a rather unsuccessful fishing trip near the pont. Despite the use of nine Soviet hand grenades, only two six-inch fish were caught and 37 Mauser rounds only yielded three pheasants. Some gunners took the lull in firing more seriously and at 23h45 the artillery commander found Lieutenant Pols, Second Lieutenant Prins and WOII van Dyk in their vehicle on their way back from celebrating in Santa Comba. These three walked the rest of the distance to their echelon area.

At 06h30 on 2 January 1976 both batteries provided supporting fire to Battle Group Bravo for an attack on Dimples. During this attack, Commandant van der Westhuizen, Major Bouwer and Lieutenant van Niekerk, in the process of moving closer to the objective, came under artillery fire, the closest round landing 50 metres from them. Not only the command element came under fire that day, the guns also came under fire from both BM21 and guns from the direction of Tunga and Hengo respectively.

After seven days of waiting, Orange was ordered to withdraw out of Angola. To cover the withdrawal, a combat team under the command of Major Louis Lamprecht, with a 140mm artillery troop in direct support (under the command of the newly promoted Captain Potgieter), was ordered to provide flank protection until Orange had broken contact and were beyond Carriango. In order to do this, the combat team advanced to Calucinga to deter possible interference from Gungo. The little force deployed an infantry company, an armoured car troop and a section of anti-tank missiles on the high ground, covering the bridge over the Cuanza River. Supporting this force was the artillery OP, 2/Lt J.P. Nel, deployed some 500 metres farther up the slope, protected by an infantry section. Close to 2/Lt Nel's OP position was a beautiful cattle farm (better described as a ranch because of its size) by the name of Quirama, which a UNITA company ransacked and occupied, giving no thought to the preparation of defensive positions. Instead, they focused on the Hereford bull to be cooked on the spit. Most of the force was under the impression that this position would be a two-day affair followed by another move southwards to safety. Once again, the gunners were the exception, and Nel's vehicle, in the dead ground behind his position, was camouflaged; he had dug in and had good command over his area of observation. Thirty targets were recorded for the defensive fire plan.

Late afternoon the next day, the force came under 82mm mortar fire during a massive thunderstorm. Captain Potgieter takes up the story:

> I climbed onto the roof of an outside farm building to see where the fire was coming from. All I could see was a Land Rover—with tarpaulin flapping in the wind—with a few armoured cars and

Unimogs hastily disappearing over the hill. On the other side of the farm UNITA panicked and was running in all directions, mainly back. I ordered the guns to fire on a target close to the bridge. The downpour increased and limited observation to a few hundred metres. While the guns were firing, the enemy mortars came closer and I took cover in an outside cement basin. JP [2/Lt Nel] could not observe the fire either and reported they were under attack from the rear. During a short break in the enemy fire, I ran up to our 60mm mortar position some 400 metres away. Luckily, they had not heard the shout over the radio to pull out. A tall corporal ran up to me; he was calm and keen to fire at whatever. He was confused and could not distinguish between UNITA running away and the Cubans attacking. Nobody could blame the man under the heavy downpour and the chaos of the contact. Luckily, I could indicate the attacking enemy to him from his mortar position, ordered him to open direct fire and to only stop when I told him to.

At that, I ran back to the old house, contacted JP and prepared for the counter-attack. Luckily for JP, the enemy fire was concentrated on the vehicles behind him. JP saw them capturing the driver, Rifleman P.J. Groenewald, who was in position at his Unimog. JP had Groenewald in his sights for some time, but shot one of the capturers instead. They disappeared over the hill and the attack refocused on the OP. The effect of the accurate mortar fire, the firing back of JP and the infantry at very short range, together with my fire from the farmhouse some 60 metres away caused a few quick casualties to them, and the enemy attack broke up.

Unfortunately, an RPG-7 rocket hit a tree above the OP section and injured the four guys in the trench closest to it. We collected a tractor and a trailer from the farmyard and JP took the injured troops to safety. Everybody was full of mud and blood; it was difficult to see who was wounded and who not. Lieb [Captain Potgieter's signaller], in the meantime, organized for the wounded troops to be evacuated.

Their lives were saved by the decision of Lieutenant Nel to hold fire until the last minute and Captain Potgieter's ordering artillery fire on the road in front of them until last light, when they could withdraw.

This action, and Captain Potgieter's leadership under these conditions, resulted in the award of the Honoris Crux medal to Captain Potgieter. During an interview with him in 2007, he humbly stated, 'The rest of them ran away; all I did was my job.'

It was during this fight that three infantry soldiers manning an Entac (anti-tank missile) jeep, found themselves cut off from the main force and subsequently taken as prisoners of war. To make matters worse Brigadier J.D. Potgieter, a gunner officer in his earlier days, was killed when the Super Frelon helicopter in which he was travelling was shot down on the way to Battle Group Orange.

To compound things for the South African defenders left behind at Calucinga, after a few hours of movement back to Silva Porto, they were ordered to return to Calucinga to hold defensive positions 'until further notice'. The trip back was slow and painful for the South Africans, as they had to witness the flow of frightened, confused refugees. Yet again, the lack of infantry involvement put the gunners in the front line own troops—the 140mm troop was expected to hold the line!

The withdrawal

For those readers who are not versed in the details of military terminology, a withdrawal is a planned and properly orchestrated movement (not always rearward) to better positions—primarily dictated by terrain. The idea is to pull back to ground of one's own choosing, which can be defended or even from where the enemy can be destroyed. It is not a retreat.

In the afternoon of 2 January the officer commanding Task Force Zulu gave his initial orders for the force to withdraw. Briefly, the orders were:

- Monday (5 January) at last light the withdrawal must be complete.
- Movement would take place without lights until the vehicles were behind cover of high ground.

- Artillery batteries supporting the two battle groups would move at the same time as those groups.
- Battle Group Bravo would blow two bridges on 5 January and move out at last light. These demolitions would be accompanied by artillery fire.
- The HQ and RHQ would move between the two battle groups.
- The task force would be in Rocades at the Cunene River by 8 January where they would stand fast for 14 days.

Major Blaauw received his orders on the morning of 3 January for movement the same night, the withdrawal to take place in steps not unlike the movement of a caterpillar. The guns would move back to positions south of Bridge 14, whereupon the first OPO would move back. This was to be followed by the next OPO and the third—all redeploying into new positions by 06h15 on 4 January. The gunners were also briefed to be ready to provide smoke for target indication for SAAF ground attack. It is rather ironic that the aircraft earmarked for this task were Harvards (T6 Texan), despite the number of jet aircraft in the SAAF arsenal. This decision was made in the light of the fact that the nearest airfield that could handle jets was Grootfontein—too far from the front line. By 06h00, U Battery (Major Blaauw) was over the Nhia River and in position. However, the OPOs were still deployed north of the river. At 07h30, Q Battery (Major Bouwer) received its movement orders and later that day Captain du Plessis was tasked to move the RHQ. During all this, both sides exchanged fire, with no losses.

Of interest here is the order given by task force HQ for the gunners to fire off *all* their ammunition before moving. This instruction was not carried out, and that night U Battery fired a deception mission to cover the preparations for the demolition of bridges 1 and 14. Once this fire mission was completed, the battery ceased fire and withdrew to a new position farther south.

A day later, both Q and U Batteries had occupied new positions north of Santa Comba and at Cela respectively, covering the withdrawal of the rest of the task force's elements.

Over the next few days, in response to the changing situation, Commandant van der Westhuizen regrouped his batteries in a typically unorthodox fashion, but one which had worked throughout the previous two months. The organization now looked like this:

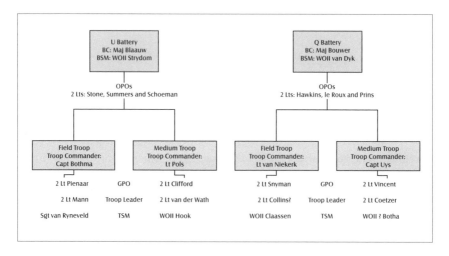

One of the reasons for this hybrid organization was the need to defend two fronts, resulting in each troop being deployed with a different centre of arc, these being:

- U Battery Field Troop: 300°
- U Battery Medium Troop: 270°
- Q Battery Field Troop: 330°
- Q Battery Medium Troop: 30° (covering the northeastern flank)

Each OPO team was deployed individually some three to five kilometres apart, and the A Echelon 2 kilometres to the west of Q Battery's medium troop. During this period, there was intelligence indicating that an enemy force had landed on the coast north of Lobito; a force was threatening Mussende in front of Battle Group Orange; a 'suicide squadron' was positioned 35 kilomteres north of Luso in the east; the MPLA had set up in Nova Redondo on the coast.

And for the second time in as many days, enemy aircraft flew over Task Force Zulu unscathed as a result of ineffective anti-aircraft fire.

On 10 January 1976, Army HQ ordered Major Laubscher and Captain Uys to return to the School of Artillery, and on 13 January 1976, they left Angola from the airport at Silva Porto for Rundu and home.

The Citizen Force mobilizes

Thursday 8 January saw the first of the gunner Citizen Force (CF) units commence mobilizing. On that day, Cape Field Artillery (CFA), ironically also the senior CF gunner unit, arrived at the Driekloof Transit camp outside Bloemfontein.

Shortly afterwards, an element of 21 Locating Battery under the command of Captain Cyril Owen-Crompton arrived. CFA's officer commanding at that time was Commandant Lionel Crook, the 2IC, Major Ian McKinney. Within two days, Crook was instructed to provide 'one fully up to strength' battery for immediate movement to Serpa Pinto. This instruction was followed by a question from the OC: 'What do you mean by "immediate?"' The answer was, 'Now, now: the aircraft are on the runway waiting!' Major Pat Finn's P (Amsterdam) Battery was the most complete in terms of personnel and was brought up to strength by personnel from the other batteries in the regiment. Major N.J. Visser, the HQ Battery commander was put in as P Battery's second in command. During all this flurry of activity, the typical 'hurry up and wait' syndrome swept in to Driekloof transit camp; the gunners were told that they would be flying at 18h00, then again at 10h00 the next day and then again later in the evening. The tendency is generally to blame the senior officers for such changes in times and instructions, but the problem usually starts with the political masters, who, by nature of their work, have better, or different, information than the troops (including the senior officers).

In this case, the South African government was deciding whether to pull out completely (a result of American and French vacillation) or whether to withdraw after strengthening the border area. It will be appreciated that while such discussions are taking place the military planners are appreciating the new situation and making recommendations. This information is passed down the chain of command to provide as much early warning as possible, especially when mobilizing part-time units which are not necessarily as fully combat-ready as their PF and national service colleagues. The SAAF did not have a large strategic airlift capability and South African Airways had to be contracted to help. All this takes time.

Finally, at 18h30 on 10 January 1976 P (Amsterdam) Battery, Cape Field Artillery marched out of Driekloof to their awaiting transport. The OC, 2IC and RSM, WOI H.W.F. Kitshoff, bade the battery farewell at Bloemspruit Air Force Base. This battery was due to fly direct to Serpa Pinto where it would take over the equipment from one of the batteries in the area and deploy thereafter. However, the political situation changed yet again, and the two aircraft carrying the battery turned back while in Angolan airspace to land at Grootfontein. On arrival, Major Finn was met by Major-General van Deventer (GOC of 101 Task Force), who asked the question, 'What do you know of 5.5s?'

'Nothing', replied Major Finn, 'but we can learn.'

Morale was high and a visit by Major Koos Laubscher and Captain Piet Uys, on their way home, helped push the morale even further.

After four days of soaking rain and mud in 'Camp Swampy', the battery moved out of Grootfontein bound for the newly created training area at Oshivello, 15 km east of the Etosha National Park. Commandant S.W.J. (Willie) Kotze, recently arrived from command of Battle Group X-ray, had been tasked with the establishment of the training area. On 15 January, P Battery fired its first training rounds from 140mm guns. CFA was a field regiment, that is, it was trained for and staffed for the use of 25-pounder guns. A 25-pounder gun had a detachment of six, whereas the 140mm G2 needed ten men—a shortage of four men per gun to start with.

In the meantime, CFA's RHQ was on its way by train to Grootfontein, followed a day later by Q (Imhoff) and R (Wynyard) Batteries—both under strength, having reinforced P Battery.

At this time, Q and R Batteries of CFA had been tasked to prepare to fly to Lobito and Silva Porto by 22 January to relieve the fire units supporting Orange and Zulu respectively. A renamed Battle Group ('Lima') was tasked to defend the western approaches to southern Angola, in this case the left flank of Zulu. The battle group comprised Cape Town Highlanders (CTH), a motorized infantry battalion; a squadron (Eland 90) from Regiment Mooi Rivier; Q Battery CFA; an AA Battery from Cape Garrison Artillery; and an engineer troop from 3 Field Engineer Regiment.

Strength of CF units

Citizen Force regiments were manned, in totality, by part-time soldiers. Although each unit was staffed by one full-time (civilian) clerk, the bulk of the administration and day-to-day functioning of the unit relied on the senior personnel taking time off from work or studies to do this work. There was a plethora of reports, returns and statements that had to be completed by certain dates (the same information that was generated by the Permanent Force units, which had full-time staff). Happily, the gunners were a close community and headquarters were sympathetic to these problems.

Once a soldier had completed his two years' national service, he was required to complete another three 'camps' (exercises) in ten years in the CF, so on completion of national service the soldier would be assigned to a CF unit—usually the unit closest to his home or intended place of study. In order to be promoted, officers and NCOs had to pass certain prescribed courses; in the case of the artillery, these courses were exactly the same as, and run together with, the PF promotion courses.

CF regiments would be 'open' on a Tuesday evening for administration and training. Here one would find most of the officers and senior NCOs attending lectures and performing administrative duties. The formal part of the evening would usually end with drinks in the mess; closing time depended on when the senior officer or mess president called it a day. In the older, more traditional units no one left before the mess president (officers) or the RSM (senior NCOs).

CF units were generally over strength (on paper). It was not unusual for a unit to have a strength of 1,500, whereas the War Establishment Table strength would be at around 700. The reason was that, when the unit was mobilized for a training camp a number of members would be allowed exemption for reasons of study, work commitment, occasional family matters, etc. Furthermore, there were the serial 'dodgers' who seldom or never reported for duty. Finally, each member had ten years' service to complete, which meant that those who were close to completion would be 'put on ice', only to be called up in the event of a general mobilization.

One of the problems that units had, once everyone had reported for duty, was the balance of musterings. For example, a unit would find that there were too many drivers and not enough technical assistants, or insufficient ordnance fitters. This often led to batteries being amalgamated and men being hurriedly trained in a new mustering.

On Friday 9 January, the national servicemen and Permanent Force gunners heard that their Citizen Force relief had arrived in Grootfontein and were busy preparing to move. As can be seen, this was a rumour because at that stage CFA had only just arrived in Bloemfontein.

On 13 January, the task force was ordered to move farther south and hold a line on the Queve River until 18 January; the move was to start at 01h00 the next morning, with the RHQ moving at 19h30 to its next position.

The next day, the gunners were once again redeployed, this time the medium battery and a field troop in support of Battle Group Bravo to the left (west) of the Queve River and one field troop supporting Foxbat to the right of the river, the OPOs having to deploy well forward to achieve good observation. The emphasis at this time was the holding of this position, and digging and camouflage was the order of the day.

Each battery had a mortar locating radar section attached. However, of the four radar sets, only two were serviceable and the other two had become expensive pieces of baggage to be towed around.

On 14 January 1976, the balance of CFA arrived at Grootfontein. This comprised the RHQ and Q and R Batteries in two trains with six hours between them. Over the next two days, CFA's Officer Commanding Commandant Crook and his 2IC, Major Ian McKinney attended an order group in Grootfontein where they were instructed to draw equipment for one battery and to this, some extra three-tonners. Equipment would be shared during training. They were to be in Silva Porto by 22 January, and the RHQ would reinforce HQ 2 Military Area's staff. They also learned that P Battery was in Oshivello undergoing a conversion to a medium battery. Also, the South African cabinet gave the SADF the instruction for the withdrawal to start on 17 January. On arrival for a recce in Oshivello, Commandant Crook met up with Commandant Ferdie van Wyk (a gunner who, shortly afterwards, became OC of 14 Field Regiment), who gave him the good news that 14 Field would reinforce CFA with seven officers and 24 other ranks.

January 16 saw, yet again, a regrouping of the artillery fire units to support the ever-changing situation. This time, Q Battery was reinforced with a medium troop from U Battery and all under Major Bouwer.

The battery deployed as follows:

- Q Battery's medium troop: 8 kilometres north of bridge 25—centre of arc: 320°
- U Battery's medium troop: 3 kilometres south of bridge 25—centre of arc: 270°
- Q Battery's field troop: 4 kilometres south of bridge 25—centre of arc: 330°.

Tiddler

Fire plans are written on a proforma and circulated to all concerned in the fire unit. The term 'tiddler' was used to denote a quick fire plan; the deliberate fire plan was known as a 'monster'. On the social side, however, a tiddler was a monthly social event held on the first Wednesday after pay day (the 15th of the month). At one time, the social tiddlers were directed by a formally distributed fire plan, which indicated the D-Day, H-Hour and the drinking times (for example, H-20, beer, rate slow; H+30, brandy and coke, rate intense, with a remark such as 'majors only'. Subalterns were discouraged from all but beer. A tiddler was for serving members only (all male) and a monster was more formal and dignified, and included the ladies.

That same night, a 'tiddler' was held in the rain and even included snacks! The next day, the news came through confirming the relief for the gunners: the 4 Field Regiment component was to be relieved by a battery from Cape Field Artillery (CFA) on 22 January and the 14 Field component by a battery from Transvaalse Staatsartillerie (TSA) on 2 February in Silva Porto. In fact, TSA arrived with three batteries. CFA would provide the relief for the existing RHQ—so they were told.

Naturally, at this news the morale was high, but as can be expected in this type of situation, discipline can decline, as was the case with the RSM (temporarily in that post), who was insubordinate and lacked self-control. This warrant officer was severely reprimanded the next day.

The task force was now spread over a bigger area than ever before and U Battery was deployed some 50 kilometres due east of the RHQ. 2/Lt Hawkins, one of Q Battery's OPOs, observed two enemy cargo vehicles approaching from Cela and opened fire on them, with the forward-most medium troop causing the vehicles to withdraw, but leaving their infantry occupants behind. These were then also engaged by the troop and consequently turned tail and hurriedly vacated the position. The reply was soon to come and BM21s and guns fired into the vicinity of Lieutenant Hawkins's OP position, the closest round landing 3 kilometres to the south. It is noteworthy here that the SA Armour immediately became involved in the small fight and, as a result, lost an officer. The same could not be said of the SA Infantry, who remained stationary throughout and observed the allied forces' infantry streaming back to apparent safety.

Back in the rear, training started for Q and R Batteries of CFA, which discovered that their first battery, P Battery, was still in the training area and, unbeknown to the OC, Commandant Crook, had been detached to Battle Group Taba, which would be operating in the Luso area. On 17 January, P Battery, busy preparing for their deployment, could not attend a parade addressed by the Minister of Defence (P.W. Botha), and at 16h30 that afternoon moved out of the training area for Grootfontein en route to Rundu.

At 11h00 on Sunday 18 January 1976, CFA's P Battery left Grootfontein for Rundu while the other two batteries continued with their training programme. This training was unusual for the Cape gunners in that there was only one set of equipment (for one battery). They were used to having sufficient for each battery, and the two batteries changed over at midday. Despite this odd arrangement, training did continue fairly smoothly because, when not training for their main role, the gunners would practise mine drills, ambushes and other such exercises. P Battery CFA left Rundu for Luso on 19 January, spending the next night in soaking rain at Catuiti.

In the Task Force Zulu area the persistent infantry problem was worsened on Monday 19 January, when Q Battery discovered that the nearest infantry were now deployed five kilometres *behind* the forward gun positions and no longer provided protection for Lieutenant Hawkins and the armoured cars at the OP position.

Brigadier Helm 'Paul' Roos, the new commander of 2 Military Area, arrived on a visit and informed the gunners that a troop of medium guns was on its way from battle group Orange to reinforce Task Force Zulu. This was good news, as van der Westhuizen needed to send a troop to reinforce the one already supporting Battle Group Bravo in their effort to hold Amboiva.

On the coast, the Angolan forces were threatening Battle Group Delta both from Nova Redondo and from the beach, landing behind Delta. This battle group dispatched a combat team supported by artillery to deploy at Vila Nova de Celas. To the east the front was quiet, with no incidents reported by Battle Group Orange.

During the night of 19 January, Q Battery's 25-pounders fired a highly successful harassing fire task on Cela and to the right of bridge 25 while Lieutenant Summers led a medium troop to Dumbi to reinforce Q Battery.

At 10h00 on 20 January, the medium troop of three guns arrived from Battle Group Orange. The leader element comprised:

•	Troop commander	Lieutenant Pieter 'Whitey' du Toit (Lt du Toit relieved Captain Potgieter)
•	OPO	Second Lieutenant J.P. Nel
•	GPO	Second Lieutenant Jaap Botha
•	TSM	Staff Sergeant Klaas Ackerman
•	TA sergeant	Bombardier Bornman
•	Transport NCO	Lance-Bombardier Valentyn
•	Ordnance fitter	Sergeant du Plessis

That same day, revised orders were issued for the withdrawal to Grootfontein, which was planned to be completed by Sunday 25 January. This withdrawal was not the final general withdrawal from Angola, as that would only be planned later. The objective here was to relieve the troops that had been in action since November 1975.

Thinning out started on 21 January after last light, with Foxbat leading the withdrawal and the gunners, still in action, bombarding Cela 'for old times sake' and moving out shortly afterwards.

Finally, the order had came through for Captain Potgieter's troop to withdraw, and they arrived in Silva Porto on 21 January to join up with the rest of Zulu.

At this point, Cape Field Artillery was only partly deployed, in that P Battery had settled down to its three-month tour in Angola; Major Harrison had left the training area and was in the process of marrying up with the Cape Town Highlanders (this was the second time in Major Harrison's military life that he had provided fire support to CTH, the first being in Italy in 1944 as part of 6 SA Division.); and R Battery (Major Ackermann) was marrying up with Battle Group Hotel. At 16h00, the balance of CFA departed from the Oshivello training area to arrive in Grootfontein some five hours later, where they were to be confronted with a traditional 'SOMFU' (self-organized military f--k-up). The RHQ and both batteries were placed on a one-hour standby at 08h00 on 22 January, but at 14h00 the intended move was cancelled. Similarly, the RHQ was readied to move to Ondangwa, only to find that this was cancelled owing to a lack of transport. The RHQ was intended to deploy to Silva Porto to reinforce the HQ of the newly formed 2 Military Area; again, this did not happen. There would be no movement before 10h00 on 23 January. Finally, at 14h15 on 23 January, CFA's RHQ and Q Battery departed from Grootfontein for Ondangwa. It may seem as if the South Africans were indecisive at this point, but this was not the case at all. Intelligence was at best sketchy; the politicians were playing for time; and the advancing FAPLA forces were increasing in size and aggressiveness daily.

By 13h00 on Friday 23 January, the gunners from Zulu had arrived in Sa da Bandeira and, once again, groupings were to change, this time however, to hand over to the relief who were waiting at Rocades. The seven-gun field battery of Major Felix Hurter that had arrived from the coast was relieved by Major Stan Harrison's Q Battery from CFA. U Battery of Major Blaauw was relieved by 2nd Battery CFA, these outgoing fire units being from 4 Field Regiment whose troops were first priority to return home. Q Battery (Major Bouwer) would have to wait until 10 February for their relief and, therefore, was deployed (one troop each) to Rocades and Mupa. At this time, all the artillery fire units were unified under the command of Commandant van der Westhuizen, who was now based at Sa da Bandeira. The reorganized artillery regiment now had the luxury of a second in command in the form of Major Hurter and under command were:

- P and Q field batteries (CFA)
- Q Battery (medium) under Major Bouwer with its two troops deployed as mentioned previously
- The RHQ and echelon under the command of Captain du Plessis (the adjutant).

It should be noted that this artillery 'regiment' was in name only, as at that stage Q Battery CFA was in support of Battle Group Golf (CTH) and deployed to the west between Cahama and Vila Roçades. R Battery CFA had been deployed in direct support of Battle Group Hotel in the Mupa area. CFA's headquarters eventually arrived at Ondangwa (the village, not the air force base), which had become the new HQ of 2 Military Area. The HQ was housed in a small government building previously occupied by the Department of Welfare and Pensions. The adjacent grounds were filled with tents, all sadly lacking replacements and none able to keep their occupants dry. This situation changed when CFA's RSM demanded new tents, much to the horror and dismay of the local storeman.

Transvaal Horse Artillery (THA) mobilized in Bloemfontein on 24 January, immediately moving to the firing range at Potchefstroom for six weeks of training.

The Permanent Force and national service gunners spent the period between 24 January and 6 February gradually moving men and equipment southwards to Grootfontein for demobilization. Q Battery remained in position to cover the withdrawal and finally handed over to Major Eddie Brown's Q Battery, TSA on 4 February.

The arrival in Grootfontein showed up the lack of concern for the returning combat troops, who had been in action since November 1975. They were assigned a far corner of the base where no facilities existed and, to make matters worse, they were not permitted into the base area until they had shaved and cleaned up! One questions this type of military absurdity. The decision was probably made by a low-level, rear-echelon staff officer who had not managed to differentiate between combat discipline and show discipline.

Major Hurter's battery left Grootfontein by train; hardly had the train departed when the battery chef appeared at the officers' coach, cap in hand for a donation of a bottle of whiskey from the majors on board, and 20 rands from each officer. After some cursory questions, it turned out that this intrepid chef had befriended his railway counterpart; this friendship was not free, however. The battery chef kept the railways' chef inebriated for the next three days and 'liberated' the latter's order book, which meant a delivery of food and liquor at the next station—a delivery probably only matched by the Blue Train on one of its five-star trips. Once loaded, the train headed off southwards and the passengers were treated to the best food available. Said Lieutenant de Villiers:

> We'd go to the lounge car at 14h00 when the troops had eaten and stay there eating and drinking on the SAR&H until the wee hours of the morning. Roast legs of lamb, beef, masses of German meat dishes, all washed down with copious quantities of beer and wine. A great change from the rat packs, most of which had had the nice bits swiped out by the rear-echelon jam stealers. At each station the chef would have arranged for more choice supplies and local delicacies to be delivered. It was an ongoing feast of gargantuan proportions.

A note on traditional battery numbering

During the period of organizing the new Union Defence Force in 1912, the South African Artillery's regiments were numbered thus:

- 1 Field Regiment (Princess Alice's Own Cape Field Artillery)
- 2 Field Regiment (Natal Field Artillery)
- 3 Field Regiment (Transvaal Horse Artillery)
- 4 Field Regiment (the training unit in Potchefstroom)
- 5 Field Regiment (Transvaalse Staatsartillerie)
- 6 Field Regiment (Orange Free State Field Artillery)

As time went on, the other units were added to this list, but this seniority still exists. Consequently, the regiments' batteries (three per regiment) were numbered 1st, 2nd, 3rd for CFA; 4th, 5th, and 6th for NFA, and so on. The senior three regiments still use this numbering.

By 10 February 1976, all the 'old hands' were home, many with stories to tell, and loves and lives to catch up on.

On 28 February, THA's advance party, comprising Major Roy Andersen (the 2IC), Captain Marciano, Lieutenants Bain-Venn, Lefevre and seventeen other ranks left Potchefstroom for Grootfontein. As with all advance parties, they spent their time drawing, begging, borrowing and 'organizing' equipment (the latter is the army term for stealing, but not for personal gain). Major Andersen and Lieutenant Bain-Venn accompanied Brigade Commander Colonel Willie Kotze, and commanders from other 72 Brigade Units on a recce to Ondangwa and Ruacana, arriving at 71 Brigade's HQ at Ruacana on 2 March. At this stage, 71 Brigade was deployed and had taken over from the original Permanent Force and national service troops in February.

There, the incoming gunners met their compatriots from CFA— Commandant Lionel Crook (the OC), Major Ian McKinney (the 2IC) and Major Stan Harrison, battery commander 2nd Battery (Q Battery). It is noteworthy that the incoming THA remarked that 'the advance party was very impressed by the standard achieved by the CFA'.

On return to Grootfontein, Major Andersen made his battle appreciation and planned the deployment of THA as follows:

- 7th Battery to Calueque—to deploy immediately
- 9th Battery to Catuitui—to deploy immediately
- 8th and 10th Batteries—to Oshivello and Grootfontein respectively.

At 17h00 on 6 March, the nearly 700-strong THA arrived in Grootfontein, to be greeted by a transit camp of thick, grey, viscous mud, but nevertheless, ready for operations. The OC, Commandant Lotz, was briefed and, with slight command changes, movement orders were given. Under the command of Captain Trahar, 7th Battery would relieve CFA at Calueque and be placed in direct support of Combat Group Lima (Cmdt J. Bosch, SA Irish); 8th Battery would move to Oshivello and convert to 140mm medium guns (only a troop was required); 9th Battery to Catuitui to relieve P Battery CFA, in direct support of Combat Group Jumbo; and 10th Battery to the Oshivello training area to relieve R Battery CFA. The RHQ would move to Ruacana and relieve the Brigade Artillery HQ (CFA RHQ).

By 8 March, THA (RHQ and one battery) was deployed under the command of 72 Brigade to the Ruacana area, where the sudden realization occurred that this was no longer a training exercise and, in the words of their quartermaster, 'the good old days were at an end'. There were no fresh rations—dry rations only; fuel, oil and lubricants were in general shortage because of the lack of transport and the distance from Grootfontein to the combat zone; and a shortage of basic cleaning material (cotton waste and cloth) for equipment maintenance. Another hurdle to overcome was the suitability of the Bedford gun tractor in the wet, muddy conditions. This was partially overcome by the use of the ubiquitous Unimog, which, although very capable of towing guns in those conditions, did not have the ammunition-carrying capacity, but this drawback was overcome by the use of vegetable trucks. 72 Brigade established a forward delivery point 40 kilometres behind the front line own troops, which was commanded by THA's quartermaster, primarily because of the quantity of artillery ammunition dumped there. Gradually, Transvaalse Staatsartillerie members reinforced THA in this endeavour.

On 8 March, the artillery units under command of 72 Brigade included:

- HQ at Ruacana staffed by Cmdt Lotz, Major Andersen, Captains Job and Marciano, Lt Marx, 2/Lt Lefevre and 9 signallers and clerks
- 7th (P) Battery THA (Calueque)
- P Battery TSA (Calueque)
- Q Battery TSA (Beranangito)
- R Battery (E Troop) TSA (Beranangito)
- 1 Battery Regiment Oos Transvaal (anti-aircraft) (Ruacana water scheme)
- 62 Battery 6 Light AA Regiment (Ruacana airfield)
- 22 Battery 2 Locating Regiment (Battery Commander Captain B.J. Klopper).

CFA had prepared five firing positions along the approach routes, from which they could cover all likely enemy approaches. Taking this a step further, 7th Battery gave these positions nicknames: Alamein, Bentley, Ellis Park, Harrison and Berry. A defensive fire plan was developed and the gunners, once again, used their initiative by plotting these targets, sending up 1,000-foot flares at each target and marking them from the OP position.

72 Brigade issued new movement orders, and on 11 March, Q and R Batteries (TSA) moved north to Otchinchau, and 7th Battery (THA) redeployed at Calueque, only to move again soon afterwards.

That same day, 1 Transvaal Scottish (1TS) reported a contact with four tanks and numerous armoured cars in the Cahama–Ediva area; the 'Jocks' withdrew (1TS was an infantry unit so did not have sufficient firepower to take on tanks). TSA's two fire units arrived in the Otchinchau area having used up all their fuel, a dangerous situation under any circumstances— and in this case, within range of an enemy armoured force. The brigade administrative area had no stocks of fuel, and drums were transported up from Grootfontein, with Captain Job spending the night of 11/12 March unloading, reloading and moving fuel to the deployed batteries. The fuel arrived in the early morning of 12 March.

Meanwhile, 9th Battery had travelled to Catuitui to relieve P Battery CFA (Major P. Finn), where they were deployed 50 kilometres north of the border. This battery was quickly to learn the term 'greatcoats on, greatcoats off', as no sooner had they been deployed than they were given orders to move back to Grootfontein. Once in Grootfontein, they received orders again to move to Ruacana via 7 Infantry Division's HQ in Ondangwa. For some inexplicable reason, the GOC of 7 Division, Brigadier Helm Roos (himself a gunner), insisted that he personally inspect the guns while en route to Ruacana. This was not the first or last time that he inspected equipment: the author underwent the same belittling experience in Bloemfontein in 1974.

On 13 March, Q Battery 7 Medium Regiment came under the command of 72 Brigade to relieve P Battery TSA, who at that stage were still deployed at Otchinchau in support of Combat Group Golf. At this time, the gunners were deployed as follows: in support of Combat Group Golf Q Battery and E Troop of R Battery TSA; P Battery THA; Q Battery 7 Medium Regiment, as well as two radar sections and three observer troops from 22 Locating Battery. Combat Group Lima was deployed at the Calueque project as the brigade reserve and, therefore, would get artillery support when required.

All fire units carried their full first-line ammunition with a full reserve either in the brigade administrative area or on wheels in the areas immediately behind the deployed fire units.

10th Battery at this stage had drawn the short straw and remained behind in Grootfontein to take over the guarding of the ammunition dump from Q Battery 7 Medium Regiment. Lieutenant Francois Reitz moved out with Q Battery on 10 March to Oshivello and the next day, 10th Battery was pleasantly surprised to move to Oshivello as well. This would be infinitely better than guarding an ammunition dump and building volleyball courts. Brigadier Roos arrived soon afterwards and informed the gunners that they were to be ready for operations with whatever was available in Oshivello, this being seven serviceable 25-pounders, an assortment of vehicles in various degrees of serviceability and 3,000 rounds of ammunition. Training and maintenance was prioritized and, under Major G. Deane's leadership and under difficult conditions they prepared for operations. Leaving behind an ingeniously built officers' mess, complete with home-made fridge and dartboard, 10th Battery arrived in Ruacana late in the afternoon of 23 March and deployed near the Calueque Dam wall.

8th Battery completed their conversion and handed their camp over to Captain M. Bester of TSA, the battery arriving in Ruacana at 17h00 on Sunday 14 March to relieve R Battery TSA. En route to Ruacana, Lt M. Gerber was left at Ondangwa to join up with 7 Division HQ. That same evening, Captain A. Kopp with his 9th Battery arrived in Ruacana: a change in deployment from the original plan because the main threat now was from the northwest. Q Battery TSA engaged the enemy in the Ediva area on 14 March. What made this and subsequent engagements unusual was that, because Ruacana was the only serviceable airfield in the area, all air OP efforts would have to be based there. The closest available officer to perform these missions was

Major Andersen, the 2IC, who had other tasks to perform, mainly that of deploying the blunt end of the regiment and expediting logistics supply. On this particular day, Major Andersen took off from Ondangwa accompanied by a second aircraft, tasked to identify surface-to-air-missile sites. Once in the loiter area, Major Andersen called Q Battery to adjust fire on an enemy patrol using smoke shells. Smoke was favoured at that time because of the height that the air OPs had to maintain to avoid ground fire. From 12,000 feet it was difficult to see an HE shell exploding. In this case Major Andersen used smoke; the rain was obscuring visibility as he was flying at 3,000 feet. Unfortunately, the target was out of Q Battery's range, but the two adjusting rounds were enough to send the patrol packing.

On Tuesday 16 March, 8th Battery relieved Majorr L. Coetzee's R Battery TSA (E Troop) at Beranangito, 100 kilometres inside Angola.

On 20 March, the Angolan forces were occupying Sa da Bandeira and making contact with South African forces at Chitado and Otchinchau. South African forces were occupying a line from Ruacana to Calueque and to a point 50 kilometres north of Calueque.

72 Brigade issued an operational order on 24 March 1976 to all units under command to commence the withdrawal to positions south of the SWA–Angolan border. This order immediately placed D Troop of TSA under command of 7 Division for further deployment. The rest of the artillery was to remain under 72 Brigade's command, supporting the combat groups. Defensive fire plans were to be prepared, as, at that stage, the Angolan forces were already deployed at Otchinchau, Cahama, Chilau and Humbe. The gunners were given the authority to record targets by fire and at least three firing positions were recced for each fire unit.

The role of the locating battery became vitally important during this withdrawal, and 22 Locating Battery was tasked to survey battery and regimental deployment areas both on the high ground on the Angolan side of the Cunene River and south of the border. The Brigade Artillery Intelligence section would keep constant watch on the movement and deployment of Angolan artillery; a sound ranging base would be established and surveyed, mortar-locating radars would accompany the batteries throughout the withdrawal; and artillery meteorological data was to be issued at 10h00 daily. What is not clear is why 'met' would only be available once a day, especially at that time of the year when air temperature and barometric pressure changed considerably between night and day.

By 18h00 on 27 March 1976, all units had withdrawn, 7th Battery THA being the last out.

Lessons learned

The gunners learned that they could not expect to fight effectively without all the equipment they were supposed to have. Coupled with this was the problem of moving equipment forward at short notice over distances of 2,500 kilometres and more without the benefit of a strategic airlift capability. This led to the forward positioning of equipment for a complete 140mm battery (and reserves) at Grootfontein.

In 1976, the Director of Artillery ordered a full debriefing of Operation Savannah. This took place in Potchefstroom, and all the gunners who had been involved received the opportunity to provide their input. A variety of subjects were covered, but the need for new long-range medium guns was particularly emphasized. Another subject that received attention was the high rate of consumption of airburst ammunition. The need for long-range observation equipment for artillery officers was also stressed, as well as the need for more training in the skill of controlling fire missions at long ranges. The successful performance of the gunners during this operation, together with the lessons learned, led to an immediate channelling of capital funding into the development of new equipment. Details of the development of the new equipment is covered in Chapter 12.

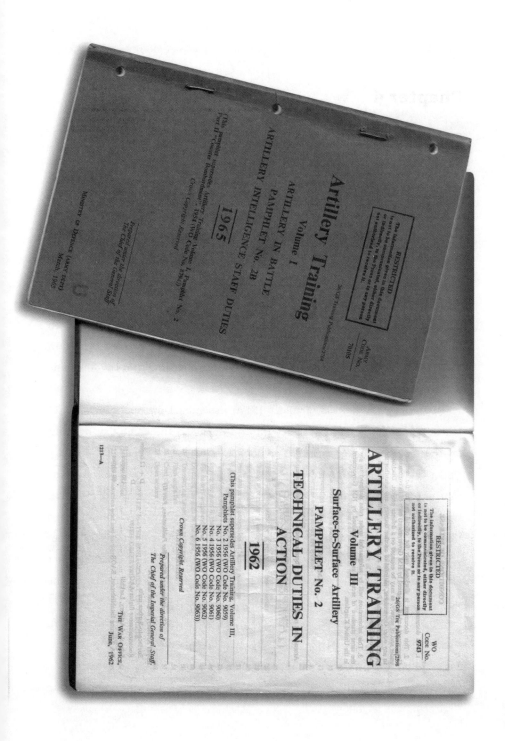

Chapter 4

Budgie, Bruilof, Seiljag
and Reindeer (1976–1978)

Charcoal in the sand: Natal Field Artillery (May–August 1976)
Operation Savannah ended with the withdrawal of the last of the South
African conventional forces in late March 1976. This southerly move and
the subsequent demobilization of units created a concern for the military
planners in that a gap was now left in the conventional warfare capability in
the theatre of operations. Apart from the armoured car troops left behind in
SWA, there was no conventional defence against anything that the Angolans
and Cubans may attempt.

5th Battery Natal Field Artillery (NFA) assembled for operations on 24
May 1976 at Lords Ground, Durban, and departed the same day by train
for the mobilization centre at Diepkloof, just to the west of Bloemfontein.
Under the command of Major Peter Hodsdon, the battery went through the
routine of medical examinations, kit issues and a limited amount of refresher
training. Within a day of arrival, Captain Rob Harvey, the BPO commanding
the advance party, left a freezing Bloemfontein for Grootfontein and other
warmer climates. (At that time, the BPO was the battery 2IC. Doctrine later
changed this arrangement, and the senior troop commander became the
battery 2IC.)

Six days after mobilizing, the main party of 5th Battery arrived in
Grootfontein. NFA's War Diary describes it as 'a shambles . . . an unbelievable
camp still in the process of being built. It is to cost R85 million eventually'.

By this time, the grouping of the incoming force, known as Combat Group
Charcoal, was as follows:

- Durban Light Infantry (DLI, Motorized Infantry Battalion) (Commandant Justin Hulme)
- B Squadron, Umvoti Mounted Rifles (Armoured Car Regiment)
- 5th Battery NFA (88mm G1 guns) in direct support
- 14 Locating Battery (1 Locating Regiment)
- Engineer Troop (19 Field Squadron).

This force married up at Oshivello where training for the primary task immediately commenced. Like their comrades in arms before them, the Natal gunners quickly found that life in the army had changed somewhat since their last training camp in Potchefstroom. To their horror, they found that they were standing to every morning at 06h00 and, despite a long, full day's training, standing down at 19h00 was not the end of the day, as lectures continued until the late hours.

This arrival in the operational area was significant for NFA, in that the unit had last seen action in South West Africa in 1915, and 5th Battery was in action for the first time since World War II.

The next peculiarity for the gunners was the flat, featureless terrain and the lack of maps, forcing the use of 'no map' drill. Major Hodsdon was soon introduced to the dangers of firing without maps when his party felt the discomfort of a shell bursting within 100 metres of their position. This was quickly corrected by the command 'more three degrees', and the next round landed a safe distance away.

For the first two weeks, 5th Battery was accompanied by Commandant Duane Jakins, the regimental commander, Major Don Guthrie, the 2IC (with an evaluation team) and Major Ron Pepler, the quartermaster. These officers were typical of the committed senior members of CF units — they were not expected to be there because only one battery was deployed, but they deployed with their troops nevertheless. Training continued and specific attention was paid to the integration of the capabilities of the mortar-locating radar of 14 Locating Battery with that of the guns.

It is ironic that no matter how well the gunners shoot during training and even on operations, 'Murphy' arrives just ahead of a VIP before a demonstration shoot. (Murphy's Law states that, no matter what, if something can go wrong, it will.) This particular occasion was no exception. The battery received a visit from Chief of the Army Lieutenant-General Constand Viljoen. NFA's diary takes up the story:

> Delta Troop . . . nearly wrote off the OPs once again. A one-round fire for effect had two shells landing short and two over. Shrapnel whined through the OP position and bits were found around the vehicles. The command to fire was followed by the shells exploding—then a lull. Suddenly, Delta's radio operator was shocked to hear Major Hodsdon's voice crackling through the air with a crisp: 'What the hell do you think you are doing?' This incident caused amusement on the gun position, especially [among] those on Delta Troop position. The major arrived on the position soon afterwards, noticeably paler, and holding a generously sized shell splinter.

On Sunday 13 June, 5th Battery, minus one gun (no. 3 gun, Sergeant Garrity), suffered two punctured tyres and had to await spare wheels from Grootfontein and moved out of Oshivello for their deployment area south of the border checkpoint at Osikango.

At this time, 2 Locating Regiment was in the process of withdrawing after completion of its three-month tour of duty.

The two gun position officers, Lieutenant Shane Jakins of C Troop, and Lieutenant D. Krige of D Troop, laid out the battery position after a careful sweep of the area. This battery position was 100 metres to the east of the main road from Ondangwa to Oshikango (Santa Clara) and 12 kilometres south of the border. The front of the gun positions was protected by Bren machine guns covering an open field of fire over a large corn field. The flanks and rear were covered by the infantry companies of Durban Light Infantry and the Elands of Umvoti Mounted Rifles. Once again, the gunners formed the front line own troops. Observation was achieved by deploying two OP parties, one on a 30-metre-high concrete water tower on the border, and the other on an identical tower 12 kilometres south of the gun position.

The objective of this battle group was to act as a mobile conventional deterrent that could be deployed anywhere in the operational area. The medium batteries had pulled out a day or so earlier and this meant that 5th Battery was now the only gunner unit deployed in the operational area.

As with all such deployments, boredom gave birth to innovation on a grand scale. Innovation leads to what is termed, 'organizing' (a military term for scrounging or thieving). Water was an issue at this time. According to Captain Johnston-Webber:

> . . . the water truck [had] to travel to the towers to fill up. However, the water pipeline from Angola to Andanua [sic], for which the water towers provided the gravity, ran past the camp and there were plans afoot to ask the water scheme's resident engineer to provide an outlet near the camp. A few bottles of whisky persuaded him that the effort was worthwhile.

The battery, realizing that they were more than likely to be in the same position for the next two months, busied themselves with organizing home comforts. Captain Johnston-Webber said:

> Behind their guns they built huge pits, supported the walls with sandbags and then lined the dug-out with tarpaulins and sails. Above them they erected tents, and so produced a cosy, communal home for the six members of the gun crew. Delta 3, with no gun to worry about, had joined their efforts to build what must have been one of the most comfortable dens around. Called the 'Owambo Spa' by the battery, those gunners soon proved the champion scroungers of the unit. They swapped their berets for stretchers from outgoing troops in Ondangwa, 'acquired' a large galvanized bath for washing and seemed to be the best off for food and drink. A good scrounger is an asset in any gun crew in such circumstances, and the men of 14 Locating hadn't been slumming it either. They had a hand-operated washing machine which found its way out of troubled Angola to their camp.

It appears that most acquisitions were sourced in military bases, Ondangwa being the primary source. A fine example of this is told by Captain John Johnston-Webber, the battery captain:

> We, as a battery, decided that we needed a mobile kitchen. I used to make a twice-weekly trip (about 200 kilometres) to Ondangwa and Oshakati. I designated one of these trips as the mission to secure a mobile kitchen. These items were in short supply. When I arrived in Oshakati, I saw a mobile kitchen standing ready to go. I told the men to hitch it up whilst I went in to secure it officially. I was informed that I could not have it, since the kitchen had been reserved for 15 Maintenance (Unit), who had requested it some time previously. I promptly replied that we had already hitched it up and that the gunners were in need of it far more than the grocers . . . a sense of urgency suddenly came over me, in that, if I wanted to avoid a showdown with 15 Maintenance, a discreet, hurried departure would be very much in order.'

The organizing went on unabated:

> Delta 1 gun under Sergeant 'Small Mike' Phillip had bought two fowls from a neighbouring tribesman at 50 cents a head. In that crew a heated discussion took up most of the day. Opinion varied as to whether to eat the fowls then, fatten them first before slaughter or keep them as layers. The egg eaters won the day . . . Sergeant Garrity was not to be outdone. His crew had also bought a pair of chickens.

The axe fell a day later when the battery commander gave the instruction that all chickens would be dead by dawn.

5th Battery were well manned during that period; the list following gives an indication of the deployed personnel:

- Battery commander: Major P.G. Hodsdon
- BPO: Captain R.D. Harvey
- Assistant BPO: Second Lieutenant J.G. 'Blackie' Swart
- Observers: Captains R.C. Lovell-Greene, T.A. Hatton, R.J.F. Prior, C.A. Cavannagh
- Gun position officers: Lieutenant S.A. Jakins, 2/Lt J.D. Krige
- Troop leaders: Lieutenant J.J. Fourie, 2/Lt M.M. Godbold
- Transport officer (not normally found in a battery): 2/Lt D.P. Fleet
- Battery captain: Captain J.C. Johnston-Webber
- Assistant battery captain (another anomaly): 2/Lt J.E. Hall
- Battery sergeant-major: WOI J.M. Wessels
- Troop sergeant majors: WOIIs T.B. de Gersigny, D.J. McLean
- Doctor: Captain J.D. Buchan.

According to the unit order part 2 of 15 June 1976, the battery also comprised:

- S/Sgts: T. Martin, D.C. Mudie, R.P. Thompson
  Sgts: P. Asbury, G.D. Campbell-Hall, C.W. Garrity, I.A. Macaskill,
  A.C. Norman, A.R. Phelp, M.J. Philip, M.J. Philip (there were two),
  L.C. 'Horse' Rogers, T. Segarius
  Bdrs: A.W. Bennet, A. Adams, G.M. Bosch, J.L. Botha, S. Brick,
  A.M.A. Campbell, C.R. Cowan, A.B. Cronjé, H. du Preez, B.K. Fowler,
  T.J. Gow, H.M. Jacobs, J.F. Kidson, U.P.M. Maquet, A. Marx, M.T.
  Naudé, T.C.V. Newton, R.J. Oeschger, H.J. Olivier, G.H. Putter, D.J.
  Potgieter, D.M. Poyers, J.G. Roth, L.M. Surgeson, P.A. Sauvage, S.J.
  Totman, G. Thompson, C.W. van Niekerk, G. van Tonder
- L/Bdrs: A.R. Burke, G.F. Lange, J.B. Leitch, N.J. Pole, R.E. Vincent
- Gnrs: H Adamson, E.V. Baker, A.J. Bester, A. Brindley, R.M.T. Carlin,
  N.M. Cassidy, C.J. Chambers, D.A. Clark, A.J.F.F. Coelho, N.J.
  Collier, B.J. Cowan, R.P. Delport, N.D. du Plessis, M.P. de Marigny,
  K.A. Dettman, R.W. Ellis, G.J. Ellis, D. Evans, L.R. Fourie, R.H.
  Gielink, G.G. Hannaford, A.S. Hattingh, R.P. Hofert, A.A. Hoogers,

G.F. Hopwood, A.C. Hill, G.P. Hitchner, F.P. Human, H.J. Ihlenfeldt, A.E. Jessiman, D.T. Kidwell, W. Kiloh, G.A. King, B. Kokkin, H.D. Kruger, H.M. Lee, I.J. Leyenaar, S.J. Little, G.J. Macatthie, S.P. Margison, D.P. McLean, B.D. Molver, M.A. Muller, W.F. Nathras, J.D. Nel, I.G. Oberholzer, W.J. Oschmann, N.A. O'Toole, J.S. Papenfus, J.P. Pretorius, J.J. Pretorius, C.J.J. Putter, I.D. Russel, G.R. Russel-Smith, L.E. Smit, M.S. Somes, G.D. Swale, M.D. Swart, W.J. Swart, M.A. Sykes, C.V. Thompson, S.D. Thorne, A.C. Thorton, M.J. Todd, B. van Rensburg, W. van Zyl, G.D. Varga, C. Vermeulen, F.L. Visagie, J.P. Visser, R.T. Walters, W.O.N. Wareing, R.S. Wassink

At 20h00 on 22 June, the battle group received a message that a group of 40 SWAPO troops were to cross the border near St Mary's Mission with the aim of raiding the Etale area. This immediately alleviated the boredom, and the gunners went onto the alert. The likelihood of the gunners being called to provide fire support was low and a number of them were deployed in an infantry role to protect the water towers, thus relieving DLI to concentrate on setting up ambush positions along the possible infiltration routes. During the night of 23 June, Captain Rob Prior, one of the OPOs, reported activity and lights flashing to the east of his position. Two days later, intelligence came through warning of a likely mortar attack on the Etale base. The guns were given a new centre of arc, and 14 Locating Battery brought their Cymbeline mortar-locating radar sets into action. Seventy rounds per gun were offloaded, including airburst fuses. Naturally, there was a downside to all this activity: the additional guard duties required gun crews, which meant that guns would be unmanned for periods at a time. On reflection, counter-bombardment by one troop would probably have silenced the mortars.

By the beginning of July, reports of insurgent movement were a daily occurrence and kept the battery focused on the job at hand. On 3 July, thoughts drifted towards home, as the Durban July Handicap was being run. For this, DLI set up a battle group tote and took bets, heavily supported by 5th Battery, during which some lucky gunners won R41 each on Jamaican Music's win.

At about this time, the urge to improve the base, combined with the usual boredom, resulted in Captain Johnston-Webber 'finding' a bulldozer. He regales the story:

> The DLI from our Combat Group Charcoal base was sent to guard a school. They found what appeared to be an abandoned bulldozer [tracked]. It appeared to be a Caterpillar D6. It was brought back to the base camp where it was serviced and used for improvements to the camp, such as bush clearing, that were strategically necessary, and digging a petrol point.
>
> I eventually commandeered the machine and set about satisfying one of my childhood desires—to drive a bulldozer. We had a bulldozer operator within the battery and I asked him to sit next to me whilst I drove the bulldozer through the camp. I had a further motive and that was to use the machine to construct a huge mound of soil. The idea was to mount a machine gun on top of the pile to improve command over its sector and, therefore, our local defence. Constructing the mound meant digging a large hole. During the 'construction works', the contractor arrived to reclaim his bulldozer, and I had not finished the task. He was very good natured when I explained to him what I was doing and he agreed to allow me to finish the job, telling me that he would return with his low-bed transporter in about two hours. We completed the job and he took his machine. The idea was good until the time came to leave the area. It was important that we left the area as we found it. Problem: I had a large pile of soil to go into a very large hole in the ground and no bulldozer. Answer: many gunners with many shovels took the place of the bulldozer. I was not popular.

On 8 July, intelligence reported that there was a military build-up in the Ongiva (Perreira d'Eca) and Santa Clara (Oshikango) areas. This was confirmed by Captain Prior, who had observed troop carriers moving around the border-post area, and new faces that had been seen. In the period between 9 July and the end of their tour, the Natal gunners at least had a taste of the war being fought. They had to step in to reinforce the infantry and support the armoured cars on occasion; they saw what anti-tank mines can do to vehicles and humans; they saw the reaction of the world news media after the search of St Mary's Mission; and they saw their comrades in DLI wounded in action. There were regular sightings of flares and other lights at night, but what they did not realize at the time was that they were observing the SWAPO build-up for bigger operations, which was eventually to culminate in the conventional operations six months later.

On 5 August 1976, 5th Battery departed the operational area: The lessons learned would be passed on to the rest of the regiment and future training and, in particular, leadership would put NFA in the top spot as the best artillery unit for a number of years to come.

Operation Bruilof—'greatcoats on'

The year 1978, some two years after the bulk of the SADF had withdrawn from the Angolan operational area, caused a vacuum that created an opportunity for SWAPO to establish a greater presence in southern Angola, particularly in towns such as Xangongo, Ongiva and Cassinga, where they established camps either in the towns or close by, where they could get protection and support from the FAPLA forces. They also established smaller bases farther south, which were final jumping-off points for incursions into SWA.

In late January 1978, after a night raid on a poorly protected army base at Etale, SWAPO captured Sapper van der Nescht. This incident naturally caused some embarrassment to the South African government and more to the army, but was not significant in its contribution to the war during that time.

In February, 14 Field Regiment was again tasked to mobilize a battery for operational duty. 14 Field Regiment was organized as follows:

- 141 Battery (P Battery): 120mm M5 mortars
- 142 Battery (Q Battery): 88mm G1 (25-pounder)
- 143 Battery (R Battery): 88mm sexton self-propelled
- 2 Medium Battery (S Battery): 140mm G2 (5.5 inch)
- 32 Locating Battery.

The 'G' series of South African ordnance

During this period, the Directorate of Logistic Services at Army HQ decided to standardize on the nomenclature of ordnance in the army in general, the artillery equipment being allocated the prefix GV, an acronym for geskut veld (ordnance, field) and thus the ordnance was named as follows:

- GV1: 88mm (25-pounder)
- GV2: 140mm (5.5 inch)
- GV3: 155mm Long Tom
- GV4: 155mm Soltam M78
- The GV5 and 6 were in concept exploration at that time
- GV7: 88mm SP (Sexton 25 pr)

The 120mm mortar was designated M5, the other mortars all being either infantry or armour systems (M1 to M4). The 127mm multiple rocket system was in full-scale engineering development and was designated FV1. A little later, the ordnance was given names as well, but, like the 'V' in the prefix, these names were never used by the soldiers on the ground.

Mona Ambriz: A historical connection here. One of the guns assigned to 2 Medium Battery was camouflaged in green and brown paint and had the name Mona Ambriz painted on the recoil mechanism. I found out that this was the gun that fired the historic first round in November 1975 and later was rescued north of Luanda by the navy. Here is the content of an email received from Manual Ferreira, translated into English: 'The story of the three 5.5 inch guns that were left under the mango trees in Ambriz is now clearer. During the withdrawal, the firing mechanisms and sights were removed and evacuated with the crews, on the SAS President Steyn to Walvis Bay. Toutjies Venter (a gunner officer who retired as a colonel) rewarded Holden Roberto of the FNLA with two hundred AK-47 rifles for the safekeeping of the guns. The guns were finally evacuated to the RSA on 11 March 1976 and were in good condition and immediately put back into service. The guns still had the Walvis Bay yellow paint on.'

This time, 2 Medium Battery under the command of Major Piet Uys was the selected fire unit. The requirement came from the lessons learned in 1975–1976, where the South African gunners were outranged by the FAPLA artillery, and this time they were taking no chances. The battery comprised eight G2 guns in two troops with all the supporting vehicles and equipment that could be gathered. The bulk of this equipment had been used in Savannah, serviced and then stored in Grootfontein. Captain Jakes Jacobs and WOIIs Claassen and Hensberg departed ahead of the rest of the battery as the advance party to check equipment and receive initial orders. The main party arrived in Grootfontein about two days later under the command of the battery commander. Captain Jakes Jacobs was the troop commander of G Troop and Lieutenant Clive Wilsworth the troop commander of the junior troop (H Troop). On arrival at 101 Task Force HQ (Grootfontein), the main party met up with the advance party and started loading equipment onto vehicles for the journey northwards to Oshivello, the training area.

At this time, the designations of some of the posts in a battery had changed, largely as a result of the move to eight gun batteries; the GPO was replaced by the troop position officer (TPO). The old section leader was replaced by the troop leader, and the battery guide became a troop sergeant-major.

To put this into perspective, the organogram below will help explain:

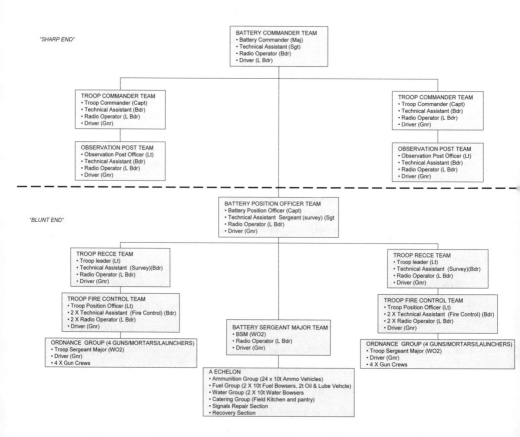

S Battery's blunt end comprised:

- BPO: Lieutenant Willie Gresse
- G Troop TPO: Lieutenant Deon Holtzhausen
- G Troop Troop Leader: Second Lieutenant Jakkie Potgieter
- G Troop TSM: WOII Sampie Claassen
- H Troop TPO: Lieutenant Ernst Kamffer
- H Troop Troop Leader: Lieutenant Ian Johnson
- H Troop TSM: WOII 'Peppie' van Dyk
- BSM: WOII Len 'Soutie' Hensberg

The battery was assigned as part of a new operation under a new grouping; this operation was code-named 'Bruilof' and would be conducted by the newly formed Battle Group Juliet, under the command of Commandant Joop Joubert, the commander of 1 SA Infantry Battalion. What was significant about this battle group was that it was the first-ever mechanized force to be deployed by South Africa. The infantry battalion was equipped with the new Ratel ICV, then just coming off the production lines. The battle group also had a squadron of Eland armoured cars, both the 90mm and 60mm models. The artillery battery sharp end was equipped with Eland 60s.

The biggest adjustment the gunners had to make was the total lack of terrain features—the countryside in that area is flat and the trees are all the same height! This necessitated 'no-map' drill to plot targets, which in itself can be a dangerous practice, as was found out. During one of the practice engagements the first adjusting round from the battery landed about 25 metres from the vehicle Major Uys and Lieutenant Wilsworth were using. Happily, the round landed in the soft sand and on the target side of the vehicle, resulting in a few nervous twitches and the order to stop.

Another problem they faced was the state of calibration of the guns. These guns had been used extensively on operations, and the barrel wear and number of equivalent full charges (EFCs) fired had not been documented. This lack of information means that a gun does not fire in accordance with the range set on the sight—an extremely dangerous and risky situation.

In 1978, a proper gun calibration exercise would have taken a full week of firing on an accurately surveyed firing range, with selected, weighed ammunition, and supported by meteorological data updated every four hours—not the thing to do immediately before an operation. This forced the battery to do a 'bush calibration', which at least removed some of the unknowns.

The plan was for the battle group to attack and destroy a series of SWAPO bases about 15 kilometres north of the border above the Etale base. The cover story was that they were going to rescue Sapper van der Nescht.

It is interesting to note that the battery had to move to Eenhana, one of the bases next to the border, via a dirt road, in order to assemble with the rest of the battle group. On the way, the fire-control vehicle, a Unimog, drove over a landmine, which exploded and flipped the vehicle over. Except for the driver, who broke a leg, there where no injuries. What is peculiar about this incident is the fact that the Unimog was the eleventh vehicle in the convoy: the first three vehicles were actually mine-clearing vehicles, which all crossed the spot where the mine was buried in the road without detonating the mine.

Another point of interest is that, once in Angolan territory, the guns had to be moved cross-country owing to the complete lack of roads. This put a lot of strain on the gun carriages, and breakages started to occur.

The total operation lasted about 50 hours—most of the gunners remember that clearly because they were awake for 52 hours continuously. Of course, they didn't find van der Nescht, as he had already been moved to Luanda by then. But they did make contact with SWAPO forces and they did realize the potential of the Ratel as a combat vehicle.

The battery returned home about a week later and within two weeks received its next warning order to mobilize again.

Battle Group Juliet

This group was the forerunner of 61 Mech Bn Gp, and the artillery battery that was eventually placed under command of 61 Mech was called S Battery (call sign Golf 49).

Seiljag: an unhappy ending

In April 1978, 32 Battalion was conducting sweeps in the central part of the operational area and required artillery support. This was a series of small operations under the name 'Seiljag'. The intention was to flush out SWAPO bases in southern Angola. Once again, 14 Field Regiment mobilized a fire unit, this time one medium troop (four guns) under the command of Captain Jakes Jacobs.

Apart from Captain Jacobs, this was essentially G Troop from the previous operation, with some minor personnel changes, those being:

- Captain Jaap Nel: the relief Air OP
- Lieutenant Clive Wilsworth: the FOO
- Lieutenant Ernst Kamffer: the TPO
- Lieutenant Deon Holtzhausen: the troop leader
- Sergeant Steve Collins: the troop sergeant-major.

During this period. the two regiments rotated annually: in 1978, 14 Field Regiment was operational while 4 Field Regiment was busy with training.

This particular operation, from the artillery's perspective, was wrong from the start. A troop was deployed independently, an organization that has no organic support and which went into action virtually on arrival from Grootfontein. 32 Battalion had deployed two infantry companies under the overall command of Major Eddie Viljoen. The operational orders were given by the battalion commander without the gunners being present, and so these were not able to provide any input into the fire plan. The battalion commander, after being advised by the air force that the Cessna 185 would not be able to loiter for the full duration of the operation, replied, 'We will worry about that later.'

The sketch overleaf shows the basic layout of the operation. Note the angle between the axis of attack to the second objective and the line of fire of the guns.

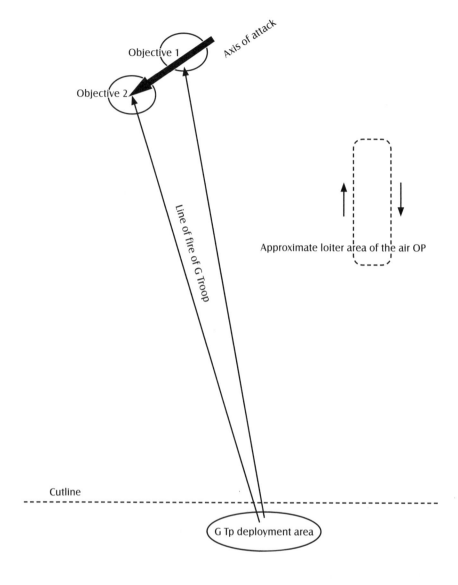

The FOO, without the 'luxury' of the rest of his team, was flown from Etale base by Puma after last light to join up with the 32 Battalion assault force. After a short night's sleep, during which time the blunt end deployed just south of the 'cutline' (the SWA–Angolan border), the assault troops began their approach (on foot) to the objective, a distance of approximately 12 kilometres. As dawn approached, Jakes Jacobs took off from Eenhana base—another unsettling experience. Either the Cessna was too heavy or the pilot was in a hurry, but the aircraft skimmed the berm at the end of the runway and damaged the landing gear on take-off. Nonplussed, the two carried on with their mission and called the FOO once in position above and behind the assault force. It is important here to consider the effect on the defending force. It is just after first light and an enemy light aircraft is circling above you—surely something is about to happen? At one stage, Captain Jacobs called the FOO to say that they were moving farther east, 'They are bloody shooting at us!'

The cutline

The cutline was a term used by the troops to refer to the border between SWA and Angola. This man-made border comprised two east–west roads, or tracks, separated by a kilometre of open grass (although, over time, scrub and trees had started growing again). This 450-kilometre-long dead-straight stretch ran between the Cunene and Kavango rivers.

Eventually, at about 11h00 the assault force was in position and the command given to commence the fire plan. Because of the density of the bush in that area the ground troops used the smoke from the artillery fire as a navigation aid. This is not a new practice and has been used by numerous armies around the world. The fire on the objective was accurate, but the element of surprise was lost, which resulted in one kill—an anti-aircraft gunner manning a 14.5mm machine gun. The rest of the base was empty and had obviously been abandoned just as the artillery fire started. On the approach, the initial fire was lifted and moved to the next target on the fire plan. It was here that Murphy's Law took over. Between the first and second series of the fire plan, the air OPs had to change over. Somehow, during the course of the morning the warning of the Cessna's loiter time had sunk in and Captain Jaap Nel, an artillery officer from the Army College, at that time was discovered in Ondangwa. Captain Nel was tasked to relieve Captain Jacobs and immediately took off (in an AM3C Bosbok) from Ondangwa. Nel did not have a copy of the fire plan, but that was not all: his map was not marked up either. Furthermore, he had not received orders or any form of briefing. In this blind state, he arrived over the target area, where the fire plan had to be transmitted to him by Captain Jacobs by radio whilst airborne, and he still had to orientate himself and identify targets. As soon as he made radio contact, Wilsworth called for the second series on the fire plan (objective 2). On the ground, the assault force maintained its momentum towards the objective, approaching from the northeast and about 600 metres from the target. The next thing was 140mm HE shells exploding in the trees above the heads of the assault force, killing a machine gunner 50 metres away from Major Viljoen and Wilsworth, and another 32 Battalion rifleman farther to the west. The order 'stop' was given immediately and the assault continued.

On crossing the cutline later that afternoon, Major Viljoen and Lieutenant Wilsworth were airlifted back to Eenhana where a quick debrief was held, primarily to determine what went wrong. It was not gun calibration, as has been claimed, but a result of the air OP changeover and a number of other contributing factors. These were as follows: the lead platoon was not on the correct route because of navigation difficulties, resulting in the assault group arriving on the objective nearly one kilometre too far to the north; one of the guns had set the wrong range on its sight—the range ordered by the TPO was 7,800 yards, but the no. 1 of the offending gun had transposed this to 8,700 yards—the data that was fired on. No one was held responsible, but some important lessons were taken to heart after that tragic incident.

Reindeer

This next operation was to be a big one, spread over a large area of southern Angola. The aftermath of this operation is remembered in Namibia each year on 4 May as Cassinga Day.

Operation Reindeer's plan included two distinctly separate attacks on SWAPO bases.

The main attack would be an airborne assault on the base at Cassinga by 1 Para Battalion supported by the SAAF. The secondary attacks would be farther south on an area by the name of Dombondola, by Battle Groups A and B supported by a medium battery and air support where needed.

The battery was once again under the command of Major Piet Uys, who would be deployed on the ground in an Eland armoured car. His two FOOs were also deployed in Elands and the two air OPs were Captain Jakes Jacobs and

Lieutenant Wilsworth, each in a Kudu light fixed-wing aircraft. Uys relates:

> Lieutenant Wilsworth had, in the meantime, contracted yellow jaundice (along with nearly half of the battery), which became worse as the date of the attack approached. On D-Day, Major Uys had no option but to request Lt Wilsworth to actually take off in spite of his sickness, and to fly his sorties as normal. Lt Wilsworth, of course, did so in spite of feeling miserable with two yellow, burning eyes.

Captain Jacobs's troop provided fire support for Battle Group A and they deployed somewhat earlier than H Troop. Lieutenant Wilsworth took off only when the supported battle group actually crossed the cutline, and that was about 14h00 in the afternoon. By the time the aircraft arrived at the contact point above the target area, the troop was deployed and reported ready. The OPOs and fire-control officers had already prearranged to adjust with smoke rounds to prevent confusion, as the OPOs would be flying at 12,000 feet, and detailed observation was difficult—one can hardly see vehicles from that altitude, never mind people. Fire was opened and the attacks went in.

The following gives an example of the way in which hurried plans had to be made. Captain Mike Cowley, an ex-Royal Artillery officer, joined 14 Field Regiment during late April, and reported in the operational area about five days before D-Day. Captain Cowley was assigned an Eland 60 armoured car, and duly prepared his vehicle for operations. Being new to the SAA and totally unaccustomed to the African climate and terrain, he determined that water would be his key to survival. This resulted in his armoured car being festooned with water bottles: the whole turret was encircled by suspended bottles. As the battle group started up to move northwards, Captain Cowley's Eland broke down. The battle group commander immediately ordered the vehicle, complete with crew, to be loaded onto a transporter and to follow the convoy. This strange configuration went through the attack with its supported unit and probably made history as the only artillery OPO to carry out fire missions from a transporter!

By 17h30, the air OPs withdrew, as fuel was running low and it was getting dark. By then, the objectives had been achieved and the ground force was busy digging in for the night. The next day, Wilsworth received feedback from his FOO, Captain Toon Greeff, as to the success of the fire missions: they had managed to hit one bicycle, which was found wrapped around a tree! It should be noted that there was no artillery support for the airborne attack on Cassinga because at that time the gunners had no light, or airborne, capability (see Chapter 12).

The Army Battle School

At about this time, the SA Army had made a decision to establish a central training capability, to be known as the Army Battle School (It is now called the Central Training Centre—CTC). This unit was set up on largely unproductive farmland in the Northern Cape between the Sishen Iron Ore Mine and the town of Postmasburg. Based on the Israeli Battle School, the firing range extended a distance of approximately 60 kilometres north to south, and 30 kilometres east to west, an area large enough to accommodate a divisional exercise. Each of the corps in the army (infantry, armour, artillery, etc.) had a permanent resident training team to provide training and related liaison functions to the units deployed for training. Originally it provided training for Citizen Force formations and their subordinate units, as well as promotion courses for Permanent Force officers (combat team and battle group courses). It had sufficient main equipment for a brigade, and personnel for skeleton forces to support courses. As lessons were learned from operations, the approach to training changed, and the inception of the annual Exercise Sweepslag proved a great success. The conventional units would complete their initial training at their home bases and then complete their training and operational preparation immediately before and during Sweepslag. In the case of the artillery, training would take place in Potchefstroom, where troops would undergo individual training (skills development) and sub-unit (battery) training using the limited range available. This meant that a battery could mobilize, move, deploy and fire. Once this phase of training was completed, the regiment would move to Army Battle School for more live firing and movement (but at a more realistic, faster pace); anti-aircraft drills; camouflage and concealment; and logistics support in the field. This training would culminate in a number of regimental exercises, both during daylight and at night, using the full spectrum of ammunition and firing at operational ranges. The accent was on night movement and night deployment, in radio silence and without lights. At the same time, PF officers on the battle group commanders' or junior staff courses would plan for the exercise and then be allocated to one of the units in the area. The gunners would inevitably be allocated to an artillery unit as regimental commander, fire support co-ordination officer or battery commander. The permanent incumbents would act as coaches or, occasionally, simply as the radio operator to the student allocated.Units would then join up with Sweepslag and take part in the exercise, which would run non-stop for two to three days. The founder general officer commanding of the Army Battle School was Brigadier Frans van den Berg, a very popular and knowledgeable gunner, who eventually retired as a Lt-General as Chief of Defence Staff.

Chapter 5

Ruacana and Katima Mulilo:
fixed fire bases

Ruacana: digging in

No sooner had S Battery arrived back at Oshivello after Operation Reindeer than the new mission was issued: to deploy a troop to the infantry base at Ruacana to support operations around the Calueque Dam complex. Immediately, Major Uys tasked G Troop to prepare to move, and by the next day the troop was on the road to Ruacana. In order to maintain secrecy the troop arrived during the night and, by next morning, had deployed the guns under tents. One must understand that these were 140mm guns, and these require rather large gun pits. Happily, the sand is soft enough to dig by hand and about two weeks later, the battery was satisfactorily dug in. This new firing position was directly adjacent to the armoured car squadron also deployed in the Ruacana base in addition to an infantry company— the company commander being the base commander. The base itself was rectangular in shape, with the long axis running east–west facing the Angolan border. Immediately to the south lay the airstrip.

This was the start of a ten-year-long deployment. When the battery first deployed there it was decided that one of the OP officers should be deployed at the Ondangwa air force base and fly air OP missions every time a light fixed-wing aircraft flew to Ruacana base or thereabouts. Lieutenant Wilsworth was the first air OP selected and duly moved with all his baggage to the SAAF base at Ondangwa. There was only one problem, however—no one had told the SAAF that a 'pongo' (SAAF terminology for anyone in an army uniform) was coming! It took some explanation, and eventually the SAAF were informed, but it was actually an exercise in futility, as the flying time from Ondangwa to Ruacana is about 40 minutes (without the normal reaction time of at least an hour before getting airborne).

This initial deployment was followed by a continuous gunner presence until 1988, when the battery was withdrawn to join 10 Artillery Brigade during Operation Hilti. This presence included the posting of permanent staff in the form of the battery commander and battery sergeant-major, who lived in the domestic area at Ruacana and worked on the base.

Early in 1979 and before the permanent postings, Captain Mike Cowley (14 Field Regiment) was posted to this battery. Shortly after arrival and the usual operational briefing, Captain Cowley, inquisitive by nature, wondered about any possible SWAPO activities at a seemingly deserted house situated on the cutline and about 8 kilometres from the gun position. Up until then, no movement had ever been seen, either by passing patrols or air observers flying in the area. Captain Cowley organized a small patrol comprising his OPO party and an infantry section for protection, and set off on foot to investigate. Upon approaching the house, Captain Cowley, with typical British aplomb, called out, 'Hello! Is anyone at home?' The reply was fast: a burst of machine-gun fire and several rounds of other small-arms fire that was close enough to graze the OPO's webbing and send the party back to the Ruacana base at the double.

On 22 March 1979, G Troop of 2 Medium Battery left Potchefstroom to relieve the outgoing troops at Ruacana, followed by Captain Willem Botha and Lieutenant Willem Gresse to take over the leadership role.

The nature of operations at that time dictated that there had to be a permanent artillery deployment at Ruacana to support the infantry operations in the area and cover the strategically important Calueque Dam. This meant that the gunners would have to transfer at least a troop commander and a TSM to permanently man the deployment.

73 Battery, 7 Medium Regiment, commanded by Major P. Moir, relieved the 41 Battery personnel for three months in 1981.

At a point in 1983, 41 Battery was deployed under the command of Captain Jaap Nel. A group of about 200 SWAPO fighters were infiltrating into SWA on

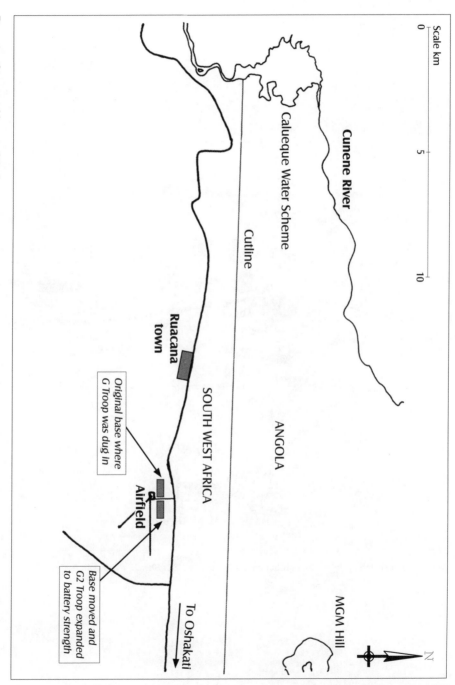

Ruacana: the general layout of the base.

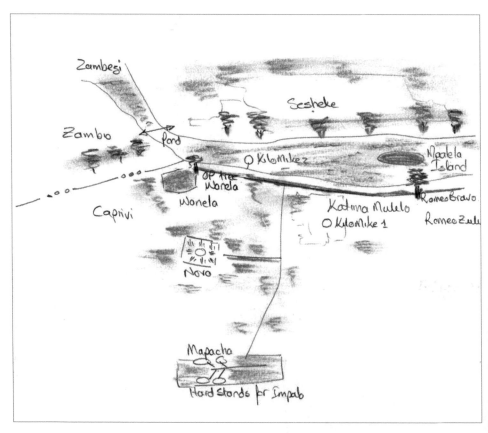

Nova base: a sketch of the Katima Mulilo base area in 1981/82. *Sketch: F.J.G. van Eeden*

a route to the east of the village of Ruacana. As luck would have it, Captain Nel was summoned to Oshakati to attend an order group (never a brief affair at that time) and had to leave his GPO, a national service second lieutenant, as acting troop commander. Late that night, the SWAPO group commenced firing mortars at Ruacana. The mortar position was quickly plotted by the Cymbeline Radar set from 4 Locating Battery, deployed with the troop. The acting troop commander wasted no time and went over to fire a counter-bombardment mission, successfully disrupting the SWAPO intentions. The group was last heard of fleeing northwards, and had disappeared before the reaction force could catch them.

Katima Mulilo: eastern outpost

In 1977, almost a year before the Ruacana deployment, Captain Pieter 'Whitey' du Toit was briefed by Commandant Vossie Nel at 4 Field to mobilize a field troop (G1 guns), move to Katima Mulilo and establish a fire base there. Captain du Toit was supported by his OP officer, Lieutenant George Gravett, his TSM, WOII 'Boer' van Zyl, and Sergeant Albert Hook. On arrival, the gunners were briefed by the commander of the area and immediately set about creating what was to be known as Golf base (phonetic 'G' for 'guns').

Here the incumbent troop could more or less develop their home as they wanted it. The local engineer troop built a berm around the base as protection against fragments and small-arms fire. The gunners dug themselves in, but the guns were left on flat ground. Golf (and later, Nova) and Katima, for that matter, were always considered by the South African troops as a great place for a paid holiday. It was, fortunately, the quietest base in the operational area in that attacks were few and far between. It was a popular stop-off for VIPs, including members of parliament, military top brass who needed a break, foreign attachés, entertainment groups and anyone else that the SADF wanted to impress, including the wives of all the aforementioned. The base was equipped with a number of boats, which were put to good use at weekends for angling and parties, and even had an SA Navy marine component to patrol the Zambezi River. Captain du Toit's troop had not been deployed for long when the tranquillity was shattered by a mortar engagement onto the main base at Katima. The troop was ready and returned fire on Sesheke in Zambia, from where the mortar fire originated. Because this troop was equipped with field guns they had to engage at maximum range, and, had to cover a target size of 800 x 600 metres—big for a field troop. Nevertheless, this counter-bombardment silenced the mortars for months to come. However, the lesson was learned that the artillery would have to cover a longer range and the decision was made to replace the G1s with 140mm G2 guns. This increase in the capability meant that the artillery could deploy farther south, hence the establishment of the new Nova base.

By August 1977, the first artillery base—named Fort Human after Major Chris Human, who played the major role in developing this facility—became operational.

On Wednesday 3 May 1978, while 2 Medium Battery were putting their final preparations together for Operation Reindeer, F Troop of 43 Battery in Walvis Bay, under the command of Lieutenant Nick Grobler, boarded a C-130 at Air Force Station Rooikop to relieve E Troop deployed in Katima Mulilo. Three months later, E Troop, under Lieutenant Jan van der Westhuizen, was back in action in the Katima area.

On 6 August 1978, Lieutenant Grobler, at that stage the battery commander, issued an artillery ops order in preparation for a likely attack on the Katima Mulilo complex. By this time, SWAPO had planned an attack that included an infantry-type assault on WNLA (pronounced 'Wenela') base and a long-range bombardment on Katima. P Battery (as it was known in the sector) was tasked with supporting the defence of the base and then to support any follow-up actions that may take place. The defence was planned in two phases, the first being engagements on the attacking force at WNLA, and the second the support of the follow-up actions by two combat teams. The time during the lead-up to this operation was well spent by the gunners of B Troop, as they recced firing positions and marked them accordingly. A Troop was to remain in Golf base for the duration. The OPO, Lieutenant Maartin Schalekamp, was tasked with carrying out air OP duties from a helicopter and, once phase 1 was complete, marrying up with Combat Team A as FOO. The gunners in Potchefstroom regarded 1978 as one of the most active years in their service on the Angolan border. It often happened that national servicemen ready to go on a weekend pass on a Friday afternoon were stopped by a phone call from Army Headquarters, informing the unit that the troops could not leave the military base and that they were to prepare to leave for the border.

On one such occasion, on 22 August 1978, Army HQ instructed 14 Field Regiment to send personnel to Katima Mulilo to man the troop of 140mm guns that were deployed there. Intelligence suggested that terrorist cross-border activities from Zambia were on the increase, evidenced by the bombardment of the main base at Katima with rockets, which led to the death of several soldiers and damage to the buildings in the base the previous night.

Major Uys, who, at that time, was the 2IC of 14 Field Regiment, was ordered to take a troop of the medium battery to Katima by air. That same evening, the troop flew to Mpacha airfield and was transported by road to Katima, only to find that the 140mm troop was still manned by a contingent of gunners of 43 Battery from Walvis Bay. The troop from Potchefstroom was intended to guarantee continued artillery support because the gunners from Walvis Bay were on the brink of returning to their home unit.

On 23 August at 10h10, the SWAPO attack commenced. Soon after the arrival of the gunners from Potchefstroom, the battery engaged SWAPO targets in Zambia, the fire being controlled by the OP officers from the top of a water tower (this was the highest point in the area). One specific 23mm anti-aircraft machine gun was very dangerous and had to be silenced, as it fired at every SAAF helicopter or aircraft that flew above Katima.

Intelligence sources indicated the presence of a SWAPO base inside Zambia and the officer commanding of 13 Sub-Area decided to send a combat team to destroy the SWAPO base. The combat team, supported by the 140mm troop advanced well into Zambia, moving through the bush. (This type of movement was known as 'bundu bashing', that is, taking a direct route through the bush using a prismatic compass and map.) When the SWAPO base was reached, the infantry commander requested an air strike, which was provided by a Buccaneer aircraft with cluster bombs. After this air strike, the infantry entered the SWAPO trenches and cleared the base. Artillery fire was not necessary, although the guns were deployed ready for any event.

On the back of the aforementioned artillery order, the results were recorded, somewhat cryptically, but sufficient nevertheless:

- Attack went ahead on 23 August 1978. Time: 10h10.
- Casualties own forces: ten members of the armour [in Katima itself].
- Attack was repulsed by artillery fire.
- Follow-up was only done the next day. It was, by then, too late, as SWAPO had removed all their dead and wounded.
- Ammunition was captured.
- Wenela and Katima were engaged simultaneously. The attack on Wenela was unsuccessful. The fire was either short or over the top of the base.
- They [SWAPO] adjusted fire on Golf [base], but without success, as the guns answered their fire too quickly.

After this excursion and the debriefing Major Uys and the troops from Potchefstroom returned to 14 Field Regiment and F Troop returned to Walvis Bay. A battery from 27 Field Regiment took over duties from F Troop, 43 Battery, from June to September 1979, whereafter 43 Battery, once again, occupied the base. It was probably a relief for 43 Battery to move into Katima, as the routine in Walvis Bay centred on either keeping the rust off the equipment or maintaining the gardens in the gunners' lines. The incident that follows is indicative of this problem.

This particular tour was not without incident, however, because during a practice shoot, the gunners managed to hit Mpacha air base. In a letter to his battery commander, van der Westhuizen explains what happened:

At the moment it is quiet. You have probably heard about the shell that landed on Mpacha? Lance-Bombardier Kriel, number 5 gun's number 3, made a laying error. As far as we can determine, he layed on the wrong aiming point. We started firing in the morning, but it went slowly as Staff Sergeant Hook and I went through [checked] the drills on the guns. We [only] recommenced firing at about 21h00 that night. It was dark [no moon] and by then, I was concentrating on the TAs, as the slow reaction time during the afternoon's shoot was caused by them. We engaged with one troop at a time. After A Troop finished, we swung [traversed] B Troop onto the exercise centre of arc. This took about half an hour before we carried on firing. Bossie [Lt Bosman] controlled the fire from Katima; Potgieter [2/Lt Jakkie Potgieter] was the GPO; and Leslie [2/Lt George Leslie] the troop leader. Leslie had already swung B Troop onto the exercise centre of arc and was busy laying A Troop onto their DF [SOS] target. At that stage, he hadn't checked the guns [it was the troop leader's responsibility to check the bearing of the guns by prismatic compass before and during firing]. After about 25 minutes and three adjusting rounds, fire-for-effect was ordered and one round landed in Mpacha.

An enquiry was held immediately and found that the number 1 on the errant gun was responsible for the 18° line error on his gun. A number of others were also held responsible, and eventually, because this occurred in the operational area and no serious damage or injury was caused, the whole incident was shelved. In fact, the only damage was to the air conditioner on the Mpacha control tower from a shell fragment. The lessons had been learned and some changes in the posting of some of the individuals took place. Happily, all those involved moved on and progressed in their careers in the artillery. It is also noteworthy that there was only one troop leader, shared between two troops—not the way the battery organization was intended, but a symptom of a lack of personnel. It was often said that one wasn't a true gunner until one had fired a round out of the firing range at some stage. Some did this better than others.

On 4 June 1981, the main party of 4th Battery, Natal Field Artillery arrived at Nova and were welcomed by Captain O'Connor, who had led the advance party, and were subsequently briefed on the situation. As is customary in most military deployments, things are lost along the way, and this particular deployment was no exception. The battery sergeant-major (of all people),

WOII Colin Hill, discovered that his personal kit had not been unloaded from the C-130 that had transported the battery in and was now underway to East London back in South Africa. WOII Hill's comment: 'Being without kit, it is a common sight to see WOII Hill with borrowed nutria, T-shirt, shorts and Staff Scheepers's size-ten takkies on his size-seven feet!'

Because Katima was the quietest, or least active, area in the theatre, the biggest problem facing commanders at that time was the troops' morale—boredom creates idle hands. The result was that sport was encouraged and troops were regularly involved in entertaining the visiting groups, who ranged from the prime minister and cabinet to business people and journalists. It was perceived by most of the SADF as being a holiday camp. On 6 June, the combined 4th and 1 Medium Battery (4 Field Regiment) rugby team lost 10–3 to the sector HQ team.

The next seven days were spent in training, the most important objective being to qualify the gun tractor drivers on the newly introduced Samil 100. Additionally, the gun crews needed to be converted onto the 140mm G2 gun, as NFA at that time was a field regiment and was equipped with 88mm G1 guns.

Early in the evening of 17 June, 4th Battery's troops were settling down to watch a movie when Sergeant Wragg and the local dominee (chaplain), in the watch tower to see the base in the moonlight, observed a light near the deserted Golf base and at 19h25 reported this observation to Katima HQ. Receiving no reply, they sent up an illuminating flare to improve their night vision. After launching a second flare and having been joined by WOII Hill, they realized that the 'light' was nothing more than a patch of white sand bathed in moonlight. Moonlight has a strange way of playing tricks with the human eye. That same night the Alpha bunker reported automatic fire from the direction of the tarred road (the main road) and this was confirmed by Delta bunker. Katima HQ replied that they had no knowledge of any South African vehicle movement between Mpacha and Katima Mulilo. At this, the movie was stopped and the battery took post, extinguishing the lights at the same time. Movement was heard near the base's main gate and 2/Lt van der Merwe (a national service officer from 1 Medium Battery) fired a round with his rifle. The ensuing silence and lack of any further activity resulted in the resumption of the movie and associated bar activities. Despite the lack of action, regular live practices were held to keep the battery combat ready, and improvements were made on a daily basis.

Tedium was interspersed with football, rugby and volleyball matches against the other units in the area and visits by dignitaries, such as Mr Vause Raw MP of the opposition party at the time, as well as Mrs Viljoen (wife of Lieutenant-General Constand Viljoen) accompanied by a group a female students—much to the delight of the troops.

On 21 July, four guns were brought out of action and towed to the SAAF base at Mpacha where they were to be airlifted out to another sector (the build-up for Operation Protea) in the operational area. As one of the Samil 100 gun tractors was rounding a bend, the door of its crew compartment flew open and Bombardier Dick Hassebroek fell out. Despite all efforts by the crews and the medical personnel, Bombardier Hassebroek died of his injuries. The four guns that were destined for deployment elsewhere ended up back in Nova base and back in action. Such is life in the army in general and in the artillery in particular. On 4 August, the same four guns found themselves back at Mpacha base. This time three of the guns were loaded into C-130s and the fourth had somehow punched a hole through the roof of one of the aircraft! It appears that the SAAF personnel who had loaded the gun decided to unclamp the barrel, and in the process of loading, the barrel suddenly elevated, causing damage to the aircraft's roof.

7th Battery, THA, under command of Major Brent Chalmers took over responsibility from NFA on 10 August 1981. 7th Battery marched in with 90 members, as there was a tendency among the CF units to call up a battery at a time in order that a troop, at least, would be fully manned. Shortly after arrival, a gun tiffy inspected the four G2 guns and made a scathing report on the condition of the main equipment. This prompted Lt P.E. Lawrence, the BPO, to write a report on this situation. The gunners admitted to their lack of proper maintenance where appropriate, and immediately set about rectifying the situation. However, on closer reading of Lawrence's report, it could be seen that the vast majority of faults were those resulting from a lack of repair on the part of the technical services. In those days (and by and large, still to this day), the gunners' maintenance tasks were limited to inspections and routine cleaning. They were not equipped or trained to carry out repairs on the guns. It is also true that the previous incumbents at Nova, NFA, had reported the same thing. This type of backbiting was a regular occurrence, especially where fire units were static and boredom crept in.

For the historical record, barrel numbers of the guns in action at that time were L 17345; L 17305; L 17326; and L 17327.

Despite the bickering and corps rivalry, the deployment at Nova was organized and well controlled. This is evident from the artillery standing operating procedure, which spelt out exactly the responsibilities of the leader element, radio nets, daily routine, casualty evacuation and numerous other procedures. In essence, the troop commander, being the senior gunner in the area, was also the fire support co-ordination officer and artillery adviser to the sector commander. This troop commander, by nature of his physical location, was also the air OP. Observation was carried out by the OPOs deployed at Wenela base, KM3 (a point 3 kilometres from Katima). Three other observation posts were established over time: KM1, the water tower in Katima; KM2 another water tower on the bank of the Zambezi River; and RB, a large tree on the eastern end of Katima overhanging the Zambezi River, which was manned 24 hours per day to provide fire control for the 81mm mortars covering the eastern approach to Katima. 71 Battery, 7 Medium Regiment, commanded by Major C. Madgwick, took over duties from THA.

Locating Artillery

In the Katima Mulilo area two radar sections were deployed, one at Nova base with the G2 battery and one farther forward in Katima Mulilo.

Radar set Cymbeline FA No 15

This British built mortar-locating radar set was purchased by the South African Artillery in the early 1970s and replaced the obsolete Green Archer, also from the UK. Unfortunately, they were not designed for the hot, dusty, rough southern African conditions, and reliability was a constant problem. However, the problem seemed to worry the gunners who did not know the equipment more than it did those who were trained to operate and maintain the Cymbelines.

Late in 1981, Captain Francois van Eeden took over the troop from Captain Julius Engelbrecht. Captain van Eeden recalls the daily routine:

. . . would start at 05h00. Up, shave and prepare for the day. My first visit would be to the joint operations centre. Here I would normally find Captain Coen Beukes [the intelligence officer] and be briefed about the incident reports for the sector operational area. I would attend the morning order group held by Sector Commander Colonel Gert Opperman, and then start my journey for the day. First stop would be at Nova base to inspect the troops and the guns and check up on the fire plan. The guns were always trained on the most probable targets in Zambia, covering the positions of their ordnance and ready to deliver counter-bombardment within minutes. In command of the guns were Lieutenants Piet Tempel and Ralph Boetger.

Once satisfied that the blunt end at Nova was up to standard, Captain van Eeden would move on to Wenela to check on the state of the 81mm mortars deployed there. As these mortars were part of the fire plan, it was essential that their readiness equalled that of the gunners. Some time would be spent up a large 20-metre-high tree overlooking the Zambezi River and debriefing the OP in that post. This OP post observed and noted troop and equipment movements on a pont that moved back and forwards across the river to the town of Shesheke. At this time, a ceasefire agreement was in place and SWAPO members had been granted an amnesty should they want to return home to SWA. South African security measures were intensified to prevent any surprises that December. On the Zambian side an increase in activity was noted, prompting Captain van Eeden to increase air observation and record new ordnance positions on the Zambian side of the river in order to improve on the fire plan.

With the Wenela inspection complete, the next stop was the OPs deployed at the other three positions (KM2, KM3 and RB) to collect their daily logs. (Artillery OPs kept a log of activities in their area of observation, as this was one of the most important sources of information for the intelligence community. The only time that logs were not kept was during fast-moving mechanized conventional operations, simply because the OPs were not in one place for long enough.) One can imagine that these static OPs were highly vulnerable, as the opposition on the other side of the river knew of their deployments—there was nowhere else they could deploy. So for the OP deployed in the tree a little deception was put into place in the form of a plastic pipe painted in camouflage colours, complete with sight unit and elevation wheel—a dummy 106mm recoilless gun.

Captain van Eeden recalled that his most dreaded visit was the OP in the water tower at KM1. The 20-metre-high construction was accessed by a narrow steel ladder (with no safety rails) and on arrival at the top one found a metal roof that served to substantially push up the temperature. Not the favourite OP position. As time went on, so the OPs manning this post would improve their knowledge of the area under observation as well as their ability to identify targets quickly. This was done by painting arrows on the underside of the roof indicating targets and their allotted numbers, and, in addition, a panoramic photograph of the area marked with targets.

Once a week, the mortars at Mpacha air base were inspected, and this trip was combined with a visit to WOII Niemand, the gunner sergeant-major in control of the army component in that base. Captain van Eeden relates a high point in that particular tour of duty:

> In December, I was joined by a few officers from the University of Pretoria doing their duty during the university vacation. One of them was an interesting character by the name of Lieutenant 'Bol' Bootha. He had almost magical powers, in that he could pull more than the proverbial 'rabbit out the hat'. He found an old Unimog body, 'borrowed' an engine and various parts from other Unimogs and stores in Mpacha, this Unimog being rebuilt into a serviceable utility [another word for a taxi] vehicle for Nova base. It was used for paragliding—it could tow someone hooked into a liberated green

'pumpkin' parachute along the road, only slowing down just before the main road. He also disappeared once without authority, being covered by his colleagues with the story that he liked to go out with the patrols around the perimeter. This time, he emerged with a PVC swimming pool, which he installed in the base, causing the displeasure of the sector commander and the sector sergeant-major [Jack Pierce]. Nevertheless, this was wonderful morale booster for the gunners.

Lieutenant Bootha's finale was the acquisition of a tractor loader backhoe (TLB, often referred to as a JCB) to effect bunker repairs at Nova. This particular machine was returned to the Engineer Squadron after complaints that it had gone missing.

This almost isolated part of southern Africa was well known for its elephant population. Often the incumbent troops would drive into the bush in a Buffel set at fast idling speed, where they could move up close to the large herds of elephants. The animals seemed to accept this strange apparition as one of them. At night, they would wander right up to the protective wall of drums around Nova base and rub themselves on this sand-filled construction.

On 18 April 1982, 142 Battery returned to their unit after a sojourn at Nova base. On 19 April 1983, Commandant Brent Chalmers, the commander of THA, issued a mobilization order for the regiment to provide two batteries for service in Katima Mulilo over the period 13 June to 14 November 1983. THA's role would be to provide fire support for Sector 70 over that period. At that time, THA were short of senior leader group personnel and were forced to make an arrangement whereby the lower ranks of the two batteries would serve for three months and the senior members would be scheduled for shorter periods, but still cover the full period of deployment, this being solved by the creation of seven leader group teams. The table overleaf shows the scheduling of these members.

Team	Battery Commander	OPO	Battery Post Officer	Troop Leader	Battery Captain	Battery Sergeant Major
1.	Capt van Rensburg	Capt Nel	Lt Legg	CO P. Swart	CO Levin	WOII Aucamp
2.	Capt Nel	Lt Legg	Lt Munnick	2/Lt Bothè	2/Lt Wepener	WOII Francis
3.	Capt Reitz	Lt Munnick	Lt A. Swart	2/Lt Philpot	CO Reynele	WOII Golden
4.	Capt MacKay	Lt A. Swart	Lt Grealy	2/Lt Smith	CO Vollmer	WOII Visser
5.	Capt Peck	Lt Grealy	Lt Carty	2/Lt Erasmus	CO Wulfsohn	WOII Twilley
6.	Capt Lawrence	Lt Carty	Lt Frisby	2/Lt Knowles	CO Milner	WOII Pretorius
7.	Capt Rimmer	Lt Frisby	2/Lt Moolman	CO MacFarlane	CO Herr	WOII Jackson

The most important issue facing the THA leader group was that of morale. What would the lower ranks' attitude be towards this arrangement? It was decided that the facts would be presented without any additions or omissions—a decision that had very positive effects in the end.

Attached to each THA battery were two radar sections and a sound ranging section from 2 Locating Regiment.

Captain Ivor Rimmer, the battery commander of Team 7, was tasked to lead an advance party to Nova base. Upon returning on 19 May 1983, Rimmer reported back to his commanding officer that the state of the base had deteriorated since their last tour in 1981, some critical items being:

- The reliance on one 220 volt generator without a backup. This single generator was intended to provide power to the operations room.
- A shortage of serviceable vehicles. The implication here was that it would not be possible to deploy a troop (let alone the battery) outside of the base.
- The concrete floors of the bunkers, ablutions and kitchen were cracked and broken, presenting a health hazard.
- There were a number of minor issues that would do no more than make

life less comfortable for the Johannesburg gunners. These included a shortage of acid for the swimming pool and insufficient glasses in the bars. War is hell.

On 16 June, Captain T. van Rensburg of 7th Battery THA took over Nova from CFA. On 25 July 1983, Captain Francois Reitz took over from Team 2, which left Mpacha on 27 August. Once again, Reitz found the serviceability of the guns to be well below that expected of operational equipment.

The greater part of his tenure there as battery commander was spent attempting to improve this sad state of affairs. The end result was that seven of the eight guns were returned to a serviceable state and the eighth was prepared to be backloaded to Pretoria for base-level repair. Despite having repaired the seven guns, the Technical Services Corps (TSC) ordnance fitter still reported that all the Nova guns needed to be returned to Pretoria to 61 Base Workshop.

At this time, the attached 1 Locating Regiment Sound Ranging Section had deployed microphones near the Mafuta gate. A point of concern was that this equipment was left unguarded, and shortly after the problem was addressed by the battery commander, a transmitter was stolen. This led to the radar section at Katima gate being redeployed to Mafuta to provide protection for the equipment.

Artillery serviceability issues were not limited to the guns. During August, two Cymbeline radar sets were reported as out of action because of a lack of spare parts. This was eventually solved by the SA Corps of Signals deploying a radar fitter to Katima.

During the second week of August the 2IC of THA, Major Frank Louw, paid a visit to the deployed battery. A parade was held and the following members were promoted:

- To sergeant: Bombardier J.C. Duvenhage
- To bombardier: Lance-Bombardiers A. Herbst and P.J. Prinsloo
- To lance-bombardier: Gunners M.J.A. Coetser and W.J. Theron.

This visit also produced a report highlighting the poor state of the guns. By this time there were four guns that needed to be backloaded to the workshops in Grootfontein and replaced with four serviceable pieces. The 2IC quite rightly expressed doubt as to whether this would actually transpire unless great pressure was applied from the operational area. Furthermore, there was a general lack of concern from Sector 70 Operations as to the state of artillery equipment. On reflection, at that stage the build-up of SWAPO and FAPLA activities 500 kilometres west of Katima Mulilo was becoming a cause of concern and the focus of attention from both operations and logistics was on the possibility of conventional operations in Sector 10's area of responsibility.

At that time, the opposing forces' deployments to the north and east of Katima and SWAPO had some 12 bases prepared and occupied in the area. It should be noted, however, that all of these bases were either training or rest camps. Added to this, the Zambian National Defence Force had a battalion of four companies supported by three artillery batteries to prevent contact between SA forces and SWAPO, part of their mission being to ensure that SWAPO troops stayed in their bases. However, despite the seeming tranquillity SA Intelligence reported that an attack on Katima could be expected between 23 and 26 August, as these were the fifth anniversary of the last attack and SWAPO Founding Day respectively.

Captain Allan Peck took over Nova from his predecessor on 5 September, immediately setting about to remove the holiday atmosphere from the battery. In order to do this, he tasked Lieutenant Raymond Bothe to attend the daily order group at the Katima HQ so that he could spend more time in the battery lines and instill discipline. Happily, the troops had only been in the base for a week so the problem was relatively easy to rectify. Captain Peck introduced a new routine that included stand-to at first and last light, 05h45 reveille and a schedule of training and base maintenance and improvements.

Once the holiday was terminated, the gunners went on to do sight tests on each of the eight guns. Here it was found that seven of the guns had, at some stage, been fitted to new carriages without any form of sight testing or alignment. To cap it all, they found that one of the dial sights and two sight clinometers were unserviceable. Furthermore, ammunition needed replenishment and 450 rounds were delivered in that period. Completing the sight tests by firing found the guns to be firing parallel to one another, but that the state of calibration was poor. Captain Peck had to request help from Director Artillery in Pretoria, as his gunners had little or no expertise in the subject, and they did not have the survey equipment necessary for such an exercise.

Once work was satisfactory, the battery commander allowed more free time, and the gunners landed fourth place in the Sector 70 potted sport competition, lost by 62 runs to 701 Battalion's cricket team and spent many happy hours on Hippo Island with the traditional South African pastime of braai (barbeque) and beer. The occasional fights between men were quickly sorted out by the use of a 50-kilogram smoke projectile.

Once again, the mortar-locating radar sets were playing up and Lieutenant Shulze, the Locating Troop commander from 4 Field Regiment, had to call in for a SAAF Alouette to lift and replace the radar set from the top of the water tower.

Captain Ivor Rimmer, the battery commander of 9th Battery THA, arrived with his Team 7 at Mpacha air base prepared to take over the battery at Nova. What he did not know as he set foot on the Mpacha hardstand was that the handing over would take 20 minutes, the length of time it took to walk from the aircraft to collecting one's baggage. The outgoing battery commander, Captain Gordon MacKay, was booked on the return flight. This would cause problems later on. Together with Captain Rimmer were Lieutenant Jannie Moolman of 9th Battery, CO R. Herr of RHQ and Sergeant F. Slippers of 9th Battery. Luckily there were a number of the leader group who remained behind from Team 6, these being Lieutenant J.L. Erasmus (8th Battery); CO R. Milner (RHQ); and Staff Sergeant D. van der Merwe (7th Battery). Lieutenant T. Knowles (9th Battery) was scheduled to arrive on 2 November.

Lieutenant Moolman was immediately appointed as artillery liaison officer at the sector HQ, a task that included the control of the sound ranging base deployed near the HQ. A number of other changes were made to improve the efficiency of the gunner effort. These were a reallocation of call signs using the doctrinal call signs rather than arbitrary nicknames that seemed to have crept in along the way; an artillery-specific state code for reporting (this had the effect of speeding up reporting by radio, which effectively reduced transmission time); and the introduction of Griddle (a random allocation of letters to grid lines on a map, each letter having a numeric value). Griddle was taught at all the training units, but seemed to be politely ignored on operations.

On 31 October, the first live firing was carried out in a troop exercise, the guns having been recently overhauled. The exercise was a success, the only issue being the state of gun calibration—the subject of ongoing concern.

On the same day, the advance party of 41 Battery arrived at Nova to take over from THA. Here the main point of concern was the lack of stock verification certificates and the possible, at that stage, unknown, loss of controlled equipment. In the end, the total loss amounted to R180.24, which was paid over to the sector HQ by the outgoing battery. That amount of money, although very little for a six-month (and more) deployment period, could have been avoided by better stock control: a valuable lesson learned for future deployments.

141 and 14 Locating Batteries, under the command of Major Piet Williams, took over Nova base on 21 September 1984, returning to Potchefstroom on 10 December in preparation for their clearing out of 14 Field Regiment on 17 December, the completion of their national service.

Chapter 6

Operations Bowler and Sceptic: covering two borders

Bowler

The beginning of 1980 was the beginning of the end for what was then Rhodesia. Political agreements had been put into place and the new state of Zimbabwe would be born on 18 April 1980.

In the meantime, the South African Defence Force was concerned over the amount of equipment that it had loaned to Rhodesia and how this equipment would be returned. It should be noted that by this time, South Africa had loaned Rhodesia Alouette helicopters, Eland armoured cars, G1 and G2 guns and numerous other items of military equipment and ammunition.

With this as background, on 11 February 1980, 14 Field Regiment tasked Major Tobie Vermaak, the battery commander of 142 Battery, to mobilize a medium battery by combining the efforts of 142 and 143 Batteries. This organization was to be known as S Battery and to marry up with a mechanized battle group (Battle Group C) for Operation Bowler. While busy with the mobilization exercise, the battery lost two of its junior leaders: Lieutenant A.D. Kotze died of his wounds from a shooting accident on 3 March, and on 6 March, Bombardier M.J. Naus was killed the same way.

Operation Bowler's objective was to protect the South African equipment being transported by road south from Salisbury (Harare) and other places in Zimbabwe-Rhodesia. This battle group would act as a reaction force should the incoming ZANU-PF attempt any blocking of the movement of the equipment. The battle group moved into an assembly area near Beitbridge and awaited further orders. Fortunately, the equipment arrived back in

South Africa unmolested, and Bowler ended without a shot being fired in anger. S Battery returned to the unit before the end of March and immediately went into preparation for the next operation in a totally different direction: Operation Sceptic in Angola.

Sceptic

After the May 1978 attack on Cassinga and other bases, SWAPO was demoralized, disorganized and lacking in both material and moral support. The Soviet government had warned them that they needed to produce results. SWAPO had learned some operational lessons from the Cassinga attack and had moved their operational HQ and a number of supporting and protection units to Chifufa. In essence, the whole infrastructure accommodated in buildings in Cassinga was relocated to a well-dispersed temporary base with no buildings at all. The complex comprised dug-in bunkers, communications trenches and defensive foxholes covering an area of 45 square kilometres. Where possible, these excavations were under the trees and covered with logs and a thick layer of sand. Track discipline was strictly applied and trees were even planted to help with camouflage. This now created a base that was pretty much impervious to artillery and air-delivered fire. Furthermore, the distance from the SWA border was increased—this base lay 180 kilometres to the north of Eenhana battalion base and thus could be warned of any South African movement in its direction.

In 1980, South African forces identified this base complex and, during April, commenced planning to destroy the elements deployed there.

Because of the distance from the border and the fact that the SWA forces were only trained and equipped for counter-insurgency operations (primarily light infantry), the decision was made to commit 61 Mechanized Battalion Group as the main assault force, with other, lighter units in support.

At that time, 61 Mechanized Battalion only had one medium troop under command, but the requirement was for a full battery. Major Tobie Vermaak, the battery commander of 142 Battery, 14 Field Regiment, was tasked to mobilize one troop and report to Commandant Dippenaar, the OC of 61 Mechanized Battalion at Omutiya. The first troop had only reported to 61

Mechanized Battalion in early April, with the reinforcing troop arriving in the area on 15 May.

The concept of operations was developed at the sector HQ in Oshakati by the sector commander, Brigadier 'Witkop' Badenhorst, together with his staff and the unit commanders earmarked for the operation. The main assault force, 61 Mechanized Battalion Group, was commanded by Commandant Johan Dippenaar, an experienced armoured corps officer. The concept was that a brigade-sized force, supported by the SAAF, would attack and destroy the SWAPO complex over the period 10–16 June 1980. This force would comprise the following:

- A headquarters located at Eenhana base
- 61 Mechanized Battalion Group in its entirety (including its organic direct support battery) and two parachute companies
- 53 Battalion—a light infantry (counter-insurgency) battalion
- 54 Battalion—also a light infantry battalion, reinforced by two companies from 32 Battalion and a parachute company
- Battle Group 10—made up of motorized and light-infantry companies from units already deployed in the sector.

The operation would be conducted in six phases—to the uninitiated, seemingly complicated, but in fact not:

- Phase 1: 54 Battalion would conduct an area operation to clean up the area inside Angola between beacons 24 and 26 to prepare the way for the administrative area and the movement of the assault force.
- Phase 2: the other three battle groups would prepare for the operation. This would occur while Phase 1 was active.
- Phase 3: 54 Battalion would work northwards and establish the administrative area while the assault force would carry out a feint on the SWA side of the cutline. From here they would move to the jumping-off point at Eenhana.

- Phase 4: D-Day. Two parachute companies would troop in by helicopter to Mulemba, refuel and deploy by helicopter as stopper groups to the north and northwest of the main objective—nicknamed 'Smokeshell' (hence the popular, albeit incorrect, name for this operation).

- All three battle groups would cross the cutline together with 61 Mechanized Battalion in the lead. At a place called Chitado the two motorized battle groups would swing left and attack Chitumbo and Mulola respectively. 61 Mechanized would attack the main objective using S Battery to provide preparatory bombardment for an hour. All the attacks would be supported by the SAAF, which would provide close air support, trooping, casualty evacuation and air observation.

- Phases 5 and 6 involved area operations (mopping up) and the withdrawal.

61 Mechanized Battalion's mission was 'to destroy the SWAPO command and control, and logistic structures in the Smokeshell and Ionde complexes on 10 and 11 June 1980 respectively. Thereafter, to conduct an area operation east of the general line Smokeshell–Dova–Mulamba, and north of the general line Dunatana–Mulavi, with Ionde inclusive, for approximately 10 days.'

Commandant Dippenaar and his senior leader group had planned an eight-phase operation within the overall operational concept mentioned above. Briefly, this would entail:

- Phase 1: movement from Omuthiya to Mulemba (Combat Team 3 in the lead followed by S Battery)
- Phase 2: deployment of stoppers and movement to the forming-up place
- Phase 3: attack on part of Smokeshell—the central part
- Phase 4: final capture of Smokeshell
- Phase 5: clearing up of the objectives and preparation for occupation of a leaguer area

- Phase 6: clearing up and an attack on Ionde by two combat teams supported by S Battery
- Phase 7: area operations, including the preparation of the runway at Ionde for demolition
- Phase 8: withdrawal—the artillery battery would cover the withdrawal and be the second-last group out of the area.

An intense period of training and rehearsal took place at 61 Mechanized's training area, the exception being the SAAF, which could not devote its full attention as it was committed to other operations at the time. In the afternoon of 7 June, the leading element, Combat Team 3 (three troops of Eland 90 armoured cars, infantry support troops, an engineer section and an artillery FOO in an Eland 60) moved off to sweep the road in preparation for the main body.

The next day at 10h00, the main body of the assault force drove out of the gate at Omutiya heading for Eenhana. At 19h00 on 8 June, the force crossed the cutline into Angola.

After a short rest in a leaguer area 50 kilometres north of the cutline, the force commenced with their approach to contact, the objective still some 130 kilometres away. There were delays of up to an hour because the gun tractors buried themselves in the thick sand on the route. According to Commandant Dippenaar:

> By 24h00 [on 8 June] all vehicles had been recovered. From Omuthiya northwards the sand gets thicker, with the thickest being probably in the Oshifitu area and Eenhana and Mulembo, and up to Mulavi. The first vehicle that drives on the sand finds it difficult enough and leaves a deep track [more like a trough]. After some 20 Ratels over the same track, the Buffels and Magirus Deutz vehicles move with extreme difficulty . . . the gun tractors overheated; the normal temperature of 90° Celsius went to 150° . . . and engines cut out.

The Ratel series of combat vehicles

Although not an artillery vehicle, the ever-present Ratel is worth a mention. Ratel (named after the Honey badger) was designed initially as an infantry combat vehicle that could carry an infantry section into battle and support that section during the firefight. The Ratel 20 was armed with a turret-mounted 20mm belt-fed cannon firing HE incendiary (one belt) and armour piercing (second belt), the selection being done by a selector switch on the gun. This main armament was complemented by a co-axial 7.62mm Browning machine gun. In the rear was a 7.62mm flexible mounted AA machine gun—although not all infantry combat vehicles (ICVs) carried these. The total crew of the Ratel 20 was eleven: a vehicle commander, gunner and driver, and eight infantrymen, who would dismount and operate on foot; the vehicle's main armament provided close fire support.

Five Ratels made up one infantry platoon (three section vehicles, the platoon commander and the platoon sergeant vehicles). The Ratel weighed in at 18 tonnes, and the six-wheeled vehicle was powered by a six-cylinder, turbocharged, diesel Büssing power unit driving an automatic gearbox. It had few design faults, one of the few being that the power pack was situated in the left rear of the vehicle, occupying space that could have been used for operational needs. The right rear housed the 750-litre fuel tank. The position of the power pack meant that debussing troops left the vehicle via two side doors—not as practical as other ICVs in which debussing was from the rear.

The 20mm version was immediately complemented by the Ratel 60, equipped with a 60mm breech-loading mortar like the Eland 60 armoured car. In fact, the Ratel was designed to accommodate the Eland turret so these could be interchanged when necessary. Shortly after this came the Ratel Command. To the army this was the last word in battlefield luxury. Fitted with a turret-mounted 12.7mm machine gun and co-axial 7.62mm, this vehicle was designed for its purpose. In the crew compartment were two forward-facing seats for the commander and adjutant faced with two map boards and places for pens, protractors and the associated paraphernalia required to command a battle. There was even a car radio that was linked into the communications harness for listening to the news—something that didn't last, as they were removed by those who felt that they belonged in private cars. Eventually there were enough for the gunners to use as command and control stations (Ratel Artillery Command, brigade, regiment and battery commander vehicles), with the artillery variants fitted with six radios, some in the turret and the rest in the hull between the seats. In 1988, the 10 Artillery Brigade tactical operations Ratel even boasted a 24-volt-powered photocopy machine! Other variants were:

- 90mm anti-tank (Ratel 90)
- ZT3 anti-tank missile (Ratel ZT3)
- 81mm mortar (Ratel 81): the mortar and its ammunition occupied the crew compartment, the mortar firing from inside the vehicle
- Communications Centre (Ratel TG): this variant was fitted with a pneumatic mast for radio antennae
- Electronic Warfare (Ratel EW)
- Recovery: fitted with a counterweight on the nose (Ratel Recovery)

This overheating was not caused from overloading because additional gun tractors, only carrying 30 rounds each, one-third of their capacity, also overheated. To put this into perspective, the area that the battle groups had to traverse is a series of parallel dunes (covered in undergrowth and trees) running west–east, with a distance of about three kilometres between them. The direction of travel was south to north, so the dunes were approached at 90° each time.

Lieutenant-General Viljoen and his Personal Staff Officer Colonel Gagiano joined the Mechanized force at Eenhana on 9 June late in the afternoon, Gen Viljoen taking up a seat in the commander's Ratel.

At 08h00, the air force attack went in—four Buccaneers, four Canberras and 18 Mirages delivering a withering amount of ordnance, the idea being that, by the time the attacking force moved in, the objective would be destroyed. The problem was that the objective had already been partially emptied of occupants.

The approach to contact did not go as well as planned, as the artillery air OP arrived overhead at 08h00, one hour later than planned. One of the tasks of this mission was to help navigate the assault force into their correct position. On reporting in, the OP found that 61 Mechanized Battalion was on the wrong road (not a difficult thing to achieve in that terrain). The result was a 5-kilometre trek northwards to reach the correct road. It should be noted that, from the air, at a height of 5,000 feet above ground level, roads were somewhat more easily identifiable than from the height of a Ratel turret— there were times that one would drive over a road without even seeing it. Despite this operation being a mechanized effort, the average speed over the distance travelled was 20 kph.

At 13h15 on 10 June, the combat teams of 61 Mechanized Battalion reported that they were in position and ready to attack. The problem was that the gunners were not: a direct result of the slow speed caused by the soft sand and thick bush limiting rapid movement. Their navigation to their deployment area was eventually aided by the air observer, and the battery went into action quickly. The first targets were complexes 1 to 4, the in-depth objectives. Unfortunately, little damage was done, as the enemy had vacated shortly before—probably a result of their early-warning system. Likewise, the air attack produced the same result. After this the gunners shifted their fire onto objectives 6, 7 and 11, the focal point of the attack. Once the air OP was satisfied that the adjusting rounds were on target, the control of fire was taken over by the FOO on the ground. Once again, the fire was accurate, but the result was poor, in that the SWAPO incumbents had by and large evacuated. There was an opinion at the time that the FOOs lifted their fire too early, giving the defenders, especially their mortars, enough time to react to the oncoming attack.

Combat Team 3 (three armoured car troops) took two and a half hours to attack, search and consolidate despite there being no resistance—although, at the time, the attackers did not know this; surprises were still to come. Following on, Combat Team 1 attacked the main objective (6 and 7), again finding no resistance.

On completion of their engagement on complexes 1 to 4, one troop was ordered by the air observer, Pieter Williams, to fire into objective 13 in preparation for the attack by Combat Team 2 (this team attacked the southern objectives, starting with 8 then 9, 10, 12 and 13). By this time, Williams's pilot, Lieutenant Trichardt, warned that their aircraft was running low on fuel and their place was taken by Lieutenant Julius Engelbrecht in another aircraft. The fight in the southern part of the objectives was another story. These complexes contained the domestic area and vehicle park. Combat Team 2 swung slightly left, that is, to the south of objective 11, as they were not absolutely sure of the position of their objective. In so doing, they arrived in a dry pan, an ideal place for an ambush.

Here the SWAPO defenders took advantage of the situation and opened fire with small arms and an 82mm recoilless gun. The attackers fought their way out, but in the process lost their momentum and were forced to move through the dry riverbed westwards to complete their attack on objective 11. To support this, the air OP shifted the fire of one troop of S Battery onto this objective. The artillery continued firing while the combat team split into their prearranged assault and fire support groups. The direct fire support group in their Ratel 90s headed eastwards and then northwards to take up their positions to the northeast of the target, the assault group moving into position to the southeast for the attack. Hardly had the fire support group arrived in their position than they made contact with the defenders. The 90mm guns had to be used at ranges from 30 to 300 metres and some of the Ratels even physically drove over the defenders. In the meantime, the assault group went into action, thinking—mistakenly—that the support group were ready and already delivering their supporting fire. This rush into the objective caused them to move too far west. On realizing this, the combat team commander ordered the assault group to turn around (to face southwards) and continue the attack. This move caused the assaulting Platoon 1 to become trapped in the middle of a nest of one 23mm and three 14.5mm machine guns. The end result of this was the loss of 12 men and two Ratels, one of which burnt out completely after a 23mm round penetrated the left crew door, setting off a hand grenade inside. Help was called for and the reserve moved in to evacuate the casualties and remove the dead. Here again, the reserve were caught by the defenders, again in an ambush, but managed to fight their way out. The remaining two available combat teams (1 and 3) were then summoned to reinforce the remnants of Combat Team 2.

Eventually darkness took over and the battlefield became silent. Only next morning could the SAAF Pumas come in to evacuate the casualties. Just after dark, S Battery ceased firing and moved back to redeploy for further fire missions. The battery's fire was not called for again. The next day dawned with Commandant Dippenaar issuing new orders, one of which was for the gunners to occupy their position of the previous day should covering fire be needed during the clean up of the objectives and the recovery of the damaged and destroyed vehicles. Clearing the objectives and evacuating casualties meant that Smokeshell was a busy place, so Dippenaar decided to move his tactical HQ—a move that was to result in his command Ratel hitting a double TMA3 mine, badly damaging the front axle and throwing out the crew, including Lieutenant-General Viljoen, still a passenger at that stage.

The planned attack on Ionde by Combat Teams 1 and 3 supported by S Battery's guns was cancelled at the last moment, as new intelligence indicated that the town had been evacuated.

For the next phase of the operation—the area operations—S Battery remained at Mulemba with the echelon to protect the stores there and await replenishment (particularly diesel) from Ondangwa.

By 30 June, the operation was over and the troops were back in Omuthiya enjoying a welcome hot shower, cold beer and hot food—not necessarily in that order.

In retrospect, one wonders if the gunners could have done more to save the catastrophe on D-Day. The answer is no. The attacking infantry had already closed with the defenders and they were too close for the battery to provide close fire support. If anything, the 81mm mortars could have helped, but given the visibility over that flat ground they may have caused more own forces' deaths.

Chapter 7

Operations Protea and Daisy: longer reach

'You can go where you please, you can skid up
the trees, but you don't get away from the guns!'
—Rudyard Kipling, from *Screw-Guns*

Before discussing the next major operation it is important to mention the lessons learned from Operation Savannah, the most important being as follows:

- The South African Artillery was outranged by the Soviet-supplied equipment.
- To an extent, they were outgunned by the firepower of the 122mm BM21 rocket launcher.
- They had been too reliant on foreign weapon supplies and, to make matters worse, were now under UN arms embargo.
- They had to modernize the artillery to be effective.

Operation Sceptic, the deep strike against SWAPO some 180 kilometres into Angola by three battle groups, saw for the first time since 1975–76 Angolan FAPLA forces mixed with and supporting SWAPO forces. The year 1980 was a particularly bloody one and the battles eventually became known by the troops as 'the winter games'. The end result was 100 South African losses and 1,447 from SWAPO–FAPLA. Despite this, SWAPO managed to regroup and, at the beginning of 1981, launched the largest-ever infiltration, in which, after a number of smaller South African sweeps, they lost another 365 insurgents. These sweeps were followed by Operation Carnation, a special-forces-type operation by 44 Parachute Brigade, 5 Reconnaissance Regiment and 32 Battalion, in which SWAPO lost an average of 225 insurgents per month. This escalating conflict, together with the FAPLA involvement in operations, was one of the contributing factors influencing the decision to launch the next operation.

SWAPO, supported by the Angolan government and the Eastern bloc, and aided by the ever-increasing Cuban presence, continued its build-up of equipment, particularly in the southwestern part of Angola. This build-up, intertwined with the build-up of Angolan FAPLA forces and the deployment of East German air defence radars and missiles, was a natural outcome of the South African military successes and was also gaining support from the world at large, and the UN, anxious to speed up the implementation of Resolution 435 (independence for SWA / Namibia), put South Africa under pressure. SWAPO bases were now protected by FAPLA forces in defensive lines, or echelons, concentrated in the Cunene province of Angola. The towns of Xangongo and Ongiva were the operational bases closest to the SWA border, with the regional headquarters at Lubango, which was also home to the air defence system and air support component of the FAPLA–SWAPO effort. At one stage it was estimated that some 23,000 FAPLA and 7,000 Cubans were deployed to intervene with South African forays into the area. Air defence early-warning radars were now also deployed to Cahama as protection against SAAF aircraft.

Protea

The FAPLA defence was organized according to classic Soviet doctrine: four defensive echelons with deep trenches connected by communications trenches and bunkers, supported by anti-tank guns, armour and artillery, all dug in. These defended localities were constructed up to a depth of 12 kilometres and covered the approach roads from the south and were protected by mines and man-made obstacles. Generally, the defence was organized as follows:

- FAPLA 19 Brigade, 500 SWAPO and about 500 semi-regular guerrillas at Xangongo.
- FAPLA 21 Brigade and a strengthened SWAPO battalion in the west between Cahama and Humbe.
- A tactical group to the north at Peu Peu.
- FAPLA 11 Brigade protecting the district HQ, the Soviet and Cuban advisers and their families, as well as the SWAPO command and control centre based at Ongiva. The town of Ongiva and the airfield were further protected by an air defence umbrella.

It was August 1981 and Operation Protea was planned to neutralize the East German–FAPLA air defences and disrupt SWAPO operations. This would be the biggest operation since Savannah, and involved effectively a South African brigade-sized formation. What made this operation somewhat different was the use of the SA Army Command and Staff Course students for both the planning and, to a limited extent, execution of the operation. At that time, the Staff Course comprised two phases: a pre-course, or distance-education phase, followed by a one-year 'residential' phase. For this operation the residential students were tasked to plan the operation, and, in typically Army College style, this was done to the finest detail, supported by detailed, annotated air photographs and good intelligence. At each stage of the appreciation the students presented their options and conclusions to the operation's commanders. Some of the students from both phases of the Staff Course would be tasked to take part in the operation—a sound method of testing their thinking and planning ability, as well as giving them combat experience. Planning called for two task forces; these were named Alpha and Bravo. Task Force Alpha was planned as the main attacking force under the command of Colonel Joop Joubert (at that time, the commander of 82 Mechanized Brigade), an infantry officer who had commanded Battle Group Juliet in Operation Bruilof, the first mechanized operation in 1978. Alpha comprised four battle groups supported by a composite artillery regiment, the battle groups being:

- Battle Group 10, a mechanized infantry unit based on 61 Mechanized Battalion under the command of Commandant Roland de Vries and equipped with Ratel 20mm, 60mm and 90mm infantry combat vehicles.

- Battle Group 20, a newly formed mechanized unit under the command of Commandant Johan Dippenaar.

- Battle Group 30, a motorized infantry group under the command of Commandant Chris Serfontein, another seasoned infantry officer.

- Battle Group 40, a light infantry battalion from 32 Battalion under command of Commandant Deon Ferreira, with its organic support.

Task Force Bravo, under the command of Colonel Vos Benade, comprised two counter-insurgency battle groups:

- Battle Group 50, a light infantry group under the command of Commandant Frans Botes

- Battle Group 60, a light infantry group of three 32 Battalion companies under the command of Commandant James Hills

The task force reserve was made up of two parachute companies under Commandant Johnnie Coetzer.

To give an idea of the proportions of this operation, the SAAF allocated 138 aircraft of which 73 were combat aircraft.

The gunners now, at last, had new equipment in the shape of the 120mm M5 mortar to provide close support and the 127mm multiple rocket launcher, which could provide large volumes of intense fire (also known as artillery strikes). At last, the deficiencies were being overcome.

The artillery regiment to support this operation was assembled under the command of Commandant Koos Laubscher with Major Jacob van Heerden as his 2IC. The regiment comprised two batteries and two troops as follows—

H Troop, 1 Medium Battery (4 Field Regiment): a BL 140mm (G2) troop under Captain Francois van Eeden with the following members:

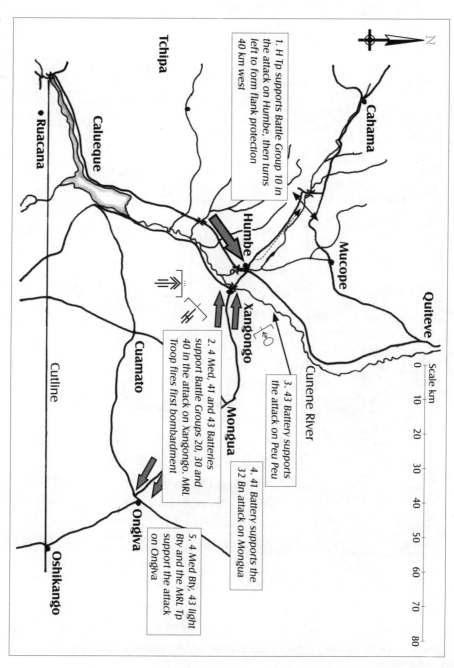

Protea: the plan for the operation.

1. H Tp supports Battle Group 10 in the attack on Humbe, then turns left to form flank protection 40 km west

2. 4 Med, 41 and 43 Batteries support Battle Groups 20, 30 and 40 in the attack on Xangongo. MRL Troop fires first bombardment

3. 43 Battery supports the attack on Peu Peu

4. 41 Battery supports the 32 Bn attack on Mongua

5. 4 Med Bty, 43 light Bty and the MRL Tp support the attack on Ongiva

N

Scale km
0 10 20 30 40 50 60 70 80

Cahama
Quiteve
Mucope
Tchipa
Humbe
Xangongo
Cunene River
Mongua
Calueque
Ruacana
Cutline
Cuamato
Ongiva
Oshikango

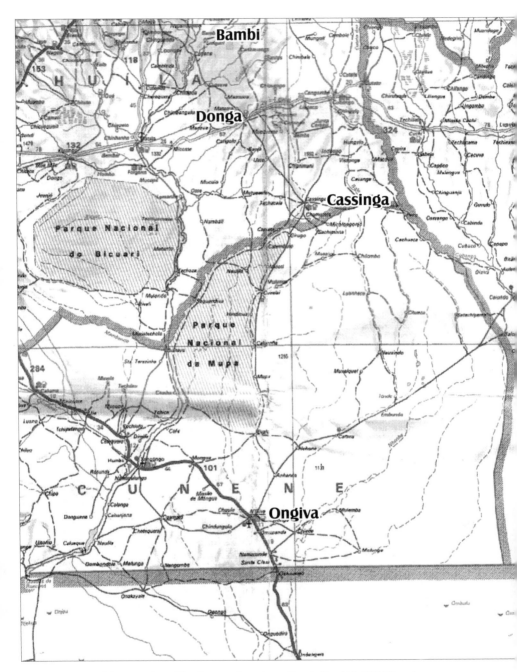

The general area of the operations. The distance from the cutline to Bambi is 360 kilometres.
Map: Cartographia Kft

- Battery captain team: Lt N.J. du Plessis, Gnrs H.S. Meintjies and J.P. van der Linde
- GPO team: Capt J. Marais, 2/Lt R.J. Boetger, L/Bdr H.V.L. Olver, Bdr D.D. Schoonwinkel, Gnr G.K. Erikson; Sgt G.J. Kruger
- Troop leader: 2/Lt P.P. Tempel
- Troop sergeant-major team: S/Sgt G.P. Hill, Gnr A.J. Stander
- Gun no. 1: Bdr J.P. Potgieter, L/Bdr N.D. Harris, Gnrs F.J. Linde, H.F. Niewenhuis, C.K. Shiller, J.H. Marx, J.J. McGeary, D.E. Kieck, W.E. Minnie, A.E. Oelofsen and N.J.J. Prollius
- Gun no. 2: Bdr S.P.J.J. van Rensburg, L/Bdr G.J. Pretorius and NCB Wiese, Gnrs W.J. Vermeulen, F.L. Kupfer, B.C. Coetzer, J.J. Pelser, J.G. Schoemen, M. van Rensburg, F.E. Oelofse and A. Lategan
- Gun no. 3: Bdr I.J. Brytenbach, L/Bdr J.J.D. Herbst, Gnrs F.H. Rudolf, F.V.E. Coetzee, D. Conradie, M. Maritz, A.B. Pruis, A.P. Lindeque, P.A. Mostert, P.L. Williams and F.A. Esterhuizen
- Gun no. 4: Bdr J.J. Roux, L/Bdr A.S. Ross, Gnrs A.J. Pretorius, J.J.A. Matthee, P.J. Odendaal, E. Escorcio, C.J. van Eeden, C.J. Kennedy, L.G. Pienaar, A. Smit and E.C.F. Prinsloo
- A Echelon: Gnr A. Dreyer (driver, 10-tonne water bowser), Gnr S.P. Lange (water orderly), Bdr S. Sauerman, L/Bdr C.J.J. Marx, Gnrs A.E. van Wyk and E.E.J. Steyn (drivers, 10-tonne ammunition 1 to 4 respectively), Gnrs B.J. de Klerk and L.R. Kotze (drivers, spare gun tractors)
- A protection element (this was not a normal, organic element in a troop or battery, but was added because of the vulnerability of this troop. All these members of the troop were assigned additional tasks such as ammunition numbers, spare drivers and spare technical assistants): L/Bdrs: W.H. du Plessis and P.J. Prinsloo, Gnrs: G. Blake, D. Gardner, G.A. Chittenden, R.A. Daws, S.P. Gouws, D.S. Jacobs, D.J. Mills, R.R. Pretorius, T.H. Sherman, C.J.M. Esterhuizen, J.H. le Roux, A. Lipschitz, N.J. Pretorius, C.A. Harris, K.R. du Toit, L.C. Botha, J. van den Dool, C.L. Kotze and G.N. Robbertse

H Troop would remain in direct support of Battle Group 10 for the operation. During this operation Bernie Pols acted as air OP for the first phase.

4 Medium Battery (BL 140mm G2) under Major Johan Potgieter was made up of members of THA, with additional manpower coming from the PF and national servicemen that were available. This fire unit had been 'thrown together' by moving B Troop of 7th Battery THA from their infantry task in Katima Mulilo, mobilizing 8th Battery THA in its entirety and combining this with PF officers from the Command and Staff Course. It is interesting to note that NFA were originally earmarked for this task. The leader group in this battery were:

- Troop commander, C Troop: Maj Tobie Vermaak from 14 Field Regiment
- C Troop: Capt T.J.J. van Rensburg (the air OP), Lts L. van Wyk and T.C.K. Wilken (GPO) (4 Field Regt), 2/Lt S.W. Burger (Tp Lr) (4 Field Regt), CO M. McFarlane, WOII S.E. le Roux, S/Sgt P.H. Jackson, Sgts J.P. Lerm and J. van Eeden
- D Troop: Lts I.W. Rimmer (FOO) and I.H.S. Stinton (GPO), 2/Lt J.J. Sippel, WOII R.A. Golden (TSM), Sgts F. de Beer, F.K. van Zyl and M.K. van Wyk
- The battery sergeant-major was WOII L. Francis of THA.

Other members of the battery drawn from 4 Field Regiment were (unfortunately their posts in the battery are not clear): Sergeants A.J. Kruger and M. Emmerich, Corporals C. van Aswegen and C. Bosch, Rifleman P.J. Ras (Ratel driver from 1 SAI Battalion), Gunners L.C. Botha, P.H. Lubbe, C.H. Minaar, E.D.F. Prinsloo and C.P. Roux. Protection was provided by a platoon from 5 SAI Battalion under the command of Second Lieutenant G.A. Wessels.

4 Medium Battery would provide direct support for Commandant Dippenaar's Battle Group 20.

41 Light Battery (120mm M5 mortar) was under the command of Major Jaap Nel, with Captains Maartin Schalekamp and Theuns Coetzee as the troop commanders, Lieutenant Piet Botha the battery captain and Staff

Sergeant Willem van Ryneveld the BSM. This battery would remain in direct support of 32 Battalion (Battle Group 40) for the duration.

43 Light Battery (120mm M5 mortar) (the only battery from 4 Field Regiment permanently based at Walvis Bay) was under the command of Major Jean Lausberg, with Captain Jakkie Cilliers as one of the troop commanders. The manpower of this fire unit was reinforced by Lieutenant Carel Laubscher, a PF officer from the School of Artillery, as GPO of the senior troop (call sign 31) and Lieutenant Pieter Botha (no relation to the Piet Botha above) as GPO of the junior troop (32). The BSM was Staff Sergeant Albert Loubser. The Walvis Bay gunners would be in direct support of Battle Group 30.

An MRL troop was also a 'come as you are' fire unit, comprising a mixture of personnel from the School of Artillery and 4 Field Regiment. Some of the personnel were:

- Captain Johan du Randt: troop commander
- Captain Willie Viljoen: GPO
- Second Lieutenant Daan Malan: battery captain
- Second Lieutenant Ossie Zaayman: technical assistant 1 (under normal conditions the TA1 is a bombardier or a sergeant)
- Second Lieutenant Enrico de Freitas: meteorological officer.

Each MRL was commanded by a Permanent Force NCO, again unusual, as this was normally the task of national service NCOs. The entire leader element of this troop had just completed an MRL conversion course at the School of Artillery and, were the only qualified MRL gunners available at that time. Second Lieutenant Zaayman emphasized an important point that had emerged from the course:

In this training course the fact that this weapon is not a standard artillery gun was emphasized, together with the need to exercise some lateral thinking in utilizing it in the bush. This would be the first time that the MRL would be used in action and we were all proud of that!

The MRL Troop remained under Commandant Laubscher's command to reinforce the fire of any of other fire units when and where required.

To make life for the MRL gunners more interesting they had to use Buffels as fire-control posts. Here they had to improvise by attaching the active wind-measuring system (an anemometer and wind vane) to the Buffel. As mentioned earlier, this vehicle was not designed for such use.

During the preparation for the operation, Commandant Laubscher issued guidelines for the local defence of firing positions to all batteries under command—something that was new to the gunners and which would remain an integral part of training in the future. These guidelines included the tactically sound selection of gun positions, avoiding local population, the use of natural obstacles and the use of dead ground (behind cover against observation and fire). Laubscher also emphasized the use of camouflage and concealment, communications security and the use of lights at night.

In terms of ammunition planning, the regimental commander (who was, at that time, the OC of 4 Field Regiment) issued instructions for the scales of artillery ammunition that was to be carried into the operation. The medium battery would carry 1,500 rounds of all types, the medium troop some 1,040 rounds. The light batteries would carry in the order of 2,000 mortar bombs each, with a total of 11,000 bombs in reserve, and the MRL troop some 288 rockets and fuses with 144 in reserve. With this planning behind him for the time being, Commandant Laubscher added a footnote to his instruction: 'Crack the head of any artillery officer that delivers the wrong type and calibre of ammunition to the wrong place.'

This operation required somewhat more equipment than that available in the mobilization stores in Grootfontein. For example, there were not enough G2 guns. During the early preparation phase, Laubscher instructed Captain van Eeden to fly to Katima Mulilo and find 'the four best guns in Nova base'. Duly instructed, Captain van Eeden reported to the sector commander and informed him of the need to backload four G2 guns to Grootfontein for 'base repair and rebuild'. The sector commander, being a professional soldier, asked no more questions. Once in Grootfontein, these guns were given a rebuild with heavy metal plates being welded onto their trail legs and towing eyes, a modification essential to ensure that they would survive the cross-country journey to Cahama and back. Furthermore, Commandant Laubscher, in his orders to his regiment had clearly stated that no gun shall be left behind or fall into enemy hands.

These forces gathered at the Omutiya operational training area and preparation started. As usual, the artillery regiment found itself without maps. This problem was overcome by duplicating air photos that were then overlaid by a grid drawn on acetate, which was then aligned to the air photos. Because of the unreliability of meteorological data the gunners would fire on a 'witness point' (a distinct feature on a photo); the point where the round landed would be measured relative to the witness point and the difference used as a 'standard' meteorological correction. This method was intended to provide the ability to achieve first-round hits on nearly every fire mission.

By this time, the South African forces had improved or replaced weaponry, improved communications, developed night movement across country, and, most importantly, improved the co-ordination between ground- and air-delivered fire, as well as all-arms battle handling and doctrine.

The point of main effort of this operation was an attack on Xangongo. This was to be followed by an attack on Ongiva to drive FAPLA out of the latter, both attacks aimed at neutralizing the FAPLA air defences and thereby creating space for the SAAF to operate.

The plan for the operation was for Battle Group 10 (Mainly 61 Mechanized Battalion) with H Troop in direct support to approach from the southwest, crossing the Cunene River at Calueque and attacking the Humbe complex (nicknamed 'Apple Pie') 6 kilometres to the west of Xangongo. This was to be followed by a turn to the west for 40 kilometres as flank protection to prevent any Cuban intervention in the attack on Xangongo (nickname 'Yankee') from the direction of Cahama. The battle group was tasked to delay any intervention for 14 days.

Battle groups 20 and 30, with 40 in reserve, would approach from the south between Xangongo and Ongiva and attack Xangongo from the east, supported by 4 Medium, 43 and 41 Batteries respectively. The MRL troop remained under the command of 4 Field Regiment throughout the operation.

Once this phase was complete, the force would then turn its attention on Ongiva, attacking from the north.

On 5 August 1981, Major Jaap Nel and his battery left their lines at 4 Field Regiment in Potchefstroom bound for Air Force Base Waterkloof in Pretoria, where they boarded an aircraft for their next stop, Grootfontein. On their arrival in Grootfontein, an operational briefing by Commandant Laubscher was followed by the collection of ordnance, vehicles and equipment, all of which was checked and packed for movement.

The next day, the battery moved by road to the training area at Oshivello, adjacent to 61 Mechanized Battalion's base at Omutiya, where administrative orders were issued to the battery commander and preparations started.

By 8 August, 41 Battery had deployed on the firing range some 30 kilometres north of the base area and had commenced acclimatization and training. It must be remembered that, although the gunners were all trained and combat-ready, they still needed to become accustomed to the featureless terrain, soft sand and thick bush that they would be encountering during the operation. This brief period of acclimatization also gave them the opportunity to complete any outstanding, or unfinished, parts of their training curriculum. Battle discipline was always enforced, and at the end of the day's firing with this particular battery, Major Nel had to punish two of his NCOs: 'Had Bdrs Taljaard and Swanepoel run around the mortar position with ammunition cases because they had left their sight-test booklets behind.' It was a drill that every number one on a gun carried his sight-test booklet with him—such was the importance of sight testing.

Ammunition was collected by 41 Battery on 10 August and packed on 20 Buffel vehicles. Just as the Buffel was unsuitable as an artillery fire-control vehicle, it was even less suitable as an ammunition vehicle. Even with the side flaps dropped down, it was still about one and a half metres high—not easy to load or lift out the 40 kilogram mortar ammunition cases.

During the period of preparation, the intelligence picture was changing on a daily basis, with new air photos continuously being updated. More and more 23mm AA gun positions were being identified and, given their firepower when used in the ground role, the South African gunners had to adjust their fire plans each day. The 23mm gun positions were becoming increasingly important as priority targets for the artillery, as the attacking infantry and armoured cars would be neutralized, if not destroyed, by these guns.

The evening of 22 August saw the gunners moving out of 61 Mechanized Battalion's training area to halt at Ondangwa for some sleep before advancing the next day via Okalongo where they refuelled before crossing the cutline.

The group was addressed by Lieutenant-General Jannie Geldenhuys (then chief of the army) and held a church parade before continuing their advance northwards at 03h00 on 24 August. Battle Group 40's forward assembly area was placed some 500 metres south of the cutline just north of Okalongo. Here, 41 Battery had to move their position southwards as Commandant Ferreira was concerned that they were too close to the easternmost FAPLA–SWAPO company localities. While the light gunners were testing mortar sights and setting up their artillery boards and maps, intelligence reports came in that day that additional 82mm mortar positions, a 122mm D30 gun position and a ZPU AA position had been identified south of Xangongo— direct threats to the impending attack.

The MRL troop lost an ammunition vehicle to an anti-personnel mine at 03h30 that morning, causing a delay, but no casualties. After a frustrating reconnaissance, the MRL troop finally went into action on the edge of a *shona*, ready to fire on target at Yankee (Xangongo).

Captain van Eeden's H Troop went into action first by delivering a preparatory bombardment on Apple Pie (Humbe) prior to 61 Mechanized Battalion's attack. No resistance was forthcoming and the gunners only fired 25 rounds, of which three were smoke. By 18h00 on 24 August, the bridge over the Cunene River was secured and the force turned west to take Uia. Once again, there was no resistance and the group continued their move westwards the next day.

The move westwards was not without incident however, as, on 26 August, contact was made with FAPLA forces moving across the main Cahama–Humbe road. Here H Troop went into action and fired 36 rounds contributing to a successful attack and the capture of two BM21 MRLs, four 23mm AA guns, two BTR 60 (destroyed), six GAZ trucks (two destroyed) and ten POWs.

At 11h15 on 24 August 1981, total surprise was achieved by attacking from the northeast and the combined air force and 20-minute-long artillery preparatory bombardment started on Xangongo, the main objective. The MRL troop continued to engage another three targets through the day before moving eastwards to a new position. Shortly afterwards, 41 Battery opened fire on their fire plan. Major Nel explains:

> At about 11h00 [more likely 12h00], the 120mm mortars started firing on the base east of Yankee [Xangongo]. It went well. So much so that the base could be cleared quickly—six enemy killed. By 11h30, the air attack on Yankee commenced [according to the sitrep, 40's attack went in at 12h50]. What a sight! The Mirages, Buccaneers and Impalas dropped bombs on the enemy in between waves of AA fire. The whole world was explosions and dust. Just after that, Combat Team 43 started their attack on the northern base, meeting heavy resistance. As a result of bad communications, FOOs not being able to see their targets and air observers taking so long to relay corrections, the 120mm engagement went very slowly. The base was eventually taken.

From here, two combat teams of 32 Battalion (Battle Group 40) launched their attacks in their sectors, Majors Jan Hougaard and Chris du Toit's teams attacking the southern and northern objectives respectively. Once again, the supporting 41 Battery was plagued by communication and observation problems—an artillery failure. Nevertheless, all targets were neutralized, but it took somewhat longer than intended. By this time, FAPLA were on the run. According to Major Nel:

> Unfortunately, the 140mm guns of Battle Group 20 fired on our own forces, killing one and wounding seven [this incident is described later in this chapter]. By 17h30, we occupied Xangongo and the engineers were on the bridge [over the Cunene River]. There were a

number of enemy killed [approximately 20], captured and wounded. We commenced consolidating. Currently, we are in one of the Russian houses. Here is plenty of Russian propaganda—a lot of photos of Russian VIPs and weaponry. Here is Angolan beer to drink and tuna ready to eat.

The tuna was provided by the Netherlands government via the UN—so much for UN neutrality. Thanks to this, the gunners could enjoy a change in diet for a while.

This attack continued throughout the day and into the early evening; by 18h00 the force could report that they had captured Xangongo. At one stage during the night, WOII Francis, the battery sergeant-major of 4 Medium Battery (G20), was totally surprised by three T-34 tanks that drove metres past his echelon. Luckily, it was dark and no contact was made. In Xangongo a FAPLA artillery battery on the move was ambushed by the 90mm anti-tank guns of Commandant Dippenaar's battle group and destroyed in its entirety. During the night, the MRL troop ceased firing after a total of four ripples and moved eastwards to their next deployment area, again becoming lost, but happily found by a section of Ratels when they were escorted into the protection of a leaguer area for the night.

While the main attack on Xangongo was developing, Battle Group 30 moved northwards to attack Peu Peu in order to prevent interference from the SWAPO–FAPLA forces deployed there. The attack on Peu Peu was supported by 43 Battery. Lance-Bombardier Frank Louw, a No 3 (layer) on a mortar at that time, continues the story:

We fired over 600 rounds of white phosphorus on the tactical group HQ, using sweeping fire [sweep and search] and 'creeping' up the base, which lay directly north of our position and was exactly as wide as our battery front. We never aimed between rounds, as we had worked out that the quarter turn on the elevation [handle] at that range adjusted the creep by 50 metres.

By last light, the defending forces had evacuated Peu Peu and deployed to the west of the town near the river. Unfortunately, last light limited the amount of clearing up the attacking battle group could do.

Just after midnight on the morning of 25 August, the MRL troop deployed 100 metres from the 'highway'—the main road from Xangongo to Ongiva, to be ready to fire on target Hotel (Mongua). At this point the little fire unit was surprised by a FAPLA patrol, who attacked them. The MRL gunners managed to drive off the FAPLA attackers, but, in the process, drew the attention of a passing mechanized infantry company on its way to the new objective. Here, the infantry confused friend and foe, and joined the FAPLA patrol in the fight until the gunners contacted them on the command radio net and requested them, in no uncertain terms, to depart the area. The only consequence of this fight was a number of empty rifle magazines in the troop. At 01h50, the task force reserve attacked Mongua.

At 05h00 that same morning, Gunner Beeton, Major Nel's signaller, once again attempted to establish radio communications with the battery, and by 07h50, was still out of contact with the mortars. The only way left to order the battery to move up was for a message to be passed through to the battle group's echelon and for the gunners to follow this tail into Xangongo. The low point in 41 Battery's part in this operation occurred a little later that morning when Major Nel, having finally made contact with his battery, gave them fresh orders at the now deserted fort in the town. To give the gunners a break he allowed them to look over the captured equipment that had been packed at this fort in preparation for backloading southwards. A small number of the battery members began picking up these items and it was here that Bombardier Grobler became the first casualty in the battery when the booby trapped item exploded, amputating his hand and mortally wounding him in the stomach. Despite the efforts of the doctors who were close by at the time, he died of his wounds. 2/Lt Philip Erasmus, and Bdrs Geertsema and van der Westhuizen were evacuated by helicopter, all wounded.

'I am bitterly sorry that Bombardier Grobler was taken away from us,' said Major Nel. That night, Major Nel was informed that the next phase of the operation, code-named Konyn, would commence next morning.

By 10h05 on 26 August, the 32 Battalion convoy, with their artillery battery (41 Battery) in support, found themselves hiding under the cover of the plentiful trees on the road from Xangongo to Mongua (operational nickname Hotel) and an hour later moving into the town of Mongua to witness the destruction wrought by Battle Group 30. The pace continued and by 15h30, 41 Battery had arrived in Evale (Taurus) after a chase of 70 kilometres across country to join up with Battle Group 50. It was here that the SAAF had established a forward airfield where, according to Major Nel, 'there [were] so many Dakotas coming and going that it [made] Grootfontein look miniscule'.

On 26 August, FAPLA issued instructions to hold Ongiva at all costs; this included instructions for removing families, money from the bank and the planting of mines on and around the airfield.

That night, Battle Group 20 formed up northeast of Ongiva and at first light on Thursday 27 August 1981 commenced their attack. Captain Cilliers directed the fire of the 4 Medium Battery from the top of a Buffel, the only raised platform available with some view of the target area and in full view of the whole of Ongiva! The limited command of the target area and the inaccurate fixation by the medium battery resulted in a time-consuming adjustment process where the command 'drop 1600' was given by the observer on more than one occasion so as to see the fall of shot. After an air attack on the objective, Major Potgieter's battery eventually fired the preparatory bombardment on the defensive positions, the rounds landing on the roofs of the buildings in Ongiva. Under the control of Captain Johan du Randt, the MRL troop fired on the FAPLA headquarters, the infantry and armour driving in at best speed with their sirens blaring and generally causing mayhem amongst the defenders. Major Potgieter, being the direct support battery commander, travelled in his Ratel 'in the shadow' of Commandant Dippenaar. This was normal practice, but what made this situation interesting was that this Ratel also housed Lieutenant Spyker Jakobs, the air liaison officer, and Loffie Eloff, the mortar platoon commander. The total radio antenna count was 13, making the vehicle resemble something like a porcupine.

By 11h00, Battle Group 20 had reached the Ongiva airfield where they came under intense mortar fire, and at the same time, Battle Group 30 captured the FAPLA HQ while the reserve was called in to help clear the airfield. The fight at the airfield continued and by 12h07, the advance was effectively stopped—not only by mortars, but also tanks, 23mm AA in the surface-to-surface role and D30 fire. The cause of the accurate fire was soon discovered, however, by locating a FAPLA OP and radar control post on top of the airfield's water tower. The 120mm gunners of 43 Battery were tasked to deal with this problem and successfully destroyed the tower and its attached radar control post. At about this time, 43 Battery's OPO team reached the town and were first to arrive at the bunker of a Soviet colonel. The OP assistant, Bombardier Hans Arler, took the honour of being first into this accommodation and 'was able to liberate many bottles of vodka (that were well used), many cans of pork and sardines (the sardine cans were the size of a tank mine) and, most importantly, a box of one gross of brand-new socks. It was great pulling on a brand-new pair of socks each morning'.

Not all went well, however, as after the airfield was secured, the medium battery's command affiliation was changed to be 'in support' of Battle Group 30. This meant that their fire would be controlled by someone who was not an organic part of the battery, as the situation would not allow Major Potgieter or his observers to move across to that group. The fire control, therefore, was taken over by Major Jean Lausberg, the mortar battery commander, who was the direct support battery commander of Battle Group 30. During the adjusting process a correction was given that resulted in a round landing on own troops, killing four, with a near miss on Captain Cilliers. This was the result of the sudden change of command and control, and the assaulting troops not being in their reported position.

During the late afternoon, FAPLA counter-attacked with T-34 tanks. The only artillery fire unit capable of stopping them was the 43 Battery firing WP bombs. Captain Cilliers, at this point, had a commanding view by positioning himself on a toilet seat and looking out of a third-storey window. One of his rounds was a direct hit on a T-34, but had little effect. The afternoon was saved by the arrival of the infantry's Ratel 90s.

By 14h00, 4 Medium Battery had moved to a new firing position south of the runway to cover FAPLA escape routes and possible interference from the north, and some six hours later fired a harassing fire shoot on the Soviet positions that had been previously bombed by the SAAF. Who was more harassed is not entirely clear because, during that afternoon, the SAAF ground teams, a medical element and a logistics element had occupied the airport building—a position some 300 metres in front of the deployed battery. As was customary for such rear-echelon organizations, the party started with lights ablaze and no knowledge of the close proximity of 4 Medium's gunners. Major Potgieter completes the story:

> I was in a comfortable position to observe the airport building and was amazed at the speed with which the gathering ducked for cover under flying half-empty Coke and beer bottles when the battery opened fire. Needless to say, it wasn't necessary to ask them to put out their lights after that bombardment.

The MRL troop spent the rest of the day in position, loaded, and waiting for further orders. None were forthcoming from the RHQ so they came out of action and withdrew to a hide in the town of Ongiva until the end of the operation.

At last light, Battle Group 30 pulled back and deployed in a position where the town of Ongiva could be dominated by observation and by fire.

During the night of Thursday 27 August, 32 Battalion (Battle Group 40) settled down for the night in a position some 20 kilometres north of Mupa (nicknamed Long Tom) in preparation for their attack on the SWAPO operational headquarters—the start of a wide-ranging sweep.

At 02h00 on Friday 28 August, after the attack on Ongiva by the mechanized force, 32 Battalion, with 41 Light Battery in direct support, commenced their approach to contact. For a change, the vegetation was not as thick as expected and the gunners arrived at their deployment area two hours early. The fire plan for the 120mm mortars was focused on four AA positions. All fire was predicted and Major Nel controlled the fire plan from behind the firing position (not usual, but tactically sound in this case). The attack commenced with an air attack from some 16 Mirages and four Impalas, followed by 41 Battery's fire on each AA position. This involved a cocktail of five rounds fire for effect of HE bombs fused with the M150 multimode fuse (this fuse was fitted with a 300 millimetre rod that, when striking the ground, caused the bomb to detonate, creating an airburst effect); white phosphorus; and finally, HE bombs fitted with the AZDM III fuse set on delay, thus causing the bombs to explode below ground level—a particularly good treatment for bunkers or trenches with overhead cover.

By the time the mortars of 41 Battery had engaged the fourth target, the barrels were so hot that one mortar experienced a 'cook off', where the charge ignites prematurely. The result was a mortar bomb that fired and landed about 15 metres in front of the firing position, starting a veld fire. Fortunately, the propelling charge could not build up enough chamber pressure so that the departing bomb did not arm itself and, therefore, did not explode on impact.

Nevertheless, it caused not a little mayhem on the mortar position. By 10h40, all firing had ceased, the end result of the attack being an anticlimax: SWAPO had fled a month earlier, leaving the base empty. A question in hindsight, given the importance of the target: why was this base not kept under surveillance in order to update intelligence?

Immediately after the attack, 32 Battalion was instructed by Chief of the Army Lieutenant-General Jan Geldenhuys, who visited them there, to ignore the next planned objective and carry on with area operations—not a job for the artillery.

The morning of Saturday 29 August brought good news for the South Africans sitting in the Angolan bush, effectively out of touch with the rest of the world—the Springbok rugby team had just beaten New Zealand 24 to 12, this at a time when the anti-apartheid movement was disrupting sports events and anything else South Africans were involved in. Futher good news for the gunners was that the planned target, 'Wynland', was indeed to be attacked. By 13h30, the battery was in a hide to the north of the objective awaiting detailed orders. Shortly afterwards they were notified that the SAAF would bomb the target and that the ground forces were to deploy as many stopper groups as possible to cover escape routes. Here the differences between the thinking of the more conventional warfare-orientated gunners and the unconventional warfare expertise of 32 Battalion came to clash. Major Nel explains:

> Commandant Ferreira deployed his battle group in packets to the north and west of Wynland. Without consulting me, he began deploying the artillery as well. I explained to him that the 120mm mortars would be useless against small groups of fleeing terrorists in this thick bush. I suggested that we deploy the gunners as stoppers with their rifles and machine guns [12.7mm Brownings]. Thereupon, he became angry and accused us of only wanting to rest and, further, that he wasn't a complete idiot.

A while later, Captain Theuns Coetzee, deployed on foot as an FOO, radioed in to suggest that the battery deploy near a dry riverbed where they could cover Major Jan Hougaard's group because this group at least had reasonable observation (400 metres).

That same morning saw Battle Group 20 attacking directly north into the town and 4 Medium Battery providing short harassing fire shoots later that night. The medium gunners finally withdrew on 1 September.

The next morning, after the air attack, Commandant Eddie Viljoen issued brief orders for 41 Battery to move immediately to the helicopter administrative area (HAA), and by late that afternoon the gunners were in the HAA and awaiting new instructions. These instructions came on 31 August when the battery was attached to Commandant Viljoen's group to support them in area operations to the south. This group also provided cover as the rearguard of the withdrawing task force.

For the next six days, 41 Battery followed the 32 Battalion group northwards, eastwards and eventually southwards to cross the cutline at 20h30 on 5 September. At the Elundu base the gunners were given a chance to dazzle the infantry with a firepower demonstration and finally they departed the operational area on 9 September.

Suppression of enemy air defences (SEAD)

Air defence is generally organized around three elements: early warning, target acquisition and target engagement. Early warning is provided by long-range radars that are in contact with a central command post. Target acquisition methods are shorter-range radars and even observers. Target engagement is carried out by both guns and missiles working in combination.

In order to provide own aircraft with the space to manoeuvre—especially to carry out interdiction and close air support to the ground troops—the enemy's air defences must be suppressed, even if only temporarily. This suppression was done by the SAAF: electronic warfare aircraft would pick up the radar signals from the early-warning radars. This would be followed by a feint air attack which would activate the acquisition radars, and another group of aircraft would attack the launchers or gun positions. But another alternative, somewhat less risky for the SAAF, was to use the artillery to either neutralize or destroy the radars and effectively 'blind' the launchers.

This operation ended with the withdrawal of South African forces on 3 September and succeeded in that about 930 SWAPO–FAPLA were killed or wounded, 250 tonnes of ammunition and a multitude of equipment captured and SWAPO activities disrupted for almost a year.

In a post-operations debrief, the Directorate Artillery presented a report, part of which contained the ammunition consumption for the deployed artillery during Protea. It showed the ammunition consumption in detail, the more important items of which are shown here. It also explained that the actual usage was below that predicted, as some targets were found abandoned and the operation only ran for 13 days as opposed to the predicted 21 days. Below is the list of ammunition consumption:

- Projectile 140mm HE: 1,517
- Projectile 140mm smoke: 26
- Fuse 213 PM 1 (mechanical time):   164 (used on both HE and smoke shells)
- Rocket 127mm HE: 155 (most fused with proximity fuses)
- Mortar bomb 120mm HE (all types):   1,505
- Mortar bomb 120mm white phosphorus: 320

- Mortar bomb 120mm illumination: 8
- Mortar bomb 120mm smoke/coloured smoke: 80

It was the light gunners who suffered casualties during this operation; these were:

Killed in action:
- Bombardier H.A.G. Grobler of 41 Battery

Wounded:
- Second Lieutenant P. Erasmus of 41 Battery
- Lance-Bombardier Geertsma of 41 Battery
- Lance-Bombardier van der Westhuizen of 41 Battery
- Gunner P.A.L. Snydert of 43 Battery

Some world firsts

Operation Protea yielded more than just suppressed enemy air defences in that theatre: the ground troops had the honour of being the first western force to capture a Soviet SA-8 missile system—and intact at that. This operation also yielded the biggest haul of foreign weaponry (in tonnage) in modern times.

For the gunners, the success of this operation had special meaning. It was an operation that was conducted without sufficient equipment; batteries were forced to exchange vehicles and personnel to fill the most serious gaps. Not even sufficient gun sights were available to 4 Medium Battery and they had to improvise by stripping two sights to make up one serviceable unit. They managed to collect a sight from, of all places, Ruacana, one day before the operation commenced. The first time the sight was fitted to a gun was in preparation for the attack on Xangongo. Another consequence of insufficient vehicles and personnel was that 4 Medium Battery could not deploy a BPO—a vitally important post for co-ordinating movement of the two troops and the echelon, as well as for the direct liaison with the sharp end. Gun tractors were overloaded: 103 rounds of 140mm ammunition were carried, although the tractors were designed for 48 rounds. Finally, the lack of accurate maps that contributed to difficulty in fixation of gun positions and targets alike had the effect of undue delays in deploying and, initially, inaccurate fire, requiring large corrections.

Captain T.J.J. van Rensburg of THA, the Air OP of 4 Medium Battery, provided critically needed gun and mortar fire control at the times when ground-based OPOs and FOOs could not see their targets because of flat terrain and the smoke and dust from the aerial bombardments. Captain van Rensburg was flown by Danie Laubscher (42 Squadron), the pilot who was awarded the Honoris Crux medal for bravery for his actions under AA fire. This pair of officers, flying in a Bosbok, succeeded in destroying a 23mm AA gun position through the use of the 68mm rockets fitted to the aircraft.

Operation Daisy

Insofar as major, or large, operations go, Daisy was almost insignificant and seldom gets a mention in the history books. The objectives were identified by intelligence gathered during Protea and were analyzed as being a SWAPO HQ at Bambi (15-35-05 E; 14-02-53 S), as well as a number of transit camps in the area.

This operation was not in the least insignificant though, as it scored another first in that it was the deepest strike since the end of Operation Savannah, and was conducted not by Special Forces, but by 61 Mechanized Battalion, supported by 1 and 3 Parachute Battalions, 201 Battalion and a company from 32 Battalion. Artillery support came from S Battery of 61 Mechanized Battalion Group, equipped for this operation with 120mm M5 mortars and under the command of Captain Bernie Pols. The SAAF provided reconnaissance and close air support for this operation.

Intelligence had identified seven SWAPO bases, the largest being protected by upwards of 1,000 men, two bases of 400 men each and the rest occupied by smaller groups with their vehicles. There were also five FAPLA positions, three of which were occupied by brigades, and finally one Cuban regiment of approximately 500 men and eight BM21s. All these positions were supported by a good early-warning system and most would be in a position to engage South African forces by artillery fire.

The 127mm FV1 Valkiri multiple rocket launcher

Despite stories to the contrary, this launcher system was not based on the 122mm BM21 'Stalin organ' and was already in the design phase in 1975. The first instructors' course was held in Somerset West, Cape Town, in mid-1979 and the equipment first became available in 1981 in time for Operation Protea.

The 127mm rocket was designed as an anti-personnel/soft-skinned vehicle munition and was fitted with only one type of warhead: high explosive anti-personnel. The fuse was either a point detonation (ground burst) or proximity (air burst). The combination of the 6,400 steel balls in the warhead and the proximity fuse delivered an awesome effect on the target, where the average coverage was two balls per square metre.

The launcher was a modified Unimog 416 diesel chassis with a 24-round tube pack and a crew of two on board. Each launcher was supported by at least one 10-tonne Samil 100 ammunition vehicle carrying 72 rockets. Although the Samil was a ten-tonner, physical space limited the vehicle to a 7-tonne payload of rockets.

Being a Unimog, the launcher had an excellent off-road capability, although it should be borne in mind that a fully loaded launcher with its crew and TOTE (equipment such as sight unit, spades, camouflage net, etc.) exceeded the designed all-up mass by 200 kilograms. In 1986, a 'bush bar' was added to protect the radiator and create space for the camouflage net, water jerrycan, spades and crew kit. This modification added another 150 kilograms to the already overweight vehicle. Despite this, these little workhorses performed exceptionally well in the soft sand of southern Angola. They were phased out of service in the 90s when replaced by the 48-round Bateleur.

---

61 Mechanized Battalion's mission was to execute a pre-emptive conventional attack against the SWAPO command post in order to achieve maximum casualties and cut off the SWAPO forces. This would be followed by an area operation for 17 days that was intended to follow and destroy SWAPO command and control, as well as its logistics capabilities. Included in the mission was the task of denial and domination of the SWAPO and FAPLA supply route and command axis from the north.

61 Mechanized Battalion, under the command of Commandant Roland de Vries, was the attacking force, with 201 Battalion providing flank protection and mopping-up operations approximately 20 kilometres to the southwest of the main objective.

Three parachute companies (from 2 and 3 Para Battalion) would deploy by air as cut-off forces to the northwest of the main objective; one was assigned the role of mobile reserve and based at the helicopter administrative area at Ionde. Special Forces teams deployed ahead of the force to monitor the

The 120mm M5 mortar

Although introduced into service to support the airborne forces, this useful ordnance was never air-dropped during operations, mainly because, at that time, the light-artillery concept (and the consequent training) was still in its infancy.

The 120mm fired two types of HE bomb: a 'standard' bomb, which, on charge 8 would provide a maximum range of 6,500 metres, and a rocket-assisted bomb providing a useful 12,000 metres. The other ammunition types were:

* White phosphorus
* Coloured smoke
* Illumination

This mortar was Israeli in design and manufacture, but was modified somewhat to suit local conditions. For example, the original sight was not suitable and was replaced by a dial sight of similar construction to that of all the other ordnance in the South African Artillery arsenal. The 120mm was equipped with a trailer for towing purposes, but it was found to be too fragile for southern African bush conditions and was subject to major modifications.

During operations the mortar was porteed on the back of a Samil 10-tonne vehicle with its ammunition, which gave it the same mobility as the rest of the force at that time.

objectives some time before the attack. S Battery would provide fire support in the form of an artillery strike on the 400-man-strong SWAPO B Battalion protecting the command post and then support the attack on the 1,000-strong protection element.

On 1 November 1981, the force penetrated through to its objectives at Bambi and Cheraquera, 300 kilometres into Angola. During the night, 3 Para jumped into a drop zone to the northwest of the objective and deployed three companies as flank protection against enemy interference from Cassinga and Techamutete.

The gunners fired 800 rounds at these targets, which may explain why no contact was made with FAPLA ground forces. A SAAF Mirage, however, did score one kill by downing a MiG-21 that had attempted to interfere with the business of the day.

This operation was completed by 20 November 1981. An operational debrief was held after the completion of the operation and, in his report, Commandant de Vries had the following specific comments about the artillery:

- Air observers arrived too late to acclimatize themselves with the operational conditions.
- Air observers are flying too high to properly identify targets and see own forces.
- The young pilots are inexperienced and the air OP training in Potchefstroom is not realistic, making it difficult for the artillery air OPs to do their job.
- Longer-range artillery is needed to bind the enemy during the approach to contact stage of the attack, the 120mm mortar is not suited to this task.

Air observers

As a prerequisite to promotion to captain, all South African artillery officers underwent observer, or OP, training as part their promotion course. This training included air observation. However, the aircraft were provided and flown by the SAAF, as the SA Army did not have its own aircraft. Three SAAF squadrons provided this capability and their pilots attended the observation training with their gunner colleagues at the School of Artillery. The aircraft used were Cessna 185 D/E (11 Squadron); AM3C Bosbok; and C4M Kudu (41 and 42 Squadron). One of the problems with the training was that it focused on the technical aspects of observation and fire control, but omitted tactical flying skills so necessary in the operational area. At one time the author experimented with the concept of flying 'nap of the earth', but found that one still had to pitch the aircraft up to observe the shot, making the slow-flying aircraft very vulnerable to ground fire. Happily, this experiment was done in Potchefstroom.

Chapter 8

Askari: near disaster

During the period between Operations Sceptic and Askari, activities in the southeastern area of Angola continued, primarily by UNITA in their efforts to maintain control of that area. UNITA planned an attack on the town of Cangamba (19-50-00 E; 14-00 S), but, lacking in expertise and equipment, required South African help in the form of artillery fire support. Thus, Operation Karton came into being. This secret operation called for a 120mm mortar battery and training support for UNITA's 76mm Soviet field guns.

Major Johan du Randt was tasked to combine what was available in Potchefstroom and form a light battery. One of the troop commanders was Lieutenant Pieter Williams; the BSM was WOII 'Penkop' van Dyk.

On arrival in the operational area, the battery first stopped off at the Special Forces' liaison base of Fort Doppies in the Caprivi, where training and marrying up was done with UNITA. From there the force moved northwards. Once again, the availability of maps was problematic and Lieutenant Williams had to use a Michelin tourist road map to navigate.

Once in the general area of deployment, the gunners were issued with 1:100,000 scale Angolan maps.

The attack by UNITA did take place and the town was occupied—for a while. The gunners fired at maximum range with rocket-assisted ammunition, Lieutenant Williams observing and controlling the fire from a position in the fork of a high tree, much to the amusement of his UNITA colleagues.

Training takes on more realism

It wasn't until the early 1980s that training became more realistic, despite the lessons learnt during Operation Savannah. By this time, the new generation of unit commanders were being appointed. Major Frans van Eeden recalls:

> The School of Artillery, under the command of Colonel Koos Laubscher, abruptly changed in the run-up to Operation Askari. He created a new generation of chief instructors, who played a major role in the change. 'White bed' morning inspections [the focus being on display discipline, such as starched sheets and highly polished floors, etc.] gave way to operational readiness, full kit inspections and the like. I recall the surprise on the face of one of my troops one morning when the officer commanding, during an inspection, asked him to explain how to calibrate a compass instead of looking at his square bed and boned boots. All ranks had to wear their webbing at all times during exercises and all were issued with full first-line ammunition to carry. Vehicles would form up on the parade ground in order of their radio call signs; Golf 9, the regimental commander for the exercise was in front, the troop commanders next, all the way down to the last echelon vehicle and 9 Foxtrot and the RSM in the back. A full inspection would be done on all tote [the equipment carried on the vehicle: radios, antennae, spades, camouflage nets, etc.]; equipment, radios and call signs [were] tested and authenticated; and movement from the base was done by report lines to report progress.

Being so flat and featureless, the southern part of Angola necessitated that the gunners improved their methods of observation. The SAAF light aircraft squadrons played their role admirably in this. Because two of the three squadrons (11 and 42) were based in Potchefstroom, the liaison between the artillery and the air force was easy and relationships were good (the pilots and the gunner officers shared the same mess). At about this time it was decided that artillery air observers should be formally graded for their ability to operate in the air—not everyone was blessed with a strong sense of balance or stomach. The artillery could not afford to have an observer depositing his breakfast in the aircraft and not being able to conduct a fire mission. Officers were graded as 'A' category (fully orientated, competent, able to fly and enjoyed the job.); 'B' category (suffers from air sickness, but can carry on with mission); and 'C' category (best not taken anywhere near an aircraft). The main reason for this was that the habit of flying in a steady figure of eight or rectangle at 3,000 feet above ground level very rapidly became dangerous with the arrival of AA missile systems in the theatre of operations. Therefore, air observation missions changed to treetop height and the pilot would pitch the aircraft up to approximately 300 feet just before the round landed in the target area, remain at that altitude for just long enough for the observer to see the shot, and dive back down into cover.

During training, candidate air observers were given only three rounds to adjust onto the target—any more than that was a failure. These air OPs and their pilots risked their lives on operations and did not get the recognition they deserved.

Before Operation Askari a small probing operation was launched by a battle group, titled A (Alpha), with a battery from 7 Medium Regiment under the command of Major H. Backeberg in direct support.

Askari

December 1983 saw the sixth large-scale cross-border operation: Askari. The main aim of this operation was to fix the SWAPO–FAPLA forces in Cahama in order to prevent them from interfering with an infantry operation to be launched from Oshakati in SWA. One clear instruction given by Chief of the Army Lieutenant-General Constand Viljoen was that Cahama was not to be attacked unless it was for the express purpose of capturing an SA-8 Air Defence system The question, of course, was where was the SA-8? This was to be done by a feint by two mechanized combat teams from 61 Mechanized Battalion Group supported by the fire from a composite artillery regiment. Why 'composite'? All this means is that the main equipment (guns) differs from battery to battery. What is significant in this operation was the

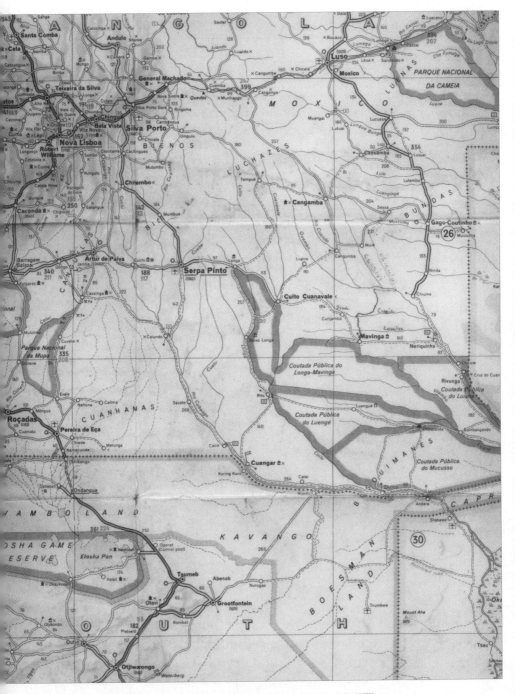

arton: the Michelin map used to navigate to the deployment area. *Source: P.S. Williams*

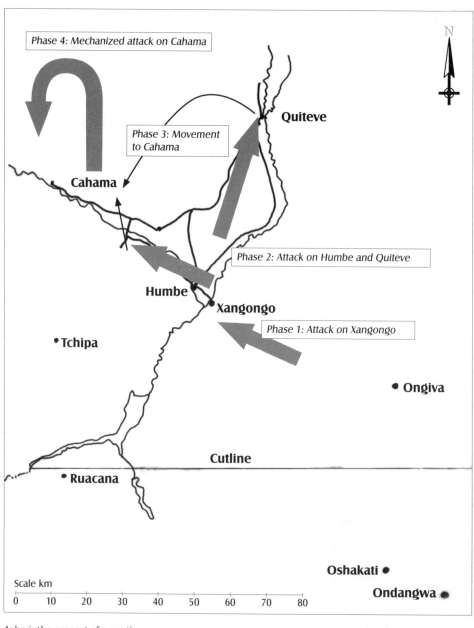

Askari: the concept of operations.

Ruacana: A composite of the base looking east. The runway can be seen on the right. During Operation Hilti (Chapter 11) 14 Artillery Regiment's A Echelon deployed in the bush south (to the right) of the runway. *Photo: A.N. Eckard*

Ruacana: A composite of the base after it had been moved eastward. In the distance MGM Koppie can be seen. By this stage of the war, the guns had fired on numerous occasions and the air threat in this area was negligible, obviating the need for camouflage. *Photo: A.N. Eckard*

Nova Base in 1982, showing the observation tower that was used for base protection. *Photo: A.N. Eckard*

Nova Base: A form of physical training not found in the manuals. It also served to relieve the boredom. *Photo: A.N. Eckard*

Nova Base: Maj Jacob van Heerden and Capt Francois van Eeden seemingly keeping fit. Note the beverage in van Eeden's hand. *Photo: F.J.G. van Eeden*

Nova Base: A very clean-looking base under NFA occupation, June 1981. *Photo: C. Hill*

Nova Base: Life was not all about swimming and videos—a G2 in action outside the base in 1983.
Photo: F.J.G. van Eeden

NATAL FIELD ARTILLERY

NCOS' FORMAL MESS

NOVA BASE

29 th July 1981

· ·

MENU   TOASTS

CALIFORNIA COCKTAIL

HAKE FLORTINE

CHICKEN IN WHITE WINE,   THE STATE PRESIDENT
STUFFED GEMSQUASH,
ROAST POTATOES,
GREEN BEANS

PEARS IN RED WINE

CHEESE & BISCUITS

COFFEE

PORT   THE NFA

· ·
· ·
· · · · · · · · · · · · · · · · · · · ·

Nova Base: NFA NCOs' formal dinner, July 1981. Judging by the state of the
wine glasses, the photo was taken at the start of the function. *Photo: C. Hill*

Nova Base: Typical accommodation in the protected bunkers. Sgt Nothard's gun detachment, NFA, June 1981. *Photo: C. Hill*

Nova Base: A G2 in its gun pit at last light. *Photo: F.J.R. Louw*

Sceptic: Part of S Battery forming up to move to their deployment area. *Photo: SANDF Archive*

Sceptic: Maj Gen Holtzhausen visiting the battery commander's team. Maj Vermaak is seated second left; Sgt Eddie Donaldson crouching right front. *Photo: SANDF Archive*

Sceptic: S Battery ready to leave Oshivello for deployment. *Photo: SANDF Archive*

Sceptic: S Battery in action. *Photo: SANDF Archive*

Sceptic: No. 2 gun firing at maximum elevation. It is not clear why the gun on the left is nearly 90° off line from no. 2 gun. *Photo: SANDF Archive*

Sceptic: No. 6 gun passing through 61 Mechanized Battalion's echelon on the cutline on its way home. *Photo: SANDF Archive*

Sceptic: Unloading ammunition before the first fire mission. *Photo: SANDF Archive*

Protea: Loading an MRL prior to the commencement of the preparatory bombardment on Xangongo.
Photo: O. Zaayman

Protea: An MRL firing the first round of the preparatory bombardment on Xangongo. *Photo: O. Zaayman*

Protea: The MRL Troop fire-control post with its active wind equipment fitted.
Photo: O. Zaayman

An AM3C Bosbok over Owamboland. Note the lack of cover for ground troops operating in this area. The south-western part of Angola was the same. *Photo: SAAF Museum*

A Cessna 185. These aircraft carried artillery observers from the beginning of operations until 1986. Some say these aircraft had more airframe hours than the Harvards that were used for training SAAF pilots. *Photo: SAAF Museum*

A C4M Kudu. Because of the side-by-side seating in the cockpit, it was easier for the air OP to communicate with the pilot, as hand signals could also be used. *Photo: SAAF Museum*

Battery Commanders' course, 1983.

Back row from left: Maj J.H. van der Westhuizen, Maj A.E. van Rhyn, Capt H.J. Steyn, Capt P.S. Williams, Maj B.F. Liebenberg, Maj F.J. van Eeden, Maj W.J. Viljoen, Capt G.H. Swanepoel. Seated from left: Maj E.H.W. Kamffer, Maj J.A. Pretorius, Cmdt J.G. Jacobs (Chief Instructor Gunnery), Col J.A. Laubscher (OC School of Artillery), Maj D.J. de Villiers (instructor), WOII A.E. Hook (Wing Sergeant Major, Gunnery Wing), Maj J. Marais. All these officers were deployed operationally during the period covered by this book. *Photo: School of Artillery*

Protea: The pile of empty 120mm mortar ammunition containers after 43 Battery's first fire mission. *Photo: F.J.R. Louw*

Karton: No. 5 mortar in action. Note how deeply the base plate has embedded itself. In cases like this, even the practice of placing sandbags under the base plate was a wasted effort. *Photo: M. Lowes*

Protea: This baobab tree formed the battery centre for 43 Battery. FAPLA troops infiltrated to a position some 300 metres behind the battery (the high ground to the right in the picture) but were chased away before doing any damage. *Photo: F.J.R. Louw*

Askari: A G4 gun engaging Cahama. *Photo: A.N. Eckard*

Askari: OPO's view of Xangongo from the water tower.
Photo: A.N. Eckard

Askari: The frequently repaired bridge over the Cunene River at
Xangongo. *Photo: A.N. Eckard*

Daisy : A 120mm mortar of S Battery in action.
Photo: F.J.R. Louw

Daisy: G41: G Troop fire control post. Note the addition of a roof to this Buffel, an attempt to make life more comfortable in a vehicle totally unsuitable for the job. *Photo: F.J.R. Louw*

Daisy: No. 2 mortar awaiting fire orders. Although the M5 mortar could be towed it was not feasible in the operational area as the trailer was not rugged enough. Mortars were porteed on the back of gun tractors together with their ammunition.
Photo: F.J.R. Louw

Askari: A G4 at night, ready to fire on Cahama.
Photo: A.N. Eckard

Daisy: The battery commander's, Capt Bernie Pols's, Ratel. *Photo: F.J.R. Louw*

Askari: The remnants of the gun tractor hit by FAPLA fire. *Photo: A.N. Eckard*

Karton: Lt Williams's detailed air photo map used for the engagement on Caiundo.
Source: P.S. Williams

Karton: No. 5 mortar about to fire a white phosphorus round.
Photo: M. Lowes

Askari: Capt Hendricks and 2Lt Eckard relaxing alongside their Ratel between deployments. *Photo: A.N. Eckard*

make-up of the Artillery Regiment. The regimental commander was Faan Bothma, OC of 14 Field Regiment; this composite regiment had three batteries, two of which had equipment never used before in combat. It was made up as:

- A regimental headquarters with 2/Lt André Eckard as adjutant.
- 142 Battery (155mm G4) under Major Ian Johnson. The G4 is an Israeli-designed and -built gun of 155mm calibre, which fires a NATO-standard M56 shell to a maximum range of 24 kilometres. These were modern guns in those days, but had severe limitations— which will be covered later. One of the OP officers was Captain Hannes Hendricks from 4 Artillery Regiment.
- A 127mm MRL troop from 4 SAI Battalion Group under the command of Major Bernie Pols, with Captain George Swanepoel as his OPO. For this operation it was titled R Battery.
- A 140mm G2 battery under Major Jakkie Cilliers. This was 61 Mechanized Battalion's organic battery. It is noteworthy that S Battery had three sets of equipment: G2s, G4s and 120mm M5s. The equipment for Major Johnson's battery came from here. One of the OPOs in this battery was Lieutenant André Schoonwinkel.
- Two Cymbeline radar sets porteed on a Samil 50.

The fourth battery, 72 Battery from 7 Medium Regiment under the command of Captain Ben Coetzee, was placed in direct support of Battle Group D, a Citizen Force group originally earmarked as the reserve. Because of the threat of the SA-8 system in Cahama, no light aircraft were allowed to fly in the area, therefore the gunners would not have an air OPO capability. Furthermore, strike aircraft were restricted to 60,000 feet or higher so no close air support could be provided. What's more, the terrain around Cahama was entirely unsuitable for the deployment of anchor OPOs and, because of the restriction on attacking Cahama no FOOs would be deployed either. To all intents and purposes the guns would be blind. However, to relieve the observation problem it was decided to release the experimental KORV system for operational use.

KORV

The acronym for Klank Oorsprong Rigting Vinder (English: sound origin direction finding), in other words: sound ranging. It was not intended as an all-encompassing sound-ranging system for use by the artillery and was eventually used by the infantry for mortar locating. In short, it was a 'cluster' of three microphones connected to a computer. It had to be orientated into grid north with the microphones in a triangle, equal distances apart and 100 metres away from the central computer. Such a cluster would take an observation team about 10 minutes to bring into action. Two or more clusters could provide fixation of enemy guns firing by plotting the bearings to the sound of the gunfire.

Another first in this operation was the deployment of the Seeker unmanned air vehicle (UAV) system. Chapter 12 deals with a development of this system in more detail. At that stage, the Seeker was a combined artillery–intelligence project that was busy with the problem of air observation. The pilot of the system at that time was Captain Sarel Buijs of 14 Field Regiment, who was assisted by Brian Rowbotham, also of 14 Field Regiment. The Seeker was instructed to deploy at Xangongo, as there was at least a resemblance of an airfield there. Finally, to aid navigation and fixation, the CSIR provided an experimental global positioning system (GPS), which was accurate enough for regimental survey purposes, but it needed 18 torch batteries to fix five points on the ground and took 15 minutes to perform one fixation.

The operational concept was as follows: an attack on Xangongo and exploitation to a point west of Humbe followed by a mechanized attack on Quiteve by 61 Mechanized Battalion (two combat teams) with their organic S Battery (140mm G2) in direct support, reinforced by R Battery 4 SAI Battalion (127mm MRL) in support; a mechanized combat team (61 Mechanized) protecting 142 Battery (155mm G4) to move to a position east of Cahama as flank protection or a blocking force. Only after the attack on Quiteve was a decision made to attack Cahama and capture the SA-8.

The attack on Quiteve

R and S Batteries, following 61 Mechanized, crossed the Cunene River and 'bundu bashed' for a full day directly north to Quiteve. 142 Battery headed westwards along the Xangongo–Cahama road to their assigned deployment area. The next morning, the attack on the SWAPO positions in Quiteve

---

Battle groups and combat teams

A battle group is based on the organization of a battalion and is also referred to as a 'reinforced battalion'. It is commanded by the battalion commander. Typically, a brigade could field three battle groups; at that time the SA Army had three full-time battle groups, namely 61 Mech Battalion, 4 SAI Battalion Group, and 8 SAI Battalion Group. The former two were each supported by an artillery battery, whereas 8 SAI would be supported by a battery made available from Potchefstroom when required.

61 Mech Battalion comprised three mechanized infantry companies, a support company, an armoured car squadron, an artillery battery (G2, and later G5), as well as an AA troop and a field engineer troop. 4 SAI was similarly organized, whereas 8 SAI, being the newest grouping, was not fully formed.

A combat team is based on a company HQ with support from an artillery troop and, when necessary, an armoured car troop. Therefore, a battle group could, in effect, field three combat teams, but one could not rely on the luxury of the direct support (guaranteed fire) from an artillery troop, as there were only two troops in a battery.

---

commenced. S Battery fired the preparatory bombardment and R Battery remained laid on a thickly wooded area northeast of Quiteve in anticipation of cutting off the SWAPO escape route. For this attack the gunners could deploy an air OP, as the aircraft would be well out of SA-8 range. This mission was flown by Major Maarten Schalekamp, who, once in the area, reported that the SWAPO main positions were clear and that the enemy was moving into the wooded area. This prompted the MRLs to engage, but to no effect. The result was the demise of a number of cattle and pigs!

During the consolidation phase to the north of Quiteve, Battle Group Commander Commandant Gert van Zyl's Ratel detonated a mine, but without injury or serious damage to the vehicle. Apparently, this vehicle was a habitual mine detonator.

Not long after this incident and the completion of consolidation, the ground troops were treated to an air display seldom seen before or since. Two Impalas deliberately streaked in at low level to entice the enemy anti-aircraft guns to fire and give away their positions. Two Mirages, flying high, were to identify the AA position and attack. The Mirages could not see the target (possibly because of their altitude) but the artillery's Cymbeline radar sets detected the bursts from the self-destruction shells fired by the AA battery, and thereby determined the battery position. A request to engage the AA battery with MRL fire was turned down by the sector HQ in Oshakati and the MRLs were instead tasked to fire on an area west of Mulondo. This accurate fire mission was observed by the radar section as no OP teams were near enough to do so.

The next move was, once again, a bundu-bashing straight line to a point north of Cahama. In fact, the point was the 20 northing line on the map, identifiable by a cutline running west–east in very close proximity.

Cahama

It is worth describing the terrain around the town of Cahama to understand the next succession of movements. Cahama lies in a hollow with a gentle slope rising towards the north and east. A circular route runs along the top of this high ground and any point along this route falls within sight of Cahama. Therefore, not a good place to be, especially during the day.

S and Q Batteries occupied their positions during the night (on the circle route) and all three batteries fired a harassing fire plan that night. Ineffective counter-bombardment was returned by the FAPLA artillery.

142 Battery remained in position while the rest of the battle group occupied a leaguer area for the handover of command of 61 Mechanized Battalion to Commandant Ep van Lil; a strange time to change command. The decision was then made to withdraw the teeth arms of the battle group to Xangongo to re-plan and reorganize, with the gunner fire units remaining behind. The sector HQ required that a specific target in the Cahama locality be engaged, and 142 Battery was redeployed for this task with the regimental HQ just 500 metres to their east. When 142 Battery fired, the FAPLA artillery returned with counter-bombardment. Bothma explains what happened next:

> The mean point of burst of the enemy fire was about 2 kilometres north of the G4 battery, but one gun—one enemy gun—had a bad no. 3 [layer] and he put a number of hits into the G4 position, setting the gun tractor alight. Fortunately, there were only a few white phosphorus shells on the gun tractor. The heat caused the plugs [fuse

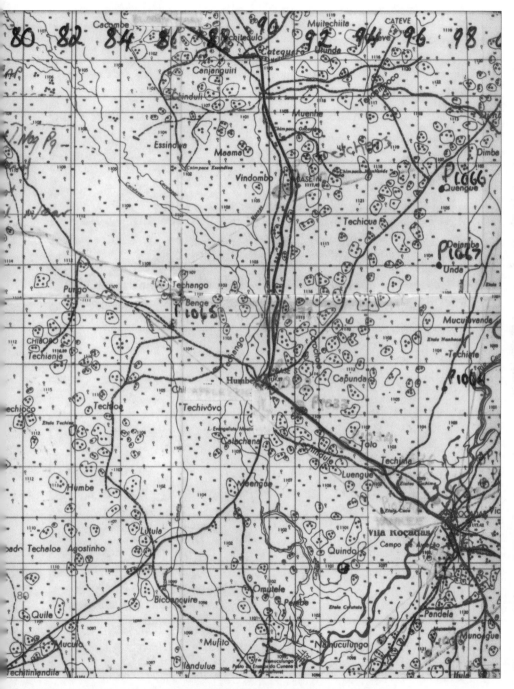

skari: 2/Lt Eckard's battle map. *Source: A.N. Eckard*

Askari: a Samil 20 fire-control post moving through the remnants of Xangongo after the first phase of the operation. *Photo: A.N. Eckard*

Askari: a G4 of 142 Battery in action at Cahama. *Photo: A.N. Eckard*

hole plugs] to shoot out and some of the phosphorus landed on the other vehicles. These vehicles did not burn but could be clearly seen at night as a result of the glow of the phosphorus. Two gunners were burnt and were evacuated to 1 Mil [1 Military Hospital, Pretoria].

To make matters worse, Major Johnson had asked that the burnt-out tractor be left behind. The reply from the sector HQ was 'under no circumstances' would any equipment be left behind. By this time the gun tractor was a twisted wreck with no wheels.

The order to withdraw came and the effort involved in physically dragging the burnt-out gun tractor back to Xangongo is worth recounting. The tractor had to be dragged (not towed) by no fewer than five Ratels forming a train— this on a tarred road. When they arrived at Uie about 18 kilometres down the road, the differentials looked as if they been cut through by a saw. They were completely smooth and flat underneath. Happily, there was a troop of tank transporters waiting for them.

One wonders now how on earth the sector HQ could make such decisions when so far away from the combat zone. This was but one of many examples of the passion for centralized control of deployed forces that was the source of many unrealistic expectations and even more unrealistic decisions.

The near disaster was saved by the very successful artillery strike on Cahama, which silenced the FAPLA guns and achieved the original objectives. The decision was made to attack Cahama from the north, the batteries deploying as shown on the maps on pages 224 and 229. What the gunners did not know, however, was that between the approach route and the deployment areas was an expanse of deep, soft sand.

The gunners were tasked to set up an 'artillery ambush' while en route to their new firing positions. Positions to the east of Cahama were occupied by 142 and Q Batteries, with Captain Hannes Hendriks, the 142 Battery OPO, deploying a KORV cluster farther west towards Cahama. Major Cilliers and his OPO deployed a second KORV at a spot previously surveyed by GPS. In Commandant Bothma's words, 'The old divisional surveyor in me ensured that every point that I fixed with GPS was marked as a bearing picket.'

Midway between the gun positions the third KORV cluster deployed together with the radar section. Fire opened with Q Battery firing three rockets on the same bearing and elevation to adjust the mean point of burst, the radars recording the point as a radar datum point.

142 Battery followed with a harassing fire shoot and immediately drew counter-bombardment: the 'ambush' was set. The three KORV clusters picked up and fixed the origin of the counter-bombardment, passed this on to the radar section who immediately passed a correction (from the radar datum point) to Q Battery. 142 Battery fired a second fire mission to confirm that the FAPLA gunners were still manning their equipment; the subsequent counter-bombardment proved this to be so. With no delay, Q Battery fired a full ripple into the FAPLA gun position—ambush complete.

At this point, the G4s' restricted mobility began to rear its head. These guns were originally designed around a self-propelled chassis / hull and only the few export guns were towed. They were designed for the Sinai Desert where the roads are somewhat harder than those found in Angola. The result was that, firstly, the hydraulic firing platform underneath the gun would catch on the *middelmannetjie* (the ridge in the middle of the road between the tyre tracks), causing extra strain on the gun tractor, which resulted in gun tractor clutches being burnt out. Secondly, the track width of the G4 was narrower than that of either the Ratel or the Samil gun tractor, which meant that the forward wheels on the gun's bogey continually climbed up the middle section of the road, eventually tearing the steel bogey open. This would then cause the forward wheels to act like ploughshares, putting an even greater strain on the gun tractors.

This problem was hastily rectified by changing the guns' four wheels for Unimog wheels, thus giving more ground clearance. A small problem, however: the gun's wheelbase was now wider than the tractor's, which meant that they still couldn't follow in the track left by the tractor and narrow bridges could not be negotiated with any speed above a slow march! The tiffies were hard-pressed to weld damaged bogeys and keep up the required speed. Major Johnson deployed 142 Battery to the northeast of Cahama during the night, placing his mechanized combat team as a protection element in a defensive position between the battery and the target area. This combat team doubled up as the battle group reserve. S Battery deployed to the north of Cahama, with Major Cilliers deploying with a combat team immediately to the west of the tarred road, and the RHQ deployed with 61 Mechanized Battalion Tactical HQ on the tarred road.

At H-Hour, 142 Battery reported 'shot' on the fire plan on the artillery radio net and at that precise moment the left-hand combat team, moving southwards about 3 kilometres west of 142 Battery, reported enemy fire to their left (east) and immediately went over to the attack by wheeling left. At the moment of contact, Major Cilliers reported sighting a company of tanks and quickly commenced firing with S Battery. Battle Group HQ gave the order to break contact and withdraw, whereupon Commandant Bothma instructed 142 Battery to cease firing and move northwards at best speed.

Enter another shortcoming on the G4: the trail spades were not large enough to prevent the trail legs from digging into the soft sand. Major Johnson, standing on his Ratel like a soap-box orator, screamed at his men: 'You do not understand the gravity of this situation!' This was prompted by a lack of haste in digging the guns out of the sand. He did, however, hold his protection element in place while this excavation was going on.

The other two combat teams withdrew with the lightning speed that only mechanized infantry can muster; so much so that Major Cilliers at his forward position and his battery behind him now formed the FLOT with a company of tanks facing him. Fate can sometimes be kind and, happily, on this day, the FAPLA tanks did not move out from the Cahama defences.

The day was still far from over, however. While this northward withdrawal was underway, 61 Mechanized Battalion's echelon was formed up, bumper to bumper, ready to move forward to replenish their combat teams. The thick sand in the area dictated that these vehicles would be road-bound at that time.

By this stage the withdrawing combat teams had arrived on the scene, clogging all movement. Finally, 142 Battery arrived after having dug themselves out of the sand, only to have to work their way through this traffic jam to their new position.

To the north of this traffic jam was a small hill or outcrop. To make the shambles worse, a BM21 started firing into the traffic from the north, and accurately at that. Lady Luck once again made her appearance—the BM21 rockets' fuses were set on delay, making the ammunition explode under the ground and, therefore, ineffectively. There was no damage or injury caused. While this was going on, Commandant Bothma and Lieutenant Eckard climbed a small outcrop to see the BM21; this was unsuccessful and, as it was, the BM21 was out of range of the G4s at that time. Shortly afterwards, the guns of 142 Battery arrived and Commandant Bothma and Eckard took turns to talk the gun tractor drivers through the thick sand and the stationary logistics convoy. Two Impalas appeared out of the east and turned northwards up the tarred road: no more trouble from the BM21 after that.

The SAAF planned to bomb Cahama on the night of 24/25 December. The problem, however, was how to identify targets from a safe altitude (to avoid SA-8 missiles) at night. To get round this the gunners offered to mark the four corners of the target area with white phosphorus (WP) shells. This was successful; the only drawback was that the WP burnt out very quickly.

At the last minute, during the planning for Askari, the planners needed to create a diversion, or draw the attention of SWAPO and FAPLA away from the main attack in the western theatre. The town of Caiundo (17-40-00 E; 15-45-00 S) lay in 32 Battalion's area of responsibility and over time had become increasingly active, in that SWAPO and FAPLA were developing a logistics base there.

Captain Pieter Williams found himself, once again, in Katima Mulilo attempting to keep himself and his troops busy. Relief came in the form of a call to the sector commander's office where Captain Williams was instructed to assemble one medium troop, move to Rundu and report to Colonel 'Falcon' Ferreira, the officer commanding 32 Battalion. In Captain Williams's words: 'The worst part of this mobilization was deciding who was to stay behind at Nova, and then to have to break the news to them. There was no shortage of volunteers.' On arrival in Rundu, the troop was instructed to leave their medium guns and take over four 120mm mortars, these having been moved up from Grootfontein for the operation. Furthermore, the troop was ordered to move northwards and meet Colonel Ferreira for orders at a point approximately 10 kilometres southwest of Caiundo. The troop immediately took to the road and travelled alongside the Kavango River through Savate, eventually turning left and swinging around to meet up with 32 Battalion tactical HQ. Captain Williams: 'We arrived one hour late.' No mean feat for a short-notice mobilization and a 300-kilometre trek, mostly in the dark without the benefit of navigation equipment.

The objective of this diversion was to draw SWAPO and FAPLA command's attention away from Cahama while Askari was underway. The gunners fired a number of harassing fire tasks on Caiundo at maximum range with rocket-assisted bombs—a range of 12,000 metres. Just after Christmas, the gunners set another 'artillery ambush'. At this time, the Seeker remotely piloted vehicle (RPV) team arrived at Xangongo airfield and immediately went into action. The battle group (minus 142 Battery, who remained in action) withdrew to Xangongo to regroup for the second attack on Cahama. Commandant Bothma relates a story about his Ratel driver:

It was interesting that, previously, we [had] crossed the engineers' bridge at night every time. This time we arrived there in daylight, and my Ratel driver—seeing it for the first time—was too scared to cross it.

Battle Group D had moved in towards Cuvelai by now and Q Battery was detached to support them.

During this period, the sector HQ instructed the battle group that the SA-8 (deployed southeast of the Cahama defences) must be captured, and captured intact at that. The new plan was to attack from the southwest—presumably to capture the SA-8 as early in the attack as possible.

142 Battery remained in position, and Captain Hendriks deployed as FOO with one of the assaulting combat teams; Lieutenant André Schoonwinkel from S Battery was attached to the second combat team.

Major Cilliers deployed with the battle group HQ, and Bothma joined up with the Seeker team at their control centre at Xangongo. At this time, the Seeker was not yet ready for operations, but was deployed out of necessity because of the SA-8 threat. As with all acquisition projects, the bulk of the manpower in that team was civilians and, therefore, not legally allowed in the operational theatre. Imagine the situation should one of them have been killed or taken prisoner.

Seeker was tasked, firstly, to find the SA-8, and, secondly, to help direct artillery fire (actually, to keep the gunners' fire away from the SA-8!) A superimposed task was to navigate the assault force straight into the SA 8 position.

Unknowingly, the battle group commander decided to hold a final order group on an enemy defensive fire target and, on stopping at this point, drew effective artillery fire. The offending battery was seen by Seeker, and 142 Battery went on to deliver counter-bombardment, the effect of which could not be determined because, at the same time, the Seeker saw the SA-8 firing a missile that was heading straight for the Seeker.

Commandant Bothma takes up the story:

> . . . strange to watch the screen and see the missile streaking towards the Seeker—a person forgets that although you are sitting many kilometres away you still feel as though you are about to be hit. Sarel [Captain Buijs] waited until precisely the right moment and dived the Seeker away. The missile destroyed itself without damage to our equipment.

A second missile was fired, produced smoke, but never left the launcher; a third missile, close enough to the RPV to detonate its warhead, damaged the aircraft. Captain Buijs managed to bring the aircraft safely back to Xangongo where it was found that the fuel tank had been ruptured, luckily from above, therefore not causing any leaks. The damage was reported to battle group HQ and the Seeker team withdrew. By this time, the assault force was breaking contact at Cahama, as they could not affect a break-in.

FAPLA radio messages were intercepted shortly after the attack in which a 'crazy Cessna pilot' was mentioned. 61 Mechanized Battalion with Major

Cilliers's S Battery now moved on to join up with Battle Group D for the assault on Cuvelai and 142 Battery remained in the Xangongo area to protect the bridge over the Cunene River. Commandant Bothma remained at Xangongo where his team joined up with the newly arrived 82 Brigade HQ. Here his biggest task was to ensure that Puma helicopter loads of G2 ammunition were lifted forward until such time that the ammunition convoy could reach the deployed S Battery.At that time, the 127mm multiple rocket launcher system had not been tested or accepted for service, and this was to cause a catastrophic failure at Cuvelai. One launcher, by accident, fired two rockets through its crew compartment. The MRL was designed with an electronic safety cut-out to prevent such accidental firing when travelling; this incident prompted further development and the situation never occurred again.

Some more on the G4s

When the first batch of G4 guns arrived in South Africa, Captain Piet Uys was appointed as the project leader to integrate the guns into the existing artillery arsenal. One of the first steps taken was to present a special gunnery course; all the instructors, i.e. officers, warrant officers and NCOs, participated. This course took place at the School of Artillery in Potchefstroom. The training staff was provided by the Israeli Army. It was a pleasant experience for all of these students to be ordinary gunners again and to become familiarized with a brand-new piece of equipment.

An incident remarkable enough to note occurred when the gun crews were expected to occupy a gun position in full darkness. In artillery jargon this is called a 'night occupation'. The gun position for the night occupation was prepared in daylight, on the General de la Rey Firing Range. When it was completely dark, the order was given to occupy the gun position.

The move towards the position was also completed in darkness and all went well. The gunners brought the guns into action, and did all the necessary technical work to prepare the guns for firing. The complete silence was suddenly broken by the senior Israeli instructor when he shouted at the top of his voice:

Please, gentlemen, can you stop what you are doing for a moment. I want to tell you something! I have been an artillery officer during my whole career and I have been through two wars in the Middle East. This night occupation that you are now doing is the best I have ever seen. I have never heard a night occupation so quietly done. The discipline is remarkable. Thank you, you can carry on!

Another design problem with the G4 was the breech. It was designed and built with a horizontal sliding breech—similar to that on a quick-firing gun (a gun that uses a metal cartridge case), rather than on a breech-loading gun (a gun that uses a bagged charge). This breech mechanism was fitted with a high-strength steel ring, which, on firing, would expand, thus sealing the hot propellant gas inside the chamber.

However, the tolerances were so fine that a grain of sand (of which there is great deal in southern Africa) wedged between this ring and the breech opening would cause a leak through which the hot gas passed—not unlike the effect of a shaped charge. The result was that the breech had to be cleaned between each round, which consequently affected the rate of fire dramatically.

This was the first and last time that the G4s were ever used in combat. They were soon replaced by the G5.142 Battery arrived back in Potchefstroom on 20 January 1984.

Cuvelai

Battle Group Delta was formed under Commandant Faan Greyling to test the defences of the town of Cuvelai. To support this, 7 Medium Regiment were tasked to mobilize a battery, this being 71 Battery under the command of Captain Coetzee. In addition to Captain Coetzee, 7 Medium Regiment's battery comprised the following leader element:

- OPOs: Captains Mike Christie and Fielies Prinsloo
- BPO: Lieutenant Niel Wiid
- A/BPO: Second Lieutenant Mark House

- GPOs   Lieutenants Mike Fish and John Harris
- TPOs   2/Lts Gordon Chilvers and Richard Harris
- BSM: WOII Fouché
- TSM: Staff Sergeant de Lange

Lieutenant Wiid picks up the story:

In the early stages of Askari, 7 Medium conducted probes to test the defences of and engage registered targets in Cuvelai. During this period there were no OPOs deployed and the guns often formed the FLOT for the most part of what was an artillery duel.

Cuvelai was well defended, and, as such, returned fire with interest and often initiated the exchange of fire. There were an estimated 6,000 FAPLA soldiers and Soviet officers defending Cuvelai with an unknown number of SWAPO.

At some stage, 7 Medium retreated with Delta to regroup. A small group supported by a 7 Medium contingent was rerouted to Mulondo where there was a short but fierce exchange of artillery fire and an equally quick withdrawal. There were 107 enemy casualties plus a number of tanks destroyed during this battle.

On rejoining the battle group, a troop of Ratel 90s and a G2 battery of national servicemen [S Battery, 61 Mechanized] joined the battle group for the final assault on Cuvelai. Both batteries were placed under 7 Medium's BPO.

7 Medium advanced with the engagement force to entice the enemy with a separate force that would perform a flanking movement once the enemy was engaged.

Not far from Cuvelai the advance force drew accurate mortar fire. 7 Medium pulled out of the convoy and deployed to provide support fire. The advance force drove into FAPLA's 11 Brigade, which resulted in a three-day battle where Delta suffered a number of casualties, including two gunners of 7 Medium wounded. 7 Medium lost a gun tractor and a Samil 20 out of action due to shrapnel from 122mm rockets. During this battle a company of Soviet tanks joined the attack on Delta. The entire tank company was destroyed. When it finally fell, Delta [including 7 Medium] took occupation of, and began the clean-up operations in, Cuvelai.

As the airstrip was destroyed by artillery fire Delta had to be resupplied by an air drop.

There was a large number of enemy weapons and vehicles captured, including a SAM-9 surface-to-air missile system and AGS-17 grenade launchers, both significant firsts.

When Delta finally withdrew from Cuvelai, they found that FAPLA had blown the bridge representing the only way home. A mammoth effort resulted in the bridge being rebuilt using logs cut from surrounding trees.

Chapter 9

Operations Wallpaper and Alpha Centauri: big results

During the latter half of 1985, FAPLA developed and deployed its forces in the east and southeast of Angola in order to threaten UNITA's main base at Jamba. This deployment was the shape of things to come, as it was a miniature version of bigger operations later. FAPLA had occupied the town of Luau in the Cazombo region and was threatening Mavinga in the southeast, a strategic town on the advance to Jamba.

Operation Wallpaper was planned to support UNITA for the capture of the town of Luau before 4 September 1985. The South African component would be limited to an artillery and anti-aircraft element to support the UNITA battalions, of which there were between five and eight, earmarked for the attack. In August, while the negotiations between the SADF and UNITA were underway, FAPLA forces launched an offensive with their 14, 21 and 63 Brigades from Luau and Lucano to capture and occupy the Cazombo salient. By the end of the month, UNITA were losing control of Cazombo and help was now critical.

This time there was sufficient early warning for the gunners to prepare for operations. No doubt because of the distance of the intended theatre from the SWA border, and the attendant logistics problems, it was decided that the artillery effort would comprise two 127mm MRLs under the command of Major Jakkie Cilliers (School of Artillery) and one 120mm mortar advisory / liaison team, being Major Theuns Coetzee (School of Artillery) and Lieutenant Leon Phillipson (seconded to Chief of Staff Intelligence at that time). The latter team was placed to integrate the 120mm mortar fire of UNITA with that of the 127mm

MRLs during the attack. Major Coetzee and Lieutenant Phillipson both underwent a short conversion course on the Soviet M1943 mortar in preparation for this operation. The manpower situation in the South African Artillery was so critical at that stage that the ordnance maintenance team at the School of Artillery was mobilized to provide crews and the various wings tasked to provide the leader element and technical personnel. This small, understrength fire unit comprised:

- Commander: Major Jakkie Cilliers with a Land Rover driven by Bombardier P. Lombard.
- MRL crews: Lance-Bombardiers P. Rossouw and G.P. van Zyl. (Note that an MRL was supposed to have a crew of two, not one each)
- Fire-control officer / troop position officer: Lieutenant W. Visser (who would travel in one of the MRLs)
- Troop sergeant-major / technical assistant sergeant: Lieutenant M.K. van der Watt (who would travel in the other MRL).

Technical equipment was kept to the minimum by limiting it to the basic meteorological equipment and an HP41-C programmable calculator for launcher firing data.

The 'troop' left by road for Waterkloof on 29 August, where they joined up with Major Coetzee's team and a Special Forces component of six Milan anti-tank teams under the command of Major D. Fourie. Later that afternoon, the gunners assembled at Fort Foot in Rundu to change into green uniforms and receive AK-47 rifles before flying on to Cazombo.

At a point some 10 kilometres south-southwest of Cazombo they joined up with the South African Tactical HQ and two SA-9 anti-aircraft teams.

By 30 August, two of FAPLA's brigades (14 and 21) had moved another 70 kilometres southwards and were faced by three UNITA battalions in the area. FAPLA air activity had increased and the first aircraft made their appearance at 16h00 on the afternoon of 30 August. The next day, the little South African force left its position at 18h00, crossing the Zambezi River at Cazombo by pont to move another 60 kilometres farther to the front.

The battle plan for the South African gunners was for the observer (Major Cilliers) to infiltrate the target area to confirm the accuracy of the MRL fire and to adjust the 120mm mortar fire. One hundred and forty-four rounds of airburst-fused rockets would be fired (six ripples per launcher) and the empty wooden ammunition boxes and associated litter burnt after the fire missions.

The launchers were loaded on 1 September and occupied their firing position; the observer team crossed the Luvua River and infiltrated during the night of 2/3 September, and joined up with the allied forces. During the day of 3 September the MRLs were in action, deployed on a road, and fired three adjusting rockets. The night was quiet, and during the morning of 4 September 1985 the first ripple of 48 rounds was fired, followed by an immediate move southwards to the Zambezi River.

This nightly routine continued until the night of 6/7 September when the last three ripples were fired before they withdrew to the pont on the Zambezi River.

The effect of this fire was the loss of a FAPLA brigade commander; 111 others were killed, untold were wounded and there was an eight-day delay in movement.

It turned out that this movement of FAPLA towards Cazombo was, in fact, a feint to mask the main advance to Mavinga. Here they had deployed four brigades supported by six BM14 and two BM21 MRLs, as well as twelve 120mm mortars and numerous helicopters and attack aircraft.

The little 'troop' flew in to Mavinga airfield during the night of 9 September to find the situation confused and 'very vague'. Within a day, they had deployed and fired another three ripples at the advancing brigades. The next night saw another ripple being fired in an attempt to slow the advance.

During this period, the scope of the FAPLA advance had been appreciated and the decision was made to reinforce the gunners' capabilities, resulting in the arrival of another two MRLs—and another Land Rover—under the command of Captain Willem van Ryneveld during the night of 14/15 September. By now, MRL ammunition was pouring in, all of it airlifted by C-130 into Mavinga. That same night, FAPLA crossed the Lomba River and immediately ran into three ripples of MRL fire and a SAAF air attack, losing 24 killed and 67 wounded. During a fire mission on the night of 25 September, Lance-Bombardier Gideon van Zyl's MRL set the undergrowth alight (caused by the backblast of the rockets). Realizing the danger that this could create, he dismounted and ran to the back of the launcher to raise the trail legs so as to move the MRL out of the way. While trying to start the engine, the tyres and fuel lines combusted. Despite this, Lance-Bombardier van Zyl managed to drive the MRL out of the burning grass, singeing his hair and beard in the process. Once out of the danger area, the fire on the MRL was extinguished. For his actions that night van Zyl was awarded the Honoris Crux.

By 26 September, the FAPLA 7, 8 and 13 Brigades were reported moving westwards in a possible attempt to outflank UNITA and then move onwards to Mavinga. Three days later, these brigades reported ready to move, but also requested authority to destroy unserviceable vehicles, the higher command duly approving this destruction. In the early afternoon of 29 September, 8 and 13 Brigades reported that their vehicles were 'in bad condition', the main problem being radiators and a lack of water. Furthermore, they reported that they could not destroy their vehicles, as they had nothing to destroy them with! At the same time, 7 Brigade reported coming under fire from 81 and 120mm mortars. And again that afternoon, 8 Brigade reported that they were being pushed back by UNITA.

During the night of 29 September, the SAAF delivered three C-130 loads of artillery ammunition to Mavinga—336 rockets and 250 cases of 120mm mortar bombs. This took place in the background while the MRL troops fired on two targets to draw FAPLA fire. The next afternoon at 17h00, the MRLs, in conjunction with the SAAF Mirage F1AZs, managed to reduce 7 Brigade's troop strength by 87 killed and 41 wounded, and shortly afterwards the engagement was repeated on 8 Brigade, this time in conjunction with Impala Mk IIs, causing 31 killed and 42 wounded. By the early evening, 13 Brigade reported that they could not move as a result of vehicle serviceability. At 20h00, the MRLs, in a pre-planned fire mission, engaged 8 Brigade, but the fire had to be stopped because the rounds were bursting too close to the deployed UNITA forces: UNITA had given the wrong target co-ordinates.

The result of this aggressive action was that, by 22h00 on the night of 30 September, FAPLA ordered 7, 25, 8 and 13 Brigades to withdraw and the Soviet advisers in 13 Brigade to be airlifted out on 1 October. In addition to the 18 officer casualties, FAPLA also reported equipment losses, these being two URAL trucks, one T-54 tank and one burnt out ammunition vehicle.

The night of 1 October saw the FAPLA brigades moving in a northwesterly direction in order to cross the Lomba River. The casualties reported by them at that point amounted to 438.

During this active period, the MRL troop tried unsuccessfully to deploy and fire by day, but was hampered by poor intelligence, the Angolan air superiority and strong winds, which affected the accuracy of the rocket fire. At this time, the Angolan Air Force started dropping incendiary bombs, setting the bush alight to remove the natural cover and expose the MRLs. This was followed by recce teams infiltrating between UNITA lines. It was later determined that FAPLA did find that troop, but why they never exploited the situation remains a mystery.

MRL ammunition was, once again, running low and another 167 rockets were delivered to Mavinga by the ever-busy C-130s.

The nightly bombardments continued until 3 October 1985, by which time the decision had been made to withdraw the MRLs. This was carried out the next day at 17h00 when the gunners, their four MRLs and two Land Rovers were airlifted out of Mavinga.

Some interesting statistics emerged from the Mavinga fire missions:

- 37 fire missions were fired, during which 3,240 rockets were consumed.
- The South African Air Force flew in 298 tonnes of artillery ammunition.
- 1,500 FAPLA were killed or wounded (there were more, but the rest were attributed to SAAF strikes and infantry fire).
- 71 vehicles were either destroyed or damaged.
- One Mi-25 helicopter was destroyed on the ground.

It was during this operation that the South African 127mm MRL earned the nickname 'Shindungu' (red-hot chilli) after the effect it had on vehicles and troops on the ground.

This operation finally proved that the judicious use of rockets in the right hands could be the deciding factor in a defensive battle.

Major Cilliers was awarded the Southern Cross medal for his actions during this operation.

During this time, the two gunner officers seconded to UNITA, Major Coetzee and Lieutenant Phillipson, were somehow led into a FAPLA company ambush while withdrawing to Cazombo. On 15 September, their Landcruiser was hit by RPG-7 fire, stopping the vehicle and killing the doctor that was on board with them. Both wounded, they crawled out and managed to take cover and evade the FAPLA force for three days, eventually being extricated by elements of 32 Battalion under the command of Colonel Eddie Viljoen. Not long after this incident, Major Coetzee related this story to the author and the most profound words of his narrative were: 'What they taught us in basic training was right—Dash, Down, Crawl, Observe, Sights, Fire.' It was that simple drill that saved their lives. These two artillery officers were awarded the Honoris Crux for bravery under fire.

The battles were not over yet, however, as 16 Brigade was perceived to be a threat to the UNITA forces. At that stage their intentions were not clear, and on 15 October the SADF planners were considering redeploying the MRLs as a precaution.

This planning came to fruition when, on 22 December 1985, Major Holtzhausen, Lieutenant Bouwer, WOI Claassen, Sergeants F.S. Botha, Pretorius and George Sinclair (TSC), Lance-Bombardiers Kruger, Dawson and Heyns, and Gunners Goewerden, T.A. Murray, van Wyk and de Quintal left 14 Field Regiment for Rundu for deployment in the Sector 20 area.

This little group formed an MRL troop that stopped 16 Brigade's activities by firing at least seven ripples (672 rockets) into that partially deployed formation. Again, all these rounds were fired at night, each night in a different position. This group had returned home by 26 January 1986.

In February 1986, the decision was made to reinforce 32 Battalion with a 'support group' comprising an anti-tank squadron (Ratel 90mm and ZT3), an MRL Battery and an AA troop (20mm Ystervark). The first elements arrived at Buffalo Base in March. In April, the MRL Battery (P Battery), under command of Major Clive Wilsworth, started training and experimenting with alternative ways of deploying. Up until that time the Unimog-based MRL had very little bush protection, and damage to radiators and power-steering systems were causing equipment availability problems. So during that initial deployment at 32 Battalion the MRLs were fitted with a heavy steel 'basket' in front of the radiator. This attachment also served as a place for the crew to store their personal kit and a spade pick. Before that modification, the MRL was already 800 kilograms overweight; the basket now took the excess weight to 1,100 kilograms when fully loaded. In July that year, Major Pierre Franken was permanently transferred as battery commander.

Arrival of the G5

On 18 April 1983, 143 Battery departed their lines at 14 Field Regiment for Middelburg (Transvaal) where they attached to 4 SAI Battalion Group as Q Battery. The first battery commander was Major Bernie Pols, with Captain George 'Swannie' Swanepoel as his BPO, WOII Giep Hill the BSM, and S/Sgts Willem van Dyk and Hannes Myburgh the two TSMs.

At that time, Q Battery was a name with a small leader element only, the new equipment being delivered to Potchefstroom. Therefore, Major Pols and the rest of the Q Battery leader group travelled to Potchefstroom for conversion onto the G5, as this training could not be done in Middelburg because of the limited size of the firing range (it was only just large enough to accommodate the range of the 81mm mortar—5,000 metres). Q Battery was finally commissioned in September 1983 by 142 Battery of 14 Field.

Alpha Centauri was yet another attempt (successful) at stopping the latest FAPLA move on Jamba. In August 1986, a two-battery regiment (the ad hoc title was 32 Artillery Group) managed to put a stop to their antics where it hurt most: in Cuito Cuanavale.

By this time, the full-time component of the South African Artillery looked like this:

- 4 Artillery Regiment in Potchefstroom with:
  - 41 Battery (120mm mortar)
  - 42 Battery (155mm G5)
  - 44 Battery (127mm MRL)
  - 1 Medium Battery (155mm G5)
- 14 Artillery Regiment in Potchefstroom with:
  - 141 Battery (120mm mortar)
  - 142 Battery (155mm G5)
  - 143 Battery (127mm MRL)
  - 144 Battery (support)
  - 2 Medium Battery (155mm G5)
- School Of Artillery provided the meteorological sections
- Q Battery (155mm G5) at 4 SAI Battalion Group in Middelburg
- S Battery (155mm G5) at 61 Mechanized Battalion Group in Oshivello
- P Battery (127mm MRL) at 32 Battalion in Buffalo Base
- 43 Battery (140mm G2) at Walvis Bay

In June 1986, planning had already started at Army HQ for an operation, called variously Camel and Suiderkruis, whose aim was for 32 Battalion and UNITA to capture Cuito Cuanavale. This was to be a night operation supported by an artillery regiment of three batteries, one each of 140mm G2, 120mm M5 and 127mm MRL.

The objective was to have the capture completed by 22 July. At that time, FAPLA's 25 and 13 Brigades were deployed in and around Cuito Cuanavale, with 8 and 16 Brigades alternately protecting the vital supply convoys on the Menongue–Cuito Cuanavale road and to the east of the latter town. During a briefing to the chief of the army later in June, the decision was made to add a 155mm G5 battery to this regiment to provide the gunners with the much-needed range and weight of fire.

Q Battery mobilized in Middelburg in July 1986 and moved by road to 32 Battalion's base at Buffalo on the western edge of the Caprivi Strip. This arrival caused a major uplift in morale for all the South African troops in the base at that time, as it was the first battery to be seen with brand-new equipment and, moreover, it was fully equipped. The battery marched in with the following personnel:

- Battery commander: Maj G.H.F. Swanepoel
- BPO: Lt J.C. Kriek
- **C Troop**
- Troop commander team:
  > Lt G.J. Andrew
  > Gnrs T.O. Miles, A.J. Kotze, M.S. Simpson
- Troop position officer team:
  > 2/Lt Valjalo
  > Bdr L. Ras
  > Gnrs A.J. Corrans, J.L. Ingram, M.J. Scheepers
- Fire-control post:
  > 2/Lt C.P. Albertyn
  > L/Bdr J.P. Fritz
  > Gnrs D.R. Evans, S.N. Ramsay, D.G. White
- Gun no. 1:
  > No. 1: Bdr B.G. van den Berg
  > No. 2: Gnr W.A. Very
  > No. 3: Gnr E.G. Opperman
  > No. 4: Gnr P.L. Vorster
  > No. 5: Gnr A. Simmenhoff
  > No. 6: Gnr C. Langlands
  > No. 7: Gnr K.H. Taka'cs
  > No. 8: L/Bdr J.H. Olivier
  > Driver: Gnr S.H. Kaiser
- Gun no. 2:
  > No. 1: Bdr J.H. Booyse
  > No. 2: Gnr R. Olivier
  > No. 3: Gnr J.H. Hauser
  > No. 4: Gnr J.A. Venter
  > No. 5: Gnr J.G. van der Schyff
  > No. 7: Gnr P.J. Vermeulen
  > No. 8: L/Bdr G.D. Hastie
  > Driver: Gnr J.W. Harmse

- Gun no. 3:

    No. 1: Bdr G.B. Webster

    No. 2: Gnr Britz

    No. 3: Gnr W.E. Brooker

    No. 4: Gnr Basson

    No. 5: Gnr Havenga

    No. 6: Gnr Dodgson

    No. 7: Gnr Jacobs

    No. 8: L/Bdr Grobler

    Driver: Gnr Manser

- Gun no. 4:

    No. 1: Bdr A.N. Taylor

    No. 2: Gnr G.S. Russon

    No. 3: Gnr O. de Wet

    No. 4: Gnr P.E. Nortje

    No. 5: Gnr N. Marits

    No. 6: Gnr A.A. Wright

    No. 7: Gnr M.J. Pedzinski

    No. 8: Gnr J.L. Kemp

    Driver: Gnr W.J. Pieterse

- **D Troop**
- Troop commander team:

    Lt K. Ashley

    Gnrs L. Gorvett, P.D. Hyde, R.L. Menezez

- Troop position officer team:

    2/Lt J.H.C. Hattingh

    Bdr R. Drotsky

    Gnrs Vorster, Cohen, P. van der Merwe

- Fire-control post:

    2/Lt A. Davies

    L/Bdr P.W. Roos

    Gnrs F.W. Kock, H.O.B. Smith, P.J. Hardy

- Gun no. 5:

  No. 1: Bdr M.J. Wilters

  No. 2: Gnr P.H. Bush

  No. 3: Gnr H.L. Bronkhorst

  No. 4: Gnr G. Cloete

  No. 5: Gnr D. Vorstmass

  No. 6: Gnr M.J. Gale

  No. 7: Gnr D.V. Brown

  No. 8: L/Bdr P.R. de Beer

  Driver: Gnr R.C. Kidwell

- Gun no. 6:

  No. 1: Bdr C.A. Pote

  No. 2: Gnr S.W. Meintjies

  No. 3: Gnr G.D.P. Roy

  No. 4: Gnr C.F. Viljoen

  No. 5: Gnr P.J.S. van der Merwe

  No. 6: Gnr R.G. Andrew

  No. 8: L/Bdr H.C. Nicholson

  Driver: Gnr T. Mostert

- Gun no. 7:

  No. 1: Bdr T. Paetzold

  No. 2: Gnr W. Venter

  No. 3: Gnr D.M. Grobbelaar

  No. 4: Gnr J.J. Snyman

  No. 5: Gnr C.J. Opperman

  No. 6: Gnr H.Z.N. van Deventer

  No. 7: Gnr A.C. Vilonel

  No. 8: Gnr A. Bezuidenhout

- Gun no. 8:

  No. 1: Bdr E. Bester

  No. 2: Gnr W.J.G. Steynberg

  No. 3: Gnr A.O. Johnsen

No. 4: Gnr P.P. Badenhorst

No. 5: Gnr J. Kruis

No. 6: Gnr D.A. Smith

No. 7: Gnr J.D.R. Naudé

No. 8: L/Bdr J.W. Lovell

Driver: Gnr W. de Jager

In the last week of July, the decision was made not to commit 32 Battalion, but instead to support and advise UNITA's 13 battalions earmarked for the task. The decision was also made to limit the South African Artillery support to two batteries. The operation would be code-named Alpha Centauri. On 31 July 1986, Colonel Koos Laubscher, Officer Commanding the School of Artillery, had formed an understrength artillery regiment at 32 Battalion's base at Buffalo in readiness for Alpha Centauri. The regiment (aka 32 Artillery Group) comprised:

- A tactical HQ under Colonel Laubscher with Major Willem van Ryneveld as the fire support co-ordination officer
- Commandant Div de Villiers, the 2IC, responsible for the deployment of the blunt end and the echelon
- WOI Cas Badenhorst, the RSM / echelon commander
- P Battery (127mm MRL), 32 Battalion under Major Pierre Franken
- Q Battery (155mm G5), 4 SAI under Major George Swanepoel
- The artillery observers were not specifically assigned to the batteries, but would call for fire from whichever fire unit was allocated by the artillery tactical HQ. Lieutenant Jacques de Villiers from P Battery was one of the observers.

It is important to note that the South Africans appreciated that an attack of this nature against well-defended positions would require a conventional assault—a type of warfare that UNITA was neither trained nor equipped for. Therefore, the gunners would have to pull out all the stops. Furthermore, the decision to limit the artillery effort to G5 and MRL fire support created a

6. MVL BESTOKINGSPROFORMA (HP 41 CV) 7 Sept.
H uur. 02h00.

PASSIEWE MET

1. Stasie hoogte .... .1160 .. m
2. Lugdruk .... 875 .. mb
3. Droëboltemp. .... 20 .. °C
4. Natboltemp. .... 16,5 .. °C
5. Relatiewe Vogtigheid .... 70 .. %
6. Virtuele temp. .... 22,2 .. °C

BALLISTIESE TEMP | 1025 | %
BALLISTIESE DIGTHEID | 84,9 | %

025
849

LYN no	TYD min'sek	AZIM ↗	ELEV ↗	SPD knope	RIGTING ↗
00	0'00				
01	0'39				
02	1'58				
03	3'16			4	010
04	4'56				
05	6'33		-		
06	9'50				
07	13'07				
08	16'23				

AKTIEWE MET

1. Drift. 28,5 _ m   Anem Spd 0 _ _ _ X 0,593
2. D.Dir 0100 _ ↗   = 0 _ _ _
                          Anem Dir 0100 _ _ ↗

Tkn 0.044 .. N 260 .. hte 1150
Tp 0.158 .. N 270 .. hte 1160
Verskil hte _ _ _ _ _

Ring _ 105 _
A/S + NR _ 10 _
Lad. temp. _ 24,7
Met lyn no _ _ 6 _
Met lyn no _ 84
Rotasie v Aarde Aft. _ +15
Rotasie v Aarde Plg. _ +0,3

BRG 4711 ↗   RNGLI 444m
ERNG 11434m
E. RNG2 10126m
RNG 10372 m
BRG 4733 ↗   EL 389,7 ↗

6/9 21h00 Tkn 038 266
6/9 23h00 Tkn 042 264
7/9 02h00 Tkn 044 260

FEC .-96 ↗
FBC -0,2 ↗

3 ripples

BRG | 4745 ↗ | EL | 389 | ↗ |

Wallpaper: a rough-and-ready shooting pro forma. Note the times of the fire missions, bottom left. *Source: J.K. Cilliers*

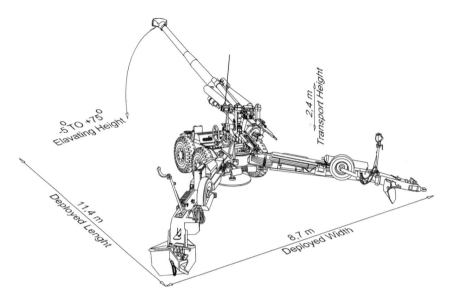

Project Boas: A technical illustration of G5 Mk II with the overall dimensions.
Illustration: Denel Land Systems

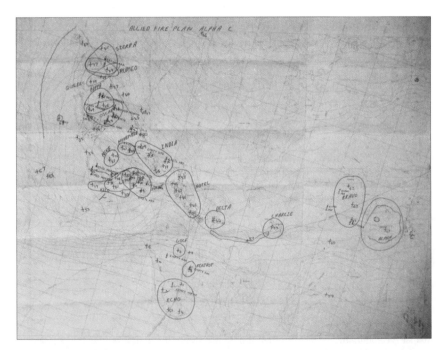

Alpha Centauri: Major Swanepoel's map of the artillery targets for the operation. Note how they have been grouped into smaller, manageable clusters. The map is a trace taken from an air photo. *Map: G.H.F. Swanepoel*

serious gap in the provision of close fire support for the attacking infantry. The G5—and even more so, the MRL—was not suited to provide the close fire support needed. The plan, therefore, was for 32 Artillery Group to provide preparatory bombardments up to a point where UNITA's mortars (120 and 81mm) would take over and fire the close fire support missions, by which time the gunners would fire on deep targets. Even if UNITA did not succeed in their attack, at least the destructive effect on FAPLA would slow down an attempt at advancing on the UNITA headquarters at Jamba in 1986.

These decisions were to bring about a dramatic increase in the amount of ammunition required by the gunners, and the consequent increase in logistics support (additional vehicles, freight aircraft, technical support, etc.). Furthermore, the G5 base bleed ammunition, which gave the G5s the ability to extend their range beyond 30 kilometres, was not yet qualified for operational use. The risks of this were considered, and finally the green light was given for the use of this new ammunition together with the new electronic proximity fuses to provide the airburst capability.

The vast number of targets identified from air photos were grouped into some 19 target areas to reduce complexity in fire planning and so that these target areas represented the shape, or footprint, of each battery's fire on the ground—this being elliptical, but varying in size depending on the range.

The result of this planning was the selection of a deployment area between 18 and 25 kilometres southeast of Cuito Cuanavale, which gave the G5s the ability to fire on targets 15 kilometres northwest of the FAPLA-occupied town.

The secrecy behind the G5 presence was paramount; consequently, the guns were flown in by SAAF C-130s at night, with the gun tractors travelling by road.

The artillery group arrived in Mavinga at 21h00 on the night of 1 August 1986, whereupon the leader element joined Colonel Laubscher for a briefing. During this it was predicted by the commander on the ground (Eddie Viljoen) that movement and deployment would be likely to occur during the night of 2 August. The following night, after fragmentary orders, the gunners moved, during which time they were reinforced by three additional Kwêvoël ammunition vehicles (mine-protected Samil 100s) and additional technical services personnel. The additional ammunition vehicles were specifically added to this group to spread the load being carried, and, although being most welcome, caused some 'hysterical' regrouping and co-ordination. All of this took place on the move, at night, without lights and in the thick bush. By 22h30 the route to the west of Mavinga had been found and the convoy managed to speed up, only to be held up again by the Withings recovery vehicles bogging down in the soft sand.

By 03h25 on the morning of 2 August, the artillery group had reached the Lomba River and by 05h00 had occupied a hide.

During this operation, the gunners were finally issued with the LandNav system, which, despite its complexity (compared with modern-day GPS), provided fixation to an accuracy of one metre at least. Its only drawback was that it needed to acquire six satellites, not all of which were available all the time, and, therefore, it occasionally caused long delays.

Sunday 3 August: the rapid movement forward to the deployment area meant there was no radio communication between the blunt and sharp ends of the artillery group; all the blunt end could do was maintain a listening watch on the regimental frequency. At 07h30, Commandant de Villiers held an order group in which he thanked the batteries and the echelon for their efforts thus far—a distance of 75 kilometres travelled through the night without lights, the only stragglers being the recovery teams. Orders were given that tracks were to be camouflaged, fires extinguished and the local defence plan activated. At this point it was appreciated that, in order to successfully occupy a firing position the batteries would have to be in position by 04h00 for their final recce of the firing positions and in action by 05h30 for first light.

During the day, Colonel Viljoen arrived at the hide and informed Commandant de Villiers that they would be moving that night over a planned distance of 35 kilometres to the east where they would occupy a new hide in preparation for a deployment. This move was planned for 18h00, but in order to complete this the group would need to be refuelled and rewatered.

What was planned and what transpired were not quite the same because the actual distance covered was 48 kilometres and not 35. The group was split into two convoys, namely the F Echelon, which left first, followed by the A Echelon, which left some one and a half hours later, with a distance of 24 kilometres between convoys. The move, although slow (average speed of 12 kph), was uneventful until the gunner blunt end arrived at the supposed 'contact' or rendezvous (RV) area, where they drove straight into a UNITA base and took two hours to reorganize the convoys in the right direction. No one had bothered to tell the artillery group of this; the shambles could have been avoided had there been guides at the base's entrance. Not all was bad news, however. Firstly, Commandant de Villiers met up with Brigadier Renato from UNITA, a soldier whom he hadn't seen since their first meeting in Lobito in 1975. Secondly the outstanding performance of WOII Giep Hill in reacting to demands on the A Echelon kept the convoys mobile—to the point that Commandant de Villiers recommended WOII Hill for a Chief of the Army's commendation. At this point, de Villiers decided to move the group forward some 10 kilometres, which was completed at 04h00 the next morning without incident. All this time, the gunners were plagued by bad radio communications (or none), especially the rear link. Commandant de Villiers commented, 'KL [Colonel Koos Laubscher] must be fuming by now—wonder when the command Buffels arrive.'

Orders were received from the tactical HQ to move to a new position 11 kilometres away, and by 15h00 reconnaissance was underway—a recce that went well with sufficient space for the echelon in the deployment area. This led to the order to move at 18h00 and at that time the gunners reported to the tactical HQ that they were mobile, only to be told to stop where they were. This created a certain amount of chaos among the troops, as by now they had vacated their position and were extremely vulnerable because everything was now packed onto the vehicles. WOII Hill's echelon was ordered to close up on the convoy—a decision made in haste because of the stop-start ('greatcoats on–greatcoats off') nature of orders coming through from the tactical HQ, and a decision that was to lead to a large number of vehicles and equipment being compressed into a small area. By the time the echelon arrived it was

22h00; by this time, the gunners were transporting some 1,800 155mm rounds (shells, fuses and charges) and more than 2,300 127mm rockets with fuses.

The artillery group moved yet again on the night of 5 August, with the main convoy an hour behind the recce parties. This time they had their parking lights on for better control, but maintained a speed of 4 kph, ultimately occupying their new position at 22h00 without much delay. After all this manoeuvring and frustration of the night moves the force commander finally confirmed that there would be a four-day postponement in the operation. At this point, a typically military self-organized incident occurred when General Jannie Geldenhuys arrived in the theatre and asked to see the gun positions. With red faces, the senior officers admitted that they had forgotten to inform the chief that there was a delay!

By 7 August, the effects of the continuous movement from one hide to another was being felt by the blunt end of the artillery group. The late arrival, during the night, of part of the echelon caused a traffic jam of note and the 2IC had his hands full trying to reorganize this mêlée into a hide that at least provided some natural cover, as they had ended up in an open area, leaving them vulnerable both to air and ground observation. The force commander arrived at 11h00 that day to see for himself and agreed with de Villiers that the next move may be problematic because of time and distance. This resulted in an order for a recce to be carried out some 30 kilometres to the west of the gunners' existing hide. Colonel Laubscher arrived at the group's hide at 14h15 and, after a brief discussion with his 2IC, authorized the movement of the 21 echelon vehicles still on the road to the hide. They had stopped after the last order to stand fast where they were, as daylight movement was deliberately kept to the absolute minimum. Finally, the blunt end moved at 18h45 and maintained a steady 9 kph. Driving with park lights on, they arrived at the arranged RV three hours later. To those readers not familiar with night movement, one of the many risks associated with this method of movement is the possibility of being heard—sound travels farther at night. In this case, the convoy was heard 6 kilometres away. On arrival at the RV, chaos, once again, ensued. This time, the echelon drivers had fallen asleep and held up the deployment by some three hours. On 8 August 1986, Colonel Laubscher issued a supplementary, or additional, order to his 2IC to deploy the regiment that same night. There were to be absolutely no vehicle lights on and the group was to travel as slowly as possible in order to keep engine noise to the minimum. At that time, there was some uncertainty regarding the actual D-Day date so the gunners remained on standby to move. The plan was that the two batteries would record their centre of arc at first light on D-1. Time on target was planned for 17h30 (Angolan time) on 9 August (D-1); the fire plan made provision for some 92 targets to be engaged until after 17h30 on D-Day. These targets included the HQ of FAPLA's 25th Brigade. One of the considerations for this time and day was that FAPLA troops had developed a routine of queuing for supper at 17h30—an opportunity not to be missed. The other was that Saturday night in Cuito Cuanavale was party night.

D-Day was finally set for Sunday 10 August. Further detailed reconnaissance was scheduled for the Friday and positions would be occupied on the Friday night to be ready for the fire plan the next day.

Finally, the preparation and jockeying for position came to fruition as the artillery group deployed without any major incidents in the right place and well in time for the fire plan.

After all the moving, reconnaissance and deploying, the fire plan almost seemed inconsequential and was conducted faultlessly, with P Battery immediately redeploying for their next engagement early in the morning of August 11. However, the engagements were not all one-sided: FAPLA managed to fire what was described as 'a most fearsome couple of BM21s that landed very close'.

The artillery fire missions caused numerous secondary explosions and fires, and during the early morning of 10 August a single G5 fired a single round at almost maximum range into a target north-northwest of Cuito Cuanavale—a speculative shot to see what sort of retaliation there might be. This single round caused a detonation akin to a volcanic explosion: the round hit an ammunition dump in the FAPLA administrative area. This pyrotechnic spectacle continued, aided by a number of battery engagements that followed, for two days. The damage to other supplies in the area was never discovered. The end result of the operation was the destruction of FAPLA's 25th Brigade and the delay of any further advance southwards for another year. It is interesting to note that, during the movement and deployment for Alpha Centauri, skeletons from the previous year's Operation Wallpaper were found, never buried, never marked. Furthermore, the fighting took place in the same area as before and would end up repeating itself a year later during Moduler.

Commandant de Villiers summarized the lessons learned (and, in fact, confirmed existing doctrine) whilst still in action:

> My concept is that the regimental commander is at the higher HQ, the brigade fire support co-ordination officer does the pre-planning and the 2IC is the commander of the blunt end. The regimental commander's appreciation allots ammunition and gives deployment guidelines. The 2IC plans on his own and gets the ordnance deployed at the right time and place with the right ammunition. The BFCO controls the fire plan.

In his closing comment, Commandant de Villiers stated that drills are essential. This meant that every single member of the artillery unit deployed had to know and understand exactly what he was meant to do, almost parrot fashion, and furthermore, understand the sequence of events from the time that orders are given to the time that they come out of action after a fire plan. This was a valuable lesson applied during training, and one that was to lead to the successes in the operations that followed.

On 15 August at 01h00, the gunners received the order to 'cease fire, hook in'. Alpha Centauri was finished. A point of historical interest is that UNITA never launched their attack on 25 Brigade and their capture of the 13 Brigade positions went uncontested.

Chapter 10

Moduler and Hooper:
the big fights

'If you want to win your battles take an' work your bloomin' guns!
Down in the Infantry, nobody cares;
Down in the Cavalry, Colonel 'e swears;
But down in the lead with the wheel at the flog
Turns the bold Bombardier to a little whipped dog!'
—Rudyard Kipling, from *Snarleyow*

The results of Operation Alpha Centauri were such that not until March 1987 did FAPLA begin redeveloping its forces in the Cuito Cuanavale area. A logistics base was established in Tumpo to the east of Cuito Cuanavale, and additional forces initially assembled along the Menongue–Cuito Cuanavale road. All battle indications directed South African Intelligence to a renewed FAPLA offensive toward Mavinga and Jamba again. The background and build-up of FAPLA forces are well documented in other works, and suffice to say that these preparations were well thought out and well prepared. By 1 May 1987, the first South African officers had arrived at UNITA's headquarters in Mavinga to plan the counter to this offensive. This resulted in the political decision to commit limited South African forces that would be controlled at the highest level: a decision that would cause problems later on.

In order to clear up possible confusion later, the broad outline of the FAPLA operation can be divided into four stages, the first three of which were countered by UNITA and South African forces under the name of Operation Moduler. The fourth stage became Operation Hooper.

- *Stage 1*: Advance to the Lomba River. This stage included the build-up of forces and the bridgehead at Cuito Cuanavale; the movement to the Chambinga high ground; and the southward advance on two axes—one between the Cuzizi and Cunzimbia rivers, the other to the west of the Cuzizi River. This advance progressed well up until the general east–west line of the Lomba River. During this stage only UNITA forces were deployed as a defence. South African deployment was limited to a handful of Special Forces teams collecting intelligence, and some training teams supporting UNITA.

- *Stage 2*: Bridgehead over the Lomba River. FAPLA forces developed defensive positions on the north bank of the Lomba River in August 1987 and then attempted to create a bridgehead close to the junction of the Cuzizi and Lomba rivers, their reserve being deployed in the vicinity of the Cusumba River. The objective from there was to advance to Mavinga and the UNITA headquarters at Jamba. At this point, the South African forces commenced their deployment to help UNITA stop the FAPLA advance. This South African contingent comprised 61 Mechanized Battalion Group and 32 Battalion, supported by two batteries and one troop (later three batteries) of South African artillery. There was, initially, no artillery regimental headquarters.

- *Stage 3*: Withdrawal and reorganization into the defence. At the end of September 1987, FAPLA withdrew in its entirety back to defensive positions close to its original (Stage 1) localities. FAPLA high command realized that its offensive was failing and changed its mission to that of occupying the defensive positions southeast of the Chambinga River and Chambinga high ground as part of a bridgehead for a further offensive against UNITA at a later stage.

- *Stage 4*: Defence of the third line. This stage was the result of South African–UNITA actions in Stage 3, and FAPLA had to withdraw yet again to more favourable ground. This defence was more of a strategic / political effort than that of an operational military necessity. This happened in December 1987 and was the main effort of Operation Hooper.

It should be borne in mind that UNITA, although proficient at guerrilla warfare and semi-conventional operations, did not have the capability to stop a conventional attack. During the build-up, South African liaison teams (Special Forces) deployed to collect information well in advance—in particular terrain intelligence.

On 22 June, Operation Moduler was approved by the South African government and the first forces began to move immediately. Initially, Defence Headquarters approved an option whereby South African forces would deploy to watch and harass FAPLA as they deployed. Special Forces provided three 'liaison' teams to do the watching and 32 Battalion was tasked with providing its organic 127mm MRL battery (P Battery), with protection elements to conduct the harassing fire tasks.

Less than a month later on 20 July, Major Cassie van der Merwe, the battery commander of Q Battery 4 SAI Battalion Group, found himself in the theatre involved in the planning and reconnaissance for possible artillery operations. The first gunner fire unit to deploy, therefore, was P Battery (127mm MRL) from 32 Battalion under the command of Major Pierre Franken, with Captain Cobus Stoltz as his BPO and Staff Sergeant Johan Rademeyer the BSM. By the end of July 1987, P Battery was in action engaging the FAPLA 16, 21, 47 and 59 Brigades at the source of the Chambinga River.

August 1987

By 4 August, 32 Battalion had commenced mobilizing its infantry and support weapons and was in the process of moving out of Buffalo Base, accompanied by additional gunner OP teams. Under the command of

Commandant Robbie Hartslief (the commander of the 32 Battalion support group), these first elements arrived in Mavinga four days later. The second artillery fire unit, in the form of a troop of 120mm mortars from S Battery 61 Mechanized Battalion Group under the command of Major Theo Wilken (the battery commander), joined Commandant Hartslief's force on 10 August. 61 Mechanized Battalion's organic battery was, in fact, a G5 fire unit, but the troops were also cross-trained on the 120mm M5 mortar, and the equipment was always ready for operations if needed. That same day, Hartslief's force joined up with P Battery in the area northwest of Mavinga, their mission to support UNITA in delaying FAPLA in crossing the Lomba River.

The 155mm GV6 Mk I self-propelled howitzer

The G6 was designed after the G5, but carried the same ordnance and fired the same ammunition as the G5. Its advantage was that, being self-propelled, it could move and deploy faster than its towed sibling. The G6 was fitted with a 12-cylinder, turbocharged, air-cooled diesel engine, giving the 42-tonne howitzer a top speed of around 95 kph on a tarred road. Despite this top speed, however, it was normally never driven faster than 80 kph, mainly for road-safety reasons. The other advantage over the numerous tracked self-propelled guns in existence was that it did not need to be transported, but could drive from South Africa right into the combat zone under its own power. The G6s used in Operation Moduler were pre-production models, which is why only three were deployed, and all three were configured differently.

Although P Battery had been in action for almost a month, very little in the way of firing had taken place; the stated mission was to 'keep an eye on FAPLA'. It would seem that by 11 August the fog of war was thicker in Army HQ than in the combat zone because, on that day, Army Operations in Pretoria asked the forward HQ in Rundu where the MRLs were deployed! The question is: why? A syndrome of commanding the battle from the rear? Over the next three days, the gunners were kept fully busy, with P Battery moving into a hide 7 kilometres southwest of the confluence of the Cunzimbia and Lomba rivers, ready to deploy to engage the FAPLA 59 Brigade as it worked its way to the Lomba River. S Battery was in a hide near Mavinga and ready to move closer to the newly formed tactical HQ, now joined by the HQ of 20 Artillery Regiment under the command of Commandant Johan du Randt (the OC of 4 Artillery Regiment). S Battery fired the regiment's first rounds

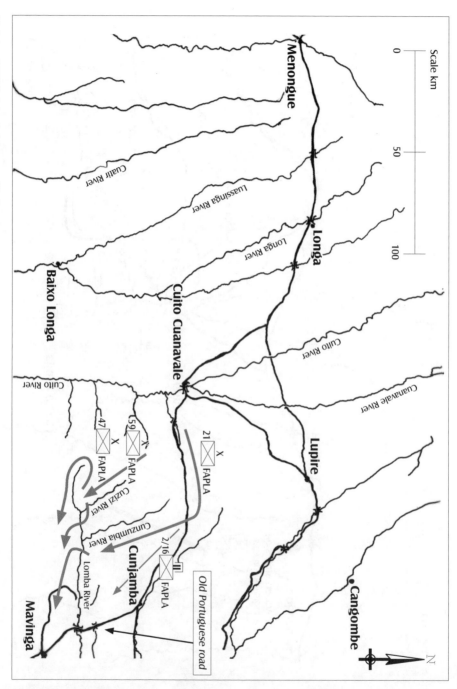

Moduler: FAPLA's intended move on Mavinga.

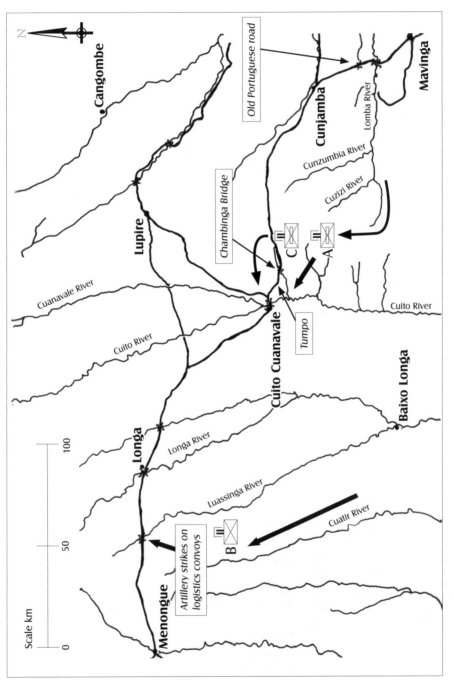

Hooper: South African deployments.

on 13 August against 47 and 59 Brigades at a range of 9,000 metres. During this time, Major Wilken moved into the area of the Vimpulo River source to recce for OP positions and, to his surprise, was confronted by a platoon of FAPLA tanks heading towards him. He immediately about-faced and moved to create distance between himself and the tanks, but was followed until last light, and was almost caught at the Mianei River crossing.

Four days later, authorization was given by Defence Headquarters to increase the South African troop strength in that area and for '1 X G5 Battery to go over to the offensive'. A point of interest here: in the same document Army HQ instructed that '. . . the safety of RSA personnel is a higher priority than the success in operations'. Ironically, the G5 Battery would not be going over to anywhere, as there were no G5s in the operational area at that time. In another instruction of 17 August 1987, Army HQ stated: 'G5 and/or MRL Battery must bombard FAPLA during their creep forward—when vulnerable.' So much for high-level control of the battlefield. One wonders what possessed the higher HQ to think that they could control the fight from Pretoria: it is clear from this that they did not even know what capabilities were deployed. Therefore, Q Battery, 4 SAI Battalion could finally mobilize to join 20 Artillery Regiment in the Mavinga area some time later.

20 Artillery Regiment was formed as an ad hoc unit specifically for this operation, its number derived from the sector in Rundu (Sector 20). Later, 20 SA Brigade would be formed around this core already deployed, with Sector 20 HQ forming the main and rear HQs. At this time, 4 Artillery Regiment was the operationally ready unit and three of its batteries were assigned (one G5 Battery each to 61 Mechanized Battalion and 4 SAI, and one MRL Battery to 32 Battalion). The other two batteries were on standby to move should they be required to. 14 Artillery Regiment was undergoing training and only scheduled to be ready in November. In fact, at that stage 14 Artillery Regiment was deployed in its secondary task—counter-insurgency operations, and individual batteries (deployed as light infantry companies) spread from Mamelodi (Pretoria) in the south to Lebowa (in what is now Limpopo Province) in the north. During this time, the two deployed batteries continuously moved positions near to the HQ of 5 Reconnaissance Regiment,

for which they were to provide fire support (the Special Forces liaison teams were units of 5RR).

Finally, on 17 August 1987, the FAPLA brigades started moving. Once authorization had been given by Army HQ for Q Battery to deploy, the detailed planning commenced. At that time, S Battery 61 Mechanized Battalion had two sets of equipment: specifically, a battery of 120mm mortars, and a battery of G5s. However, not all equipment was duplicated, as it was never the intention to deploy two batteries from this source. There was only one set of echelon vehicles and one set of gun tractors (the 120mm mortars were porteed on the back of the gun tractors when used).

Furthermore, there was only sufficient personnel for one battery. Army Operations planned for Q Battery to provide the personnel and S Battery to provide the equipment to form the newly authorized battery. This concept was communicated to Director Artillery Colonel Koos Laubscher, who wrote to Army Operations to spell out the implications of this. In essence, the problem was twofold. Firstly, there was a personnel problem. All Q Battery's senior personnel were already deployed: Major van der Merwe, the battery commander, was deployed as an OP officer in P Battery; WOII Hannes Myburgh, the BSM, was deployed as ammunition master, and commuted between Mavinga and Rundu most of the time; Staff Sergeant Willem van Dyk, one of the TSMs, was acting as BSM for P Battery; and, finally, two national service officers, OPOs, were deployed with the 120mm mortars of UNITA. Secondly, handover of equipment was an issue. A proper handing and taking over of equipment would have to be done, and this meant that Major Wilken would have to be withdrawn from his deployed S Battery to issue the equipment to Q Battery. Furthermore, there was not enough supporting equipment or vehicles for two batteries so Q Battery would have to provide its own. As it was, WOII John McCormack, the BSM of S Battery, found himself away from his troops and his primary job, in that he had to supervise the handover of the G5s and related equipment to Q Battery in Mavinga. Colonel Laubscher also indicated in his report the initial ammunition requirement for this new battery, which was as follows:

- 1,350 projectiles on the gun tractors and in the echelon
- 700 rounds as first line reserve in Mavinga
- 700 rounds as second line reserve in Grootfontein
- Fuses would be a 60:40 mix of SA8513 (proximity) and PDM572 (point detonating)
- Charges would be a similar mix, with charge 3 making up the greater number.

While Colonel Laubscher was arguing the case for Q Battery's equipment, Major van der Merwe was on foot shadowing 59 Brigade at the Vimpulo River, where, on calling for fire, found that he had no radio communication with S Battery, or anyone else for that matter. Wasting no time, he immediately ran some 5 kilometres back to the mortars and ordered a fire mission. On the same day, the innovative Major Franken decided that more experience was needed at the sharp end, and personally deployed as an OPO to follow 47 and 59 Brigades.

Despite the arguments over Q Battery's equipment in Pretoria, preparations were underway for the reception of that battery's personnel in Rundu, and on 18 August Major van der Merwe withdrew to Rundu to receive his people.

The pace of the battle stepped up on 19 August when, at 13h45, S Battery engaged 59 Brigade with 32 rounds of mortar fire, followed at 00h05 the next morning by P Battery firing a ripple of 192 rockets on 59 Brigade, one more ripple at 01h00 and a rapid move back into a hide 5 kilometres southwest of the Lomba River source.

Keeping to a time-honoured South African tradition, once again the gunners were the FLOT—this time for four days!

During the period of 21 and 22 August, the artillery component was reinforced with the arrival of Commandant Jan van der Westhuizen, a gunner officer stationed at the Directorate Artillery at Army HQ, with the appointment of artillery adviser to UNITA. On 22 August, 94 personnel of Q Battery arrived in Rundu under the command of Lieutenant Rob McGimpsey, the BPO. In the combat zone both P and S Batteries moved into hides approximately

11 kilometres southwest of the confluence of the Cuzizi and Lomba rivers, and 300 kilometres to the south, nine Samil 100 gun tractors and 30 Samil 100 ammunition vehicles left Buffalo base for Mavinga.

It was quiet on the day of 24 August. Commandant du Randt reconnoitered for an assembly area 8 kilometres west of Mavinga for the newly arrived Q Battery. P Battery remained static in a hide and Major Wilken at the tactical HQ helped with Q Battery's deployment planning.

At 06h00 the next morning, P Battery fired a ripple from each troop on 47 and 59 Brigades respectively. Some days later, electronic warfare (EW) intercepts provided the result of these fire missions: 'Five tanks are destroyed; a complete artillery battery barring one man are killed; and a complete infantry company is destroyed.'

That same day, S Battery exchanged their gun tractors with Q Battery—probably not a smart move because on 26 August one vehicle mysteriously burst into flame, with the 120mm ammunition on the cargo deck eventually exploding. There were no injuries. Lieutenant Rob McGimpsey, the BPO of Q Battery, gives his first impression of Angola:

> The many field gun exercises at the Potchefstroom range and the integrated exercises at the Army Battle School training terrain could not compare to what lay ahead in waiting in the open battlefields of Angola.

While this pyrotechnic display was underway, FAPLA convoys were on the move to replenish or reinforce 47 Brigade. The artillery component was three BM21s, two BM14s and eleven 120mm mortars. To this was added a 66 Brigade convoy moving to reinforce 16, 21 and 59 Brigades with seven BM21s, three BM14s, eight D30s, twelve 120mm mortars and 47 other guns. All told, the reinforcement or replacement artillery equipment alone was four times more than that deployed by the South African gunners.

That night at 20h15, P Battery fired the first of three ripples; the second was fired less than an hour later and the last at 06h15, leaving little time to occupy their hide before the FAPA (Angolan Air Force)–Cuban aircraft were expected. The reply was just three rounds of inaccurate counter-bombardment on the vacated firing position.

Ripple

A term unique to the rocket artillery. The South African MRL could either fire individual rockets from selected tubes on the tube pack or a 'ripple', meaning all 24 rockets. The electronic control system fired the 24 rockets in series with a one-second interval between them. The fire orders for the rocket batteries were the same as for the guns, and the command '24 rounds fire for effect' meant that a ripple was to be fired.

Between 26 and 28 August, the SAAF C-130s flew in the eight G5s to Mavinga where they were taken over by Q Battery, who were hiding just to the west of Mavinga. During this period, P Battery had moved at least three times to be in a position to engage 47 and 59 Brigades. On the night of 30/31 August they deployed in a position some 15 kilometres southwest of the Lomba–Cuzizi confluence, from where, at 07h50 on the morning of 31 August, they fired a full ripple, pinning down 47 Brigade. While P Battery were busy, it was the turn of the medium gunners of Q Battery to commit; and this they did by deploying 18 kilometres southeast of the Lomba–Cuzizi confluence. As expected, the occupation of their first position in Angola did not go according to the book by any stretch of the imagination.

Lieutenant McGimpsey sums up that first performance:

In Mavinga, I was given a Buffel, radios and a LandNav . . . My navigational training was done on a basic compass and a map, making use of local landmarks and the resection method of fixation. Standing on the Buffel and looking for landmarks . . . was impossible. Adding to these unexpected surprises, I received a contingent comprising elements of medical, air force, anti-aircraft and a 32 Battalion protection element as well as many, many lost UNITA [men].

From Mavinga Q Battery moved off to a hide to the northwest of Mavinga, just south of the Lomba River. To make matters interesting, McGimpsey—and most other officers and senior NCOs—had had no training on the LandNav whatsoever; therefore, this was done on the move. This was but one example of the lack of integration that abounded in the SA Army at that time—a consequence of the passion for secrecy and the resultant 'empire building' by staff officers and operational commanders at all levels in the hierarchy. Upon arrival in the hide, Major van der Merwe radioed deployment orders to his blunt-end commander for action the next night. This move was to be the first in which Q Battery and all its supporting elements would deploy as a whole. This was not an easy job for a 22-year-old lieutenant on '. . . the first night that all the guns and supporting elements including and not forgetting the lost and uncontrollable UNITAs [sic], who had to marry up and understand various drill, formations and similar field tactics relating to blunt-end matters'.

The battery arrived at the assigned grid reference some hours later, but the LandNav displayed a different set of co-ordinates, indicating that the group should move 2 kilometres south. As there was no other method of checking in that pitch-black night, the BPO trusted the new technology and duly moved south, whereupon the battery went into action. Daybreak revealed that they had deployed in an open *shona* and the whole battery was exposed for the whole world to see, including the MiGs. The rest of that day was spent camouflaging and praying that this day would not go down in the history of great military disasters. Their prayers were answered: despite the low passes of MiGs over the position, they were not detected. In hindsight, it is quite possible that the Angolans did not suspect the presence of the G5s because they had not yet fired a single round; furthermore, flying at 500 knots at low level over that vegetation is not conducive to good observation. By occupying this position Q Battery could reinforce P Battery's fire on any of the three FAPLA brigades. The deployment was in time and in the right position for Q Battery's two troops to engage 47 and 59 Brigades respectively. Under the command of the OPOs, Lieutenants Koos Brytenbach and Nick Prinsloo, the first round was fired at 07h50 on 31 August 1987. Captain Mark Brown of 4 Artillery Regiment, an OPO, spent this period to the east of the old Portuguese road to Mavinga accompanying a sapper team to reconnoitre possible crossings on the Lomba River and to record potential targets.

September 1987

September 1987 saw, yet again, an increase in activity. FAPLA were determined to cross the Lomba River, and 20 SA Brigade even more determined to stop them. One should bear in mind that, despite the name, 20 Brigade was not much more than an overstrength battle group. The greatest firepower lay with the three artillery batteries, but the teeth arms were, by normal conventional warfare standards, seriously lacking. At that stage, the infantry component of the South African ground forces comprised three motorized companies from 32 Battalion, as well as elements of the support company and a company from 101 Battalion. 32 Battalion was not trained as a conventional force—their expertise lay in guerrilla warfare, and 101 Battalion was a counter-insurgency unit. The armour component was the anti-tank squadron (Ratel 90mm and Ratel ZT3) from 32 Battalion's support group.

On 1 September, Q Battery was occupying a hide 11 kilometres south-southwest of the Cuzizi–Lomba confluence in readiness to deploy to engage 21 Brigade, and at 07h50 that morning, P Battery fired two troop fire missions on 47 Brigade. Electronic warfare intercepts provided the results of those engagements: two logistic vehicles destroyed and six people wounded. From here, the battery came out of action and moved to a position 4 kilometres south-southwest of the Cuzizi–Lomba confluence to engage 47 Brigade. Later that night, Q Battery's readiness paid off when they fired an 80-round harassing fire mission on 21 Brigade and moved immediately thereafter to deploy for an engagement on 47 Brigade. That same night, S Battery had redeployed some 7 kilometres southeast of the Cuzizi–Lomba confluence to cover a possible crossing of the Lomba. Two nights later, 47 Brigade was hit by three ripples from P Battery; and 21 Brigade was harassed by 160 rounds from Q Battery. September 4 was a sad day for the gunners. That night at 22h45, the sitrep OPS/331/04 Sept 87 from HQ Rundu to SWATF 31 (SWA Territory Force—Operations) bore the news that Commandant J.C. du Randt of 4 Artillery Regiment had been killed in action.

Du Randt had been reconnoitring the Lomba River in a Bosbok of 42 Squadron when the aircraft was shot down by a missile. The pilot attempted an emergency landing on the floodplain of the Lomba River and ended up upside down in the mud. UNITA troops were on the scene quickly and recovered the two bodies and all the information on board. This was the last time that a manned light fixed-wing aircraft would be used on the battlefield, and the incident accelerated the deployment of the SAAF's Seeker Unmanned Air Vehicle System in the theatre. Commandant van der Westhuizen was the nearest senior gunner in the area and took over immediately.

The gunners' pre-planning and flexibility were highlighted during the next three days, during which P Battery moved into a new firing position each night and engaged 47 and 59 Brigades, firing full ripples to good effect. Q Battery fired on a large vehicle concentration by the use of a 'sweep and search', by firing six rounds per gun per target. The next day, they split into two troops to deploy apart from each another and fire on 21 Brigade, and then merged once again to take on 47 and 59 Brigades. S Battery deployed in direct support of the 32 Battalion anti-tank squadron to stop 21 Brigade. These missions resulted in FAPLA vehicles being burnt and an obvious slowdown of their advance. In another fire mission Q Battery fired 108 rounds on 21 Brigade. By 5 September, the gunners were expecting four C-130 flights with MRL and G5 ammunition to replenish the dwindling stocks. On 7 Sep Q Battery's position was detected and engaged by a BM21. The gunners fired back immediately, set four vehicles alight and silenced the BM21.

The next three days saw the gunners constantly moving and firing from late afternoon and through the nights. Q Battery split its two troops and engaged separate targets, and conducted a sweep-and-search mission on 47 and 59 Brigades. S Battery was deployed in direct support of 32 Battalion's anti-tank squadron, which was deployed to destroy the FAPLA armour of 21 Brigade at the Cuzizi-Lomba confluence. Later in this period, S Battery redeployed to support the reserve at the Lomba River crossing. This fire and movement resulted in the burning of numerous FAPLA vehicles and at least one silenced BM21 in the process.

By this time, ammunition was running low again: the gunners were waiting in anticipation for four C-130 flights of MRL and G5 ammunition.

At about this time, FAPA air activity escalated to the point that Q Battery was hunted almost daily and always during engagements. The battery did receive warnings when the MiGs were approaching, but often only when these aircraft were about to strike. On one such occasion a single aircraft dropped a bomb at low level, striking some 200 metres to the front of the battery position. Lieutenant McGimpsey describes the scene:

> We all saw this yellowish smoke billowing out through the trees and, fortunately, the wind blew it away from the gun position. We then realized that the enemy was using dangerous chemicals—we can only assume that it was mustard gas. The smoke drop from treetop height was no target indication.

Needless to say, camouflage and concealment improved dramatically during that period, and eventually nuclear-biological-chemical (NBC) protective equipment in the form of gas masks and the uncomfortable 'noddy suits' were issued to all.

Air defence

As stated earlier, the offensive South African air defence capability was poor, to put it mildly. This was largely the effect of the arms embargo and the availability of funding to undertake expensive development in this environment. The South African Anti-Aircraft Artillery was equipped with a 20mm single-barrel gun mounted on the back of a mine-protected 2-tonne vehicle, and the Oerlikon-Contraves 35mm twin-barrel system. Both sets of ordnance were coupled to radar systems and the serviceability was generally good. The problem was that the 20mm was not a match for fast, attacking aircraft like the MiG-21 and -23; and the 35mm was too sensitive to operate in thick bush. 32 Battalion had additional AA means in the form of captured 23mm twin-barrel systems but, although an excellent gun system, it lacked any form of radar guidance. The SAAF deployed the old Cactus mobile missile system, but in limited quantities. The biggest limitation lay in the SAAF interdiction capability—not through aircraft, but because of distance and the associated loiter time. A Mirage F1 needed 30 minutes to reach the combat zone and longer to reach Menongue, whereas FAPA only took 10 minutes. The SAAF radar coverage was also limited and did not include the combat zone. UNITA, on the other hand, had been given Stinger shoulder-launched surface-to-air missile (SAM) systems, and used them to good effect on occasion. An irony here: the South Africans were not allowed to get near these systems despite the fact that they knew about them and saw them in action. These circumstances led to the South Africans—the gunners especially—perfecting the art of passive air defence by means of limiting vehicle movement to nighttime, the careful use of lights, radio silence and camouflage at all times. It could be said, however, that the thick bush and tall trees in the eastern part of Angola made the camouflage of vehicles and equipment a relatively easy task.

One can safely say that one of the factors that contributed to the artillery's success during Moduler, Hooper and Packer was their tactic of changing positions constantly and at irregular times, together with the rapid movement between firing positions. Furthermore, most of the movement and deployment was done under the cover of night without lights and, more often than not, in radio silence. This was the result of realistic tactical training, particularly in Lohatla, but it was also born out of necessity because of the lack of air superiority. They could not move during the day because FAPA aircraft were constantly overhead.

By this time, 20 SA Brigade had been reinforced by the arrival of 61 Mechanized Battalion, which became the task force reserve and named Battle Group C. Their role was to destroy two FAPLA brigades.

Ammunition remained a point of concern, but had not reached critical lows yet. An entry in the sitrep of 8 September stated: 'Expecting a C-130 with 7,000 kilograms G5 ammo tonight.' Meanwhile, the three batteries once again were moving and firing.

An example of the sound co-ordination of the fire and movement of the artillery regiment can be seen in the sitrep of 9 September. S Battery was positioned to support an attack on a company defensive position, with P Battery ready to fire the preparatory bombardment. UNITA attacked prematurely and the FAPLA force withdrew to the north. S Battery fired on the withdrawing troops and, in turn, drew effective counter-bombardment from the north. Immediately, this light battery came out of action and moved southwards, with Q Battery taking the cue and delivering counter-bombardment, thus silencing any further FAPLA fire that night. Having successfully completed that fire mission, Q Battery then took on a newly identified command post of 21 Brigade, and S Battery moved up closer yet again.

The next night at 18h30, Q Battery fired on the mobile bridge positioned for the crossing of the Lomba, successfully hitting that piece of valuable equipment. It was inevitable that this fire mission would cause some response, and shortly after, the battery found itself the subject of a bombardment by a D30 battery—fortunately it was inaccurate. The G5s promptly returned fire, destroying two D30s and detonating their ammunition. Their night's work was not yet done, however. In the early morning of 10 September, FAPLA attempted to establish a bridgehead yet again, only to be chased away by 32 and 101 Battalions supported by Q Battery firing proximity-fused ammunition that caused heavy casualties. This contact was repeated the same day when a FAPLA platoon attempted a crossing, and still later, three vehicles tried and two were lost in the process.

The MiG problem was to be short-lived because by this point, the UNITA commander attached to Q Battery had had enough and stated that next time his AA missiles would be successful. A MiG was soon shot down by a Stinger and crashed 2 kilometres away from Q Battery's position. From that day, the skies above the battlefield were strangely quiet.

Also on 10 September, a FAPLA group was chased away, this time by S Battery, while attempting to cross; and S Battery subsequently destroyed an enemy 120mm mortar.

The pace of the operation continued unabated between 11 and 16 September. In this period we note at least five fire missions by Q Battery from at least four different positions. These included the destruction of two vehicles and 160 rounds fired on 47 Brigade; harassing fire tasks on 47 Brigade; the support of Battle Group B's attack on 47 and 59 Brigades, leaving upwards of 250 casualties; and the engagement of an identified forward HQ. By the nature of its role, P Battery was not as active, but nonetheless continued firing and moving against 47 and 59 Brigades. They fired 384 rockets on the former and a ripple into the identified HQ. It must be remembered that each occupation of a firing position was preceded by the occupation of a hide and the loading of tube packs. By this stage in this operation, P Battery had honed their loading skills to the point where they could fill a tube pack in ten minutes—no mean feat in the dead of night. S Battery was not as active, as it remained in position for longer periods, but nevertheless supported Battle Group B in their attack on 47 and 59 Brigades.

By now, 59 Brigade had been reported in a position some 5 kilometres northwest of the Cunzimbia–Lomba confluence, where they were prevented from interfering in the Battle Group B attack by Q Battery. The attack on 47 and 59 Brigades resulted in a number of 32 and 101 Battalion troops being reported as missing. Fortunately, however, these missing members walked into P and Q Batterys' positions on 14 September, from where they were moved back to their respective units.

Finally, at the end of this period, six MiGs attacked the old artillery firing positions, but missed by a distance of 700 metres; the gunners had vacated the positions the previous night.

On 17 September, P Battery occupied a new hide 4 kilometres farther east of their last position and awaited the next move from 21 Brigade, who obliged by attempting a crossing with three tanks, one infantry company and accompanying soft-skinned vehicles. Major Hannes Nortmann, the squadron commander of 32 Battalion's anti-tank squadron (Ratel 90mm and Ratel ZT3), waited for the group to concentrate before ordering the gunners to fire. The result of a ripple from P Battery and harassing fire from Q Battery was that by 18h00 one tank was burning and many infantry were reportedly left lying in the target area.

At 09h45 on 19 September, P Battery fired 96 rockets on a helicopter seen landing in 21 Brigade area. No more helicopters were seen after that. Late in the afternoon of that day, P and Q Batteries engaged FAPLA infantry and vehicles, destroying all the vehicles. Good news flashed through the artillery regiment that day when it was announced that the SAAF Seeker UAV team had arrived in Mavinga.

Unfortunately, bad news followed and 20 September 1987 became a black day for the artillery. During an intense fire mission, one of Q Battery's G5s, after 11 rounds, mistakenly loaded a charge bag without first having loaded a shell. The gun was fired and the charge bag, having no chamber pressure, simply popped out of the barrel, setting the veld alight. The fire was quickly extinguished and the barrel washed out. However, upon loading the next round the rammer failed to seat the shell properly, whereupon the crew rammed the shell for a second time and completed the loading process. On firing, the shell detonated in the barrel (aka 'a barrel premature'), killing Gunner William Beekman and wounding six others; these were:

- Second Lieutenant J.Z. Oosthuizen
- Gunner C.N. Lourens
- Bombardier C.J. du Plessis
- Gunner J.J. Jacobs
- Gunner H.J. Coetzee
- Gunner K.R.T. de Melo

A board of inquiry was held, which confirmed that the combination of the bad ram and some remaining hot, unburnt charge was the cause of the catastrophic explosion. That night at 20h35, P Battery fired 96 rockets as counter-bombardment on a BM21 of 21 Brigade. There was no further counter-bombardment after that.

22 September: at midday, one of P Battery's troops fired an accurate mission on 59 Brigade; unfortunately, the results could not be seen at that time. During the night, Q Battery fired yet another series of missions on 59 Brigade and, according to the sitrep, BM21, mortar and small arms ammunition burnt for three and a half hours that night. Radio intercepts indicated that a D30 gun and an AA missile system were both damaged during this engagement.

24 September: at 10h00, the observers reported enemy movement north of the Lomba River in the 21 Brigade positions and engaged this target with Q Battery, damaging two soft-skinned vehicles and killing a number of FAPLA troops. At the same time, Major Franken arrived at the UNITA positions on the Lomba River between the Cuzizi and Cunzimbia confluences, where he was tasked with observing 47 Brigade's possible attempt to cross, and, if necessary, engage this force. Here we see mention of the first 155mm carrier shells being delivered and filled with propaganda pamphlets; some 500 rounds were expected to be delivered by 26 September. It was either this delivery or the arrival of the prototype 155mm HE sub-munition (cluster) that prompted the rumour (in South Africa) that the South African Artillery now had a nuclear capability. This rumour went as far a 7 SAI Battalion

in Phalaborwa, where some infantryman actually saw the shell—purple in colour—in a 'very strong metal case'. The standard NATO colour for HE sub-munition is purple; a nuclear or chemical round is normally light grey. One wonders at the origin of the story of someone from either the SADF or Armscor opening a case containing a nuclear round in front of a group of infantrymen in a base where any form of artillery presence is non-existent! It is noteworthy that the artillery formed the front line own troops for nearly six days, and both MRL and mortar batteries fired daily and through the night to slow the enemy advance.

On 25 September, intelligence issued a report to the effect that the FAPLA brigades were expecting helicopters to evacuate the Soviet advisers from their forward positions and move them back to the relative safety of Cuito Cuanavale. Having been warned, the gunner sharp-end teams plotted the most likely landing zones for this evacuation. Major Wilken, at that time observing the 21 Brigade area, plotted four such targets and allocated two 120mm mortars to each target. The wait was not long. On 27 September, three Mi-25 gunship helicopters clattered into the target area. Eavesdropping from the electronic warfare section gave the indication that the gunships had landed, and Wilken opened fire on all four identified targets. Success was quick: within seconds, a huge explosion was heard as one of the helicopters blew up. Similarly, Franken tried the same tactic, but without the confirmation of a secondary detonation. Two of the three gunships escaped, carrying the Soviet command with them. On the same day, Captain A. Piercy of 3 Squadron SAAF was hit by an air-to-air missile; returned to Rundu with his damaged Mirage F1CZ; and landed at high speed, collapsing the nose wheel gear. The accidental ejection at ground level paralyzed Piercy.

During this time, the allied forces were positioning themselves to follow up the withdrawal of the FAPLA brigades, which by this stage, were reduced to around a third of their original strength. On the night of 27/28 September, 21 Brigade managed to extricate themselves in complete secrecy under cover of darkness.

The next night saw the leader element of 20 SA Brigade hosting President P.W. Botha and an entourage of ministers and top SADF brass. At this briefing the decision was made to switch to a more offensive posture because FAPLA, it was felt, still had strong forces east of Cuito Cuanavale and could still start up their offensive yet again. It was agreed that the FAPLA brigades east of the Cuito River must be destroyed to prevent them launching another offensive in 1988.

The FAPLA situation at 30 September was that 47 Brigade was deployed to the south of the Lomba River with the river to their backs. 59 Brigade was effectively behind them on the north bank of the Lomba, deployed from here to the northeast. 47 Brigade had made contact with 59 Brigade and commenced evacuating casualties northwards over the river. Watching this activity was Major Franken, who by then had deployed his observation post on a small piece of high ground northwest of the Lomba-Cuzizi confluence. From this position he observed FAPLA once again attempting to create a crossing by laying logs down as a road across the marshy floodplain. Added to this was the arrival of a TMM heavy mechanized mobile bridge. This construction work led to two possible deductions: either 59 Brigade was going to attempt a southwards crossing, or 47 Brigade was about to break contact and withdraw northwards. The conclusion was that the latter was the most likely given that 21 Brigade had already pulled out. Therefore, the decision was made to attack and destroy 47 Brigade while still in position.

That day, the SAAF and the gunners continued pressurizing 47 Brigade, the result being an order for 47 Brigade to commence withdrawing. The whole time that planning went on, the gunners, under the control of Major Franken, fired at individual vehicles and anything else they could see, destroying at least eleven vehicles. The SAAF reinforced the artillery fire with 250kg pre-fragmented bombs, causing heavy casualties and damage. As 47 Brigade started their withdrawal northwards the opportunity for the allied attack presented itself.

Q Battery has its first close call

The continuous movement and deployment of Q Battery meant that they needed a continuous resupply of fuel. One night, the battery was tasked to pack up immediately and move into a new position, this without having refuelled for some days. Despite the low fuel stocks, the battery duly moved westwards and then northwards, nearer the Lomba River. On deploying that night in preparation for a first-light fire mission, the commander of the 32 Battalion protection element suddenly became aware of enemy activity some 800 to 1,000 metres in front of the gun position. This information was immediately passed on to the BPO, who duly informed Major Wilken for further verification. Meanwhile, the attached UNITA elements were behind the gunners collecting used 'lumo sticks'. Some hours later, the verification came back—a FAPLA brigade was indeed deployed 800 metres in front of Q Battery! This message was immediately followed by the order to come out of action and move southwards until the diesel ran out. During this hasty withdrawal the vehicles that did run out of fuel were towed by the recovery vehicles and anything else that could handle the load. This shambles was a blessing in disguise because, firstly, had the gunners been refuelled they may have deployed farther north and driven straight into the FAPLA brigade, and, secondly, had UNITA been in front they would have made contact and most probably withdrawn through the gun position with the FAPLA forces right behind them. This could have resulted in the capture of the entire Q Battery. The consequences are not difficult to imagine.

October 1987

During the preparation for this attack, Major Franken kept an eye on the FAPLA build-up of vehicles and equipment at the crossing point. Using principally the firepower of Q Battery, he managed to cause large-scale damage and destruction to that target; this included the destruction of an SA-9 air defence system. The almost continuous fire on that crossing stopped 47 Brigade and they moved back into their prepared positions. By this time, 47 Brigade had effectively been cut off from the rest of the FAPLA forces and were desperately low on food, fuel and ammunition. What made matters worse for the commander of 47 Brigade was the order issued by higher command for his brigade to withdraw back across the Lomba River and join up with 59 Brigade. A fatal decision as it turned out. At 08h00 on 3 October, Battle Group A (the full 61 Mechanized Battalion and G Compay 32 Battalion) attacked

47 Brigade from the east along the river line just as this brigade was forming up in their attempt to cross back over the Lomba River from south to north. The attacking force of mechanized infantry and anti-tank vehicles was guided into position by Major Franken, who was still in position across the river at his observation post. S Battery were deployed to provide counter-bombardment if 21 Brigade's artillery were to mix in. Supported by P and Q Batteries, they managed to halt 47 Brigade's movement, and accounted for the following FAPLA losses:

- 12 tanks, of which 4 were in good condition
- 7 BTR-60 infantry troop carriers
- 3 BMP tracked infantry combat vehicles
- 5 BRDM reconnaissance vehicles
- 85 soft-skinned vehicles
- 3 x 23mm AA guns
- 2 D30 field guns
- 2 SA-9 AA missile systems
- 1 ZSU 23/4 AA gun system
- 45 bodies
- 9 prisoners of war, including 1 captain.

This battle was by no means one-sided. Despite the UNITA attacks on the southern sector, FAPLA actually surprised the attackers by their tenacity. Commandant van der Westhuizen continues:

> Only a handful of 47 Brigade's vehicles managed to cross the Lomba; the rest were either stuck in the mud or shot out by the artillery and armour. Major Franken was on the grandstand, and he controlled the artillery fire. He told us exactly what was going on and what was burning. It was also here that we found our first SA-8 system and it was recovered.

The complete allied force moved into hides where they replenished, repaired equipment and rested.

The next day, Commandant van der Westhuizen, being the next senior officer in the tactical HQ, was ordered by the brigade commander to organize the recovery of FAPLA equipment from the now deserted 47 Brigade position. Accompanied by two SAAF colonels sent to inspect the captured missile systems, Commandant van der Westhuizen reached the closest UNITA base after two nights' travelling. His story continues:

> After I had inspected the UNITA base, I decided not to camp there and we set up camp about 500 metres to the south of them. That same night, I took the engineer and the commander of the workshop troop with me to inspect the battlefield to plan our action. The next morning at 06h00, I sent the air force personnel with a guide to do their job, as they would not wait for nightfall, while I was sorting out my plan of action and orders. The problem was that we could only work at night because the MiGs were bombing 47 Brigade's vehicles and equipment by day so that UNITA could not use them. The air force team arrived back in camp at 9 o'clock and had been talking for about five minutes when the MiGs came over and bombed the UNITA base. They dropped six 1,000-pound bombs onto the base and one stray bomb landed exactly 200 metres from us. Ten minutes later, the air force team left the area back to the tactical HQ.

The clean-up continued, with the engineers checking for mines and booby traps and the tiffies driving or towing vehicles to a point some 7 kilometres to the south. Commandant van der Westhuizen recalls one personal incident:

> As I was inspecting a BTR 60 that was intact I got the fright of my life. The drill was to inspect the vehicle inside with a torch and try to start it. If it started, one would sit on the vehicle to direct the driver, as no lights were allowed for obvious reasons. As I was inspecting the BTR 60 I saw that there were clothes and pieces of canvas lying on the front seat. I climbed in through the turret and, as I was about to sit on the driver's seat, it started to move. The seat came alive.

The next moment I was standing outside next to the BTR without having touched the turret. On closer inspection, we found a FAPLA driver in the BTR. He was sleeping in the front seat! He had a big shrapnel wound in his right leg and could not walk. He already had a high fever and through an interpreter, he told us that his commander, a Russian, had told him to stay put, that he would send an ambulance for him. He was taken away by UNITA.

After five nights' work, the recovery party had extricated 16 tanks, of which 12 were driven away after they had been pull-started. Commandant van der Westhuizen continues:

We used them to pull out the others, as well as the vehicles that were stuck in the mud. We also recovered two brand-new BMP1s of which one had 3,000 kilometres on the speedometer, and hundreds of AK-47s, about 80 logistics vehicles, 23mm AA guns, BM21s, etc.

All the captured equipment was handed over to UNITA for reuse later. Despite their close proximity to the Lomba River, the recovery party could not drink or even wash in the water because it was strewn with dead bodies, some of which were already putrefying in the heat.

On 7 October, Army HQ issued an instruction to 4 SAI Battalion Group (aka 62 Mechanized Battalion Group) to mobilize to join up with 61 Mechanized Battalion in Rundu. A tactical headquarters would also be required and 4 SAI would be issued with the necessary Ratel command vehicles for delivery to the combat zone. To this battalion group an MRL troop was added—presumably until arrival in the operational area where it would be placed under command of the artillery commander. The cover story for 4 SAI was that it was moving out from its home base in Middelburg to participate in Exercise Sweepslag III at the Army Battle School. To make this more plausible the first-line ammunition would be drawn from Army Battle School ammunition dump. 4 SAI's organic battery (Q Battery) accompanied this convoy, but without their G5s, as these had been provided by S Battery and flown in to Rundu from

Omutiya (S Battery's home base). However, Q Battery's G5s were flown up from Waterkloof to Mavinga to replace S Battery's mortars.

The build-up of South African forces continued and the airfield at Mavinga developed into the brigade admin area. In early October, the gunner component increased still further and consequently was authorized to brigade status. At this point, Commandant van der Westhuizen was sent home to be with his wife at the birth of their child; his post was filled by Artillery Brigade Commander Colonel Jean Lausberg, with Commandant Ian Johnson as his 2IC and Commandant Francois van Eeden as the brigade fire support co-ordination officer. The artillery brigade now looked as follows:

- Artillery Brigade HQ deployed with the Brigade tactical HQ
- P Battery, 32 Battalion (127mm MRL)
- Q Battery, 4 SAI Battalion Group (155mm G5)
- R Battery, 4 Artillery Regiment (120mm mortar)
- S Battery, 61 Mechanized Battalion (155mm G5)
- I Troop (127mm MRL) 4 Artilleryy Regiment (4 Locating Battery had converted to the MRL and thereafter became 44 Battery)
- J Troopp (3 x 155mm G6)
- B Echelon at Mavinga airfield.

The period between the end of the destruction of 47 Brigade at the Lomba River and the middle of October was spent planning for the next stage of the operation (Stage 3) and the positioning of forces to carry out that part of the operation. The batteries that could move redeployed farther northwards and gradually, within days, were followed by the now replenished, and newly arrived, fire units. So by 17 October, an OPO was deployed on the high ground north of the Chambinga Bridge to monitor 21 and 25 Brigades; an OP party had positioned itself 5 kilometres from 59 Brigade; and Captain Anton Boschoff had infiltrated 59 Brigade's positions. Finally, the other OPOs were positioned at the watershed at the source of the Mianei River. By then, Q Battery was deployed in the dense bush south-southeast of the Mianei–Vimpulo confluence—less than 10 kilometres from 59 Brigade.

By early morning on 18 October, P Battery had reached a position at the source of the Mianei River; S Battery were to the south of the Mianei source; and Q Battery had deployed during the night to the south of Lucaia source. That morning three MiGs attacked Q Battery, once again to no effect.

At this time, Captain Phillip van Dyk (call sign G59, the troop commander of I Troop), while observing FAPLA's movement, had a close shave with an 82mm mortar bomb. The bomb landed on the nose of his Ratel in front of the driver's windscreen and detonated, but luckily there were no injuries.

On 19 October, 25 Brigade reached the Tumpo logistics base and 21 Brigade had deployed in 59 Brigade's old positions, west of the Cunzimbia River. By this time, the focus of planning was to isolate 59 Brigade to prevent interference with the South African and UNITA artilleries and to soften up 59 Brigade for a ground attack. Planning also addressed how to prevent the other FAPLA brigades from crossing the Chambinga Bridge to deploy on the tactically important Chambinga high ground. While this was happening, FAPLA's Tactical Group 2 crossed the Vimpulo River with six tanks within 2 kilometres of Task Force Delta. This movement was outside the observation limits of the gunner observers so the G5s of S and Q Batterys shelled this tactical group using EW intercepts and shelling reports. (A shelling report is sent by the unit being shelled and briefly describes where the shells are impacting and the nature of damage.) This fire effectively stopped the movement of the tactical group and the sustained fire finally prevented it from reinforcing 59 Brigade. The problem of radio communications came to the fore that day when Commandant Les Rudman (Special Forces) called for artillery fire on the Chambinga Bridge. Because the OPO had not yet reached his position he could not control the fire. The nearest link to the South African force was a UNITA patrol that was positioned north of the bridge. This patrol passed on the fire mission via no fewer than nine radio stations, the message finally arriving at the fire support co-ordination centre, who duly activated the guns. As there was no OPO present, the gunners asked the UNITA patrol to report the fall of shot in relation to the bridge. The third round was a direct hit. This fire mission, through a total of 12 radios lasted until darkness took over. The traffic flow over the bridge was halted.

Q Battery was attacked by two air strikes the next day but, once again, no damage was inflicted. Again, Tactical Group 2 was engaged and forced back into its hide in the dense bush. Intelligence was confirmed that FAPA was intent on neutralizing the G5 batteries. This resulted in the deployment of Q Battery in positions far enough away from the rest of the allied forces to prevent possible collateral damage in the case of air attacks. At this point, Special Forces deployed a team to observe Cuito Cuanavale air base so that the gunners could dominate it by fire.

This northward movement of both forces had now placed Cuito Cuanavale within range of the artillery brigade's medium guns, an opportunity not to be missed. Q Battery took advantage of the opportunity despite being reduced to six guns because of serviceability. On 20 October, they deployed a three-gun troop to a position 10 kilometres south of the Vimpulo–Mianei confluence to be able to engage the air base at Cuito Cuanavale. The serviceability problem was not a constant factor—one must bear in mind that these guns had been firing almost every day since their arrival in the theatre and most of those rounds were fired at full charge. Added to this was the daily movement to new positions, all of which was done without the benefit of roads. No amount of engineering or design could predict that kind of wear and tear on the equipment and so there was a shortage of spare parts for these guns. The other troop remained in position for the time being.

G6's baptism of fire

At this time, the G6 project was in its final stages of development and four engineering development models had been built. These guns were presented to the artillery for them to evaluate with a view to pre-production models being built for initial deployment (six pre-production model guns were to be built). The project team was, at that stage, nearly the strength of a troop and included logistic vehicles, a Ratel fire-control post (a Ratel command vehicle converted into an FCP by adding an AS80 fire-control computer and the latest radios) and a Ratel recce vehicle equipped with a gyro navigation system.

About six months before the manufacture of the engineering development models, the South African Artillery set a requirement that the G6s be equipped with a gyro laying system (a radical departure from the traditional dial sight system then in use on other guns). This gyro system would find north and, therefore, speed up the deployment time dramatically. The irony is that the incumbent commander of the School of Artillery strenuously opposed this sighting system and the result was that the engineering development models were equipped with 'long neck' dial sights very similar to the sights on the American M109 howitzer. Unlike their British or Israeli stablemates, this sight worked on a 'zero line' and the gun was laid by means of deflections left and right of this zero line. This is fine when the fire-control system produces such information, but the AS80 computer produced a map bearing that was applied to the gun sights (the British method). However, this now meant that the troop leader standing behind the guns would be given a bearing, but the fire-control post would have to manually convert that bearing into a deflection to be applied to the sights.

The evaluation of the four engineering development models was called Exercise Zenula (Zenula was the name of the G6 project), and was planned as a full rehearsal of a pre-emptive strike together with 61 Mechanized Battalion Group. The gunner evaluation team comprised:

- Colonel Koos Laubscher (Director Artillery)
- Commandant Ivor Rimmer (OC THA)
- Major Jaco Breytenbach (10 Artillery Brigade)
- Major Francois van Eeden (School of Artillery)

During the preparation for this evaluation exercise, Operation Moduler was in its early stages and the Director Projects (then Brigadier Philip du Preez, an anti-aircraft gunner) after consultation with Director Artillery suggested that the G6 troop would be ideal to provide fire support during this operation. Armscor and Lyttelton Engineering (the developers) were somewhat reluctant, but the final decision rested with the project officer, Faan Bothma. In Commandant Bothma's words, 'Could there ever be a better developmental evaluation opportunity?' The scene was then set for the entry of G6 into combat. It should be noted that not only the guns, but also the logistic packages were to be evaluated. Preparations began under difficult circumstances (mainly the lack of a war establishment table for a G6 troop or battery, which meant that supporting equipment was not readily available in store), and the troop mobilized. On 23 October 1987, the troop was placed under the command of Major Jakkie Potgieter, with Bothma, although the senior, placing himself in the post of BPO so that he would be able to maintain close contact with the civilian team members and the equipment. Staff Sergeant Thys Franken was appointed as the troop sergeant-major. WOI Dirk Venter, the project sergeant-major, was tasked to provide logistic support from the home base, Potchefstroom. Before this, WOI Venter was the RSM of 14 Artillery Regiment, and the most resourceful and dependable sergeant-major in the corps at the time. He was among other things a driving and maintenance instructor of some repute, who did not abide fools easily.

(*Author's note.* As a candidate officer at the School of Artillery in 1969, I was tasked, together with two other COs, with towing some guns out to the ammunition proof range one morning. I drove a Jeep towing a breech-loading mortar fitted to an old 6-pounder undercarriage. On arrival at the proof range, I discovered that the mortar was missing and immediately about-turned to look for the missing equipment. I found the mortar on the side of the road where it had unhooked itself and rolled. Staff Sergeant Venter arrived shortly afterwards, and, after my stammering about this dreadful loss, his reply was, 'Welcome to the artillery, son.')

Commandant Bothma gave WOI Venter brief instructions (more like guidelines) over the telephone something like this:

Here is the [movement] authority: get drivers from 10 Artillery Brigade, and vehicles from 4 Vehicle Reserve Park. Load ammunition at Jan Kempdorp and Witbank. Add the existing personnel and vehicles at 10 Artillery Brigade and meet the G6s at Langklip Station [a deserted railway station between Upington and the SWA border] at 17h00 on 24 October. Fill up the diesel bunker at Upington.

The G6 convoy took a day to reach Langklip Station from Pretoria (a distance of 870 kilometres), and on arrival were greeted with a hot meal and hot showers—such was WOI Venter's organizational ability.

A formal movement order was issued by Major Potgieter tasking the troop to move in two packages. The first was the ammunition vehicles that had to stop in at De Aar in the Northern Cape to take on ammunition; the second package was the gun group and the balance of the echelon, which would leave Potchefstroom on 26 August. The two packages were commanded by Lieutenants Juressen and J.G. le Roux respectively. They were to meet in Upington and be ready to leave from there for Rundu the next day. For security reasons the gun crews were issued with grey overalls to match those of their civilian colleagues, and the cover story for this expedition was that they were going to Tsumeb to do trials. Finally, the two packages should move sufficiently far apart so as not to be associated with each other. They would be separated by a four-and-a-half-hour time interval. To the casual observer, this arrangement may seem rather amateur, but in fact these vehicles would be moving between numerous other convoys all bound for Grootfontein and destinations beyond. Commandant Bothma flew to Rundu to attend a planning session and Major Potgieter took command of the convoy from Langklip Station to Rundu. Because of the nature of the intended evaluation a number of civilians deployed with this troop; these were engineers and technicians, most of whom had dual appointments. For example, Fanie Potgieter was an Armscor engineer who was also a no. 1 on a gun. In fact, most of the gun crews were civilians.

During the mobilization and packing of logistic packages one of the Lyttelton Engineering Works' senior staff members uttered some famous last words: 'There is no need for a spare power pack, as we have never had problems with them before.'

The fire-control post Ratel retired before reaching Rundu and the AS80 computer was hastily fitted to a Ratel 60mm provided by 61 Mechanized Battalion. This replacement vehicle was provided by Theo Wilken (battery commander S Battery) in exchange for a 'chopper tent'. This was the start of endless communications problems because the Ratel 60 was only fitted with one VHF radio, which had to be supplemented by a manpack HF radio. The plan for the G6 troop (call sign 60) was split into two phases:

- Phase 1: in support of 4 SAI Battalion Group at Quito (Cuito), north of Mavinga.
- Phase 2: deny the enemy the use of an airfield west of Quito in order to force them to use an airfield farther away from own forces, thus shortening the loiter time over own forces.

Bothma flew directly to the tactical HQ at Mavinga to meet with Colonel Roland de Vries, the brigade commander, and Colonel Jean Lausberg, the artillery commander, for a planning session. The troop joined up with a logistic convoy at Rundu and 'hit the road' to Mavinga. To those unfamiliar with the southeast of Angola, the road to Mavinga is a track wending its way between the trees in sand that is not unlike fine beach sand. This plays havoc with gearboxes and engine cooling systems because vehicles travel in low range throughout the 300-odd-kilometre journey. On the road to Mavinga, the unexpected—at least to some—happened: a G6 power pack suffered a catastrophic failure and the gun had to be hang-towed to Mavinga. By the time the troop had arrived in Mavinga the strength had been increased by the arrival of Sergeant Barry Schmulian, a vehicle fitter with a Withings recovery vehicle (a Samil 10-tonne 6x6). The other technical services personnel were:

- Sergeant Chris Strydom, an ordnance fitter who had left the PF and (with great difficulty) called up for the task;
- Sergeant Rudolf Nortje, an ordnance fitter working for Lyttelton Engineering Works and a serving member of the CF, again, called up;
- Sergeant Piet Minnie, a PF ordnance fitter;
- Corporal Labuschagne, a PF ordnance fitter; and
- Corporal Ernie Badenhorst, a CF NCO from Sandock Austral.

With one gun out of action, the troop was now only three guns strong. Sandock Austral, the G6 hull developer, flew a team in with a spare power pack and the unserviceable gun was returned to action at the end of the operation. Major Potgieter joined up with a combat team from 4 SAI Battalion Group to act as FOO (call sign Golf 65) for the first phase of the operation. At this time, 4 SAI wanted the G6 troop's technical maintenance team to join up with their light workshop troop, but Bothma would, for very good reason, have none of it. This would have complicated the recovery and repair of the guns and the tiffies would have been used for repairs on all vehicles.

At last light, the combat team and its G6 troop formed up on the edge of a *shona* as the rain started to pour down. Seeing the infantry Ratels bogging down in the *shona*, the gunners decided to use a route that they knew the G6s could traverse. Unfortunately, one of the Ratels crossed the G6s' track and in the ensuing braking and swerving one of the guns naturally bogged down. Sergeant Schmulian immediately moved in to recover the stranded G6 and, while in the process of unreeling the winch cable and nursing an upset stomach, was interrupted by a 4 SAI recovery team equipped with an MAN 8x8, a kinetic cable and boundless wisdom. This team wasted an hour and damaged their MAN. Twenty minutes later, Sergeant Schmulian recovered the 46-tonne G6 as he intended to in the first place.

Once mobile, the troop reached its first deployment area in time and commenced with a predicted harassing fire task, coming out of action immediately afterwards and moving to the next position to support 4 SAI's attack on the northern elements of FAPLA to the east of Cuito Cuanavale.

Just as the troop was about to move, the UNITA protection element, a princely amount of ten men, poured out of the tree line and assumed position on top of the guns. Within a hundred metres of the start, the first of the technical difficulties occurred: a G6 bent a steering arm to the point that it could not move further. It should be appreciated that the bush is thick and in order to move to deployment areas this troop, like most others resorted to bundu-bashing (creating their own road through the bush by driving over trees and shrubs). Although the largest trees were avoided, there were times when thick trunks were hit and vehicles and equipment were badly damaged. The spare steering arm was fitted and the troop moved on. Within another 200 metres, the next gun suffered the same fate, and, to make matters worse, the only spare had just been used. The technical support team came to the fore and straightened the steering arm as far as they could and reinforced it with steel angle cut from wheel rims. During evaluation, steering arms never suffered damage, but in this bush the tight turns that were needed caused the front wheels to turn out of the protection of the front armoured bow plate, and tree trunks would enter the open space and cause damage. The lesson was learned and drivers were instructed not to turn tightly.

As a result of these delays the troop could not deploy in time to support 4 SAI and effectively 'lost' their troop commander, Major Potgieter, to 4 SAI.

The allocation of sharp-end personnel

During operations, the troop commanders and OPOs, although having their assigned fire units, could also call for the fire of any other artillery fire unit within range when engaging ad hoc targets. The RHQ would authorize the use of a battery of troops and allot ammunition for that specific fire mission. In the case of fire plans, the fire control would normally be allocated to a sharp-end officer, usually a battery commander. One of the sharp-end officers was authorized to control the fire of the entire regiment for a period of time depending on the tactical situation and his location. This is normal artillery practice and allows for rapid reaction and flexibility in terms of the type of ammunition that is best suited for the task.

This marked the unsuccessful end to Phase 1 and the move to positions to execute Phase 2, neutralizing Cuito Cuanavale air base. The G6 troop deployed far to the west of own forces so that it could engage the target with maximum charge but without having to use base bleed projectiles. On the way, another eleven UNITA troops were added to the party, bringing the total protection element to 21 men. The only problem was that, just as in Savannah some 12 years earlier, they preferred to sit and watch the fire missions rather than deploy to protect the guns. During the night an OP officer came onto the air and established communications. On this OPO, Lieutenant Charles Fuchs of S Battery, protected by a UNITA section, had placed himself in a tree and could see the airfield clearly. His appreciation of the time of flight of the projectiles and the movement of aircraft was immaculate: at one stage, an Mi-8 helicopter landed and opened its doors to disembark passengers as the rounds hit. The helicopter never moved again. On another occasion a helicopter approached the airfield and, at the last moment, changed plans and landed in a *shona*. Unfortunately for them, the OPO was quicker on the uptake—helicopter and 155mm rounds landed at the same time. From this time on, there was (mostly) friendly banter between the field gunners and their anti-aircraft comrades as to who had shot down the most aircraft.

FAPA consequently moved their operations to Menongue some 160 kilometres to the west. This naturally decreased their loiter time over the South African forces, but the immediate disadvantage was that they now flew directly over the G6 gun position (up to six sorties per day). To counter this, the gunners moved to a new position each night and camouflaged before first light. Nevertheless, one morning four MiGs attacked a clump of bushes two kilometres away from the gun position. Just then, a trigger-happy UNITA soldier fired off an SA-7 missile at aircraft number two, whereupon aircraft three and four broke left and attacked the SA-7 position, luckily ineffectively. The result was that in future deployments Commandant Bothma deployed UNITA at least 500 metres away from the gun position.

One of the G6 drivers, Bombardier van Heerden, a well-padded young NCO, did a practical demonstration of how to open a 'ratpack' (ration pack) when the replacement national servicemen arrived to take over. He would immediately throw away the 'dog biscuits' (a hard, dry, slightly sweet object, which, theoretically, expanded when dunked in coffee—in practice it fell apart) and, when questioned, replied that, should one get hungry later, there was danger that one may be tempted to eat them!

The general area where the G6 troop deployed was on the route between the sharp end and the rest of the deployed artillery fire units. So by default it became the transit camp for OPOs withdrawing for a period of rest (recreation was not thought of during this operation). During this period, malaria started claiming its victims and at one stage the Rinkhals ambulance, full of feverish patients, tore off its front axle and suspension. This led to the suffering casualties having to endure the ambulance being hang-towed behind a recovery vehicle. To aggravate this, the helicopter that was sent to casevac the sick turned around because the pilot claimed that the landing zone was not where the gunners had said it was (bear in mind the accurate navigation systems that the G6s were equipped with).

WOI Sampie Claassen had established an ammunition point very near the first G6 deployment area and the G6 troop sergeant-major was given a map from there to the ammunition point to collect the troop's ammunition. Four nights later, Commandant Bothma briefed the guards and the UNITA protection element to expect the ammunition convoy during the night. Midway through his briefing WOI Claassen came onto the air asking where the convoy was. Bothma found the missing convoy in a UNITA base 5 kilometres away from the ammunition point, sitting around enjoying a braai of buffalo meat with some Special Forces operators. Apparently the TSM could not find the ammunition point and his radio batteries had run flat. The braai ended rather abruptly and by first light next morning, the loaded convoy was back in the gun position.

The Director Logistic Support of Army HQ contacted Commandant Bothma, enquired after the troop's welfare and asked if they required anything specific. The answer given was 'beer, meat and a chaplain, please'. All requirements arrived by air that same night and the next morning the fires were lit and a church service held.

A bit of innovation here: the 155mm projectile pallet (four rounds) is made from a 6-millimetre-thick square steel plate and a steel bar with a screw-on lifting eye: an ideal braai plate when inverted and sunk into the sand, leaving about 200 millimetres clear for the firewood. It is a well-camouflaged, virtually invisible 'gun position', but suddenly wafting above the trees is the white smoke from the braai fire. As Commandant Bothma puts it:

> This naturally attracts unwelcome visitors — in the form of a patrolling flight of MiG-23s! The previously tranquil gun position came alive in an instant; some people shovelling sand on the fires, some attempting to blow the smoke away and others simply running for their foxholes. Happily, the MiGs took no interest in the smoke and flew on.

Bothma admits to an error of judgement at this point. The excess beer was put into the ambulance for safekeeping. Soon after this he found the medical officer, who could only be described as 'incapable', sitting with his feet hanging out the back of the ambulance and singing at the top of his voice. Not even the chaplain could get any sense out of him.

Until that stage Commandant Bothma had stuck to the principle of no daylight movement or deployment. Without warning, the gyro navigation system in his Ratel expired, leaving him with no accurate means of fixation. This meant the G6 troop would deploy close to its old positions so as to make survey easier. This also meant that the FAPLA artillery could also plot these positions, and this was proved shortly afterwards when a 122mm D30 gun opened fire on them. Luckily, the D30's fuses were set on delay and the rounds buried themselves deep into the earth before exploding. No damage was caused.

Q Battery's second close call

One of the few prominent terrain features in this theatre of operations was the Viposto high ground, a bluff-like hill that dominated the countryside to its west and a favourite spot for OPs of both sides of the conflict. After the rout of 47 Brigade, the allied forces moved northwest following the FAPLA withdrawal, and, within a short time, occupied the Viposto high ground. By now the gunner HQ was focusing its efforts on the town of Cuito Cuanavale— the nerve centre of FAPLA's operation. In order to engage Cuito Cuanavale the G5s of Q Battery needed to deploy on the Viposto high ground, not only to reach the targets 39,000 metres away, but also for early-warning and local defence reasons. While they were busy with a fire mission on Cuito Cuanavale, a message came through to Q Battery that a FAPLA tank force was on its way to attack the gun position and that preparations should be made to defend the position. This defence included using the G5s in the direct role (open sights, à la Tobruk in World War II) and deploying anything and everything that could shoot, including the 20mm AA guns and Stingers. The battery waited, and by last light, nothing had happened. The next morning they were ready for a first-light attack—still nothing, so they came out of action and moved away to a new position. Later that day, a report came through from Major Hannes Nortmann (32 Battalion's anti-tank squadron commander) that the enemy tank force had moved through the evacuated gun position just after the gunners had left.

November 1987

The arrival of Colonel Jean Lausberg, the commander of 10 Artillery Brigade, in the operational area coincided with the allied requirement to progress from a purely defensive mode to a more offensive, or aggressive, posture. Colonel Lausberg had been promoted in January 1987 into the top operational post in the artillery, having taken over from Colonel Felix Hurter. His last operational post had been in Operation Protea as a battery commander, but he had gained a vast amount of planning and staff experience in his previous post as chief instructor at the Army College. Supporting him were two experienced and capable gunner officers in the shape of Commandants Ian Johnson (at that time, the SO1 Logistics at 10 Artillery Brigade) and Francois van Eeden (SO1 Training at the School of Artillery).

In his artillery appreciation during early November, the new artillery commander spent some useful time on his main considerations for planning the artillery's role and eventual organization for the battles to follow. These were:

- Enemy ordnance and offensive capability: FAPLA had their ordnance deployed to cover all possible fronts (or approaches). They would fire defensive fire missions on approaching assault forces and, therefore, would need to be neutralized at an early stage. Consequently, the South African Artillery would have to deploy observers in positions where they could see FAPLA's firing positions and achieve accurate fixation of these positions by cross-observation. Counter-bombardment of enemy artillery was, therefore, first priority.

- Air defence missile systems: The SAAF would not be used in any preparatory strikes, and there was an urgent requirement for the capture of SA-8 and SA-13 systems. Furthermore, these missile systems posed no threat to ground forces. The conclusion was that the gunners would focus on air defence guns, as these could, and would, be used in the ground defence role against own troops.

- Command and control: The Soviet passion for centralized command and control of their artillery was well known and was the main reason for the ineffective use of firepower thus far. As far as own command and control was concerned, the answer lay in centralizing control of fire and decentralizing the command of movement of the fire units. In the scheme of things, this meant that there would be an artillery brigade fire support co-ordination centre to control and co-ordinate the fire and two regimental HQs, each supporting the task forces (brigades) so that the combined fires of both regiments could be called for when necessary. This was the first time that two regiments would be deployed on one operation since World War II.

- Organization: Here, the decision was made to form an artillery brigade, a decision that was to be the foundation for artillery operations the following year. The deployed 10 Artillery Brigade would look like this:
  - Brigade HQ (Colonel Lausberg) supporting a divisional HQ
  - 20 Artillery Regiment (Cmdt Johnson) in support of Task Force A
  - 4 Artillery Regiment (Cmdt van Eeden) in support Task Force B

Colonel Lausberg's rationale behind this organization was that Task Force A was a motorized / light infantry formation and would require 120mm mortars for close fire support and G5s to provide the counter-bombardment. Therefore, Q and S Batteries were allocated together with a meteorological section. Task Force B comprised the mechanized forces and, therefore, required the mobility of the long-range ordnance as well the high volume of firepower of rockets. Therefore, P Battery was assigned and strengthened by the addition of R Battery (G5), I Troop (MRL), J Troop (G6) and a meteorological section.

- Chemical warfare: Own forces maintained a purely defensive posture in this form of warfare and the best the gunners could do was to plan for increased fire on potential FAPLA chemical delivery means (specifically their artillery).
- Artillery strikes: Intelligence reports had already shown that certain objectives, or targets, were psychologically damaged as a result of artillery fire. Coupled with this was the requirement to minimize own forces' casualties and the destructive effect of combined artillery

and tank fire. The conclusion made was that the gunners would be employed to destroy enemy targets in a co-ordinated effort with the armour, leaving objectives to be cleared or cleaned up by the assault forces.

Finally, this concept of artillery operations would require a tremendous logistic effort, with the supply of ammunition being paramount. To this end the artillery brigade commander assigned WOI Stapelberg to co-ordinate ammunition in Rundu and WOI Claassen at the brigade admin area at Mavinga. WOI Claassen would push ammunition forwards by means of two convoys under the command of WOI Jan Viljoen and WOI Frans Botha, assisted by S/Sgts 'Kuifie' Swanepoel and Butch Hairs respectively. These convoys would also be geared to change their missions as and when required by the ammunition demand, that is, a convoy must be able to be rerouted at short notice.

Moduler continued until mid-November 1987; by then, the worst of the fighting was over and some new strategies needed to be worked on to drive FAPLA back to Cuito Cuanavale.

At the time of the heaviest fighting, the SAAF were flying in loads of rockets each night from Rundu to Mavinga; the logistic lines were seriously straining to keep up with the artillery ammunition consumption. When the author arrived in Rundu on a Saturday afternoon at the end of November, he met up with Commandant 'Civvie' Britz, the staff officer (SO1) Logistics at 7 Division. Britz's first comment was, 'I hate gunners!' Initially taken aback by this remark, Major Wilsworth gradually realized that it was said in jest, as, eventually Commandant Britz finished his statement, 'We load C-130s full of rockets every night and all you bloody gunners do is shoot them away!' This was the start of a long working relationship.

By late November, the national servicemen had to be rotated as their time was completed and the replacement intake was ready for operations. Also, the PF personnel had had three months, and more, of combat and needed to be replaced. The withdrawal of FAPLA forces back to their old prepared defensive positions to the east of the Cuito River was the trigger for Operation Hooper to be launched at the end of November with a new mission: to drive FAPLA back over the Cuito River and prevent its logistics support from operating. An important factor in this operation was that FAPLA was occupying by this stage prepared, deliberate defensive positions, like those during Operation Protea, but with far more armament. Another crucial factor was terrain. FAPLA had the advantage of an existing infrastructure in the form of tarred roads (despite their condition) and towns (specifically, Cuito Cuanavale). With the exception of the Cuito Bridge, the bridges over the numerous rivers had all been destroyed by that time. Any attack on these positions would not be as quick or easy as the attack on 47 Brigade.

As for FAPLA logistics support, the town of Menongue had developed into a depot where all supplies coming in from the harbours to the west were processed for further delivery to the divisional log base 30 kilometres northwest of Cuito Cuanavale. Menongue also boasted an air base that could handle all the military aircraft (including strategic transport) operating in the region. Menongue's geographical position in relation to the combat zone gave the MiG-23s a 30-minute loiter time over the target area. Supplies were transported by road from Menongue to Cuito Cuanavale in convoys protected by 8 Brigade up to the Cuito Bridge. There were other crossings over the Cuito and Cuanavale rivers in the form of fords or places where ponts had been stationed. Most of these crossings, however, were really only suitable for personnel on foot.

In terms of high, dominating ground, the town of Cuito Cuanavale was built on a high feature that dominated the whole Tumpo area by observation and by fire. To exploit this, FAPLA had deployed 54 artillery pieces, including M46 (130mm), BM21, D30 (122mm), and BM14 (MRL). Direct fire could be brought down on the Tumpo area by 23mm AA guns and T-54/55 tanks. (There was also a limited number of T-62s there.) It goes without saying that air defence radars were there aplenty.

Between the Cuito and Cuanavale rivers another high-terrain feature dominated both the west and east banks of the Cuanavale River up to Tumpo, making it an ideal place for artillery observation. The Chambinga high ground between the Cuatir and Chubinga rivers effectively cut the combat zone into two flat plains to its east and west. It was the right size for a brigade-strength defensive position. The foliage to the east of the Chambinga high ground was thick bush leading to forest on the high ground itself. To the west the flora thinned out somewhat, creating open manoeuvre area. FAPLA had organized its defence on the Soviet defensive doctrine with two echelons and a reserve. These were:

- First echelon: 21, 25 and 59 Brigades. These covered the security zone immediately to their front. 21 Brigade deployed three battalions each in defended locality connected by a communications trench, the whole defence facing east; 25 Brigade deployed three battalions and occupied an area of some 9 square kilometres and faced east and southeast; 59 Brigade comprised four battalions covering the north and northeast, occupying some 20 square kilometres of ground. Each brigade was supported by an anti-tank reserve of five tanks each. The artillery support came from two batteries, one D30 and one BM21 fire unit deployed between 25 Brigade and the Tumpo area.

- Second echelon: This defence was based on a tactical group under Cuban command in the Tumpo area and comprised 3 Tank Battalion (the mobile reserve); three infantry battalions (2/13, 1/66 and the remains of 47 Brigade); and a territorial battalion for area operations deployed in the Anhara Lipanda area. This echelon was supported by a battery each of D30s and BM21s, reinforced by three M46 guns for counter-bombardment.

- The reserve: This defence was deployed on the west bank of the Cuito River and comprised the forward command post of the 6th Military Region; 52 AA Brigade with SA-6, SA-8/9, SA-3 and SA-13 air defence missile systems; 13 Brigade, responsible for the protection of the area west of the river; and a Cuban regiment deployed in the area of the source of the Tiengo River.

- The artillery regiment of some 54 ordnance under Cuban command.

At this stage, all the South African forces had withdrawn to Mavinga, leaving only the two G5 batteries and one 120mm M5 battery deployed to harass the remnants of the FAPLA brigades. Furthermore, the FAPLA regional HQ had withdrawn farther west out of the now empty Cuito Cuanavale to a position out of range of the G5s. The Cuito Cuanavale airfield was out of action for anything but helicopters—these also keeping well to the west. It is ironic that, by this stage, the gunners were deployed within metres of the positions occupied by them during Operation Alpha Centauri more than a year earlier.

December 1987

By the end of November, S Battery's men had had their fair share of fighting and were ready to be relieved and return home at the end of their two years' national service. Their relief came from 2 Medium Battery, 14 Artillery Regiment. 2 Medium Battery, however, were not up to full strength and had to fill up their capacity from other batteries, 143 Battery specifically. One such ex-143 gunner was Chris Turner, who describes his entry into the theatre:

> The next day [30 November], we packed all our kit again, got on the Kwê's and went back to the airfield at Rundu. It was about 17h30 and the sun was drifting down over the treetops. There a Transall C-160 was waiting for us (the camouflaged type of my dreams) with its engines running. I saw a Mirage F1 standing in front of its hangar with a cover over the canopy. We had to form a straight line to board the aircraft through the small door to the rear starboard side; the pilot was most anxious in case any of us walked into the spinning propeller. I was the last to get on and when I got inside I found there were no seats left, so I had to sit on top of the pile of *balsakke* [canvas kitbags] and webbing that had been loaded into the rear of the aircraft. It was dark by now and we had to cover the windows

with fabric discs. Apparently this was to reduce the chance of being detected by patrolling MiG-23s. We took off and made our way to the base at Mavinga, about 260 kilometres north-northeast of Rundu. Before we landed at Mavinga we were advised that the aircraft would only be on the ground for four minutes, so we had better make sure that we and all our stuff were off pronto, or whatever wasn't off in time would be going back to South West with it. When we reached Mavinga, we suddenly dropped in a spiral towards the earth. It might have been nice if they had explained to us beforehand that this was a measure taken against any possible anti-aircraft attack. We landed and the aircraft had hardly stopped when the cargo door opened. We had to get our kit out with a dash of speed because the aircrew were true to their word, the engines didn't slow down a fraction and we basically flung the last few things off as the door was closing and the C-160 started to move forward again. I think before we even had time to take in our surroundings it had gone.

A day or so later, the newly arrived crews had their first taste of the realities of war. Gunner Turner continues:

Later that morning, we were told to dig foxholes. We teamed up in pairs, and in the middle of our excavations this horrible crackling sound went over our heads, followed by a slapping explosion some distance in the bush behind us. Someone yelled, 'Klim in julle gate!' [Get in your foxholes!] and I dived into mine head first, my rifle pegging up to the bipod in the sand next to me. Scenes from all the Vietnam movies I had watched flashed through my head—of smoke, bangs and horrible little men charging towards me, screaming dementedly about what they would like to do to my worthless body after they had turned it into a sieve with their bayonets. But the two bangs were about all it was for the time being. Turned out they were a couple of BM21 rockets [the famous Stalin's organ], which FAPLA had randomly fired in our general direction. They were also known as *rooi oog* [red eye], I think because I remember them emitting a red glow as they approached. We came to learn that this would be typical of most of FAPLA's artillery bombardments in the weeks to come. They didn't seem to have any observation posts to direct their fire; they couldn't even establish our precise positions. So they just took potshots at wherever they thought we were.

That afternoon we moved again, to a position somewhere southwest of Cuito Cuanavale, although I'm not sure how far from it. Here we brought the guns into action in battery formation about 30 to 40 metres apart. I think this position was a short training or evaluation phase so the OPs could see whether we were up to scratch or not. We erected bivvies again (which were improving gradually) and otherwise kept ourselves occupied by reading, digging foxholes or ammo pits or preparing food from our ratpacks.

I started carving miniature skulls with my pocket knife out of sticks I picked up, and stuck them to the inside of our gun tractor's cab using wax from an old B53 radio battery. It looked like a headhunter's cave after a while. There were these weird moths about, which we called 'piss moths' because they would excrete a fluid on your skin that burnt if you didn't wash it off right away. They would also fly straight into a fire.

On 6 December 1987, Captain André Eckard arrived in Grootfontein en route to Rundu and Mavinga. On enquiring about the next leg of his journey he discovered that there would be no flights to Rundu that day or the next for that matter. Choosing from a wide range of activities, Captain Eckard opted for dinner at the well-frequented Meteor Hotel where a 600-gram garlic steak cost R16.00. Next morning, he reported to the air force base at 06h30 in the hope of finding a flight to Rundu, only to discover that the SAAF opened for business after 08h00. That day started with a pork-rib braai. Finally, he managed to hitch a lift on a convoy bound for Rundu where he arrived at 13h15 and met WOI Claassen and Major Cassie van der Merwe at the Fort Foot Special Forces base.

At 00h30 on 7 December, Captain Eckard flew out of Rundu in a Puma helicopter bound for the logistics base at Mavinga and a two-hour road trip to Q Battery's position. Finally, after receiving orders Captain Eckard set off to his allocated OP post, initially by Ratel, then by Ural truck courtesy of UNITA, finally completing the last 12 kilometres on foot. In Captain Eckard's words, 'What an incredible pace!'

For the next three days, the front was quiet and this gave Captain Eckard time to properly orientate himself and observe the FAPLA activities. Despite the quiet, the newly arrived OPO made use of the time to keep FAPLA busy by engaging opportunity targets and mastering the art of concealment every time the FAPA MiGs appeared.

The rate of firing increased on 12 December, when a radar unit was engaged by a single gun from G Troop (S Battery), the target yielding three clearly visible hits and something that burnt for four hours afterwards. (The operations log of 20 Artillery Regiment reads: 'Target hit, fire burning, looks like missiles.') Later, the target yielded some 41 killed, 85 wounded and 34 vehicles damaged. Added to this was a successful fire mission on 59 Brigade and numerous engagements on Cuito Cuanavale itself. Personal contact was always high on the agenda for the South African gunners, and, on the same day, Captain Eckard received a visit from Commandant van Eeden and Commandant Schalekamp (the commander of 14 Artillery Regiment).

On 15 December, the UNITA troop protecting the OPO made contact with FAPLA no fewer than six times, leading to the decision to withdraw from the OP position to safety. All was not lost, however, as an exhausted Captain Eckard managed to find another suitable position where he engaged 59 Brigade with intense fire in support of UNITA.

20 Brigade now had fresh troops throughout and 20 Artillery Brigade / Regiment now comprised:

- An RHQ now under the command of Commandant Francois van Eeden from the School of Artillery.
- Q Battery, 4 SAI (155mm G5), the relief battery commander being Lt André Oosthuizen (142 Battery) with Sgt 'Tos' Atkinson as his BSM

- R Battery, 14 Artillery Regiment (120mm mortar) under the command of Major Sarel Buijs (141 Battery).

- S Battery, 61 Mechanized Battalion (155mm G5) now commanded by Major Willem van Rhyneveld (2 Medium Battery).

- An MRL troop made up of the junior leader element from the School of Artillery.

The B Echelon remained at Mavinga now under the command of WOI Albert Hook. Logistic co-ordination in Rundu was the responsibility of WOI Sampie Claassen.

The 155mm GV5 Mk II howitzer

Arguably one of the finest South African military products ever developed and built, and, for some time, the best-towed howitzer in the world, this ordnance was designed in the late 1970s and went into production in the early 1980s. Its design was based on the Austrian GCT 45, but 'South Africanized' to suit local conditions. The G5 had a maximum firing range of 39 kilometres at sea level on charge 3 with a 42-kilogram base bleed projectile. Although a towed howitzer, it was equipped with a four-cylinder diesel engine driving its four main wheels in order to manoeuvre in confined spaces, especially in the southern Angolan bush. The engine also provided power for the hydraulic systems to open and close the trail legs, steer the trail wheels and raise or lower the firing platform. Weighing in at 14 metric tonnes, this equipment was manned by a crew of eight and towed by a Samil 100, 10-tonne gun tractor.

The G5 fired the following ammunition:

- High explosive (point detonating, delay or proximity fuse)
- White phosphorus
- Red phosphorus (with a time fuse)
- High-explosive cluster (a round with 72 bomblets, specifically for anti-armour use)
- Screening smoke
- Coloured smoke
- Leaflets

At this time, the gunners had four observation posts deployed: one (call sign 35, Major Robert Trautmann) overlooking 21 Brigade in the far northern sector—the right flank; another (call signs 25 and 25A, Captains Rendo Nell and André Eckard) to the right of centre observing the remnants of 16 and 47 Brigades; a third (call sign 15, Capt Adolf de Wit) to the left of centre watching 25 and 59 Brigades; and the fourth (call sign 45A, 2/Lt Piet Koen) keeping an

eye on the town and airfield of Cuito Cuanavale from the southwestern end
(left flank) where the Chambinga River flows into the Cuito. Call sign 15 was
no farther than 4 kilometres from 25 Brigade at that stage. A short time later,
an additional OP (call sign TV) was deployed at the confluence of the Cuito
and Cuanavale rivers, behind 21 Brigade. Major Trautmann relates:

> On 17 December, we left [the UNITA forward base near 21 Brigade].
> A strong fighting force escorted us. I got the impression from this
> force's armament that they were not very happy in taking us north
> of the Cuatir River. Some of the armament I noticed among the
> approximately 150 troops were 14 machine guns, 8 LAW anti-tank
> rockets, two 82mm mortars and 20 RPG-7 anti-tank rockets. We
> crossed the Cuatir River and moved north and then west to exactly
> north of the 21 Brigade positions.

Major Trautmann was to find that his observation post would be a tree that
he would occupy for the next five weeks. He spent his first week struggling to
identify shapes in the thick bush, eventually using dust and smoke to help. The
identified targets were engaged by the G5s and recorded for future missions.
At 17h30 in the afternoon of 21 December, the SAAF attacked identified anti-
aircraft positions in 21 Brigade's defended locality; the defenders only fired
back after the aircraft had left. This simply confirmed the observations and
Major Trautmann responded with a fire mission from the G5s, destroying two
23mm guns and causing an unknown number of casualties. FAPLA's routine
had already caused them many casualties up until this point, and yet they
never deviated from it. Major Trautmann continues:

> . . . I would notice between five and six o'clock each morning some
> FAPLA soldiers coming down to the Cuatir River to fetch water and to
> wash. As it was never cost-effective to fire onto them I only recorded
> the target. One morning when it became light, there were at least 45
> FAPLA in the river. Again, the G5s did their thing—at least 15 to 20
> never drank water again.

This occasional firing must have had an effect on 21 Brigade because a battalion of approximately 250 men crossed the river in search of the offending observation post, stopping to bed down very close to the observation post. The next morning, this unit moved back to 21 Brigade and attempted to cross the Cuatir River at exactly the spot recorded (and engaged daily) by the gunners. Utter chaos ensued as the first G5 troop opened fire with airburst, followed by the second troop and the MRL troop. UNITA elements watching closely counted 78 dead or wounded in the riverbed. A downpour of rain held up the carnage for a while; when it stopped, Major Trautmann could not believe his eyes: the FAPLA commander sent the rest of his men across that river in single file; more than half never reached the other side.

This fire mission caused FAPLA finally to react. This they did by artillery and air attacks, reinforced by infantry patrols. The MiGs dropped bombs anywhere from between 300 and 8,000 metres; the artillery shells landed between 200 and 3,000 metres away. The air attacks were responsible for more casualties to FAPLA than to UNITA or the South African forces. Major Trautmann says: 'I got the impression that the Cuban pilots who flew the MiGs could either not read maps or were not really bothered with the fact that they were bombing their own people.'

In December, Commandant van Eeden was relieved in the line by Colonel Jakes Jacobs, the commander of the School of Artillery; accompanying him was Major Deon Holtzhausen (the 2IC of 14 Artillery Regiment) as the replacement 2IC. These two officers' tenure was to be short-lived: Major Holtzhausen became ill and had to be evacuated and Colonel Jacobs was recalled for urgent matters. This gap was filled once again by Commandant van Eeden, who remained in the post until the end of Operation Hooper.

This war, like all others, saw men experiencing highs, lows and excruciating boredom. In the period between 17 and 25 December, Captain Eckard experienced the feeling of loneliness when he was advised that he would be remaining in position when others were being relieved; he experienced the relief of being joined by Rendo Nell; the feeling of desperation at finding that his rations had been stolen; and relief from boredom by distilling his own liquor and having a Christmas Eve 'dinner'. And worry overcame him when it was rumoured that FAPLA had infiltrated the base and he heard the sounds of small-arms fire close by, followed by seeing 'ghosts' later that night. A point worth mentioning here is that, unlike their predecessors in other wars, the South African OP officers in the late 1980s did not deploy in between, or with, own forces as such. The gunner OPs deployed with UNITA protection elements well forward, and, on occasion, between enemy lines. Added to this was the fact that the UNITA troops were not conversant in English, making communications extremely difficult. Furthermore, the OPOs were deployed in a similar fashion to Special Forces, a task for which they weren't trained. Long marches into and out of positions, carrying rations, ammunition and the vitally important radio masts and batteries was the order of the day.

It was not only the OPs who were bored. Gunner Turner tells of the life of a G5 crew member:

At night we would just lie in our bivvies and read or sleep. We made little diesel lamps by using two ratpack tins of different sizes and a piece of string for a wick. They gave enough light to read by. Barnard (our number 6) gave us some amusing entertainment one night by singing about Frylinck (our number 5), and his singing wasn't too good either. Frylinck kept telling him to shut up, but it went on and on. I think the tune was that of 'Rosanna' by the Art Company, and he was just making up any crap that came into his head as he went along.

We made sure our emplacement was dug in. The shells and charges each had to have their own pits and these had to be covered by a canopy made from branches and leaves. We had to have foxholes next to the gun and trenches in front of it. The *spoorplan* [the route made through the gun position by vehicles] had to be covered every day with fresh leaves and branches, and the sand piled up around the foxholes, trenches and pits. Our bivvies also had to be covered.

Every day there was aerial activity, with the MiGs patrolling periodically and our Mirages giving the bridge at Chambinga the occasional revving. Once, I saw an F1 'toss bombing'. He came over really low and then pulled up sharply. Suddenly, this small black object flew out from under the fuselage and forward in an arc towards Cuito. We heard the bomb land with a distant thud. Apparently, some guys from our echelon saw a dog fight between two Mirages and two MiGs over their position. A Puma flew over at low level, probably for a casevac. A few times, the MiGs dropped 1,000-pound bombs in the surrounding area in the hope of getting us with a lucky hit, but fortunately their luck was out. The bombs made a hell of a bang though, and guys who had seen where they had landed said that they literally cleared the bush by about a 25-metre radius. I heard that our water bunker driver had driven past such a bomb one day, which had not exploded, and stopped to take a look. The tail was sticking out of the ground and he studied the Russian writing and the fins. Then he got back in his vehicle and drove on for several kilometres to the *shona* where he filled up the water bunker with water, then returned along the same route. When he passed where the bomb had been, there was just a large crater there.

Gunner Turner gives us an impression of life on the guns:

A fire mission could last anything from ten minutes to more than an hour at a time, and this would generally be repeated from two to six times a day. This meant we probably fired between five and 30 shells a day. Next to my new pit for my charges was a tree, and on the trunk I began to carve with my pocket knife a record of the charges we had used. I had two columns, one for the charge 2 zone 5s and the other for the charge 3 zone 6s. By the time we eventually left that position, my 'logbook' had almost reached ground level, a reflection of how many rounds we had fired there. I often wonder if the tree is still there, with people wondering what all the numbers on the trunk mean. We certainly fired off many, many rounds. In fact, towards the end of February, some guy came along wanting some spent percussion tubes to make some trophy or other. We dug

around in the sand behind the breech of the gun and within no time
at all had filled the lid of a charge 3 container to the brim.

The last day of 1987 saw the gunners firing a full ripple of MRL fire on a
FAPLA air defence radar site, D Troop of Q battery firing at another radar
position (here, call sign TV, the OPO, was positioned some 26 kilometres
from his target), call sign 45A (2/Lt Koen) firing 56 G5 rounds on one target
and Captain Adolf de Wit scoring 23 kills during a fire mission.

January 1988

At midnight on 1 January the observers received a fire plan indicating that
192 rounds per gun would be fired during the attack on 59 Brigade. The
day wore on, with UNITA only managing to overrun the outposts by 08h00.
This attack was answered by some BM21 fire and two MiG sorties, neither
of which were accurate or effective. The G5s were in use continuously and
barrels were wearing quickly. On 4 January, S Battery reported that their
guns were reaching the end of their barrel life.

On 5 January, there was an increase in activity: Captain Eckard engaged a
BM21 battery with R Battery and the MRL troop, resulting in two BM21s and
three vehicles destroyed, with numerous secondary explosions following. To
make life more interesting, FAPA MiGs bombed the easternmost company
of 59 Brigade and finished off by strafing the position occupied by Captain
Eckard with 23mm cannon, but, happily, they missed by some 300 metres.
Captain Eckard's words were 'quite exciting'. The end of that day saw 59
Brigade burning and another four MiG sorties in the area.

On 7 January, a 300-man-strong FAPLA battalion moved around to the
east of Major Trautmann's OP position in an attempt to drive the UNITA–
South African group into the river. However, good UNITA intelligence came
to the fore and the group moved out five minutes before the FAPLA battalion
occupied their position, the rear elements making contact. As soon as the
allies had broken contact and withdrawn to a safe distance, Major Trautmann
ordered a fire mission onto their old position, forcing FAPLA to evacuate after
a number of casualties.

This attack was to cause a five-day period of inactivity; consequently, the OP team deployed in a new position just in time for the attack on 21 Brigade. Not all the South African OPs were close to FAPLA lines, and, in some cases, they were upwards of 20 kilometres from their target areas. Call sign 45A, who was deployed southeast of Cuito Cuanavale, found himself with a distance of 12 kilometres between his position and the bridge over the Cuito River. Lieutenant Piet Koen, at that time 45A, and with one gun permanently allocated to him, prevented FAPLA from using the Cuito bridge during the day, and at night they could only cross without lights. To make things more uncomfortable for FAPLA, the road bridge was partially destroyed and their mobile bridge, brought in to speed up the river crossing, was also destroyed by Lieutenant Koen's efforts. After this, FAPLA brought in two amphibious cargo carriers, which also succumbed to the excellent fire control of Lieutenant Koen and the accurate G5 fire. These were the only two amphibious cargo vehicles that FAPLA possessed.

In another incident, Captain Eckard, call sign 25A, produced good results over a distance of 34 kilometres from the target, using only a pair of standard-issue binoculars. The artillery had instituted a number of SEAD (suppression of enemy air defences) measures, one of which was simply observing and recording FAPLA air-defence radar antennae—a task made easy by the fact that they always deployed on high ground and above the treetops. One morning, the sun just in the right position, Eckard spotted a radar antenna on the western side of the Cuito River—an observer-to-target distance of 34 kilometres. Within minutes, the G5s were on target and palls of smoke were seen emitting from the position; 15 minutes later, the last of the explosions had abated, observed by all the OPs in the area. It turned out that not only was the radar destroyed, but with it went an ammunition point, a fuel installation, 42 vehicles and some 40 personnel casualties.

It must be stated, however, that, despite the hardships experienced by the OPOs and the successes that they achieved, they were still berated by the regimental commander for either wasting ammunition or not being constantly on the air. Tempers were becoming short on both ends of communications lines, and observers in particular were starting to feel ill—more than likely from the unending monotony of the ration packs and lack of any fresh fruit (or fresh anything, for that matter). The UNITA ration pack was occasionally a break from the routine in that it contained more spicy food and always provided mielie meal (corn) porridge.

The artillery fire units remained the prime targets for FAPA, and from the outset the gunners had their work cut out in applying passive camouflage and concealment methods. This effort paid off during both Moduler and Hooper— one water tanker was damaged and was repaired within five minutes.

Another form of deception was to wait until the FAPA MiGs were virtually overhead; at this point, a battery would fire a white phosphorus round into a FAPLA position, whereupon the Angolans would bomb their own troops—usually 25 Brigade. This went on almost unabated until the 25 Brigade commander threatened to fire on his own aircraft if they entered his area. FAPA, to their detriment, did not fly in overcast weather conditions, especially if Menongue air base was clouded over. During the period covered by Operation Hooper, the weather favoured the South African forces, in that low cumulus clouds prevented flying for the latter part of almost every day. This naturally gave the gunners the opportunity to move that most essential of commodities: ammunition.

The ammunition supply chain started in South Africa at the rail sidings of the various ammunition depots around the country. From there, ammunition was transported by rail to Grootfontein where, at the rail head it was unloaded either onto road transport for direct delivery to Rundu or to stock in the ammunition dump. From Rundu, the ammunition was transported either by road or by air to Mavinga—a distance of some 300 kilometres, with no developed roads. The lack of roads caused a high attrition rate of the ammunition: nearly half of every load would arrive damaged at Mavinga. Therefore, the decision was made to fly in all the artillery ammunition from Rundu. The gunner warrant officer responsible for the regiment's ammunition supply was the RSM of the School of Artillery, WOI Albert Hook, a second-generation gunner whose father had been RSM of the School of Artillery in the 1970s. WOI Hook explains the effort involved in moving logistics support forward:

The guns' echelon areas were approximately 160 kilometres from the brigade administrative area in Mavinga. Owing to the air threat, our logistical routes became very long, not only in distance, but also in time. We were forced to do our convoy movement within 100 kilometres of the combat zone during the night. The average speed of the convoys was 15 kph.

This slow speed and long distance made a logistics run a journey of some seven hours up to the A Echelon area. The last leg, from the echelon area to the gun positions, took another four hours—all of this excluding stops for repairs, leg stretches, etc. This had to be accomplished at night without the benefit of roads. WOI Hook again:

> The roads were so bad that all the paint on the cold-drink cans wore off. The only way of determining the difference between a cold drink and a beer was to open it and taste!

Sergeant Louis Swart, a convoy commander in the B Echelon, describes a typical logistics convoy:

> Most of the time the only sleep that we got was in the open air next to the convoy, or, if it was raining, which was most of the time, inside the cargo vehicle. In such cases, it was better not to sleep at all because of the discomfort inside the vehicle. Owing to the actions of our guns [the almost continuous firing] we were constantly on the tortuous roads, taking ammunition to the front. One usually started off by preparing a convoy of six vehicles, but by the time you began the movement it had grown to 20 because of other elements joining in. It seemed that they believed in the navigational capabilities of the gunners.

The incidents described above happened during the troop replacement stage. The gunners were deployed with fresh troops and protected by UNITA companies; the others were busy finishing off training in the Mavinga area in preparation for the push against the FAPLA remnants. At 10h00 on 13 January, the weather, ammunition stocks and assault forces were ready and the east–west attack on 21 Brigade went in. The artillery opened the attack with a fire strike on the main objective. This strike comprised 160 G5 rounds and 120 MRL rounds, the G5s firing at rate intense. On completion of this serial of the fire plan, one troop of G5s continued covering the objective until the infantry's 81mm mortars could take over. R Battery (120mm mortars) provided covering fire for UNITA's attack on 25 and 59 Brigades to prevent them from interfering with the main attack. Colonel Jacobs continues:

After the initial strike the rest of the regiment was ready and waiting on all known enemy artillery positions, of which there were eleven. That meant we had, in some cases, single guns laid on an enemy battery. All observers had been made responsible for certain enemy batteries and the moment one became active the gun trained on it was used and the superimposed fire unit joined in. In this way the enemy artillery was effectively neutralized and, in some cases, destroyed.

Navigating a mechanized force in Angolan soil was very difficult at that time. The bush was so thick that one could only see to a distance of around 4 metres in front of the vehicle. During the attack on 21 Brigade the G5 troop that remained firing on the objective did so specifically so that the assault force could navigate by using the smoke and dust as a reference point. Unfortunately, the bush was so thick that this became a futile exercise and the force had to rely on the artillery observers as their eyes and ears. Here, Major Trautmann, deployed behind 21 Brigade, and Staff Sergeant Vermaak (call sign TV), a Special Forces operator deployed as an artillery observer in the delta between the Cuito and Cuanavale rivers, were successful in navigating the assault force into the main objective.

By 15h00 that afternoon, the weather cleared and with this came the MiGs. As the South African forces were still on the move and, therefore, highly vulnerable to air attack, the only option open was to use the tactic of 'MiG roulette'. Staff Sergeant Vermaak was in a position closest to the approach route of the FAPA aircraft, and on hearing an incoming aircraft would put a 120mm mortar on standby with a white phosphorus round laid on 25 Brigade. As the aircraft passed over his head, he gave the order to fire and, lo and behold, the MiG would attack 25 Brigade. This tactic worked successfully for the next 24 hours when the mechanized assault force handed over to the UNITA occupying forces. During this attack, the gunners also put a stop to enemy tank reinforcements moving up from the Tumpo area, thus giving the South African tanks space to manoeuvre; the end result was 14 T-55 tanks destroyed. By the next morning, the defensive positions in the 21 Brigade locality were found to be abandoned together with large numbers of vehicles and equipment. At this point, the assault force turned south to make sure that the area was clear of FAPLA forces. During the lull in firing after the attack, Staff Sergeant Vermaak reported a large concentration of FAPLA moving over the open area at the confluence of the Dala and Cuanavale rivers. The G5s immediately engaged this target, a troop each firing to the north and south of this concentration, effectively pinning them down. Staff Sergeant Vermaak then ordered MRL fire into the centre of this concentration, thereby destroying the FAPLA force. After this battle, the mechanized forces withdrew and the FAPLA artillery immediately commenced firing on the UNITA occupying force. This effort was quickly silenced by 20 Artillery Regiment, but, unfortunately, not for long, as, unbeknown to own forces, 8 FAPLA Brigade was deploying from Cuito Cuanavale to relieve 21 Brigade, which it successfully completed on 15 January in a night of heavy rain and bad visibility. The visibility remained bad on 16 January, preventing the artillery observers from seeing the FAPLA reinforcement action, and consequently UNITA's withdrawal from the former 21 Brigade positions. In effect, the wheel had now turned a full 360°, and FAPLA were back in their positions occupied on 11 January. Planning had already started for the next attack on 59 Brigade (the alternative being 8/21 Brigades), and the gunners spent the next two weeks replenishing ammunition and continuing sporadic fire missions. After heavy losses, 59 Brigade tried to regain their old positions two days after the attack. They were not successful.

The losses were:

- 450 personnel (estimated)
- 14 tanks (of which 4 were from 3 Tank Battalion, the only 4 serviceable)
- 4 BRDMs
- 1BMP1
- 2 BTR 60s
- 1 B10
- 7 23mm guns
- 9 BM21s and 6 D30s
- 1 each SA-9 and SA-13
- 8 echelon vehicles.

Commandant Francois van Eeden was tasked by Director Artillery to mobilize for two tasks in the operational area, the first being to relieve Colonel Jacobs, and the second to escort two civilian teams into the area for an investigation. These civilians had been working with the gunners for years in the development of the new equipment and systems and they are worth mentioning here. One team, from Teklogic (Pty) Ltd, investigated the performance of the AS80 Fire Control Computer and comprised Johan Marx and Johan Joubert, with Braam Lotter from Armscor. A second team investigated the concept of containerization of ammunition, comprising Johan Niemand (Armscor), Gary Devlin (ESD (Pty) Ltd), Ad Dietrichsen (Somchem (Pty) Ltd) and Gert Pieterse (Naschem (Pty) Ltd).

To illustrate the point that the gunners had worked hard, in the period 1 December 1987 to 28 January 1988 the regiment had fired a total of 13,089 rounds of ammunition, an average of 221 rounds per day. No surprise then that the guns were sorely in need of spares and repairs. The breakdown was as follows:

- Q Battery: 3,984 rounds (of which 1,932 were fired on maximum charge)

- R Battery: 2,944 rounds (of which 1,702 were extended-range bombs)
- S Battery: 5,062 rounds (of which 2,688 were fired on maximum charge)
- I Troop: 1,099 rockets.

Wear and tear was also taking its toll on clothing. In late January, 20 Artillery Regiment required 182 pairs of combat trousers, 356 pairs of socks and 256 pairs of underpants, to list but a few.

On 28 January, Colonel Jacobs was relieved by Commandant van Eeden. By this time, it was not only men who needed rest and replacement, of the 16 G5s in action, at least one (R5205) required a barrel replacement, as it had fired 935 equivalent full charges.

Equivalent full charge (EFC)

Because howitzers fire at different charges, a standard had to be introduced to measure the number of rounds fired by a barrel. In the case of tank or other fixed charge ordnance one merely keeps a record of the number of rounds fired to determine when the barrel is likely to need replacing. In the case of the G5 and G6 the lowest charge (charge 1) was in the order of 0.2 EFC, and the highest (charge 3) 1.3 EFC. This means that a single charge 3 round would wear the barrel 1.3 times more than a standard full charge.

By this time, planning was well underway for the replacement of the Permanent Force and national service incumbents with Citizen Force elements. As Regiment Potchefstroom Universiteit (RPU) was not yet fully converted to G5 equipment one of their batteries would deploy with G2s— another logistic challenge for the gunners because this equipment had not been used in this theatre until this point. In the meantime, 5,000 rounds of 140mm ammunition were on their way, half of which were base bleed HE. (Not many were aware that a base bleed round had been developed and tested for the G2 gun.)

Fatigue was becoming widespread and this was taking its toll on efficiency generally. The artillery OPs were spending upwards of five weeks in position, often without any backup or relief; logistic convoys were slowing down and missing their scheduled arrival times; and repairable gun parts were left lying around and not being sent back for repair.

Battle Group Bravo: December 1987 to February 1988

While the action by 20 Artillery Regiment was continuing in the east, P Battery of 32 Battalion withdrew southwards to Rundu to regroup and change personnel. Major Pierre Franken went on well-earned leave for three months and was replaced by Major Clive Wilsworth. The national servicemen (from 4 Artillery Regiment) were due to return home after their two years' service and were replaced by the national servicemen from 143 Battery (14 Artillery Regiment). The battery regrouped with an organization called Battle Group B, which comprised:

- A tactical HQ under the command of Commandant Jan Hougaard HC (32 Battalion)
- A motorized rifle company from 101 Battalion
- An 81mm mortar group from 32 Battalion
- P Battery (127mm MRL) with a meteorological section
- An electronic warfare team from 5 Signals Regiment
- Two engineer sections from 2 Field Engineer Regiment
- An anti-tank group from 32 Battalion
- An anti-aircraft section from 32 Battalion (SA-3 Missile)
- A mobile air operations team from the SAAF under Major Hennie Louw from the Central Flying School Langebaanweg (which even included a Methodist padré)
- Two medical teams.

Battle Group B's mission was to (author's war diary of 143 Battery):

. . . disrupt the enemy logistics route between Menongue and Cuito Cuanavale from 21 December 1987 until 16 January 1988 by means of MRL fire strikes, mine laying and the demolition of the bridge over the Longa River.

The concept was to engage the logistics convoys with artillery fire strikes, reinforced by SAAF strikes: a classic indirect approach. During the period

Wallpaper: A multiple rocket launcher being loaded; the extra help is being provided by UNITA troops. *Source: DOD Archive*

Alpha Centauri: Lt J.A. de Villiers resting between fire missions. *Photo: J.A. de Villiers*

The MRL course of March 1986. Barring the junior NCOs, all the others were involved in operations.

Standing from left: Lts K.M. Roos, A. Boschoff, T.J. Booyens, J.F. de Villiers, D.B.J. Schoonwinkel, S.G. Clark, M.C. Schoonwinkel, A.N. Eckard, J.A. de Villiers, E.J. Munnik and R.A. Nell. Seated middle: WOII A.E. Hook, Capt G.S. Steyn, Capt M.G. Bennet, Col J.A. Laubscher (OC School of Artillery), Maj F.J.G. van Eeden (course leader), Capt C.C. Laubscher, Capt C. Oosthuizen and Capt C.S. Wilsworth. Front: S/Sgt A. van den Berg, Bdr J.R. Whitehead, Bdr B.M. Knott and Bdr S.P. McCurty. *Photo: School of Artillery*

Alpha Centauri: P Battery preparing for the operation: stable parade at Buffalo Base. *Photo: P. Nortjie*

Moduler: Lt Rob McGimpsey; the mobilization phase. *Photo: 14 Artillery Regiment*

Alpha Centauri: The fire plan for the engagement of Cuito Cuanavale. Note the nicknames for the groups of targets. *Source: G.H.F. Swanepoel*

Moduler: No. 3 gun of Q Battery on the move. *Photo: F.J.G. van Eeden*

Moduler: A Q Battery gun tractor and G5. Most of the rivers in the eastern area of operations were bounded by floodplains such as this. *Photo: F.J.G. van Eeden*

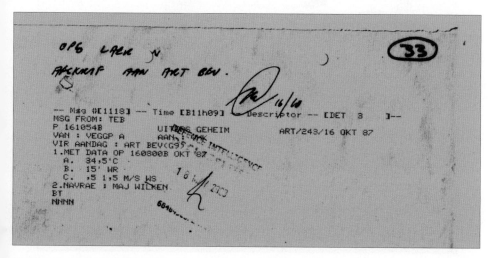

Moduler: A meteorological message from S Battery to the Artillery Tactical HQ. Note the ambient air temperature. *Source: SANDF Archive*

No. 1 launcher of 143 Battery during the final training exercise at the Army Battle School, October/November 1987. *Photo: Author*

Moduler: Capt Phillip van Dyk after the direct hit from an 82 mm mortar. Note the scar on the front deck of the Ratel. *Photo:* Uniform *magazine*

Moduler: The G6 Troop on the road to Grootfontein. On the left is the Ratel fire-control post that did not make the journey. *Photo: H.G.S. Bothma*

Moduler: G6 crew awaiting the order to move. *Photo: H.G.S. Bothma*

Moduler: A G6 in action. It was relatively easy to camouflage vehicles and equipment in the thick bush east of Cuito Cuanavale. *Photo: H.G.S. Bothma*

Moduler: The puff of smoke that follows the opening of the breech after firing: the function of the fume extractor. *Photo: H.G.S. Bothma*

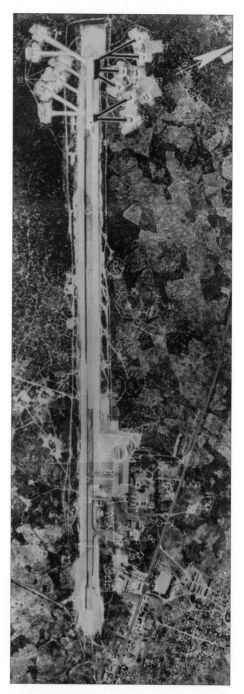

Alpha Centauri: An annotated air photo taken by the SAAF of the airfield at Cuito Cuanvale. The hexagonal annotation in the centre shows an air defence battery and its radar. The buildings at the south-eastern end were within range of the G5 battery. In Operation Hooper the G5s destroyed a number of aircraft on the airfield.

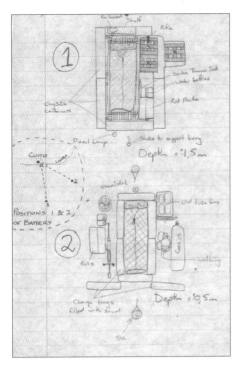

Hooper: Gunner Turner's rendition of life in S Battery's gun positions in early 1988. The sketches show the layout of his rest position. It always interesting to observe the creativity of gunners when building their accommodation; note the use of empty cartridge containers, pallets and old fuse boxes. The word *staaldak* was the general term used by all for the Kevlar combat helmet and dated back to the days when a steel helmet was first issued. The literal translation is 'steel roof'. *Sketch: C. Turner*

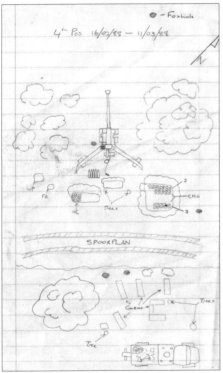

Hooper: H Troop's gun no. 5 firing position. Gnr Turner has indicated the positions for the charges, white phosphorus and HE shells, as well as the fuses. *Sketch: C. Turner*

Hooper: S Battery's gun no. 5 position. Note the dates at the top of the sketch indicating the length of stay in that position. *Sketch: C. Turner*

Hooper: Gnr Turner's sketch of his gun crew's 'ammo tree'. The number of rounds fired per charge and per fire mission were carved into the tree. This must have saved an awful lot of paper. *Sketch: C. Turner*

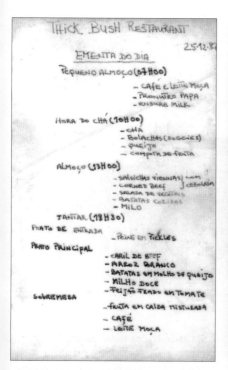

Hooper: Call sign 25A's Christmas Eve dinner menu. *Source: A.N. Eckard*

Moduler: A BM21 after the attack on 47 Brigade on the Lomba River. Note that it is still loaded with rockets. *Photo: SANDF Archive*

Hooper: In order for the OPOs to identify the various air defence radars deployed by FAPLA they were issued with a set of photocopied photographs. *Source: F.J.G. van Eeden*

Hooper: January 1988. A water-stained pen sketch of P Battery being kept busy doing refresher training during the long periods of inactivity. Note the beards and hair length. *Sketch: Author*

Hooper: 'Under the nets'. P Battery commander's Ratel in the Ponte Verde area. At this stage the battery was waiting for the FAPLA convoys to start moving. *Sketch: Author*

Hooper: 'Perpetual Motion'. Two MRLs of P Battery moving northward to the deployment area in December 1987. *Sketch: Author*

Hilti: No. 5 gun tractor with its ammunition offloaded and ready for action at Tchipa before 27 June 1988. *Photo: C.D. Turner*

A detailed view of no. 5 gun S Battery in June 1988. Immedietly to the front of the layer's seat is the sight unit; in front of that is the metal housing for the gun display unit. The gun display unit has been removed and is to the left of the water bucket. Note the shell on the loading tray ready to be rammed. *Photo: C.D. Turner*

Hilti: No. 5 gun of S Battery in action, 27 June 1988. *Photo: C.D. Turner*

Packer: The change of gunner commanders. A pleased Cmdt van Eeden hands over to Cmdt Hattingh. *Photo: SA Museum of Military History*

Hilti: 24 Artillery Regiment in the assembly area at Oshivello preparing for action. *Photo: Author*

Hilti: Crater examination at Eenhana. Maj Hennie Steyn (Arty SO2 Ops) gives an idea of the size of the crater. *Photo: Author*

Hilti: 10 SA Division exercise to the west of the operational area. Unfortunately, the area covered by the division was too vast to capture on film. The target area is in the *shona* in the centre of the picture; the dust is coming from the tanks of 81 Armoured Brigade moving out of cover to the target area. The gunners were deployed to the south (left of the picture). As is the norm with all military exercises, there was a large party of visitors. *Photo: Author*

Packer: An MRL of 191 Battery in action north-east of Cuito Cuanavale.
Photo: SA Museum of Military History

Hilti: A new design for a special tool to repair a Ratel engine! 14 Arty Regt Light Workshop Troop in the A Echelon south of Ruacana.
Photo: Author

Packer: A gun crew of Q Battery RPU.
Photo: SA Museum of Military History

Packer: 155 mm HE shells ready for loading.
Photo: SA Museum of Military History

Left: Hilti: The crews of the 10 Artillery Brigade Tactical HQ keeping themselves gainfully employed. L/Bdr Prophet (the artillery intelligence clerk) on the left, has been nominated as the scorer. *Photo: Author*

Hilti: Col Jean Lausberg, the OC of 10 Artillery Brigade taking a break during an exercise. *Photo: Author*

Hilti: 10 SA Division Tactical HQ on the move. The two Ratels in the foreground are the 10 Arty Bde Tactical HQ (Divisional Fire Support Co-ordination Centre) *Photo: Author*

Hilti: View from the water tower at Oshikango. The Angolan border is on the bend in the road, the road leading to Ongiva. This was the same tower used by NFA's OPOs during Operation Budgie (Chapter 4). *Photo: Author*

120 mm mortar: S/Sgt Claassen next to an Israeli Defence Force 120 mm mortar in the Negev Desert. *Photo: H. van Niekerk*

120 mm mortar: The first air drop, Waterkloof Air Base. *Photo: H. van Niekerk*

120 mm mortar: The original 'Tico' car used as the prime mover. *Photo: H. van Niekerk*

120 mm mortar: The mortar and some of its ammunition after landing. *Photo: H. van Niekerk*

155 mm development: A G4 on display at the School of Artillery, Potchefstroom. *Photo: Author*

155 mm development: An M2 Long Tom (G3). *Photo: Author*

Project Boas: Test firing the new ammunition in Antigua. *Photo: C.P. van der Westhuizen*

Project Boas: The M57 design 155 mm shell (left) compared to the original M56 design. *Photo: Armscor*

Project Boas: Col van der Westhuizen, Col Paul Lombard (OC of the School of Artillery) and Brig Frans van den Berg at a test firing in Schmidtsdrift. *Photo: C.P. van der Westhuizen*

Project Boas: An experimental development model G5 firing at Schmidtsdrift. Col van der Westhuizen stood on the trail leg to prove to the designers that troops could, in fact, stay close to the gun during firing. Note the length of the firing lanyard. *Photo: C.P. van der Westhuizen*

Project Boas: A G5 firing at full charge during testing at Alkantpan. *Photo: Armscor*

Project Boas: 155 mm sub-munition (cluster) shell at the target end. *Photo: Armscor*

Project Zenula: The first pre-production model G6 on trial on the Potchefstroom firing range. The new camouflage paint scheme was only applied from this point onward. All South African G6s were painted in this scheme. *Photo: Author*

Project Boas: Col van der Westhuizen explaining the operation of the G5 to the chairman of Armscor at the Defendory Exhibition in Greece, just before being thrown out. *Photo: C.P. van der Westhuizen*

Project Zenula: A troop of G6s on user trials at Riemvasmaak, Northern Cape. *Photo: Armscor*

Hibiscus / Zenula: An MLZN converted into an ammunition vehicle for the G6. The size of the vehicle can be judged by the person standing on top of the ammunition. This photo was taken in the Arabian Desert during the G6 marketing effort in 1990, a week or so before the Iraqi invasion of Kuwait. *Photo: J. Craig*

Project Furrow: Course photograph taken at Kentron South in May 1979.

Standing from left: unknown, Sgt C. Brits, Sgt E. Donaldson, WOII S.P. Claassen, WOII C. Badenhorst, 2Lt B. Rowbotham, Lt N. Loubsher, WOII H. Pretorius, S/Sgt W. van Ryneveld, Bdr R. Trautmann, unknown. Seated from left: Capt A. Greeff, Maj J. van Heerden, Maj C. Bouwer, Maj J. MacGregor (project officer), Col P. Lombard (Director Artillery), Col C. van der Westhuizen (general manager Kentron South), Maj J. Laubscher, Maj Grobler, Capt C. Roux and Lt C. Wilsworth. Inset left: Sgt M. Louw, inset right: unknown. *Photo: Kentron South*

4 to 15 December, P Battery's equipment was checked and the vehicles sent in for repair. This repair work was long overdue: this equipment had been in action since June under extreme conditions. Furthermore, the battery drove the 300 kilometres from Mavinga to the Rundu assembly area with fully loaded tube packs. How the suspension lasted can only be ascribed to sound German engineering by Daimler Benz on their Unimogs. During this period, Johan Kriek and Staff Sergeant André van den Berg arrived as OP officer and BSM respectively. On 6 December, the OP officers were withdrawn from the assembly area to Fort Foot Special Forces base in Rundu for marrying up and later insertion by air. The Buffel 'command' vehicle that was previously used by Major Franken was declared beyond local repair and the incoming battery commander immediately set about finding a replacement (preferably a Ratel). Eventually, Ratel R 8571 was found, and, by sheer coincidence, happened to be the observer vehicle used by call sign G65 (Major Jakkie Potgieter from the G6 troop that had deployed during Operation Moduler). This well-used vehicle had to have an engine replaced, however, before being put back into service. On 15 December, the OPOs flew out of Rundu with their Special Forces escort to deploy on the Menongue–Cuito road, only to arrive back two hours later as a result of a 120 kph headwind that caused the Puma transport helicopters to turn back with low fuel. An extract from the war diary of 143 Battery (P Battery) is paraphrased as follows:

---

16 December. The following problems confronted the Battery:
No one yet arrived to check the met[eorological] set.
1 x MRL requires main firing cable.
No MRL signals tiffy.
No MRL ordnance fitter.
No sign of replacement technical equipment from WOI Claassen.

A note in the remarks column reads: 'It is now the time to activate a permanent SAA unit in Rundu area with its own mob. stores.'

On 16 December, Battle Group B moved out of the assembly area and travelled 90 kilometres before occupying a leaguer area for the night. The tiffies (Technical Services Corps) worked throughout the night repairing the battery's vehicles, and the next day the MRL signals and ordnance fitters finally arrived. From this point on, the battle group was limited to night movement because of the possibility of observation and, of course, attack from the air. By 24 December, the battle group had advanced to a point 1.5 kilometres south of Gimbe (a UNITA base), where it occupied a leaguer area to prepare for the main mission. During this time, FAPA air activity was constant, but, luckily, they flew at high altitude and the possibility of observing vehicles under camouflage nets was about zero.

By 25 December, P Battery had seven serviceable MRLs thanks to the superb efforts of the technical personnel, who worked tirelessly by day without the benefit of spare parts and workshop facilities. Not only were MRL spares in short supply: Christmas Day was spent wondering when torches and lumosticks would arrive. It is important here to understand the necessity for such equipment. The battery would deploy at night, without lights and in radio silence. All the preparatory survey and prediction calculations would be done under torchlight because the battery was not equipped with standard artillery fire-control posts (Samil 20) with the luxury of an illuminated work area inside, but with Buffel mine-protected vehicles designed to carry an infantry section. These Buffels carried all the technical equipment, including a wind gun and an anemometer with a pneumatic mast, the required radios and additional batteries, topped up by a crew of five with their personal kit, weapons and a trusty spade or two! The lumosticks were normally attached to the rear of each vehicle near the rear axle so as to be seen by the following vehicle and hidden from enemy observation.

At this time, intelligence had determined that the first FAPLA convoy was 80 kilometres north of Menongue, heading into Battle Group B's area of responsibility and under the control of the Russians. A fire strike on Menongue was planned but postponed the next day, as the convoy was still too far away.

By 27 December, the Cubans had almost one division deployed between Cuito Cuanavale and the Menongue area. This led to the drawing up of a withdrawal plan. The two MRL troops would leapfrog each other in a southerly direction, covered by the 81mm mortars and the anti-tank group, with the tactical HQ in control. This plan was supported by a defensive fire plan, which was circulated to the two troops. B Troop deployed into its first firing position in readiness for the withdrawal, should it happen.

Both HF and VHF communications between sharp end and blunt end were, at best, weak to non-existent, and a VHF relay station was set up with help from the electronic warfare team. Eventually, the Special Forces stick could communicate by radio their observations of the convoy movements directly to the battle group's intelligence officer. On occasion, communications were achieved by Special Forces transmitting to Fort Foot in Rundu, which would relay the message to 32 Battalion ops room and then on to the battle group.

What is curious about the FAPLA convoy movements was that they stuck to routine throughout this operation.

The battle group was joined by a UNITA battalion that included a Stinger AA missile platoon. It is interesting that UNITA would not allow the South African troops anywhere near, let alone see, a Stinger missile.

By 30 December, the battery's morale had begun to drop because of inactivity, but suddenly reversed when news came in that FAPA had dropped bombs on their own forces at Baixo Longa, and, to add insult to injury, the AA guns at Baixo Longa fired back! More good news came from UNITA: they had shot down two FAPA helicopters.

New Year's Eve was enjoyed by the consumption of braaied fillet steaks flown in by a SAAF Puma and lukewarm Fanta Orange.

After a ten-day stay in Gimbe, orders were finally given to move closer to the deployment area on 4 January 1988. P Battery started moving at 19h30, collecting the UNITA anti-aircraft teams along the way and occupied a hide at midnight.

Hides / leaguer areas

Whereas mechanized infantry and armour units occupy leaguer areas, the artillery uses the term 'hide'. A hide is occupied as an interim position either before or after occupying a firing position. It is an area where crews can rest, maintenance can be performed and certain replenishment can take place. In the case of MRLs, loading is often done in a hide before deploying in a firing position.

On the morning of 5 January, the sound of helicopters was heard and from out of the east came two Mi-8s flying low. Despite orders to the contrary, UNITA opened fire with an RPG-7 and small arms. Naturally, the helicopters circled back and returned fire, but, luckily, some 500 metres north of the hide. It was interesting to note that after that incident it was no longer necessary to issue instructions to dig in or keep helmets close at hand.

The FAPLA–Cuban convoys were somewhat slower than originally predicted despite their adherence to routine. Once again, P Battery had to 'stand fast' until 6 January when it moved farther north at 23h30, arriving in the deployment area at 03h30. Because of the time, it was decided to occupy another hide and wait to see developments. At 15h30 on 7 January, Lieutenant Kriek issued fire orders and the battery deployed at 20h00. Two hours later, the OPO issued a time to be ready for 04h30 in the morning. This created a problem in that if firing only commenced after 04h30 there would not be enough time to come out of action, move and occupy a hide before first light. Vehicle reliability played a big role in this concern because a breakdown could leave a vehicle exposed to air observation right through the next day. Furthermore, the firing position was in a *shona* covered with waist-high grass and, therefore, out of the tree line. Staying in that position would leave the battery vulnerable to attack from helicopters.

This particular night was overcast and rainy, but by 06h15 the cloud cover had started lifting and the battery came out of action and moved some 4 kilometres south into cover to remain on 30-minute standby to deploy.

There was no activity until 9 January when the OPO reported that 22 vehicles had crossed the bridge at Cuatir. This triggered the battery recce teams to move out to survey a new firing position. The recce teams tried a new approach: they moved by vehicle during the day (to save time later), but very slowly to avoid making dust and singly to reduce potential target size, rather like a step-up or caterpillar movement. During this movement, a lone MiG-23 circled around at about 2,000 feet, presumably from an aborted landing, but, true to form, did not see the recce teams. As the day wore on more reports of convoy movement came in and by 17h45, there were 170 vehicles stopped at the Cuatir Bridge. By 18h40, the target co-ordinates for

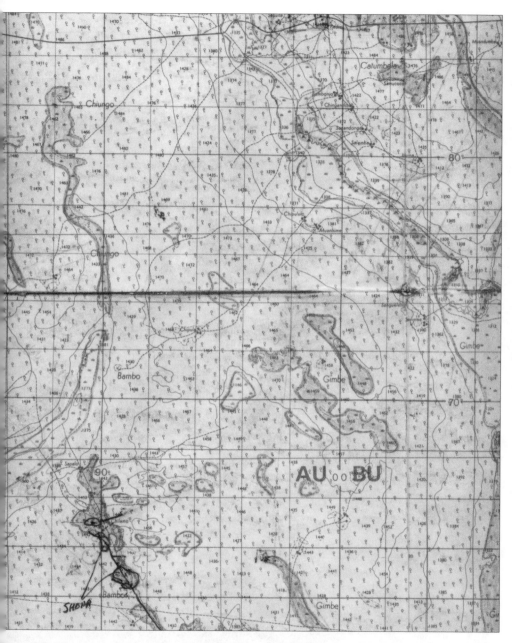

ɔoper: P Battery commander's operational map. Note that only black ink was used. To keep lights to the minimum
 night, the red dome light in the Ratel's turret was used to read with. This precluded the use of a red pen to
ark targets. The FAPLA convoys repeatedly stopped at exactly the same position en route to Cuito Cuanavale.
is was the target that the battery fired at at least twice. The target is marked in black at the top of the map.
urce: Author

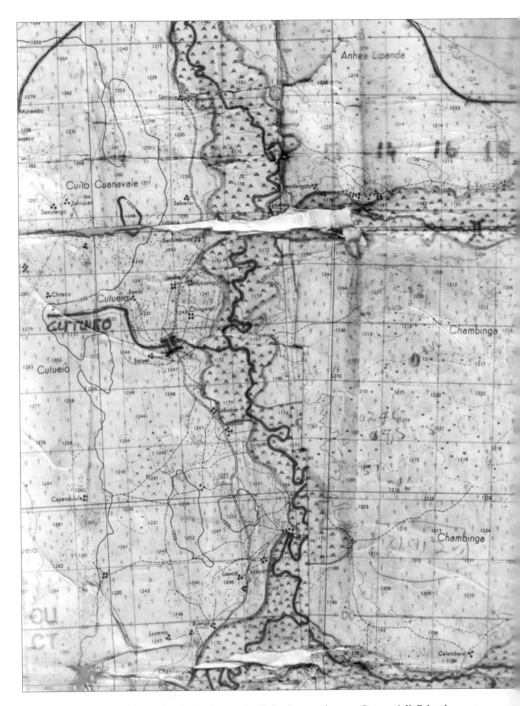

Hooper: Captain Eckard's map showing targets in the Cuito Cuanavale area. *Source: A.N. Eckard*

the convoy were sent through. These are worth noting: head of convoy 990 853 TU, tail at 940 850 TU—a spread of 4,000 metres! However, these co-ordinates meant that the firing position would have to be moved 7 kilometres east in order to reach the target.

The battery 'bundu-bashed' to the deployment area, and at 03h05 on 10 January 1988, fired the first ripple of 192 rockets into the convoy with all rounds on target. This was followed by a second ripple, which landed 2 kilometres north of the target. It transpired later that the target co-ordinates were not accurate and the convoy was hit at the middle and the tail end rather than the head and middle; nevertheless, enormous damage was done.

After this engagement the whole battle group moved south to Ponte Verde some 100 kilometres away to await further orders. By 11 January, only six MRLs were serviceable, and two days later, the battery was down to four—all with mechanical failures, such as radiators leaking and steering rods bent.

On 13 January, a Puma arrived to evacuate Sergeant Myburgh (his father had passed away), Gunner Joines (appendicitis) and Gunner Schutte (broken arm from a Unimog steering wheel).

At about this time, Lieutenant Kriek and the Special Forces team had withdrawn back to Ponte Verde and Lieutenant Kriek subsequently flew back to Pretoria to attend a Permanent Force officer selection board. The battery position officer, Lieutenant Stuart Clark, received a signal to the effect that his promotion to captain would be effective from 1 February.

The tedium of the wait at Ponte Verde was occasionally broken by short training sessions, rain, which benefited personal hygiene (i.e. showers), a game of softball in which the battery's NCOs beat the officers 13:1 and the arrival by air of an AS80 computer, which was neither asked for nor even usable in an MRL battery.

Apart from the vehicle serviceability problem the other point of concern was the reliability of meteorological data. The radio sondes had not been calibrated and could not be relied on to provide accurate upper air readings. The results of the first fire mission led to the decision to use only 'bravo met' (meteorological readings taken by measuring ground-level air pressure, and wind speed and direction by tracking a balloon with a gun theodolite (at night with a lumostick attached to the balloon). At this position the battery commander compiled his post-operational report and some points in this report are noteworthy:

- Equipment state. The state of the MRLs was such that Major Franken recommended that they be withdrawn to undergo fifth-line repair [i.e. complete overhaul and refit].
- Ballistic wind-measuring equipment: both unserviceable.
- Vehicle serviceability. On arrival in the assembly area [north of Rundu], the serviceability was 34 per cent. All vehicles were sent to the Light Workshop Troop (LWT). The battery commander's Buffel was classified as beyond local repair.

32 Battalion's excellent intelligence officer, Captain Herman Mulder, together with the replacement battle group commander, Commandant Flip Genis, arrived by helicopter on 19 January, and by the evening of 22 January, the group's tactical HQ was on the move to a new position in Gimbe (14-53 S; 18-15 E). This HQ comprised:

- The battle group commander team in one Ratel
- The intelligence officer team in one Ratel
- The mobile air operations team and the padré, Chaplain Don Williams, in one Ratel
- Two EW vehicles (included in this group was a Chilean pilot, specifically to listen to the FAPA radio transmissions): two Casspir vehicles
- The battery commander team in one Ratel
- A Casspir ambulance with the doctor on board
- A 10-tonne water bowser from P Battery driven by Gunner de Beer.

This group arrived at Gimbe at 01h30 next morning, camouflaged, and slept until mid-morning.

By 09h00 on 23 January, reports came in that FAPLA's 8 Brigade was escorting a convoy of approximately one hundred vehicles eastwards from

Cuatir (14-35-30 S; 18-03-00 E) and the Special Forces team had made contact to the east of Luassingua in the same area. The next day, intelligence reported a convoy of 200 vehicles, including some ten T-55 tanks on the road in the Luassingua area. Shortly afterwards, another report arrived identifying T-62 tanks and M46 guns in this convoy. The tactical HQ came to the conclusion that this was a Cuban battalion, as M46 guns were the exclusive preserve of the Cubans; the guns were being used to fire speculative bombardments well in front of the convoy and 'white faces' were reported seen by UNITA.

An extract from the battery commander's diary reads:

25 Jan 88. (i) Enemy: 6 x MiGs (-23s) and 2 x SU-22 overhead and clearly visible. Quiet for rest of day. (ii) Own: issued warning order to B Troop plus BPO and two ammo vehicles to move to Gimbe in anticipation of 8 Brigade convoy.

On 26 January, the battery was dispersed as follows:

- Battery commander and B Troop at Gimbe
- A Troop's leader group at Ponte Verde
- Battery sergeant-major and the A Echelon at Ponte Verde
- Four MRL crews returning to Ponte Verde from Rundu after having been quickly trained on 120mm mortars, and accompanying the mortars.

That same day, the FAPA air activity in the Gimbe area moved up a notch, with helicopters flying low over the local population (who were UNITA sympathizers) and firing 'Gatling' guns at them (the Soviet 23mm equivalent to the multi-barreled Gatling). And shortly after this, three MiG-23s broke cloud cover and flew low on their way back to Menongue. Tension was starting to build in Battle Group B.

In the period 28 January–6 February, the now more agile B Troop engaged three more convoys of 8 Brigade from the same firing position with total success, thus proving the accuracy of Battery Met. On 30 January, intelligence reported the bombardment of 28 January was on target, covering the eastern half of the convoy. FAPA helicopters were busy in and around the now static convoys for 45 minutes and EW intercepts heard FAPLA reporting that 'the enemy is using Kentron weapons'. (The 127mm MRL was manufactured by Kentron South in Somerset West, Cape Town, and its ammunition by Somchem Ltd right next door.) It was a mystery why FAPLA, despite having been rocketed four times at the same place, did not change their routine. The last convoy to be engaged comprised eleven tanks, seven guns, five rocket launchers, 128 logistics vehicles and three ambulances, and not once did they retaliate with counter-bombardment.

On 3 February, the gunners occupied a hide 10 kilometres north-northwest of the tactical HQ, where another warning order was received about the movements of 8 Brigade. Once again, they were forming up at Cambumbe ready to move. Preparations were made and ammunition was moved forward to replenish that fired some days earlier. The MRLs were loaded to speed up reaction time. During the morning, artillery and mortar fire were heard emanating from the northeast; the closest round exploded approximately 10 kilometres away. Later that morning at 10h00, in clear skies the thinned out battery watched as three MiG-23s and two MiG-21s attacked the tactical HQ, an attack lasting 20 minutes and wounding a 32 Battalion mortar number.

A day later, after deploying in anticipation of FAPLA convoy movement, the gunners occupied a new hide after bundu-bashing for a distance of about 6 kilometres. The MRL troop now had a circular route between firing positions and the men were becoming accustomed to the area, which was, in fact, not difficult to navigate in because of the shape and size of the numerous *shonas* in the area. Unfortunately, during the night/morning move to this new hide, one of the diesel bunker vehicles suffered a brake lock-up and had to be left out in the middle of a *shona* for the day until the tiffies could attend to it the next night. The crew was brought in with the rest of the troop, as they could not have protected the vehicle by themselves. The stricken vehicle was kept under observation throughout the day, as the hide was not more than 2 kilometres away. It was repaired late in the afternoon and rejoined the troop at last light. That same day saw yet again another air attack on the 32 Battalion AA positions protecting the tactical HQ, still deployed at Gimbe. A SA-7 missile was fired at the AA gunners, but because it did not launch properly it skimmed along the ground leaving a trail of white smoke and providing perfect target indication for the attacking MiGs. So much so that they returned later in the day; the statically deployed tactical HQ was saved by the overcast weather that moved in during the day. It is ironic that UNITA's Stinger missiles were not deployed that day, as they could quite possibly have downed two MiGs.

The activities of the night of 4 February are taken from the battery commander's diary:

2000B, B Troop deployed at 970 635 AU (18-10-30 E; 14-47-00 S) to engage 8 Brigade convoy comprising the following:

- Total 167 vehicles
- 2 battalions of 8 Brigade
- Assembled in area 970 852–970 848; 000 857–000 852
- 4 x T-34s, 4 x T-54s, 3 x T-62x, 1 x BRDM-2, 2 x SA-9s, 1x SA-3, 6 x 14.5mms, 2 x D30s, 1 x 76mm, 1 radar, 2 x BM21s, 3 x BM14s, 9 diesel bunkers, 6 troop carriers, 119 log vehicles, 3 ambulances
- Fired at 2330B. Came out of action immediately. No CB.

Without fail, the FAPLA–Cuban convoys were on the move again the night of 5 February. This time, a Cuban convoy comprising 46 logistics vehicles, three SA-3 missile systems, six diesel bunkers and some 37 other vehicles was reported at Cuatir. This target was 3 kilometres long from east to west and the width some 500 metres. B Troop moved from their hide south and westwards, this time to deploy in Bambo (875 675 AU), and at 04h40 in the morning of 6 February, fired one ripple, scooting immediately afterwards. By 16h00 that day, the convoy was still stationary and vehicles were still burning. A helicopter (Mi-8) flew in and out, presumably collecting casualties. B Troop spent the day preparing for a repeat performance that night. A note in the P Battery diary:

Congratulated 2Lts Lamprecht and Wilken for three successful fire missions. Am satisfied with the performance of this troop as a whole.

In another note: Referring to fire mission of night of 6 February, we believe that this is the first time that the Cubans as a whole have been under MRL fire.

On 7 February, Major Franken, having returned from leave, took over the battery from Major Wilsworth (who became the battle group 2IC) and prepared for the next strike: Menongue air base.

The leader group within the battery was changed to suit the new role and looked like this:

- Captain Stuart Clark—troop commander B Troop (127mm MRL)
- Lieutenant Cobus Stoltz—troop commander A Troop (120mm mortar)
- Second Lieutenant Fortune—TPO A Troop.

The role of the battle group 2IC is support: arranging the echelon's movement and the logistic support of the combat elements (F Echelon). This includes the evacuation of casualties. No sooner had command of P Battery been handed over than the new battle group 2IC had his hands full arranging a casevac resulting from an unfortunate incident. Two of the AA gunners—their gun being deployed close to the wreck of a FAPA An-26 transport aircraft—in a moment of boredom climbed into the cockpit of the aircraft. The booby-trapped instrument panel exploded with the result that Second Lieutenant Wessels lost both eyes and both hands, and Gunner Wilding lost a foot. Captain (Dr) Whiting, the medical officer, on the first day of his first operation, ran to the wreck to help the two badly wounded gunners, in the process stepping on an anti-personnel mine and losing a foot. The tactical situation being what it was the wounded had to wait until dark before a Puma arrived to evacuate them. The worst day during the entire operation was again the result of not complying with standing orders.

The strike on Menongue airfield was carried out by B Troop on the night of 13 February; they fired two ripples into the air base. UNITA claimed that the fire mission was a success, but the next day the sky was yet again full of FAPA aircraft, now flying low and looking for Battle Group B. It must be appreciated that an MRL troop cannot cover a well-dispersed airfield; there are just not enough rockets for the size of the area. That same morning finally saw a reaction from the Menongue inhabitants. For the first time in the operation Battle Group B aroused the interest of FAPA when two MiG-23s flew over the positions at low level, presumably on a search patrol. They did not attack and neither did they return.

Major Wilsworth and Captain Clark flew out from Gimbe to Rundu on their first leg of their homeward journey during the night of 16 February, arriving at Waterkloof on 18 February.

On 18 February, P Battery moved out again to interrupt the movements on the Menongue–Cuito Cuanavale road, where between 18 and 26 February the convoys were struck at least five times by B Troop, and the small base at Luassingua came under the fire of A Troop. During this period, a Mirage F1AZ was shot down and Special Forces were tasked to look for the pilot, assuming that he had ejected. By 20 February, FAPLA and their air force colleagues were observed working their way through the wreckage of the downed Mirage. As they were within rocket range, Major Franken delivered a fire mission of 48 rockets on them, causing a reported 143 killed.

By this time, FAPLA must have had an inkling as to the whereabouts of the battle group because southward movement was reported by UNITA, and, on 26 February, the battle group HQ was shelled by an M46 gun and elements were rocketed by a BM21. As a final gesture, A Troop, accompanied by an anti-tank troop and an infantry company, deviated from their route home to mortar the battalion base at Baixa Longa.

By the end of February, Battle Group B was home in Rundu.

February 1988

Back in the eastern part of the theatre, after 21 Brigade's rout from their positions in January, FAPLA forces appeared to enter a state of panic and assumed that all their brigades were going to be attacked. 21 Brigade had withdrawn to the Tumpo area and had begun re-equipping with equipment already pre-positioned. At the same time, they sent out recce patrols to determine what was left in the old defensive positions. Once again, UNITA had proven that they could not hold a position, and by the end of January, 21 Brigade were back in their old position and reinforced by additional elements. Furthermore, 59 Brigade had been instructed to develop their defences farther east by deploying a battalion to the source of the Chambinga River.

FAPA at this point had initiated night operations by dropping illumination flares, and the FAPLA ground forces had started preparing positions to the west of Cuito Cuanavale for a likely attack and eventual occupation by UNITA–South African forces.

On the other side, the South African forces had five problem areas:

- UNITA's inability to hold ground. This was the fundamental cause of the ebb and flow of this war. No sooner had the South Africans left a defensive position than it would be evacuated by UNITA and reoccupied by FAPLA. This had an effect on the next two problem areas.

- FAPLA could continuously improve its defensive positions, particularly east of the Cuito River. Here FAPLA could develop minefields and defensive fire targets.

- Serviceability of equipment. The South African equipment, especially the main equipment (guns, vehicles and tanks), was sorely in need of repair or replacement from the continuous use. For example, on 30 January only seven G5s out of 16 deployed were serviceable.

- Casualties. South African troops were suffering from malaria and, in some cases, jaundice as a result. Combat casualties were minimal (for example, there were no South African casualties during or after the attack on 21 Brigade).

- FAPA's air superiority and the weather. Bad weather (low cloud and rain) kept FAPA away from the battlefield. Therefore, weather conditions were critical as a factor for planning. As it was, FAPA were almost continuously in the air with flights of three MiGs at a time, and reaching the main supply route. The question was when they would reach the brigade administrative area in Mavinga.

The next objective was the neutralization of 59 Brigade: this formation was the main threat in the defence of Mavinga and Jamba. The plan was for a five-phase attack, the D-Day depending on the all-important weather conditions.

In the period leading up to the attack on 59 Brigade, the gunners kept themselves busy with opportunity targets, one of which was the bridge over the Cuito River. One round managed to damage the bridge sufficiently to stop transport from using it. Another was eight rounds of rocket fire from call sign 51 on the crew attempting to repair the now damaged bridge. Not all went the way of the artillery though. On 31 January, Captain Rendo Nell's OP position was attacked; an attack that was stopped by fire from Q Battery. More personnel changes were being carried out, and Major Deon Holtzhausen arrived on 4 February to take over as the 2IC of the regiment in Commandant Swanepoel's place; and at the same time WOI Steve Collins took over from WOI Albert Hook as RSM.

At 08h30 on 14 February 1988, the attack on 59 Brigade went in with a feint on 21 Brigade by UNITA, supported by the artillery firing a preparatory bombardment and a similar action by 4 SAI on the northernmost battalion of 59 Brigade. By 11h00, the allied forces had made contact, drawing FAPLA defensive fire, and by 17h30, both 4 SAI and 61 Mechanized Battalion had reached their limits of exploitation and joined up on the objective. FAPLA launched a counter-attack on the 59 Brigade positions, which resulted in the biggest fight of that day ending at dusk at 19h00, with both sides withdrawing. FAPLA lost some 230 personnel and 13 armoured vehicles as well as five BM21 MRLs amongst others. The South Africans did not get away scot-free this time; they lost four killed and eleven wounded, together with three Ratels and two Olifant tanks.

The gunners started the next day at 07h00 by firing on the Tumpo positions and then shifting fire onto 21 Brigade's positions in support of UNITA. At 11h00, the South African artillery began firing on 59 Brigade, and at 14h40, a BM21 battery opened fire on 61 Mechanized Battalion as it was deploying in a cut-off position behind 21 Brigade. Within ten minutes, three of the BM21s had been silenced by the G5s. By nightfall 4 SAI were withdrawing to the high ground at the Cuatir source and during this move, the gunner battery commander, Major Riaan Theron, observed a number of green flares lighting up the evening sky. This was normally a signal to the FAPLA gunners to fire on a registered defensive fire target so 4 SAI prepared for a bombardment. This never came, however, as the FAPLA guns had been destroyed by Q Battery.

The result of this attack was the withdrawal of the bulk of the FAPLA–Cuban forces westwards over the Cuito River, with a small force remaining behind dug in around the Tumpo base, and the change of the Cuban commander at Cuito Cuanavale.

It should be said, however, that not all the firing was done by the South African gunners. In his diary, Commandant van Eeden noted: 'HQ area engaged by D30, total 48 rounds fired. Total 48 aircraft over own forces, followed by another 44 the next day.'

Tumpo: Hooper draws to a close

Whilst the rest of the force were maintaining and repairing their equipment, 16 February saw the G5 gunners in action once again, delivering harassing fire on the withdrawing FAPLA forces. P Battery deployed northeast of the now vacated 59 Brigade positions to cover the clearing up of the battlefield. At 01h00 on 18 February, the gunners fired an intense bombardment on Tumpo to reinforce a UNITA recce patrol.

On 19 February, during an air attack on a FAPLA convoy at Cuatir, Major Ed Every was shot down. The wreckage of Major Every's Mirage F1 was quickly found by the Cubans in the area, who set about collecting souvenirs, only to be caught red-handed by a South African patrol, who called for artillery fire. The resulting 96 rounds of rocket fire from T Battery were reported to have caused some 143 FAPLA–Cuban casualties, which were removed in two truckloads. The FAPLA occupation of the Tumpo base became the next objective for the allied forces for two reasons. Firstly, Tumpo could still be used as a bridgehead for a renewed attempt at Mavinga by FAPLA after the rainy season. Secondly, by occupying Tumpo the allies would be in a position to command Cuito Cuanavale by fire and, therefore, make the town and its adjacent airfield untenable. As it was, the airfield could only be used by helicopters using the western end of the facility. Therefore, FAPLA would have to withdraw to Menongue, the next town and airfield of any consequence.

By neutralizing and occupying Tumpo, UNITA could control the situation and release the South Africans, who could then withdraw from the theatre. So planning commenced for the attack on Tumpo. The terrain in that area favours the defender by far, in that the high ground lies to the west of the Cuito River and commands all the approach routes. FAPLA had had time to dig in and develop a well-planned defensive locality complete with minefields and registered defensive fire targets, all observed from the west bank of the river. Movement on the western side of the river was screened by the west bank.

Whilst planning was underway the gunners spent their time harassing FAPLA deployments and making another bit of artillery history. The G5s fired the first operational cluster ammunition on two D30 guns deployed east of the Cuito Bridge. The ammunition functioned correctly, but the observation distance was too long to determine the outcome of the shoot accurately.

The position and layout of the Tumpo defences made the South Africans include deception (once again) as a major factor in their attack plan. Among others, this included a dummy gun position where S Battery were deployed at that time. The five-phase attack on Tumpo began at 11h00 on 24 February with the UNITA 4th Regular Battalion attacking the forward FAPLA elements, supported by S and Q Batteries. At 05h50 the next morning, the G5s opened their fire plan by engaging the FAPLA forward command post. R Battery fired an illumination round to help 32 Battalion in the southeastern portion. This light revealed nothing more sinister than some FAPLA troops withdrawing in a hurry. A mark of this attack was the accuracy and flexibility of the FAPLA artillery fire: they fired accurately on 61 Mechanized Battalion and UNITA forces, causing casualties and delays all along the way. The South African artillery observers, however, managed to silence two of the nine detected firing positions on the west bank by mid-afternoon.

The result of this attack was a withdrawal on both sides. At last light, FAPLA had more than 700 troops crossing the river towards the west bank; and the allied forces were moving back into hides to plan the next move. The artillery kept up firing through the night and the following days, focusing on the Cuito Bridge, where the concentration of FAPLA forces was to be found.

The second attack on Tumpo was planned as an armoured night attack on 29 February 1988. This attack was to culminate in the destruction of the Cuito Bridge, followed by a withdrawal. The main force this time was 61 Mechanized Battalion and a reinforced tank squadron (F Squadron plus two troops from Regiment Molopo), 32 Battalion, an engineer section, and two regular battalions from UNITA. The rest of the force comprised a reserve and a bridge destruction team.

In terms of equipment serviceability, the South African forces were by now worse off than they had ever been during these operations. The gunners were down to 12 serviceable G5 guns out of 16, and three available MRLs. The rest of the force suffered equally.

On 29 February, Regimental Commander Commandant van Eeden issued an instruction to his G5 battery, headed 'AA use for 155mm HE rounds'. Strange as this may sound, it was to be an experiment in deflecting enemy aircraft from own forces whilst in contact. During the previous attack, the FAPLA artillery had fired 972 rounds at own forces; of these, three direct hits caused two South African deaths and three vehicles burnt out.

The objective of this experiment was to provide counter-bombardment as support to own forces that would be pinned down in the final battle while under the threat of air attack.

The plan was to deploy two G5s in a roving position about 10 kilometres away from any other battery. One gun would elevate to 1,316 mills (74°) and lay in a westerly direction—the expected direction of air attack. The SAAF Mobile Air Operations Team would provide the approach height and direction, and the gun would set the time fuse to burst at preset heights of between 15,000 and 25,000 feet above ground level. For safety, the predicted point of burst on the ground was to be sent through to HQ to keep own forces out of that area. The idea was that a 155mm round would burst in front of an approaching enemy aircraft and scare off the pilot. At 01h00 on 1 March, the second attack commenced with 61 Mechanized Battalion in the lead. Twelve hours later, after numerous stops, air attacks, minefields and accurate FAPLA artillery fire, the attackers were still in the objective area, fighting their way out and attempting to recover damaged tanks and infantry combat vehicles. All the while, 20 Artillery Brigade kept up the pace by providing covering fire and counter-bombardment. It was especially difficult for the gunners to provide covering fire during the extraction of the vehicle casualties, as the main threat was a number of well-camouflaged 23mm guns that were responsible for the damage to the Ratels. The close proximity of these guns to the South African forces meant that covering fire had to be provided by the infantry's 81mm mortars, as both 120mm and 155mm ammunition safety distances were compromised.

The carefully selected Tumpo positions had the effect of halting the first two attempts at driving FAPLA out of this area and resulted in the allied forces, yet again, withdrawing to repair, reorganize and re-plan to allow UNITA to occupy the east bank of the Cuito River. Again, the teeth arms could move back to perform these activities, leaving the artillery to deal with opportunity targets and harassing fire tasks. The gunners made use of the apparent quiet to change OP teams, as some had been in action for months on end.

This period also saw the gradual withdrawal of the Permanent Force and national service components of the South African forces, their replacements coming from the partial call-up of 82 Mechanized Brigade under the command of Colonel Paul Fouché. On 3 March, Q Battery moved back to the brigade admin area, leaving R and S Batteries and I Troop to provide cover.

In the west, Battle Group B, by using the firepower of the 120mm mortars of A Troop and the MRLs of B Troop, gave 4 Battalion of 36 Brigade at Baixo Longa a roughing up, mainly as a deception action intended to confuse FAPLA as to the direction of the next attack. FAPLA casualties were reported and the entire 82mm mortar platoon was destroyed. They were only resupplied by helicopter on 14 March.

On 4 and 5 March, 4 SAI and 61 Mechanized Battalion began demobilizing, and Operation Hooper finally drew to a close.

Chapter 11

Packer, Hilti and Prone:
last rounds

'Ubique means that warnin' grunt the perished linesman knows,
When o'er 'is strung an' sufferin' front the shrapnel sprays 'is foes;
An' as their firin' dies away the 'usky whisper runs
From lips that 'aven't drunk all day: "The Guns!
Thank Gawd, the Guns!"'
—Rudyard Kipling, from *Ubique*

Hooper was replaced by operation Packer, which saw the national servicemen and Permanent Force personnel being replaced by Citizen Force units. The two medium batteries were to be replaced by the entire RPU; this brought them the honour of deploying as a regiment for the first time. Under the command of Commandant Chris Hattingh, RPU mobilized in Bloemfontein on 20 February 1988, the day the city recorded its highest rainfall in living memory and became isolated from the rest of the country, a phenomenon that was to delay mobilization of 82 Brigade. By 24 February, the personnel of RPU's G5 battery and all the sharp-end personnel had arrived in Rundu and commenced deploying. RPU arrived in the theatre with two batteries, one hurriedly trained and equipped with G5s and the other with G2s. In addition, RPU was reinforced by A Troop 191 Battery (19 Rocket Regiment) equipped with 127mm MRLs, Q Battery (182 Battery) of 18 Light Regiment (120mm M5) and a meteorological section from 1 Locating Regiment. Commandant van Eeden was then relieved by Hattingh on 13 March. The first battery to deploy was 182 Battery under the command of Captain Jan Borret.

> **The Citizen Force component of the South African Artillery comprised the following regiments (their parent formations in parenthesis):**
> Cape Field Artillery (71 Brigade)
> Natal Field Artillery (84 Brigade)
> Transvaal Horse Artillery (72 Brigade)
> Transvaalse Staatsartillerie (8 Armoured Division)
> OFS Field Artillery (earmarked for the future 73 Brigade)
> Regiment Potchefstroom Universiteit (82 Brigade)
> 7 Medium Regiment (7 Infantry Division)
> 17 Field Regiment (PA) (81 Brigade)
> 18 Light Regiment (44 Parachute Brigade)
> 19 Rocket Regiment (8 Armoured Division)
> 1 Locating Regiment (8 Armoured Division)
> 2 Locating Regiment (7 Infantry Division)

March 1988

During the first half of March, the main focus of the artillery was the preparations for the third attack on Tumpo, which was to occur on 23 March. Q Battery RPU spent each day delivering harassing fire with varying degrees of success. Given that the intention of harassing fire is to demoralize the enemy, with material damage as a collateral success factor, Q Battery achieved success in both aspects: direct hits on two GSP ferries on the Cuito River, a direct hit on the Cuito Bridge, a direct hit on troops on parade and either direct hits on, or destruction of, radar sets, vehicles and ammunition dumps. Although these successes would appear to be of a material, or physical, nature, one should also consider the psychological impact of the direct hits—especially on the parade ground mentioned above. It should be noted here that Q Battery were in action before their conversion to G5 was completed—a new take on the meaning of 'on-the-job training'.

For the newly arrived gunners, all was not as it was intended to be, as RPU's G2 battery found out. This fire unit received a delivery of 155mm ammunition and, therefore, had to lie low for some days because they only had a small quantity of ammunition on their gun tractors. During this time, FAPA kept up their strikes on the gunners but, again, to little avail. The FAPLA artillery continued with counter-bombardment, but also with no result. Two guns from Q Battery were deployed separately from the parent battery in order to create confusion as to the actual location of Q Battery. Staff Sergeant W. Pretch, at that time in command of the two guns, relates:

> . . . we were a small group: 23, including the medic . . . our gun positions were a favourite target of the enemy's counter-bombardment . . . On one of the more restful days, my Ratel driver was sitting in his chair very bored with life, and said, 'I am now so bored I wish FAPLA would take a few shots at us.' . . . The enemy did not disappoint him. His words were hardly cold when we received counter-bombardment. He was the first man into his hole. We were constantly worried by the danger from the air, and, because of the nervousness which was caused when the MiGs were in the air the following phrase was coined, 'When the MiGs are in the air a cigarette lasts three draws, one to light it, one to smoke it and the last one before you put it out.'

Commandant Hattingh, as part of the preparation for the third attack on Tumpo, deployed infiltration observers well forward of the South African FLOT. On 20 March, one observer was deployed on the high ground north of the Cuito Cuanavale confluence after UNITA had chased elements of 36 Brigade off this feature. To strengthen the gunners' observation over the front, 4 Recce Regiment deployed teams to the west of the Cuito River to identify artillery targets.

The mission of 82 Brigade was to destroy the FAPLA forces east of the Cuito River or drive them off the east bank by 20 March 1988. To accomplish this, the plan, in broad outline, was as follows:

- 32 Battalion, reinforced by elements of Regiment Groot Karoo (RGK), would attack the FAPLA positions south of the Tumpo River at first light, after which an artillery OP team would be deployed to cover the west bank using the firepower of the 81mm and 120mm mortars.
- A 'groundshout' supporting operation in the south of Anhara Lipanda would mask the actual armoured attack.

- There would be a north-south attack by the two tank squadrons of Regiment President Steyn on the main objective (66 Brigade). The rest of this main force would consist of an armoured car squadron of Regiment Mooirivier and a mechanized infantry company of Regiment de la Rey supported by a UNITA regular battalion.

As part of the vital deception plan, B Company of RGK (Mechanized Infantry) was tasked to build dummy artillery positions north of the Vimpulo source. The plan was that 182 Battery would fire smoke into this position to simulate gunfire when FAPA MiGs appeared. This activity was designed to draw attention away from the actual firing positions.

After some weather-related delays, the attack commenced on 22 March. To the South African gunners the presence of Cuban leadership was now becoming obvious because at 05h15 on that day, the OP team on the high ground to the east of Tumpo came under FAPLA artillery fire and less than two hours later 182 Battery was shelled, the fire moving ever closer.

Operation Displace was really the withdrawal of all units out of southeastern Angola and involved a tremendous logistic effort to bring out all the equipment and vehicles left behind.

By early May, SA forces had arrived in the demobilization area near Rundu, having effectively stopped the FAPLA forces and driven the bulk of the remaining forces over the Cuito River.

Operations Hilti and Prone

The returning Permanent Force personnel from Operation Hooper had hardly put their bags down on returning home when they were summoned to 10 Artillery Brigade's HQ for a new tasking. Towards the middle of May 1988, Majors Wilsworth (at that stage, the BC of 145 Battery, the titular support battery of 14 Artillery Regiment and the only battery not deployed) and Hennie Steyn (a staff officer in 10 Artillery Brigade HQ in Potchefstroom) were called to the brigade commander's office where they were given a broad outline of the situation in the Angolan operational area. Each was allocated a post in the evolving operational artillery brigade headquarters, these being operations and intelligence respectively. Accompanying these appointments came a set of guidelines for planning, written in longhand by Colonel Lausberg. At that stage, the guidelines covered the future operation in brief and the preparation for operations in detail. The focus of preparation was a training exercise on the Potchefstroom firing range, which included realistic target preparation— particularly for the observers. The lessons learned in the previous year were emphasized: rapid movement, camouflage and concealment, night movement and navigation, to name but a few. Work started immediately, but within a few days the two majors' appointments were switched and Major Wilsworth accompanied the brigade commander to Pretoria where they were to meet the nucleus of the newly formed 10 SA Division, whose commander was Brigadier Chris Serfontein and Chief of Staff Colonel Roland de Vries. The group gathered at the Army College, where de Vries, in conjunction with Deon Steyn, the SSO Intelligence, gave the gathering an updated briefing. It was there that most of the assembled officers and warrant officers realized the scale of the future operation. It would be the first divisional deployment since World War II. One of the crucial success factors was the identification and location of FAPLA–Cuban artillery.

Colonel Lausberg arranged regular briefings and feedback sessions with his commanders in Pretoria, and the enthusiasm with which the CF members undertook their duties was something to behold. Commandants Bol Bootha and J.J. van Heerden of 17 Field Regiment and TSA respectively attended every session and often brought their subordinate commanders and RSMs with them. While this activity was going on, the conventional units that took part in Hooper were to take leave, repair their equipment and regroup to redeploy under the command of the new 10 SA Division in the western part of the SWA operational area. This division was not formally constituted but was based on the HQ of Sector 10 in Oshakati and reinforced with a conventional warfare component. The troop list comprised the standing counter-insurgency battalions in the sector, together with their supporting forces (e.g. engineers, signals, workshops, etc.), reinforced by the addition of the 20 Brigade troops and elements of 81 Armoured Brigade. This was possible, as the eastern theatre was now occupied by 82 Mechanized Brigade, albeit understrength.

The artillery batteries that had withdrawn were, at that stage, only about 50 per cent combat-ready, as their personnel were given leave, equipment needed maintenance and repair and there was also a change of national servicemen at that time. Out of this seemingly loose arrangement of sub-units, order was established by the operational deployment of 10 Artillery Brigade under the command of Jean Lausberg. This brigade initially comprised a tactical headquarters manned by PF and national servicemen, a main or static HQ based in Oshakati and a rear HQ in Potchefstroom. 10 Artillery Brigade's tactical HQ comprised two Ratel 12.7mm command vehicles, one being the operations cell (call sign Zero Golf) manned by Colonel Lausberg; Major Hennie Steyn, the Artillery SO2 Ops; an Ops officer (2/Lt K. Hollenbach); an Ops clerk; and a driver. The other was the artillery intelligence cell (call sign Zero Golf One) manned by Major Wilsworth, the Artillery SO2 Int. (divisional artillery intelligence officer); an artillery intelligence officer (2/Lt D. Bothma); an artillery intelligence clerk (L/Bdr Rob Prophet); and a driver. The main HQ was a duplication of the tactical HQ, but also had the personnel and logistics cells added. The brigade sergeant-major was WOI Sampie Claassen.

On 16 June 1988, Lausberg issued his second warning order to 10 Artillery Brigade for Operation Hilti. In this order the complete (artillery) organization for battle was set out, and read as follows:

- 10 Artillery Brigade Tactical HQ comprising artillery operations and intelligence cells
- 10 Artillery Brigade Main HQ duplicating the tactical HQ
- 14 Artillery Regiment with its HQ and the following under command:
  - P Battery (155mm G5 from 4 SAI Battalion Group)
  - Q Battery (140mm G2 from Cape Field Artillery)
  - R Battery (127mm MRL from 32 Battalion)
  - S Battery (120mm M5 from 4 Artillery Regiment)
  - A meteorological section (1 Locating Regiment)
  - A light workshop troop
  - A signals troop

> - 17 Field Regiment with its HQ and the following under command:
>   P Battery (155mm G5 from 61 Mechanized Battalion Group)
>   Q Battery (140mm G2 from 17 Field Regiment)
>   R Battery (140mm G2 from TSA)
>   G Troop (127mm MRL from 4 Artillery Regiment)
>   A meteorological section (2 Locating Regiment)
>   A light workshop troop
>   A signals troop
> - 181 Battery (120mm M5 from 18 Light Regiment)

4 Artillery Regiment, being the unit under training, was held as reserve and earmarked to relieve 17 Field Regiment for Operation Florentine later if necessary. 10 Artillery Brigade was given the mission to 'ensure the effective employment of the artillery system in support of 10 Division's capture of the area under dispute before 31 December 1988'.

An unusual addition to the standard equipment carried by each gun crew was a chainsaw—a result of the lessons learned the previous year. This tool would save hours of effort and frustration during the deployment of the batteries generally and the G5s in particular, because of their long barrels and the overall length of the gun.

The gunners were expecting to deploy at least one of the regiments in the eastern half of the operational area where thick bush and tall trees prevailed. Another factor that was addressed was the possibility that this operation may see the possible capture of South African guns. This led to training specifically aimed at 'spiking', or destroying, the guns. Emphasis was placed on the identification and training of infiltration observers and forward observation officers for deployment with the tank regiments. The concept of infiltration observers was not new; it had been practised during operations since Savannah. This time, however, the selection of such teams would be based on fitness and stamina as well as the technical ability of the officers and other ranks making up the infiltration teams. The infiltration observer teams would either walk or be airlifted to their deployment areas between, or even behind, enemy lines.

WOI John Boulter was tasked with setting up a system where first-line ammunition was to be pre-packed and prepared for air supply to the batteries in case of an emergency.

The day of 25 July was set down as the date the brigade would move. The brigade HQ staff (Colonel Lausberg, Major Wilsworth, and WOIs Claassen, Boulter and Hickey) were booked to fly from Waterkloof to Ondangwa, and 14 Artillery Regiment were to move by road from their position at Army Battle School to the training and assembly area at Oshivello.

P Battery of 32 Battalion arrived in the sector during May. The following are the names of members of the battery:

- Maj P. Franken
- Lt G.J. Stoltz
- 2Lts W. Dekker, C. Fortune, E. Honiball, A.J. Lampbrecht, J.J. Loots and A.E.J. Wilken
- Sgt J.N. Rademeyer
- Bdrs A.H. Bach, C. Bezuidenhout, H.C. de Wet, F.J. de Meyer, C.L.N. du Toit, E.C. Dyason, C.H. Eckhart, A.M. Fernandez, P.J.W. Kotze, H.J. Lategan, L.R. Schoeman and T.D. van Rooyen
- L/Bdrs G. Botha, B. Burton, J. Bezuidenhout, R.F. Eidelman, R.F. Ellithorne and J. Els, E.H. Engelbrecht, M.J.A. Kruger, D.W. Nunan, M.C.D. Oates, L. Pieterse, G.J. Rademeyer, S.L. Stoltz, A. Strydom, D.S. van Dyk, D.C. van Eeden, M. van Rooyen and S. Waters
- L/Cpl C.M. Bonthuys
- Gnrs R.H. Brown, L.A. Coetzee, R.M. Combrink, S.J. de Bruyn, P.W. Denyschen, W. Dye, H.M. de Beer, J.C. Homan, R.J.A. Janse van Rensburg, P.J. Janse van Rensburg, G.S. Joines, W. Joubert, R. Kendall, G.P. Louw, W.W. Macleod, P. Morillion, C. Oosthuizen, J.H. Pretorius, G.A. Shaw, S. Schutte, J.J. Spies, C. Steenkamp, J.S. Turner, R. van As, C.J. van Niekerk, G.S. Venter, P.W. Vickers and M. Weber.

Attached to this battery was a meteorological section comprising:

- Lieutenant K.R. Moult
- Bombardier R. Brandt
- Gunners P.P.J. Buys, A.R. Riley, J.D. van Aswegen, D. Wells and C. Wilmans

The question might be asked as to why a division was deployed. It was anticipated that the two Cuban divisions, supported by the Cuban–FAPA air forces, would attack from the Cahama area in a southeasterly direction, taking Oshakati and Ondangwa, thence on to Tsumeb and Grootfontein. The intent was foreseen as the destabilization of SWA in order to help SWAPO take over. To support this, ground forces would be supported by no fewer than 32 MiG-24s flying in waves of eight.

Some confusion exists as to the correct name of this operation. Initially, the operation was code-named Hilti, but as more and more units deployed the name was changed to Faction, Prone, Excite and finally Agree, the latter being the pull-out of troops after the ceasefire.

There was another 'anomaly of war' at that time. Deployed under the command of Sector 10 in Oshakati was a battery of G1 guns under Major Carel Laubscher. This was intended as the 'pocket artillery' of the sector commander and was the brainchild and personal tool of Colonel Eddie Viljoen, now the sector's chief of staff. Although they only had G1s, which were about to be phased out of operational service, this battery did some sterling work, the highlight being the bombardment of Ongiva airfield one night in March 1988. They fired 130 rounds fire for effect that caused untold mayhem, and enemy radio reported that they were being engaged by G5s.

During this period, the artillery brigade concentrated on finding the Cuban and FAPLA artillery. Attending the joint intelligence centre meetings daily and analyzing the reports from the deployed OPs provided the gunners with a comprehensive, sensible picture of where the enemy was.

During the quiet period leading up to the final battle, numerous bits of information came into the divisional HQ, some of which could not be confirmed. Two such unconfirmed reports are worth mentioning. First, a large, winged missile system was seen being unloaded in the Lobito harbour. The only conclusion that could be reached was that the Cubans had unloaded an anti-ship missile system for use on land. The only activity that came of that was increased interest in the goings-on at Lobito. Secondly, very large transporters were observed moving southwards from Luanda; their cargo was long and cylindrical in shape—possibly Scud systems. These were never seen or reported again.

For those who had recently come out of operations in the east, life in the divisional HQ was not an unpleasant experience because the village of Oshakati comprised the sector HQ, the divisional HQ in a large hall where the stage was used for daily command briefings, accommodation under roof for all, a hotel, some shops and a steakhouse restaurant run by the incumbent troops where all ranks could get a break from the normal army rations in the mess. This little oasis in the featureless terrain of Owambo was a natural stopover for passing unit commanders and staff, who would usually have every good reason to stay for a night. Despite the intensity of planning and preparation, there was time for socializing, and a strong camaraderie among staff officers and commanders quickly developed at all levels.

Someone must have thought that the gunners in the Divisional HQ were under-employed because at one stage in April, a set of 1:50,000 gridded air photos were handed over to 10 Artillery Brigade with the instruction that they were to be annotated with nicknames for the topographical features. Naturally, this task went to the artillery intelligence cell, who set about marking up 247 master maps, each with about 30 features (roads, intersections, pipelines, *shonas*, villages, riverbeds and power lines, to name but a few). Each feature had its own unique nickname so this kept the gunners busy for some weeks thinking up names from South African towns, battles and characters, and even battles from the Falklands War and North Africa. The annotated maps were then sent back to 4 Survey and Mapping Regiment in Pretoria for printing. In typical military fashion, the printed maps arrived at the time when the units were thinning out and going home. In the middle of June, a sitrep came in from 54 Battalion at Eenhana, reporting that they had been engaged by rockets from a northerly direction. Within a day, 10 Artillery Brigade sent out a team to do a crater analysis in order to determine the line of fire and the type of ammunition that had been used, as there was some uncertainty about this issue and the gunners needed to make sure that there wasn't some new equipment being deployed against them. The analysis was that it was a Chinese-built 106mm rocket launcher, probably used alone.

Once the detailed planning was in place and the brigades were prepared, there was time for a divisional tactical HQ movement exercise. The main aim of this was for the younger members to become accustomed to cross-country movement, quick convoy orders, immediate action drills, crew interaction and radio procedures.

The ever-creative Colonel de Vries took charge of this exercise, and one afternoon in August 1988, the convoy of 54 vehicles (mostly Ratel 12.7mm command) left Oshakati heading northeast towards the cutline (not to be crossed) and thence farther east. Responsibility for convoy navigation was changed after every stop in order to give as many officers as possible the opportunity to practise. Needless to say, at one point late in the first afternoon, almost half of this group ended up doing a U-turn on the wrong side of the cutline, luckily without incident. This three-day exercise concluded with the juniors being given the command and navigation tasks; the senior ranks were told to relax and shut up for the duration.

Late in May, a divisional firing exercise was held in the unpopulated semi-desert area to the south of Ruacana. Here, the two conventional brigades, supported by the SAAF, conducted a rehearsal of the planned mobile defence of the operational area.

One additional task for the G5 gunners was to experiment with a chaff round. The concept was to fire a shell loaded with aluminium foil to detonate at an altitude where it would be picked up by enemy air defence radar. The radars, once active, could then be located and identified by the SAAF, who would then pass the target data back to the artillery for further attention. The first attempts were less than successful. As is typical with any experiment, there was no instruction manual explaining how tightly to pack the foil into the carrier shell. The early results were observed as a large, silver-coloured lump ejected from the projectile and hitting the ground in a cloud of dust! However, this experiment did eventually succeed, and the chaff was ejected and dispersed as originally intended.

On 17 June, the build-up of forces across the Cunene River in Task Force A's area of responsibility caused the issue of an operational order—the first from this newly constituted South African formation. The mission of this brigade-sized force was to secure for the South African forces the vitally important area between Calueque and the South West African Water and Electricity Commission (SWAWEK) installation. This was to be secured until the end of August 1988.

Under the command of Colonel Migo Delport (at that time the commander of 32 Battalion) this operation would begin with the assembly, regrouping and deployment of units as well as reconnaissance activities. The second phase would constitute offensive operations aimed at dominating the no-man's-land on Task Force A's front, an area bounded by the Ruacana Falls to the west and the Cunene River to the east, the SWA–Angolan border being the southern limit immediately to the front of Task Force A. This phase would include limited operations against small enemy concentrations. Finally, the third phase would include the occupation of deliberate defensive positions in the area, but only if offensive operations turned out to be unsuccessful.

The task force's intelligence summary indicated that the Cuban–FAPLA forces were concentrated around the village of Tchipa, with the brigade HQ deployed at Omagobo and protected by an infantry company. It was also reported that 37 tanks were near the HQ. In Tchipa there were two Cuban–SWAPO infantry companies surrounded by a minefield, the SWAPO troops forming the first defensive line and the Cubans occupying the second. The weaponry in this locality included eight T-54 tanks; four BM21 MRLs; a battery of six D30 guns; a battery of M46 guns; two SA-6 anti-aircraft missile launchers supported by SA-7 and SA-16 launchers and controlled by a Flatface Radar; an anti-tank platoon with B10 recoilless rifles; and a number of 82 and 120mm mortars. A number of BRDM 2 and BTR 60 armoured personnel carriers were also noted. In front of this defensive locality, the Cubans had positioned a tactical group-sized advanced post that stretched from Muququete to Nambua in the shape of a half moon, once again deployed in first and second echelons, with SWAPO in front of the Cubans. These troops were fed daily from a central kitchen set up in Tchipa; the rations were delivered by vehicle. Here the weaponry comprised an SA-9 missile launcher with its associated Flatface Radar, three BMP-1 recce vehicles from the Cuban recce platoon, and a number of BRDM 2s were observed. The rest of the force was on foot. This advanced post busied itself with probes and speculative actions to determine the South African capabilities.

Another advanced post was noted at Techonofeu, which comprised a Cuban–SWAPO battalion and two Cuban recce platoons similarly armed as the Muququete–Nambua group, but with the addition of an SA-6 missile launcher.Of particular interest to South African intelligence was the development of a road leading in the direction of SWAWEK. It was appreciated that this route was being prepared to accommodate a large force. The two Cuban recce platoons undertook the reconnaissance of SWAWEK and Chitado. The reserve element of this force included a Cuban battalion deployed at Kanumififa. Again, a Flatface Radar was observed in this area. The only source of water in this area was a hand-operated pump; this was protected by a Cuban infantry company and an SA-6.

In addition, there was a force deployed in the Rotunda-Hende area, of which very little was known at that time except that there were two Cuban–FAPLA tactical groups from the 80th Cuban Brigade in the Humbe-Catequero area. Explosions were heard emanating from this area and the assumption was made that the Cubans were busy with earthworks.

Finally, to the east of the Cunene River FAPLA 19 Brigade was spread around the area to the South of Xangongo.

By this time, FAPA had started landing MiGs at Cahama, which, if refuelling facilities were deployed, could interfere with any ground operations.

By 21 June, Task Force A was made up of the following elements:

- A tactical HQ
- 32 Battalion under the command of Commandant Jan Hougard, with six infantry companies and support elements
- 61 Mechanized Battalion under Commandant Mike Muller with two mechanized infantry companies, an armoured car squadron, a tank squadron, two 81mm mortar groups (eight mortars), its organic anti-tank platoon (Ratel 90mm) and a tank-destroyer troop (Ratel ZT3)
- 51 Battalion (traditionally based at Ruacana) under Commandant Leon Lambrechts with three infantry companies and a support company
- 102 Battalion with two infantry companies and an additional intelligence-collection capability
- 10 Artillery Regiment under Commandant George Swanepoel (14 Artillery Regiment were still mobilizing in Potchefstroom), which by now had been organized by assembling what fire units were available. The organization by necessity had included changing some of the batteries' titles and call signs. 10 Artillery Regiment now comprised:

  - S Battery (155mm G5—ex-S Battery 61 Mechanized), the BPO being Lieutenant Charles Fuchs
  - K Battery (140mm G2—ex 51 Battalion at Ruacana); this fire unit was understrength by two guns, the BPO being Lieutenant Gerhard Snyders
  - A Troop (127mm MRL—ex-32 Battalion) under Major Franken
  - B Troop (120mm M5 mortar—ex 32 Battalion) under Lieutenant Kobus Stoltz
  - A meteorological section
  - An anti-aircraft troop (20mm Ystervark).

By 24 June, Swanepoel had organized and allocated his sharp-end personnel as follows: two anchor OPOs would be deployed at Chambambi and Calueque respectively. Lieutenant André Claassen (call sign 55A) would deploy with 701

Battalion at Calueque, and Lieutenant Anton Jacobie and Sergeant Sanders (call sign 55B) would deploy with the mortar observers on the high ground (MGM Hill) north of Ruacana. Both observers would be responsible for locating enemy artillery and surface-to-air (anti-aircraft) defences, setting up radio relay stations to improve communication between the mobile observers and the blunt end, and to act as listening posts for any enemy air activity. Lieutenant Claassen was also issued with a Q Star long-range night-vision set—not normal artillery equipment, but vital at that time.

The rest of the sharp end would be mobile and comprised:

- Major Theo Wilken (call sign 49)
- Second Lieutenant Renier van der Westhuizen (call sign 45A)
- Second Lieutenant Piet Koen (call sign 45)
- Lieutenant Alwyn Vorster (call sign 45B)
- Captain André Schoonwinkel (call sign 59)
- Second Lieutenant Pieter Botha (call sign 15B)

Major Wilken's observers would link up with 61 Mechanized Battalion, and Captain Schoonwinkel was to remain with 51 Battalion.

The operation commenced on 26 June, with 32 Battalion deployed for wide reconnaissance, covering the whole of no-man's-land. 61 Mechanized Battalion deployed three combat teams, one 'armour-heavy' and two balanced by infantry and anti-tank capabilities, this force being the mobile, quick reaction / attack capability.

The entire artillery effort was based on the support of 61 Mechanized Battalion for this operation. The other battalions—light and motorized infantry—were tasked with performing counter-insurgency tasks on both sides of the border.

10 Artillery Regiment opened fire during the night of 26 June on Fire Plan 'Ysbreek' and Commandant Swanepoel's post operation comments provided the following results:

Target M 5000	Something burning for about four hours after engagement.
Target M 5001	Explosions started about 3 hours after completion of fire plan. Flames increased—suspect ammunition dump.
Target M 5004	Something ignited. The SA-6 did not fire after the MRL engagement.
Target M 5008	Plenty of smoke (white and black) after the fire mission; burnt for some time afterwards.
Target M 5009	Direction 6,400 mills, left 1,500 metres; something burning. Rounds possibly off line and hit some other target.
Target M 5010	Vehicles burnt during mission. Could not get any more feedback after OP withdrew.
Target M 5015	Something burnt for a short time.

A suspected SA-6 position was confirmed by cross-observation from three observers when it fired a missile. This was the subject of considerable attention by the gunners. Commandant Swanepoel reported that no enemy artillery fire was forthcoming during the fire plan.

The next day at 06h00, 61 Mechanized Battalion made contact with the now advancing Cuban tactical groups, and suddenly the gunners had their hands full as the advancing Cubans swept down on three axes of advance. The G5s engaged no fewer than eight targets that afternoon, and the G2s five. All of these targets were plotted by the observers while on the move and in the usual flat, featureless terrain. That day, S Battery (G5) fired a total of 640 rounds and K Battery (G2) 66 rounds, succeeding in helping the armour and infantry in driving the Cubans back. Commandant Swanepoel could not commit his MRLs that day because the infantry was too close to the enemy for safety and the M5 mortars could not deploy within range in time. It was also found that the speed of movement and deployment of the G2 battery limited their participation in this battle and resulted in the G5s bearing the brunt of the fire missions. This also meant that the amount of fire that was potentially available could not be used.

Nevertheless, one of the most satisfying results of the artillery intelligence efforts came on 26/27 June during these engagements. Intelligence had reported that an SA-6 battery was deployed very close to the Cuban HQ at

Tchipa, and the analysis of typical Soviet deployments showed that there should be an artillery command post / HQ very close by. To confirm this, the gunners launched a meteorological balloon, beneath which they attached aluminium foil. Within seconds, the SA-6 battery's radars became active and shortly after six SA-6 missiles were fired. Major Franken, Lieutenant Alwyn Vorster, Lt Anton Jacobie and the ever-present Lieutenant Piet Koen observed this activity and replied with six hours of almost continuous fire. The result was silence from the Cuban gunners throughout the night and the next day, leading to the conclusion that the command and control systems had been destroyed or that HQ of the 80th Artillery Division had been neutralized.

Gunner Chris Turner, who, with the rest of S Battery, had returned from leave after Operation Hooper, was a member of the crew of gun number 5. He relates the blunt-end view of the battle at Tchipa:

> That afternoon, we were instructed to hitch up the guns and prepare to move. We were briefed that we were to attack a large base at Tchipa, where there were also Russians and Cubans. There was also apparently an Angolan air force base at Xangongo. We advanced steadily through the bush. At one stage, we stopped for our commanders to confer with each other and I remember seeing one guy running through the bush with a machine gun belt over his shoulder, with the sun reflecting off it as it swung about. There were some curious-looking Ratels that had joined us. They were painted in camouflage and had weird rocket launchers on the turrets. Then we moved on again. At about four that afternoon, we reached our position, about 10 kilometres south of Tchipa. We deployed the guns. The sun was just starting to set when we were ready. Suddenly, a strange sight met our eyes. A met balloon (used by the meteorology guys to measure wind movement) was released way up front with what looked like long strips of tin foil hanging below it. Then long trails of smoke shot up from the ground at the balloon. We were all pointing at this phenomenon and remarking about it, when suddenly the order for battery fire mission was given, quickly followed by the

bearing / elevation, ammo and load commands. Without wasting any time, we were ordered to fire. Basically all hell broke loose. I don't know how many rounds we fired, but it was a lot. We could see the flashes of our exploding shells in the sky above the bush in the distance. We continued with this until about 8 or 9 o'clock, when we were ordered to ceasefire. We hitched up the gun, loaded the ammo and equipment and prepared to move off. We made our way through the dark bush back to our original position, where we deployed the gun again. Apparently, on our first barrage we had taken out the entire Angolan artillery command, with the result that we didn't receive any return fire. The trails of smoke that we had seen were SAM8 launchers which were also blasted into oblivion. After we got back we went to sleep, but we heard later that Peter Moynihan from one of the other guns had left his R4 rifle behind, and they had to go back with a Ratel and fetch it.

Next morning, I awoke to a drumming sound in the ground. The sun was up. Suddenly, a frantic shout rang across the bush '*Kom by julle kanonne; julle maatjies word gerev daarvoor!*' (Get to your guns; your buddies are getting revved up front there!) We ran to the gun, with Schmullian getting the bearing, etc. on the radio as we ran. When we got there we practically threw the projectile and charge into the breech, and commenced firing for all we were worth. This continued throughout the morning, with the occasional 'victor victor' alarm in between, although no aircraft came over at that time. However, somewhere between midday and one o'clock we got another 'victor victor', camouflaged the gun again and took cover in our foxholes. We waited till eventually we heard that familiar hissing sound approaching. With the bush being much lower here we had a much more open view of the sky, which was clear, and after a while the MiG 23s swept into sight. I think I saw six of them. Some of them were camouflaged and some were that light-grey colour. They approached from a north-northwesterly direction, passed us on our western flank and headed southeast, where they disappeared from sight. Shortly after that, we heard a number of thuds from the direction of the bridge and our anti-aircraft there going berserk. The MiGs appeared again and headed back in the direction from which they came. It was a terrible feeling; we knew that they had dropped those bombs on our guys somewhere, but we didn't know where or how many.

This was probably the first and last one-on-one fight with the Cubans. The battle groups managed to extricate themselves after some clever firing and manoeuvring against the Cuban force that was arguably the strongest and best organized thus far. This short exchange between forces did not culminate in any victory for either side, but the South African Infantry and Armour did learn that the Cubans were not a pushover by any stretch of the imagination. So much so that there was, at one stage, a very real threat that the SA forces could have been outflanked by the Cuban armour on the western side. This outflanking manoeuvre was stopped by placing the entire artillery's fire on this force, with the destruction of eight Cuban vehicles and some 300 casualties.

The battle ended on 27 June 1988 when, by noon, all South African forces had withdrawn to positions south of the Cunene River. This was the last exchange between the South African gunners and FAPLA or the Cubans. The withdrawal from the Namibian Operational Area began in early 1989.

The last rounds after 12 years and seven months of action were fired by the G5s of S Battery 61 Mechanized Battalion Group during the late morning of 27 June 1988.

The withdrawal of Task Force A from the Calueque area allowed the Cubans, FAPLA and SWAPO to move farther south, but there was no further build-up of forces. What the South Africans did not know at the time were the intentions of the Cubans after the battle at Tchipa. Because of this, the build-up of forces south of the cutline continued until August 1988, when the Cairo talks, aimed at the cessation of hostilities and the implementation of UN Resolution 235, commenced. The decision to withdraw all troops from Angola was made by Cabinet at the end of June in preparation for the peace talks. There were, however, some exceptions and limited numbers of troops were to remain behind to observe the Cuban–FAPLA activities. These teams were to provide early warning of any build-up or further southward movement of those forces. So the gunners still had OPO teams deployed to the north of the cutline—the only high ground from where observation could take place.

On 1 July, 10 Artillery Regiment planned for the troops to leave. Most of them had been in action for eight months, albeit not constantly. The first to go was B Troop (P Battery) who returned first to Rundu to hand back their M5 mortars, and then home for a well-earned rest. They returned on 17 July to Rundu where they collected their MRLs, thence on to the Sector 10 theatre for deployment. A troop left the theatre on 21 July, their MRLs being stored in Ondangwa in the B Echelon until their return on 1 August. Similarly, the other fire units left and returned for the next phase of operations.

The intelligence community was monitoring the situation across the border on a daily basis and providing battle indications of a potential full-scale attack by the Cuban forces. This changing situation resulted in the continuous regrouping of the South African forces, and the gunners were no exception. Major Carel Laubscher's 141 Battery, based in Oshakati, and still equipped with 88mm G1 guns, was the next to be re-assigned. On 1 July, 10 Artillery Regiment HQ issued a warning order to 141 Battery to prepare for a conversion to G2 equipment. The battery's A Troop would move to Ruacana with their equipment and ammunition, where they would undergo a conversion course onto the medium guns. This was intended to bring the battery at Ruacana up to full strength and provide a short-term relief while the latter went on leave. By 1 August, the conversion was complete and the gunners now had a complete G2 battery deployed, one troop in Ruacana and one in Oshakati. During this period, Major Laubscher prepared a new defensive fire plan for the Oshakati defences. It should be noted that this battery was originally trained on M5 mortars and had already undergone one conversion to the G1 equipment before deploying in Sector 10 initially. This battery maintained its M5 capability by keeping its mortars close at hand, thus being able to change roles almost overnight. The perceived threat to the South African forces meant that 61 Mechanized Battalion was deployed over the whole of

Sector 10's area of responsibility (south of the cutline), with combat teams responsible for sectors within the theatre. Happily, this did not last long, as 4 SAI Battalion Group were already mobilizing together with 81 Armoured Brigade and other units. By the beginning of August, 10 Artillery Regiment had completed their leave and had redeployed to cover the appreciated approaches. The RHQ under Swanepoel deployed in the Oshakati area. S Battery (Wilken) deployed in direct support of 61 Mechanized Battalion to cover the Oshakati approach. Farther east lay P Battery's B Troop, where Major Franken covered the Ondangwa approach. A Troop of 141 Battery deployed their G2s in the Ombalantu area to the northwest of Oshakati. Here Nico van Rensburg took over as troop commander. K Battery, now a troop of 141 Battery remained deployed to cover the Ruacana approach and was reinforced by the detachment of Lieutenant André Oosthuizen (141 Battery) as BPO. They were, however, prohibited from deploying in the 51 Battalion base (Hurricane base) at the Ruacana airfield because they needed to be mobile at all times and could become vulnerable to attack in that position. K Battery's fire was reinforced by B Troop of P Battery (127mm MRL).

The OPOs remained virtually unchanged, with Lieutenants van der Westhuizen, Verster and Koen all deployed in S Battery's area. Lieutenant George Conradie prepared himself as an infiltration observer to deploy when required; and Verster attended a forward air controller course before returning to S Battery. The OPO teams in the west were reinforced by the attachment of an OP officer from 141 Battery, bringing the total up to four officers and one sergeant.

The counter-bombardment policy became active, so fire units did not need higher authority to fire back if fired upon. At the same time, fire across the border was prohibited except in the case of counter-bombardment, but any enemy force seen crossing the border could be engaged and destroyed. All local settlements were declared no fire zones. Despite all the operational preparations, the shortage of serviceable G2s was still a cause for concern and the decision was made to send Major Laubscher and his BSM, WOII André Bothma, back to Potchefstroom to resolve that problem and help with the mobilization of the rest of 14 Artillery Regiment.

In the village of Oshakati at that time, adjacent to the sector HQ and sharing the facilities with 141 Battery, was 10 Armoured Car Squadron (Eland 60 and 90mm) under the command of Major Garth Rogers. This sub-unit provided the mobile reserve for the sector as well as escort duties, mobile roadblocks and rapid-reaction tasks. Being an integral part of Oshakati's defences, this squadron was required to exercise the defensive fire plan from time to time. On 13 July, 10 Artillery Regiment instructed K Battery, under the leadership of Lieutenant Oosthuizen, to move from Ruacana to Oshakati with a troop of G1s to support 10 Armoured Car Squadron in practising the defensive fire plan. In order to fill the gap left behind, S Battery was tasked with deploying in the Ruacana area.

The hiatus after the battle at Tchipa started to influence morale and, more especially, discipline. In an inspection report of 22 July, 10 Artillery Regiment's commander commented on the general lack of discipline: troops were unshaven, dressed in a mixture of camouflage and 'browns' (the nickname given to the dark, earth-coloured combat uniform of the time) and some were found wearing cut-off T-shirts or no shirts at all. More important, however, was the issue of functional, or combat, discipline, and here it was found that ammunition was dirty and, in some cases, covered with oil as a result of a spillage in the back of a vehicle. This ammunition was supposed to be ready for use in a fire plan. The consequences of that could have been catastrophic to the offending gun crew because the combination of oil and a covering of sand could have caused a barrel premature on firing. In the G2 battery two guns were unserviceable and little effort was made to correct this deficiency. All of this was addressed by disciplinary action and the situation was resolved quickly. On the positive side, the anchor observers who had remained in position after the last battle maintained round-the-clock surveillance and were constantly sending intelligence reports back to the blunt end. However, there was a lack of intelligence feedback to 10 Artillery Brigade HQ in Oshakati, more from a lack of manpower than anything else, and this was solved by detaching 2/Lt W. van Wyk to 10 Artillery Regiment as intelligence officer. The build-up of South African forces reached its peak in the last week of July when the bulk of the mobilizing units and HQs arrived in Oshivello. 10 Artillery Brigade was, only now, a fully fledged operational formation, as the incoming units either started training or deployed directly. 14 Artillery Regiment moved by road from Potchefstroom with the following elements:

- The balance of the RHQ
- 41 Battery (120mm M5) of 4 Artillery Regiment, under the command of Maj Niek du Plessis with the following personnel:
  - Lts D.J. Kock, J.J. Scheepers, W.P. Steyn
  - 2Lts R.M. Benade, A. Duckitt, M.J. Hilditch, D.H. van Aswegen, D.G. van der Merwe, T.J. Wood
  - S/Sgt S.H. Maritz
  - Bdrs C.J. Barnado, K.S. Barrington, P.J. Botha, J.J. du Plessis, C.H. du Toit, P. Kedian, P. Labuschange, G.N. Melville, W. Rautenbach, R. Sassenberg, H.N.J. van Heerden
  - Gnrs M. Amdur, T. Aucamp, A. Barcher, S.W.F. Barnard, I.D. Basson, M.S. Basson, A.J. Dekker, C.J. du Toit, W.A.L. du Toit, J.H. Bezuidenhout, M. Bezuidenhout, R. Bezuidenhout, D.J. Boness, A.M. Botha, T. Botha, F.J.W. Bronkhorst, D.C. Brown, J.J. Buitendag, J. Byrne, M.E. Carpenter, M.J. Carreira, L. Clarke, L.G. Cooper, C.L. Cronjé, G. Cronjé, L.A.F. de Carvahlo, A.R. de Luca, P.L. de Meyer, H.R. Dieperink, G. Dornet, S. dos Santos, D.H. Dyers, W. Edwards, C.B. Elbourne, E.A. Engelbrecht, J.A.M. Engelbrecht, P.J.L. Erasmus, G. Evans, K. Fletcher, L.S. Fourie, D.M. Fowlds, L. Friguglietti, T. Frohbus, H.J. Greeff, J.A. Grobler, J.G. Groenewald, C. Hattingh, T. Haywood, A.A. Herbst, B.J. Herholdt, E.H.B. Herman, A.R. Hibbert, A.C. Hills, J. Huddlestone, B.M. Jacobs, P.V. Juta, M.H. Karow, C. King, S.M. Klopper, M. Koekemoer, W.E. Koekemoer, M. Koutandos, S. Koutandos, D. Kruger, P.P.F. Kuhn, F.M. Kukard, G.A.P. le Roux, A.G. Lennox, G.J. Louw, G.F. Marais, J.A. Maritz, N.G. McCraken, D.R. McFarlane,

Hilti: the concept of operations.

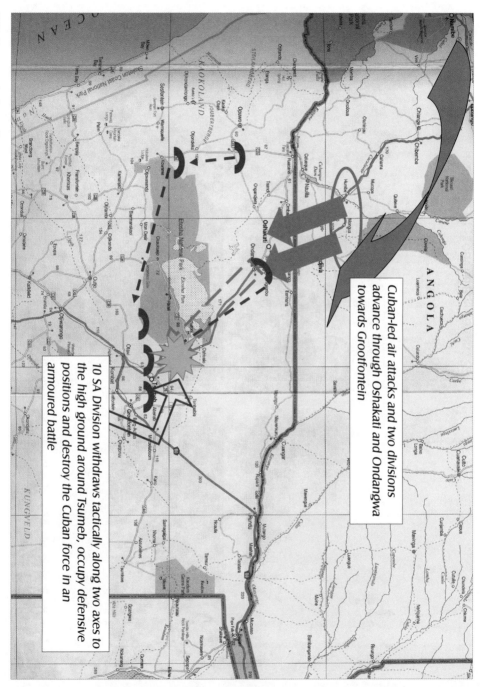

Cuban-led air attacks and two divisions advance through Oshakati and Ondangwa towards Grootfontein

10 SA Division withdraws tactically along two axes to the high ground around Tsumeb, occupy defensive positions and destroy the Cuban force in an armoured battle

No. 5 gun in a firing position just south of Ruacana airfield after firing the last rounds at Tchipa on 27 June 1988. S Battery had withdrawn from Angola and occupied positions to counter any southward movement of the Cuban forces deployed near the Cunene River.

Sketch: C.D. Turner

A.J.M. Mendes Da Ponte, J.F. Naudé, H. Nieman, J.
Oosthuizen, C.R. Panther, W.R. Penhall, A. Peyper, J.A.J.H.
Pieterse, A.G.W. Pretorius, A.L. Pretorius, W.A.P. Putter,
K.M. Robertson, S.J. Rossouw, L. Salmon, S. Scheepers, G.
Schutte, B.E. Silksone, A.N.J. Smit, P.J. Smith, D.J. van
der Merwe, F.W.J. van der Merwe, S.K. van Ginkel, C.S. van
Wyk, B.J. van Zyl, F.J.J. Venter

- Q Battery (155mm G5) of 4 SAI Battalion Group, under the command of Major Cassie van der Merwe (this fire unit having had a rest and refit after Hooper and Packer)
- Major Jaco Breytenbach, attached to this group as the 2IC, but intended for deployment elsewhere

While 14 Artillery Regiment was on the move, 17 Field Regiment and Transvaalse Staatsartillerie (TSA) flew in from Pretoria to form the nucleus of the second regiment. During the period 24 to 27 July these elements began arriving in the Oshivello training area.

In the divisional main HQ the permanent staff of 10 Artillery Brigade HQ were reinforced by a contingent from NFA and 2 Locating Regiment under Commandant Richard Lovell-Greene (NFA). This was a blessing because it gave them a chance to get home occasionally and helped tremendously in that they could deploy both main and tactical HQs concurrently, and reinforce the logistics effort using RSM Mick Rumble (NFA). At the same time, the Army Command and Staff Course moved into the 10 Division HQ to help, and gunner students were allocated to 10 Artillery Brigade for the duration. These were Commandants Maartin Schalekamp (SO1 Ops, tactical); Bossie Bosman (SO1 Log. in the main HQ); and Nic Taljaard (Log officer at 14 Artillery Regiment). Not all the students actually occupied those posts, but were used to help with the division's operational planning. 14 Artillery Regiment was mobilized in full and deployed some elements immediately. It is important to understand that the bulk of the combat element of 14 Artillery Regiment was already deployed and the regiment was actually properly activated by the addition of its HQ and its full support elements.

14 Artillery Regiment was then made up of:

- A tactical headquarters under the command of the newly appointed Commandant George Swanepoel
- P Battery—a 120mm mortar battery under the command of Major Niek du Plessis
- Q Battery—the G5 battery from 4 SAI under the command of Major Cassie van der Merwe
- R Battery—the MRL Battery from 32 Battalion under the command of Major Pierre Franken
- S Battery—the G5 Battery from 61 Mechanized Battalion under Major Theo Wilken
- T Battery—the G2 battery normally stationed at Ruacana, under the command of Captain André Schoonwinkel
- The Support Battery
- G Troop of 44 Battery—an MRL troop under Lt Koos Brytenbach.

Fortunately too, 96 members of 1 and 2 Locating Regiments with three met sets and a hydrogen generator were flown directly from Potchefstroom to Ondangwa on 22 July, reinforcing the meteorological and artillery observation capabilities. The elements that deployed later (P Battery, Q Battery, G Troop, and the main HQ of 14 Artillery Regiment under the command of Lieutenant Nico van Rensburg) were ordered to move under the command of 10 Artillery Brigade on 24 July to arrive in Oshivello by 28 July.

The second regiment was titled 24 Artillery Regiment, as it comprised a mix of personnel from 17 Field Regiment and Transvaalse Staatsartillerie forming one battery, and Cape Field Artillery forming the second battery, both equipped with 140mm G2 guns. This unit was commanded by Commandant Bol Bootha of 17 Field Regiment, with Major Jaco Breytenbach (10 Artillery Brigade) as his 2IC. During the operation Q Battery from 4 SAI Battalion Group and G Troop were moved under the command of 24 Artillery Regiment, thus balancing the firepower of the two regiments.

By October 1988, 10 Artillery Brigade had started thinning out its units in the western operational area, the deployed batteries in the east having withdrawn during April 1988. TSA and 17 Field Regiments demobilized on 4 and 11 September respectively, and CFA's battery left the operational area on 12 October 1988. By 19 October, all the gunner units were out, the only exception being S Battery of 61 Mechanized Battalion which moved back into its base at Omutiya in preparation for the final withdrawal in early 1989.

As far as can be ascertained, the South African gunners only lost three guns during all those operations, none of which were captured. The first, near Luso in 1975, was a G1 with a damaged muzzle brake and barrel; another was a G5 that suffered a barrel premature during Moduler; and the third was an MRL that became unserviceable during Hooper and was badly loaded onto a cargo vehicle returning to Rundu.

The last out

The last out was S Battery, 61 Mechanized Battalion Group. They moved by road from Omutiya to Walvis Bay for sealifting back to South Africa on board the SAS *Drakensberg*. It is rather ironic that both the first in and the last out—albeit under different conditions—were lifted by the navy.

Chapter 12

A bigger punch:
the development of new equipment

Contrary to popular belief, Operation Savannah was not the trigger for the new-generation equipment in the South African Artillery. This need had already been identified in 1968 and formalized in 1973 when the gunners set the requirements to modernize their equipment in line with the army's upgrading programme. One must also understand that it not just the guns, mortars or rocket launchers (i.e. ordnance main equipment) that make up the artillery. The objective of any artillery is to put an appropriate amount of fire into the right place as and when it is needed. In order to achieve this we need to determine the following:

- The exact location of the target on a map, ideally accurate to within 10 metres, but 100 metres usually suffices. This includes the height above sea level.
- The exact location of the gun position and its height
- How much of what type of ammunition is required
- The meteorological conditions
- The characteristics of the ammunition on the position (i.e. charge temperature, projectile weight, etc.).

If any of these factors cannot be determined, the round will be less likely to hit the target. Ideally, a first-round hit with the maximum amount of the appropriate ammunition is required.

In the early 1970s, the army had committed itself to reorganizing the conventional forces—a subject that had been neglected for years. In brief, the design was for a corps (1 SA Corps) with two divisions (one infantry, one armoured), a Mechanized Brigade (Permanent Force) and a Parachute Brigade, supported by corps troops. This corps would operate in conjunction with the unconventional forces made up mainly of the commando groups placed territorially throughout South Africa and SWA. The gunners would have to modernize to be able to support this formation, as most of the brigades were either mechanized or armoured—largely modelled on the Israeli Army. A third division (9 SA Division) was planned, but only partially established.

In the West, artilleries had already developed and fielded 155mm guns, some of which dated back to World War II. An example in the USA is the M2 155mm Long Tom, and in South Africa the G3. There were also a number of modern 155mm gun systems (e.g. the British FH70 and the US M109) all using the same M56 pattern projectile and NATO standard charges and all were equipped with 39 calibre barrels. (The calibre of the tube / barrel is 155mm and the length is measured in calibres, hence 39 calibres = 6,045mm.) Multiple rocket launchers, on the other hand, were the speciality of the Soviet or Warsaw Pact countries so there was no international standard rocket or missile.

The South African Artillery identified a requirement for a gun that reached a range of 24,000 metres if it were to counter the Soviet-supplied forces that were becoming a conventional threat.

In the environment of fire prediction or ballistic calculation, the Royal Artillery was developing the British Artillery Target Engagement System (BATES), an early-generation fire-control computer.

In terms of target acquisition, the South African Artillery lagged even further behind. The Green Archer Mortar Locating Radar was becoming obsolete (it dated back to the 1950s) and increasingly difficult to maintain. There was no means of night observation and, other than well-planned survey schemes, no accurate means of target fixation.

Armscor

In the early days, this organization was known as the Armaments Board, the Armaments Development and Manufacturing Corporation and later as the Armaments Corporation of South Africa. For the purposes of simplicity, the term Armscor has been used in this book. Initially, Armscor was charged with not only procurement (acquisition) of armaments, but also their manufacture. Over time, the manufacturing was transferred to the private sector and parastatal companies (Denel business units). Lyttelton Engineering Works (LIW) was just such a company. LIW dates back to the 1940s when it assembled and, in some cases, manufactured, artillery equipment (3-inch howitzer) and small arms.

In order to keep up with the momentum of mechanized forces, the artillery equally needs to move rapidly from position to position. At that time, the field gun tractor was the famous Bedford, and the medium gun tractor the Magirus Deutz—both of which were becoming long in the tooth. All other transport in battle was the Land Rover 110-inch wheel base for observers, and various other forms of Land Rover for recce and fire control. The infantry was already in the process of developing the Ratel ICV. The gunners would have to keep up somehow.

With this as background, in 1974, the South African Artillery embarked on an upgrade programme that was to last for more than 30 years. It should be borne in mind that the development of military systems is a costly and time-consuming process. The main reason for the seemingly long development period was cost: the budget simply did not allow for overnight development. Another factor was the international arms embargo in force throughout the 1970s and 1980s. In order to obtain technology, South Africa had to resort to gun running and other 'illegal' activities, on a grand scale.

What operation Savannah did for the gunners was to bring home their shortfalls and reinforce their operational requirements. In an article written specifically for Dr Gerald Bull, the 'father of the G5', Lieutenant-General (ret.) Joffel van der Westhuizen wrote:

My colleagues' and my artillery life had a 'before and after Savannah' character. Before Savannah, the South African Artillery [Field Branch] found itself as an extension of the Royal Artillery, and our drills, equipment, procedures, and even our traditions were British-based. We were primarily a supporting arm for the infantry and armour . . . in November 1975, 14 Field Regiment, of which I was the OC, stood on Angolan soil. For the first time since World War II, we fired our trusty old G1 and G2 guns in anger at an enemy. Against our guns [were] the 130mm medium gun (M46) and the 122mm rocket launcher [the 'red eye'].

And exactly because of this to-and-fro firing, our lives in the artillery made an about-turn and the British yoke and blinkers bit the dust. We learned with unbelievable speed that the artillery can fight independently and aggressively, whilst it must still be prepared to provide fire support to the infantry and armour. At the same time, it must be able to protect itself and especially its gun crews. Later, we even deployed a single gun well forward, engaged the enemy and withdrew before they could shoot back. Actually, guerrilla tactics with a gun.

Artillery firepower: with increased and intense firepower, the enemy is physically and psychologically disrupted [and] own forces can overcome terrain with minimum losses. For example, what was intended as an attack on Bridge 14 became an advance just because we saturated the enemy in that area with fire. It was these engagements that made the troops call the G2s the 'tools removing red eye'. It was the lack of weight [explosive power] of the projectiles that made us deploy observers far forward to make sure that every round counted.

The night is your friend when your catapult is smaller than your enemy's. We literally crept up in the darkness, deployed well in front of our infantry, fired on registered targets and were gone by first light.

A gun without a round is like kissing your sister: it's there but leads to nothing! Thanks to the loggies and sergeant majors we could always shoot, even though it was desperate at times: a few times even with captured equipment and the enemy's own ammunition. It is not just the replenishment of first- and second-line ammunition that counts, it is the overall maintenance of man, steel and tyre on the front line that keeps a force in the fight.

Strategic mobility means wheels, and that main equipment on tracks can miss a whole war. We moved every man and thing from Potchefstroom to as far as north of Luanda by rail, road, air and sea. And we brought it all back again, including an arsenal of captured equipment.

Tactical mobility, or movement on the battlefield itself, keeps surprise on your side and compensates your shortcomings, especially inferior range. We visited Angola in the rainy season, unfortunately, and on many a day had to de-water and de-mud the guns before we could fire. To move in and out of gun positions required more than just gun tractors: it required muscle power. And then the ground was uneven, bushy and criss-crossed with rivers. We fought on a front of 800 kilometres, from the Atlantic coast to just short of the Zaire and Zambian borders, deploying in terrain that gave a new meaning to 'cross-country'.

We were forced to move around as we did not have ballistic flexibility or inherent mobility, meaning the movement, or flight, of the shell in the direction of the enemy. Here we came second, and badly at that. However, the farther, wider and higher one can fire from a single position, the less one has to move tactically, and how much more an opportunity there is to deny the enemy's freedom of movement. On a hot day, with the wind behind us, we could attain 16.5 kph, whereas the Russians could reach 26 kph with the M46 and 20.5 kph with the 122mm. The higher a gun fires, the closer one can hide behind high ground, fire overhead and reach the enemy on the opposite slope. With the exception of the mortars, there was no other ordnance that could get that right. There was many a day when we yearned for an inherent upper register [high-angle] capability.

Thus was born the user's requirements for the new-generation artillery equipment somehow to be acquired. Added to this were three indelible imprints made on the gunners of that era. First, the acceptance by NATO forces that 155mm was the optimum calibre for the artillery, as this size shell could also carry a nuclear, biological and chemical (NBC) filling and provide a formidable conventional round. Secondly, the Soviet doctrine of massed artillery firepower meant that the force that could use its inherent mobility would be more than likely to win the firefight. And thirdly, the international boycotts and flour bombs on rugby fields meant that the South Africans would have no choice but to pull the proverbial rabbit out of the hat and produce their own armament. Given this context and the lack of any defence industry in South Africa, the call was made to develop the ordnance and ammunition as a system at the Space Research Corporation (SRC) in Canada and to industrialize and deliver 56 guns by South Africans, in South Africa by March 1978. In Lt-General van der Westhuizen's words, 'a mouthful'.

Taking chances: the development of light (airborne) artillery

Despite the army reorganizing its conventional capabilities there was a large contingent of resistors, who unfortunately found themselves in the senior ranks at that time. The 'RC factor' (resistance to change) was widespread, and ignorance of fast-moving conventional operations was rife. Furthermore, this old school of counter-insurgencyunconventional warfare soldiers maintained an almost xenophobic attitude to the Israelis and would not accept that their successes in three wars since 1956 were mainly attributable to highly manoeuvrable ground and airborne forces, well commanded and supported by good communications systems. Gradually, the SA Infantry Corps would split into the mechanized versus the motorized factions—the motorised being seen as the bottom of the food chain. Nevertheless, the handful of the 'converted' managed to successfully transform almost half the army into an effective conventional force in short shrift. By 1976, the first conventional brigade had deployed to cover the withdrawal from Angola.

During 1972 and 1973 the Director Artillery and his staff searched the world for a light artillery system, in effect to replace the already aged 25-pounder and to increase the mobility and flexibility of the field gunners. During this period, they visited a number of countries, specifically Italy, to look at the

OTO Melara 105mm light gun, the favoured solution to the requirement. France had a rifled 120mm mortar, but difficulties arose in establishing a contract. In 1973, a contract with Israeli Military Industries was signed for the purchase of, initially, 36 120mm mortars from Tampella Industries. In February 1975, four gunners and one tiffy were detached to Israel to train on the 120mm Tampella mortar. They were Major Chris Bouwer, Second Lieutenant Herman van Niekerk, Staff Sergeant Sampie Claassen, WOI Toon Greeff and the tiffy was Sergeant Rautenbach.

This team spent three weeks in Israel with the Israel Defence Forces (IDF) in intensive training in the Negev Desert on the 120s. In the words of Lieutenant van Niekerk, 'there was very little they could really teach us . . . but they had nice women in the base!' The comment about learning very little was not a result of extreme arrogance, but should be seen in the light of the simplicity of the weapon. All South African officers and senior NCOs were exposed to the 60 and 81mm mortars during courses, and, therefore, all that was new about the 120mm would have been its sighting system and firing tables. On their return from Israel, nothing happened in the light artillery environment for some time. Promises were made about gunners attending parachute courses, but little developed in terms of the operational doctrine for this new concept. There were good reasons for this. Firstly, the situation in SWA and Angola was occupying military planners' minds. Secondly, the climate in the artillery was changing as a result of the requirement to upgrade the corps' capabilities in general. Furthermore, the Israeli-made 120mm ammunition was not entirely reliable or safe. One instance of this was the propensity for fins to break off during firing. Therefore, the South Africans would have to improve on this ammunition and develop a production capability. All this excitement contributed to the delay in establishing the airborne artillery capability.

Operation Savannah came and went, with the important result being that the gunners conducted a major debriefing and strategic planning session in which all who could make a contribution did so, thus forming the foundation for the revamp of the South African Artillery. The artillery's success in

Savannah made them the 'darlings' of the defence force and resulted in their future requirements being given top priority.

In 1977, training on the newly delivered 120mm M5 mortar began at 141 Battery. There were a number of problem areas that needed to be resolved on this new equipment. The two of major importance were the sight that was provided by the manufacturer and the removable trailer. The sight unit was not equipped with a telescope or optical viewer, but instead with an open sight where the layer had to align a white arrow with a far aiming point. This led to inaccuracy in laying for azimuth, and this inaccuracy was unacceptable to the gunners. The complete sight unit was eventually replaced by a dial sight that was operated similarly to those fitted to the rest of the ordnance. The trailer was a flimsy affair: the axle and wheels were the rear assembly of a Citroen 2CV, and it was debatable whether this equipment would survive combat in southern Africa. Throughout operations, the M5s were ported on the back of Samil 100 cargo vehicles, and it was not until years later that a complete new rugged trailer was commissioned into service.

By 1978, an eerie silence still hung over the airborne artillery, and Captain van Niekerk was then the battery commander of 141 Light Battery. Many official requests to develop the airborne artillery concept were ignored.

In 1980, in sheer frustration, Captain van Niekerk took a staff car and travelled to Army HQ to attempt to gain some momentum for the airborne artillery concept. He found an empty office, sat down and diligently wrote a complete instruction in the format of a telex. This instruction tasked the air force, army air supply, Waterkloof air base, 44 Parachute Brigade, Director Artillery and 14 Field Regiment to jointly plan for, and execute the air supply of the 120mm mortars at Air Force Base Waterkloof and to follow up with the operational applications thereafter. During his immediately previous posting, van Niekerk had been aide-de-camp to Chief of the Army, Lieutenant-General Constand Viljoen, so he knew who to lobby to achieve some haste in this pursuit. Within a day, back at 14 Field Regiment, van Niekerk was called to the OC's office and briefed on this secret task by Commandant Hurter and Major Vermaak, the 2IC. Van Niekerk's comments are worth recording here:

I should have kept a copy of that telex . . . it was one of the best cons I did in my life and nobody suspected it . . . I think no one could even imagine that such a stunt would be pulled in an army that was that well regulated.

Captain van Niekerk takes up the story again:

Very quickly, the Light Battery was taken notice of and parachute training for the gunners commenced . . . to the absolute grief and ultimate horror of the infantry. It is true that the instructors at the Parachute Battalion were rather 'offish' and tried to fail as many gunners as they could . . . just for the sake of doing so . . . they proved themselves to be real a---holes . . . but all their efforts were in vain—the gunners qualified and the Light Battery established itself.

At Air Force Base Waterkloof in Pretoria on 7 April 1980, the first air drop of airborne South African Artillery was carried out right next to the main runway. Four mortars with ammunition were dropped successfully by a C-130 Hercules, and the concept was established. At that stage, the gunners had no lightweight, air-droppable vehicles so old airborne vehicles that were not used by the infantry were converted for use by the artillery. These were known as Ticco cars, after the officer who came up with the original concept. They were initially three-wheeled, but were soon modified to be four-wheeled. Powered by a 12-horsepower petrol engine, they were not a great success, but nevertheless served a purpose in the interim until the new-generation airborne vehicles were produced. The M5 mortars went on to prove themselves time after time on operations, and only in the near future will they be replaced by the new 105mm light entry ordnance (LEO) light gun.

The search for more firepower:
Project Boas and the birth of the 155mm guns

The story starts in 1970, when, during October that year a North American company by the name of Space Research Corporation approached Armscor and the SADF to invite them to a firing demonstration of new 155mm ammunition. This invitation and another shortly after to demonstrate the same system in South Africa were not accepted by either party at the time. No doubt the seed was planted, however, in the minds of the forward-thinking gunners, as the story will reveal.

In 1973, while the South African Army was reorganizing itself, the gunners conducted a study on the state of the artillery and here they found that they needed 232 field guns and 84 medium guns, although only 183 and 52, respectively, were available.

To add to this problem, only 54 self-propelled 25-pounders (Sexton) out of a fleet of 140 were available for use. The Sexton was a 25-pounder mounted on a modified Sherman tank hull used in the latter part of World War II; parts were not available for the nine-cylinder Pratt and Whitney aero engine, and the aviation fuel used was expensive.

To set the theme, at that time the NATO / Western countries' armies were equipped with 155mm gun / howitzers of 39 calibres, for example, the US M109, the British FH70 and the French F3. These guns could attain a maximum range of 19,500 metres with M56 projectiles on charge 10. One of the few guns with a longer barrel was the US M2 155mm Long Tom, at 45 calibres.

These were the guns used for the development work to come. Soviet–Warsaw Pact equipment tended to lag behind, and in any event, it was not available in South Africa.

Therefore, in 1974 the gunners identified the need to replace the entire arsenal of artillery ordnance. By tracking NATO artilleries' improvement programmes and the potential conventional threat posed by the neighbouring countries, the requirement was set for a gun that could provide a high rate of fire, higher mobility and a 24,000-metre range.

High mobility

In the artillery context, high mobility does not necessarily mean the ability to move the ordnance quickly from one place to another, but to rapidly shift the fire from one target to another. This means that the gun needs to fire at long ranges to provide depth, or reach, and to be able to traverse over a wide arc to the right and left to cover a wide area.

The following year (1975), the first group of artillery personnel left South African shores to evaluate potential replacement equipment. This group studied 12 different systems in Italy, Israel and France. In France they identified the GCT F3 towed 155mm system as the best option. Further, they recommended that 155mm would be the optimal calibre, as all the NATO countries were using such equipment and common ammunition. The optimum barrel (tube) length seemed, at that time, to be 39 calibres.

In December that year, the international arms grapevine finally made Space Research Corporation aware that South Africa was now serious about its artillery upgrading requirements, and targeted this country as a potential customer for their new 155mm extended range full bore (ERFB) ammunition. That year also saw the commencement of hostilities in Angola and the gunners went into action with what they had. This war, and the Soviet BM21, triggered a more serious look at the shortcomings in firepower and, in 1976 the chief of the SADF issued an instruction that 20 'long-range' guns be procured, together with 12,000 high explosive and 2,500 white phosphorus rounds. Added to this was the requirement for 50 per cent of the fuses to be proximity fuses. All this was to happen in three weeks.

The sense of urgency prevailed, and Minister of Defence P.W. Botha briefed the Cabinet on 19 January 1976 (while the troops were changing over in Angola). Here he warned of the need for self-sufficiency in the arms industry, the lack of balance in the SADF capability and the serious lack of effective weaponry in the army in particular. This stimulus, together with the success that the artillery had achieved in Operation Savannah, put the artillery's requirements at the top of the priority list on the SADF budget.

Brigadier Frans van den Berg, a gunner who was the most technically competent officer at that time and who had attended the Royal Artillery Long Gunnery course at the School of Artillery at Larkhill some years earlier, was selected to head a team to negotiate the purchase of the new equipment. The French government could not satisfy the original requirement, as they were concerned they would reduce their own inventory of F3s and would not be able to replace them in time should the need arise. Furthermore, they were at the receiving end of political pressure to adhere to the arms embargo (despite the sale of Mirage F1s to South Africa a year earlier), so that was the end of any further negotiations. The next available source was Israel, and Brigadier van den Berg started up negotiations with Israel Military Industries, in particular Soltam, the manufacturer of the M68 towed howitzer. By this time, the South African requirement had grown from 20 to 32 guns (one regiment of four batteries). Even in the 1970s the design and manufacture of military equipment was a global affair. In fact, global co-operation in this field goes back to the 19th century. To illustrate this international co-operation, the M68 howitzer was designed and developed by Tampella in Finland, modified by Tampella Israel and manufacturing was undertaken by Soltam in Israel.

In Israel the South Africans also negotiated a deal with the IDF in which they would buy six 130mm M46 Soviet guns as an interim measure until the new guns were delivered. This ordnance, together with ammunition, had landed in Israeli hands during the Yom Kippur War of 1973. Because this was an interim solution, a deal was negotiated with a provision for a guaranteed repurchase. In the end, these 'appro guns' never saw action in South Africa and eventually returned to Israel.

The M68 howitzer was limited to a range of 21,000 metres with its 33-calibre barrel and the South Africans finally decided upon the M71, a 39-calibre version of the same gun. A towed gun, it was somewhat less expensive than the self-propelled version and (theoretically) could be used in southern African conditions. The howitzer used standard NATO (M56) 155mm ammunition, which was fairly readily available internationally.

South Africa wanted 32 howitzers, which would have equipped one regiment as an interim measure until the G5s establishment and delivery of the M71 commenced in 1977, the first battery (2 Medium Battery) being established at 14 Field Regiment in 1981. In South African service this gun would be known as the G4.

Canadian origins: the G5

Because of SRC's involvement in the Martlet Project, they had developed a 155mm projectile that could attain longer ranges than those of contemporary ammunition. This projectile design was known as extended range full bore

(ERFB) and was longer and more streamlined than its predecessor, the NATO standard M56. The new projectile was given the nomenclature of M57—this still stands today. At that time, the M57 could outrange the M56 by 6,000 metres using the same propelling charge.

The South Africans, having only secured 32 modern guns, had to continue searching for other options to satisfy their requirement and, in October 1975, the CIA in Pretoria was approached. The CIA was already involved in Angola supporting the FNLA, so this request by South Africa was pursued and supported in the USA. However, the Americans had to honour the arms embargo so they decided on an indirect approach to supporting this requirement—they took the route of arranging introductions to various arms dealers who could help. By November 1975, the first exploratory talks were held in Bangkok between Deneys Zeederberg of LIW, Piet Smith of Armscor and a retired colonel, John Frost, an arms dealer. Colonel Frost recommended the Space Research Corporation.

Negotiations between Armscor, the SADF and SRC commenced in February 1976, while the South African Army was planning its withdrawal out of Angola. These negotiations, held in South Africa, centred on the acquisition of the ERFB ammunition. However, during these discussions, the SRC team leader mentioned that they (SRC) had ten surplus US M2 155mm Long Tom guns, which, provided an agreement could be reached on the ERFB ammunition, would be added to the contract.

In March 1976, SRC and Somchem began contract negotiations to industrialize the filling of the new ERFB projectiles and the manufacture of propelling charges. At the same time, a visit by the South Africans to France, the USA and Canada was discussed and planned. This trip was almost cancelled by the minister of defence, who was concerned that Canada may cause security problems for the South Africans.

After a submission to parliament in May, priority was placed on the artillery, and things began to kick into top gear. On 11 May, the project team was appointed and by 26 May, final contract negotiations were complete. Finally, in July the contract related to Project Sherbert III was concluded and SRC sold 30,000 shells, gun barrels and drawings for the GC-45, a new howitzer, to Armscor. The result of Project Sherbert III was named the GC-45 (Gun-Commercial 45), because of SRC's need to market it internationally. Therefore, it can safely be said that the G5 was conceived in July 1976.

Already at that early stage, the GC-45 showed that longer ranges from 155mm howitzers were possible and it was this characteristic that convinced the gunners to support the contract.

The first drawings and data packs did not arrive in South Africa by formal delivery, or courier. In fact, they were carried across the world by Piet Olivier from Armscor in his suitcase. A collection of drawings and gun barrels in no way constitutes a new artillery system; design had to perfected to the point that the concept would be able to serve South African military needs. These needs were unique to the African subcontinent and included the following:

- The system would have to be moved rapidly over long distances (Pretoria to Grootfontein is 2,000 kilometres by road) and would need to be airlifted in a C-130 Hercules. Therefore, the physical size and weight were critical.
- The climate of the operational area varied from hot, wet summers to cold, dry winters.
- The systems would have to operate in dense bush and between tall trees. This meant that the howitzers would need to travel and deploy over short distances without the use of their gun tractors and would, therefore, need their own power and transmission systems.
- The mud and dust of the operational area would cause a high attrition in moving parts and, in particular, breech mechanisms would need to be simple and robust.
- Furthermore, this new howitzer would be firing at far higher charges than existing 155mm equipment and would need a far stronger recoil system than that currently available.

These are but a few of the design criteria that would be applied to the new system. At the same time, the South African gunners, having listened to and studied their Israeli counterparts, realized that the howitzer would need to move rapidly from one firing position to another in order to maintain the element of surprise, and avoid counter-battery fire. This, together with the long strategic distances and reasonably good road infrastructure in southern Africa, gave birth to the wheeled self-propelled ordnance that would be known as G6.

At that time, Armscor comprised a procurement agency and a number of subsidiary business units specializing in the design, development and manufacture of military hardware. One of these subsidiaries was Lyttelton Engineering Works (now known as Denel Land Systems), a manufacturer of rifles and other small arms, based in Lyttelton, Pretoria, which had recently begun with the production of 90mm guns for the Eland armoured car. The country was not short of good engineers at that time, but it should be noted that these professionals did not have a wealth of experience in developing military equipment. Armscor appointed Dr Willem Barnard as the lead engineer to develop the new systems and Piet Olivier as the programme manager.

Dr Bull established a separate company to SRC in Brussels, called European Poudreries Réunies de Belgique (PRB), which would be the contact with Armscor. Armscor, at that time, did not have the expertise in artillery development, production or operations and needed someone from the military to provide the very important users' inputs. This was resolved by the SA Army seconding Commandant Joffel van der Westhuizen to Armscor. Commandant van der Westhuizen was to mothball his uniform, pack his family and household, and move to Brussels for an indeterminate period. To all intents and purposes, he now worked for Armscor—or rather a front company set up for the purpose. Commandant van der Westhuizen was accompanied by four other South Africans from the defence industry.

The contract between Armscor and PRB would see the early development of the GC-45 gun in Canada. This would be a joint effort, with PRB retaining the rights to market the eventual product internationally. During development, SRC would assist the South African defence industry to gear up for the industrialization and production of guns, ammunition and peripheral equipment. This was to be no mean feat as, at that stage, only small arms were manufactured, together with the 88 and 140mm artillery rounds. Initially, SRC would ship empty projectiles to South Africa for filling by Somchem and gradually the projectiles would be cast and finished by Cementation for filling.

The overall programme was given the name Project BOAS, which would be segmented as follows:

Project BOAS: Acquisition of 155mm artillery systems

FOREIGN ACQUISITION	LOCAL ACQUISITION
PROJECT SHERBET I Acquisition of G3 guns	**PROJECT STARLIGHT** Industrialization and production of G5 guns
PROJECT SHERBET II Acquisition of 155mm M57 projectiles and M11 charges	**PROJECT GHOST** Development of charges by SRC and Somchem
PROJECT SHERBET III Development of G5 guns	**PROJECT ACTION** • Development of white phosphorus projectiles by SRC and Naschem • Development of illumination and smoke projectiles by SRC and Swartklip
PROJECT BURROW Procurement of G4 guns and ammunition	**PROJECT CABBAGE** Acquisition of gun tractors
PROJECT FACTOR Development of proximity fuses	**PROJECT OLIM** Industrialization and production of charge M10 and M11 by Somchem
PROJECT GALLOWS Development of charge M10	**PROJECT GONG** Industrialization and production of M57 projectiles by Naschem

PROJECT BULB Acquisition of test equipment **PROJECT DÉCOR** Development of M82 percussion tube **PROJECT BUZZARD** Development of self-propelled artillery system (G6) and the base bleed projectile	**PROJECT PDM 572** Production of PDM 572 fuses (point detonating) **PROJECT ZENULA** Development and production of G6 systems by LIW

The 155mm G3

One of the spin-offs from the G5 project was that the Space Research Corporation had acquired a number of US 155mm Long Tom howitzers for development and testing purposes. Armscor needed 155mm ordnance to test their new ammunition, and the gunners needed equipment to bridge the gap in the interim. Therefore, six of these were bought from SRC and shipped to South Africa. To the South African Artillery these enormous monstrosities were the 'new generation', despite the fact they were World War II vintage. What they did have was the 'new' 155mm calibre and a far longer range than anything the gunners had seen before. Two guns were used as test devices by Armscor and kept at the Schmidtsdrif Test Range, where the early testing was carried out, and four were delivered to 4 Field Regiment for operational use and named the G3. The first live firing of these guns occurred on 8 November 1976 on the firing range in Potchefstroom. These guns, however, were never to see action and were eventually disposed of. One example stands at the School of Artillery.

SRC had a friendly relationship with Dr Bird, the prime minister of Antigua, a tiny island in the eastern Caribbean to the north of Venezuela. Here, the firing trials would take place out of sight of enquiring eyes until international politics changed that arrangement.

Piet Olivier, the Armscor programme manager for the project, relates how test firing took place in Antigua:

The firing range was over the sea, but, unfortunately, it was on the flight path of aircraft approaching and leaving Antigua as well as over the route used by shipping and even fishing boats and luxury yachts. Firing would be held up regularly while we waited for clearance to continue.

Of interest is that the vertex height (apogee) of a GC-45/G5 projectile at full charge and maximum elevation is in the order of 57,000 feet (17,300 metres)—somewhat higher than that of commercial jet aircraft.

Contracting between the parties was, despite the high risks, seemingly casual by international standards, but Armscor had covered themselves by ensuring that payment would only be made after delivery. So the stage was set for the biggest acquisition programme in South Africa for years to come.

One of the considerations that the South African gunners gave was for both 155mm and 175mm equipment, the 175mm intended to provide the 40,000 metre range. During development this requirement was set aside, because it was realized that the 155mm, 45-calibre gun would produce the same result.

To the northwest of Kimberley in the Northern Cape province lies a stretch of land called Schmidtsdrif, which is typical Northern Cape semi-desert, gently undulating and covered with scrub. This was the site selected by Armscor and the SADF to establish the firing range needed to test the developing gun. Although it had the length of 60 kilometres specified for the tests and was uninhabited, this forlorn piece of real estate had one interesting feature—the main tarred road from Kimberley to Douglas ran almost through the middle. Although this was not an insurmountable problem, it did mean that firing had to be rigidly controlled, as the Douglas road would have to be closed to traffic during firing.

In the early days of test firing there was nothing in the way of permanent facilities at Schmidtsdrif, and the test and calibration equipment had to be transported by road from Pretoria for every shoot. This resulted in the sensitive equipment being damaged in transit and having to be repaired before each test firing.

As the development progressed, the engineers built different forms of prototype guns for the various tests. One of the early models was a G5 barrel fitted to a G3 cradle and trail. After a day of firing this 'assembly' developed major cracks and the technical support team spent the entire night welding and patching so it would be ready for the next day's firing. This occurred not once, but on numerous subsequent shoots until the new G5 cradle and trail were designed and available for testing.

It should be noted that until this point no other Western country had fired a 155mm gun on such a high charge so no data was available to give the designers guidance as to the stresses imparted by this tremendous recoiling mass. Later, the G6 would suffer the same problems, but for different reasons.

This development occupied the workforce of no fewer than 24 different organizations, from the SADF, as the customer, and Armscor, to the contracted companies developing the new charges, projectiles, fuses, sights and all the associated equipment that the new gun would eventually need to deploy on operations.

The sighting system was based on the British No. 9 Dial Sight rather than the US sight simply because the older guns were British and sights could be adapted more quickly and cheaply than having to produce an entirely new system. Furthermore, the gunners would not have to be trained on a new system and neither would the technical assistants who had to calculate the gun data for firing. All that was changed was the sighting scales (the main and top scales); these were to be graduated in millimetres rather than in degrees and minutes.

Until such time as the South African industry was able to manufacture, or indeed, build prototypes, all the parts and equipment had to be shipped in from various places in the world. The harbour of St Johns in New Brunswick, Canada, became the main 'export' hub for this clandestine supply chain, and from here the initial 55,792 M57 projectiles, 16,605 charge M11, gun barrels and other parts were loaded onto Safmarine ships bound for Antigua. One such ship was the SAS *Tugelaland*, a South African ship registered in New York. The *Tugelaland* left St Johns and some time later berthed at Antigua, where she unloaded some of her cargo. Immediately after unloading, she diverted to Cape Town where she unloaded the rest of her contraband. To maintain security, it was arranged that SRC would paint all the parts or assemblies in yellow and mark them as 'agricultural equipment'—after all, what self-respecting customs official knows the difference between an elevating gear and a harvester gearbox? Or so they thought. For some time, things went more or less according to plan and shipments became regular and uninterrupted, until one fine day in Antigua when the captain of the *Tugelaland* was overheard by a dockworker saying that he was bound for South Africa. The consequent embarrassment to the Antiguan government caused a complete rethink as to what route would be used in the future as well as the urgency to establish an infrastructure in South Africa. From then on, all testing would be done at Schmidtsdrif.

This security breach resulted in talks being reopened with the Israelis. An arrangement could not be made despite the relations between Israel and South Africa and an alternative had to be found. The Armscor team managed to secure a 20-minute interview with King Juan Carlos of Spain, in which his majesty agreed to allow shipments to pass via Spain, with the proviso that Armscor help develop the fledgling Spanish arms industry. This was the birth of the Santa Barbara company, which now manufactures a 155mm 45-calibre howitzer bearing a remarkable resemblance to its South African parent. For reasons best known to the army, new South African equipment had to have animal names. Hence the Ratel (honey badger); Eland armoured car (an eland is a buck) and, in the case of G5 the Luiperd (leopard). Despite all efforts, the gunners (or anyone else, for that matter) never used this nomenclature, but stuck to the name G5. The defence business internationally is a small world and manufacturers find out quickly who has new products and who is selling to whom. Despite South Africa's isolation and the fact that their defence business was a relative newcomer, word quickly spread that development work was underway, particularly in the artillery field. This news came to the ears of the Hellenic Armed Forces and initial negotiations started. The Greek government invited Armscor to exhibit the G5 at the Defendory Weapons Exhibition in October 1981. Under difficult conditions, mainly security-related, Armscor set up their display stand and the new G5 gun was announced by Chris Venter, at that time the Director Artillery. To say that the sh*t hit the fan is probably an understatement. Within hours, the South Africans were asked to be off the show premises by daybreak the next day. A hasty withdrawal ensued and by the next morning there was not a sign of the G5 or any other South African presence. Needless to say, the international media had something to report on for weeks afterwards.

The opposite, however, happened in another part of the world. Iraq, already embroiled in its war with Iran, needed better artillery firepower in their efforts to move the Iranians back off their border. Through Dr Bull of the SRC they made contact with Armscor. Negotiations commenced and led to the sale of some 200 guns to the Iraqis. Iraqi artillery officers spent a lot of time at LIW and Armscor providing inputs and requirements for the development of the FF551 towed howitzer. Why FF551? The need for security prevailed and the name G5 could not be used. The Iraqis required so many changes to the original design that the final product bore very little resemblance to the original South African pre-production model. Therefore, someone at LIW came up with the name 'Farouk Ferrari 551'—the name stuck. Happily, these requirements came before the South African guns were to go into production and most of the Iraqi-inspired changes were applied to the G5. Examples included a bigger diesel engine—this was changed from a two- to a four-cylinder Deutz engine that would power the whole system, and the addition of a driver's seat—the G5 can be driven over short distances into its gun platform before going into action and the Iraqis wanted the driver to sit for this task.

The first three G5s were handed over to Captain I.R. Johnson of 142 Battery on 21 May 1982 and the first course for gun crews began on 24 May. Because there were only three guns available, and curiosity about this new gun had got the better of everyone outside of the artillery, on the day that training started, one G5 was dispatched under the command of Lieutenant Danie Crowther to Army Battle School for an exhibition and demonstration.

In 1983, four gunners clandestinely flew to Iraq to train the artillery instructors on their new FF551: Commandant Danie de Villiers, Captain

John Alcock and WOI Albert Hook, under the command of Commandant Jakes Jacobs. Training took place just outside Baghdad and the gunners were housed in luxury on an island in the Euphrates River.

Being SADF property, the Schmidtsdrif Firing Range was also used as a general training area, and at about that time, 10 Anti-Aircraft Regiment and the School of Anti-Aircraft were being moved from Cape Town to Kimberley. Other units were also moving to this centre and the army was using the range for the training of divisions and brigades in river-crossing operations (Schmidtsdrif borders on the Orange River and this was used to full effect to create realism during bridge building and river crossing). So Armscor had to find a more suitable place to establish a permanent test range.

In the middle of the Northern Cape on another remote, sparsely populated plateau stood the mining village of Copperton. The copper market had shrunk and the copper mine was rapidly reducing its output and retrenching its staff. Just to the west of this village lay a relatively flat, bleak, uninhabited area of semi-desert. This 60 by 15 kilometre strip of land was to become the new Alkantpan Test Range. Armscor acquired the property in 1987 and immediately set about building a suitable infrastructure for test firing. This included surveyed observation towers, laboratories, ovens for pre-heating ammunition and a control centre. The village of Copperton would become the domestic area and would include a guesthouse for visiting teams.

Testing the new gun did not always run smoothly, especially when testing the high charges. Such testing includes pre-heating charges in specially designed ovens to bring them up to as much as 60° C. Loading a hot charge into an already hot chamber can lead to catastrophic situations. On more than one occasion a gun 'cooked off' and the barrel exploded before firing. Fortunately, though, because of sound safety procedures and well-built shelters, no one was ever injured or killed.

World first: 39 kilometres is reached

Finally the day came when a test gun was brought into action, loaded with an M57 base bleed projectile and charge 3 (previously M11). The round landed 39,600 metres from the gun position, and South Africa went into the record books. They now had achieved the longest range from a 155mm gun. However, this range was achieved at an altitude of about 2,500 feet above sea level, so the standard sea-level maximum range in the firing tables is actually 37,400 metres.

While the main equipment was being developed, the build-up of the logistic support package followed at a similar pace. Once again, this practice was new to the South African defence industry and new disciplines, such as logistic support analysis, concurrent engineering and integrated logistics support began to influence the daily lives of the engineers and gunners alike.

Q Battery, 4 SAI Battalion Group, were the first operational fire unit to take delivery of the G5 in October 1985, and Major George Swanepoel was the first battery commander to take it into action, during Operation Alpha Centauri (see Chapter 9).

The G6 was only delivered after the ceasefire and South African production models have never been used on operations.

Project Furrow

The massive firepower of the multiple rocket launcher was already appreciated before the first contact in Angola, and in 1974 Project Furrow was authorized to commence. Furrow was mandated to develop a multiple rocket launcher for the South African Artillery. This system would be deployed to deliver artillery strikes on soft targets—ideal against logistic points or convoys, airfields, concentrations of troops in open trenches or even in the open. In the absence of a missile development capability in South Africa, the CSIR was initially contracted to perform the research and development to satisfy the SADF's requirements. Shortly afterwards, it was realized that further development and later production would need to be undertaken, and the CSIR was neither mandated nor geared to perform such work. This gave rise to the establishment of Kentron, an Armscor affiliate, with facilities in Pretoria and Somerset West in the Western Cape. Kentron was to manufacture and integrate the new systems.

The gunners wanted a system that would be transportable by air in a C-130, have excellent cross-country performance, and could be reasonably concealed among other similar vehicles. This led to the selection of the Mercedes Benz Unimog 416, 2-tonne chassis as the basis for the launcher vehicle. Being a light vehicle, the 'Mog' would have to be stabilized during the firing and this was solved by the addition of two hydraulic trails at the rear of the vehicle. The tube pack was designed and built with 24 tubes, coupled to a hydraulically powered traversing and elevating system and equipped with a standard dial sight as fitted to the G5. The crew cab was fitted with a steel canopy to protect the crew from blast and the electrical firing unit from the environment. This little package had few limitations; the only one of note was the limitation to top-traverse.

The scientists quickly found an answer to the problem of selecting a rocket that could fit the requirements for range and cargo / warhead-carrying ability. Kentron had already developed the V3 air-to-air missile for the Mirage F1CZ. This was a 127mm calibre which, with relatively minor modifications, could be used successfully. The warhead contained 6,400 steel balls cast in a resin sleeve (to save weight) and filled with RDX TNT explosive. There were two fuses available: a direct action and a proximity fuse. During operations the proximity fuse was the most effective, and very few DA fuses were ever used. The body of the rocket that houses the motor was originally an extruded aluminium tube specially treated against the heat build-up from the rocket motor. During testing, however, it was found that the rockets became unstable during flight and, therefore, caused an unacceptable dispersion at the target area, together with safety risks. To overcome this problem, extrusion was dispensed with in favour of a more sophisticated casting process that guaranteed a consistent wall thickness and consequent improved balance and stability. This was to become the new method of manufacturing rocket bodies.

The MRL was manned by a detachment of two. The no. 1 was the detachment commander, the no. 3 the layer and driver. Each launcher would be supported by a Samil 50, a 5-tonne ammunition vehicle that could carry 48 rockets and fuses. Such was the nature of the war that the Samil 50 was never used in combat: being a 4x4 vehicle, it could not keep up the pace. Samil 100 (10-tonne) cargo vehicles were used instead, as they were 6x6 configuration and could carry 96 rockets and three crew to load the MRL. Somehow, someone in the media gave the new MRL the tag 'Vorster organ'—a name derived from the BM21 ('Stalin organ')—as many thought at the time that the FV1 was a copy of this ubiquitous Soviet weapon. Nothing could be further from the truth; there was no similarity between the two launchers. This name was never used in artillery circles.

Testing of the MRL was conducted at Swartklip, the anti-aircraft firing range some 6 kilometres along the coast to the west of Kentron South. Here, the navy was called in to help, as the target area was in False Bay where fishing boats plied their trade and leisure boats were aplenty. The St Lucia Test Range in the nature reserve in the north of the Natal province was the alternative to Swartklip and did not have the restrictions of the False Bay range. The first instructors' course was held in May 1979 at Kentron South. The group of gunners and technical people were to witness, for the first time, that mind-blowing, ear-splitting roar of a rocket being launched. In those days, the practice of systems engineering was almost unheard of in the SADF. This meant that the first course did not involve any formal instruction or lectures, but the students had to develop the operational doctrine for the new MRL system. The mix of students meant that a number of different issues could be addressed at the same time and so the group was split into a number of syndicates to set about writing the manuals. These groups were allocated as: tactics and deployment; gun drill; artillery technical (computation of firing data); and technical maintenance. This work would eventually be published formally as the doctrine, or battle handling, of the MRL system.

Project Dibula

Observing the development of artillery in other parts of the world, and in particular the Royal Artillery with its BATES system, the South African Artillery saw the need to modernize the process of fire prediction, or computation. In the 70s and early 80s, computers were something new and unfamiliar to most mortals. However, there was a definite need to improve accuracy and speed of calculation, thus project Dibula was born. The arms embargo and other trade sanctions imposed on South Africa at that time severely limited access to contemporary computers, and the desktop computer did not exist.

Project Dibula addressed the problem of automating the ballistic prediction, or computation, in the artillery. At that time, Kentron was equipped with advanced computers to calculate the external ballistics of the new rockets, and, once the artillery's requirement presented itself, a small group of engineers and mathematicians broke away and formed a private company, Teklogic (Pty) Ltd, the forerunner of today's African Defence Systems / Thales. Teklogic was duly contracted by Armscor to develop a stand-alone ballistic computer that could survive the rigours of the combat zone and improve the computing time and accuracy that the new artillery systems would need. The result was the AS80 fire-control computer, a ruggedized desktop machine powered by the 12-volt electrical systems of the fire-control posts. The AS80 was unique at that time, as it was the only Afrikaans-language computer in existence.

The problem was that the English-speaking gunner technical assistants had to adapt. This was to cause much merriment and a certain degree of frustration to all as the abominations of terminology and resultant delays in communication were felt by all concerned. The AS80 was eventually replaced by the AS2000 digital artillery command and control system. As has been mentioned earlier in this book, the artillery's accuracy and 'first-round hit' capability is heavily dependent on the ability to measure and compensate for meteorological conditions.

During the early 1970s, ballistic upper air conditions were measured by launching a meteorological balloon filled with hydrogen with a radio sonde attached. The sonde would send back temperature and air density readings as the balloon rose through the atmosphere. The balloon would be tracked by a theodolite and readings for azimuth and elevation would be taken (by hand) at regular intervals. These readings would provide wind speed and direction for input into the ballistic calculations. The Locating Battery would provide a 'met telegram' every two hours throughout the day. With the advent of the new systems this rather ponderous exercise was identified as a shortcoming in the artillery's capability for a number of reasons:

- Hydrogen cylinders are dangerous and difficult to replace in the operational area.
- The new guns fired much farther and consequently far higher than before; therefore, balloons would need to be tracked at higher altitudes, farther than could be seen through the telescope of a theodolite.
- Speed and accuracy of calculation needed to be improved.

The Cape Town-based company Diel Electronics, under the direction of Bernard Dieboldt, was contracted to provide the solution, and here the S70 'met set' was developed and manufactured. This new system was fitted into a wheeled container that could be towed by a 3-tonne truck. The antenna could automatically follow the radio sonde and a bank of Hewlett Packard computers provided the calculating capability. To alleviate the hydrogen problem, a hydrogen generator was developed that could be deployed in the B Echelon behind the combat zone.

Gun tractors: Samil 100

The introduction into service of the G4 and, to a limited extent, the G3 created yet another strategic and tactical problem—how to move this heavier equipment? The existing Magirus Deutz tractor was reaching the end of its life cycle and, in any event, was not powerful enough to pull the new equipment, especially in the SWA–Angolan operational area. Tractors assigned to G4s had to have their towing hooks modified to the right height, and the guns' barrels, in the travelling position, projected forward of the towing eye so they could not be towed without having to remove the tailgate of the gun tractor. The domino effect continued: with the tailgate removed less ammunition and equipment could be carried, and that which was carried habitually fell off on rough roads.

So the need for a new gun tractor was identified and, once again, Armscor looked around the world. Because of the arms embargo South Africa could not import complete vehicles, especially those that were obviously destined for military use. This gave birth to the local Samil (from South African military) family of vehicles, which were to perform sterling service for the next 30 or more years. There were three basic chassis variants: 2 tonnes (Samil 20), 5 tonnes (Samil 50) and 10 tonnes (Samil 100). All were powered by Deutz diesel air-cooled engines with from four to ten cylinders depending on the power requirements. Engine and chassis production was entirely local. The Samil 100 was also modified by replacing the soft-skinned cab with a mine-resistant armoured cab to protect the driver and vehicle commander. This variant was named the Kwêvoël (Grey loerie) and also served as a medium recovery vehicle, 10,000 litre diesel bunker, water bunker and general cargo carrier, among others.

The Samil 100 6x6 medium gun tractor was specially designed for the G5 and was fitted with a well-organized ammunition store and a crane for lifting the projectile pallets (four projectiles) on and off the tractor. The crew compartment had sufficient space for six crew members (the gun no. 1 was stationed with the driver, and one ammunition number was stationed at the rear of the tractor as an anti-aircraft sentry and to keep an eye on the gun behind). A 12.7mm (.50 cal.) H2 Browning machine gun was fitted on a ring to the crew compartment roof for local protection. As lessons were learned on operations and training these vehicles were modified, particularly in the area of bush protection. These vehicles were introduced into service in 1980 and proved themselves repeatedly on operations: there was very little that nature could throw in a Samil 100's way.

Project Zenula

Once development work on the G5 had got underway, the next task was to address the problem of self-propelled artillery. The artillery required a gun that could support the mechanized brigades and which would, therefore, need to be armour-protected, highly mobile, quick into and out of action and have the range and performance of the G5. This led to the launch of Project Zenula, the development and production of the G6.

Learning from the experience of Operation Savannah and from the South African Armoured Corps, it was decided early on to mount the gun on a wheeled hull rather than a tracked version. This would not only save initial costs, but the gun would not need to be transported to the combat zone because it could move under its own power on roads. Furthermore, the maintenance costs of wheeled vehicles are somewhat lower than those of their tracked brethren. The concept was put together over a weekend in a snowbound Canada by van der Westhuizen and an SRC engineer.

While in the USA on the G5 development phase, the Armscor engineers discussed the subject with their American and Canadian colleagues. The South African engineers were adamant that a vehicle that potentially weighed 35 tonnes could not be wheeled: there were just not any tyres that can take that weight! Not so, it turned out. Very close to SRC was a Canadian logging company that moved such loads on wheels on a daily basis. This group paid the logging company a visit and discovered, to their amazement, that it was possible. 'The only tyre that can cope with this load is a Michelin 21.00-25X. Get hold of Michelin and find out', was the reply from the logging company. A telephone call to Michelin set the development on its way.

Once the development of the G5 barrel and top structure was underway, more thought was given to G6's uniqueness and the characteristics of self-propelled (SP) artillery. In this design, the new SP gun would be turreted and, therefore, the barrel's recoil would need to be shorter than that of the G5. Furthermore the fumes that would pour out of the breech would need to be reduced. In order to speed up deployment time the sighting system would have to be drastically changed. The new SP gun would need to carry its emergency ammunition and that ammunition would need to be readily available. Having made the decision to commit to a wheeled vehicle, the gun would need to be stabilized somehow.

In 1980, an experimental development model was shown to curious onlookers just outside 14 Field Regiment's lines. That turretless model was fitted with a set of weights where the turret would eventually fit and the stabilization was by means of two vertical hydraulic cylinders and flat base plates. The general shape of the hull was, by and large, similar to the final production model. To the layman, the G6 is essentially a G5 on an SP hull. It shares the same ammunition as the G5 and its ballistics are exactly the same as that of the G5. The development of the G6 was not without its particular problems, the most significant being the rear differentials and the recoil system. During road tests it was found that the centre axle had a habit of overheating and seizing. Improved ventilation and stronger material eventually solved that failing. The recoil system could not be identical to that of the G5 because of the limitations imposed by the turret size on the recoil length. The most serious problem was the reliability of the recoil system during sustained firing in very hot conditions. The system would overheat and destroy the oil in the recuperator thus preventing the gun from fully running up (returning to the firing position). To solve this recoil problem a new recoil system had to be designed. Probably the most difficult of the design problems that the engineers had to deal with, this took until 1991 to solve. One of the modifications was the addition of a cooling fan fitted externally that would be powered by the auxiliary power unit.

The original sight unit intended for the G6 was a long-necked dial sight used on the US 155mm M 109. However, this sight had no commonality with the G5 or the MRL sight and, being manually operated, made deployment a lengthy process. The answer was found in a gyro sighting and navigation system. Once the gun sight had been calibrated, the co-ordinates of the next firing position were typed in and the gun could navigate itself. On arrival at the gun platform, the centre of arc bearing was given by radio to the crew, entered into the gyro sight and the turret was simply 'steered' into that bearing. GPS was added later.

Each G6 carried its own emergency ammunition, 64 complete rounds stored in the nose of the vehicle and in a fireproof store at the rear of the crew compartment in the hull. First-line ammunition was carried on a Samil 100 ammunition vehicle and would be dumped behind the gun when in action. This ammunition was pushed through from outside along a trough, or chute, by the two ammunition numbers outside. The problem of stabilization of the 42-tonne gun in action was overcome by two sets of trail legs, one set behind the front wheels and one set at the rear, all powered by the hydraulic system from the driver's compartment. The turret was electrically driven, as was the elevating system, precluding the use of hand wheels for laying the gun. An auxiliary power system was fitted to the turret bustle and provided electrical power when the main engine was switched off. To make driving easier, particularly during rough conditions, the G6 was fitted with an automatic gearbox with six forward gears and two reverse, as well as electrical selection of differential, and longitudinal transmission locks in high and low range. All of this meant that this gun could be brought into action and ready to fire within one minute.

Project Hibiscus

Along with the guns and rocket launchers under development there was also a requirement for a longer-range, accurate, high-yield artillery system. This gave rise to Project Hibiscus—the development of a surface-to-surface missile with a 300-kilometre range capable of delivering either a conventional or nuclear warhead. The project integrated an Israeli missile, which was tested at the new Overberg Test Range on the Cape south coast. At the same time, the SAAF was developing a 'smart bomb' to be launched and guided by a Buccaneer, and it was determined that the subsequent H2 bomb was more feasible than a missile system and the whole project was subsequently terminated. Not all efforts were wasted though, as Hibiscus at least contributed to the development of a prototype heavy transporter vehicle nicknamed the MLZN (*Moerse Lorrie Zonder Naam*—'huge lorry without name'). This vehicle served as the basis for a G6 ammunition vehicle as it shared a number of parts (engine, transmission, axles and wheels). Like the G6, its cargo capacity was 15 tonnes and it was fitted with a crane to load and unload cargo. Like its forerunner, it never saw service in the South African Army.

Project Gharra

At the time of the development of the gun and launcher systems, the artillery realized that the days of manned air-OPO aircraft were numbered. FAPLA was introducing more and more sophisticated AA systems, and aircraft were being forced to fly either at very high altitudes or at treetop height, neither being suitable for manned artillery air observation. Operation Savannah brought attention to the problem of long distances from observers to targets. An observer needs to see detail in order to determine the type and amount of fire to deliver to the target. In 1977, an Israeli officer was sent to the School of Artillery to attend a meteorological course. Here he showed Major Faan Bothma and Lieutenant Roelf Louw a collection of brochures containing the latest Israeli military developments—one of which was an 'unmanned reconnaissance aircraft'. Once this information had been seen by the gunners, Major Bothma developed an operational requirement, based on the Israeli information, for such a system. The differences, however, were that the South African requirement was for an aircraft that would only fly out to a range of 60 kilometres, but that could loiter over the target area for a longer period. Furthermore, the gunners required a smaller aircraft that would not need a runway from which to operate and would have the optical capability and associated software that would assist with target acquisition and engagement.

Colonel Paul Lombard, the commander of the School of Artillery (and, at that time, the Director Artillery) handed in the requirement to Army HQ for further action. Together with army intelligence, the gunners embarked on the development of a medium-range remotely piloted vehicle (RPV) system. In this text the more modern term 'unmanned aerial vehicle' (UAV) is used.

Armscor's subsidiary, Kentron, was the only company that was able to undertake such an endeavour at that time, and was consequently contracted. The arms embargo by then influenced all acquisition and development activities, and the South Africans had to turn to a friendly country for help. Armscor made contact with Israel Aircraft Industries, a company which was not only willing to provide assistance, but also arguably the forerunner in UAV development at that time. The first airframes were Israeli-designed, but as time progressed, a South African-modified design was used. Given that the new UAV would be operating within or even alongside artillery and tactical intelligence units, it would be expected that it would be rugged and capable of deploying in unprepared terrain. Unfortunately, this was not the case and the eventual Seeker UAV system would be reliant on reasonably flat runways with at least 100 metres of take-off.

During the development phase of the project, Captain Sarel Buijs of 14 Field Regiment and a number of short-service officers were detached to the project to provide the necessary users' input. The project team had been tasked with testing the system by flying a reconnaissance mission over Maputo, Mozambique, and here the first operational casualty (a pre-production model) was suffered when the UAV was shot down.

Given the physical growth and complexity of this system, the new Director Artillery, Colonel Joffel van der Westhuizen, made a decision to terminate the gunners' involvement on the project because it was realized that the artillery did not have the ability to sustain such a system. Therefore, Project Gharra was now an army intelligence project—but not for long.

There had always been rivalry between the army and the SAAF, and this came to the fore once again when the SAAF was arguing for the ownership and control of the new UAV system. At that time, the SAAF was concerned with air traffic control in the combat zone and felt that such control should be centralized under the Mobile Air Operations Team (MAOT), a SAAF team deployed with the battle groups or brigades. The SAAF even insisted that the pilot of the UAV should be a qualified SAAF pilot. This lobbying was topped off by Brigadier Dick Lord of the SAAF, who opined that 'if the good Lord had intended the army to fly, he would have painted the sky brown'.

Another operational requirement was developed in July 1986—to the outsider a seemingly irrelevant need—this time for a fire-control officer's checking instrument. Until that time, safety on the firing range was the responsibility of a dedicated, appointed safety officer whose only job was that of checking safety. A combination of a lack of sufficient personnel and the decision to spread the responsibility across the entire fire unit generated the requirement for this particular equipment. Fire-control officers used to make up their own safety templates out of any material that they could find, and scales were not always the same. To reduce this risk the artillery came up with a requirement for a Perspex or plastic template that provided the safety distances, ricochet traces and minimum and maximum ranges for all ordnance on the corps at that time. The result was a factory-made 1:50,000 and 1:100,000 scale that could be easily carried, stored and used by all involved in the business of artillery fire control.

Project Ignite

Ignite was initiated in February 1987 to address the serious shortcoming in the ability to fix targets. It was not a major project, but did nevertheless produce a useful observation aid. In short, it was a laser range finder mounted on a rotating bezel to provide a bearing (azimuth), the whole of which was mounted on an adapter plate and fitted to the outside of a Ratel turret. This and a number of other projects devoted to upgrading already developed systems, such as the fire-control computer, sound ranging systems and meteorological systems, were later amalgamated into one. To this was added the development of a new observation capability (manpack, vehicle-based and UAV), gun-control computers and the 'digitization' of the artillery regiment. This project, however, only started after the period covered by this book. In summary, the development of the new-generation equipment was typically South African pioneering work, and the speed of both the development of the equipment itself and of the industrial infrastructure set new world records, some of which remain to this day.

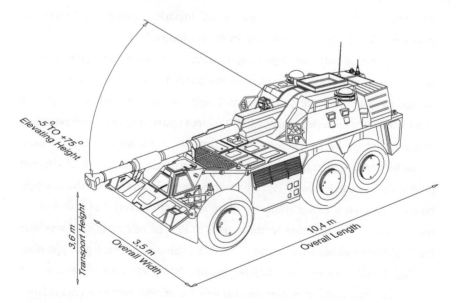

Project Zenula: A technical illustration of the G6 Mk I with the overall dimensions.
Illustration: Denel Land Systems

Epilogue

Twenty-two years after the events one wonders about the value of all this effort. The South African Artillery started operations as a poor relative of the British Royal Artillery, with not only genetic tactics and equipment, but inherited traditions. In essence, there was nothing fundamentally wrong with any of these traits—the error lay in the lack of modernization, a result of the lack of funds allocated to beefing up the artillery's influence on the conventional battlefield.

War is a great leveller, it is said, and the expression 'what this army needs now is a war' held in those early days as much as it does for the modern South African National Defence Force of the 21st century. Soldiers become complacent in peacetime and despite all the best intentions, this complacency cascades down through all the levels, from command and control at the top levels to training, discipline and equipment maintenance at the lowest level.

The 13 years of war caused a fundamental change to the South African Artillery's doctrine, training, equipment, logistic support—and even its character. Strangely, little changed in its traditions.

The concept of batteries deploying in static positions for extended periods of time received a rude awakening on the battlefields of Ebo, Santa Comba, Bridge 14 and Quiramba. Regimental fire missions would no longer be conducted with batteries deployed 300 metres apart, and defensive positions would no longer be connected to each other by cable for communications. These battlefields dictated that OPOs would no longer arrive at their selected position in a vehicle, slowly set up their equipment and spend the daylight hours sitting on a camp chair. No more would OPOs retire at last light to the ritual of a mess dinner in the wagon lines. The reality of that war was the frightening experience of BM21 rockets exploding in your gun position; digging foxholes or trenches before you ate; being dirty for weeks on end despite the proximity of water; and infiltrating on foot between enemy lines with all the equipment you could carry and with no one to talk to in your own language.

The lack of modern means of delivering accurate, massive fire was identified by some forward thinkers before the commencement of hostilities, and was given a powerful boost after Operation Savannah showed the potential of the artillery to influence the battle. Under severe international embargo, the gunners, together with their civilian counterparts in the almost non-existent defence industry, rallied to develop some of the most modern and sought-after ordnance in the world. This effort took less than ten years—a record by any measure.

The operations around Xangongo, Cahama, Ongiva and Evale brought the gunners into contact with the new operational concepts of mechanized warfare and fast-moving, rapidly changing pace of advance, attack and outflank. Here they had to reconsider their communications as a means of command and control. Here they had to deploy far earlier than other forces and move faster than ever before. They had to acclimatize to new vehicles, such as the Ratel Command, and perform observation over flat terrain from the turrets of their vehicles or from the right-hand seat of an aircraft. More emphasis was placed on night occupations and radio silence during deployment, and movement became the drill.

All the lessons learned thus far were put into practice in training, especially when units were in their final stages of training at the Army Battle School. There, the troops learned passive anti-aircraft measures, what to do when an enemy aircraft warning went out —this was practised while both on the move and in firing positions. Long-distance night moves were practised without radios or lights. Emphasis was placed on alternative positions and their occupation as quickly as possible. And of course, the troops were given a taste of working for long hours and even days without sleep.

By 1986, the development of the new systems had reached the point where they were being delivered to front-line units, and the CF units were either receiving troops already trained on this equipment or who were undergoing conversion courses. The CF units were by this time already earmarked for the allocation of new systems. For example, 18 Light Regiment was already equipped with 120mm M5 mortars and the supporting equipment for them to deploy by air drop or air assault, and 19 Rocket Regiment was ready for MRL operations.

The much-improved training and tactical deployment were put to the test on the operations in the eastern sector of Angola in 1986 through to 1988 and culminated in the final battle around Tchipa in June 1988.

By 1988, there was only one G1 fire unit deployed and the rest of the faithful guns were being phased out, a number of which were destined for museums or for deployment as gate guards. Some of those old guns still serve on ceremonial duties for salutes and military funerals.

This story will not be complete without a mention of, and a deep sense of gratitude to, the wives, mothers and sweethearts of the gunners who served in that period. The wives of the PF gunners also sat at home wondering when, if ever, they would see their men again; they spent countless months raising the next generation, managing the home finances, and helping build the morale of the troops who were in training or waiting to go 'to the border'. The ladies of the CF artillery regiments were, in some ways, worse off than their PF counterparts, as they were not as well informed about the situation or accustomed to that way of life. In particular, there were those who suffered financially, despite the moratorium on salaries and wages, when their men were dismissed from their regular employment while away on duty.

In those 13 years, the South African Artillery, despite its shortcomings, played a major role in the events that contributed to the peace and democracy that followed. The corps—and the men and women who served it—grew up, matured and took its place in the world of the 'black art' as one of the best artillery forces ever seen.

Select bibliography

10 Artillery Brigade: Lines Books 1983 to 1989

4 Artillery Regiment: Lines Books 1963 to 1989

14 Artillery Regiment: Lines Books 1974 to 1989

Bothma, Lt-Col H.G.S.: Personal notes

Cilliers, Lt-Col J.K.: Personal notes

De Jager, J.: Personal notes

De Villiers, Col D.J.: Personal notes

Dippenaar, Maj-Gen J.M.: Personal notes

Eckard, Lt-Col A.N.: Personal notes

Gillings, WOI K.G.: Personal notes

Heitman, Helmoed-Roemer: *War in Angola—The final Final South African Phase*. Ashanti. Gibralter. 1989

Hill, WOII C.: Personal notes

Holtzhausen, Col H.G.: Personal notes

Jacobs, Col J.G.: Personal notes

Johnson, Brig-Gen I.R.: Personal notes

Kruys, Brig-Gen G.: 'The Events at Ebo, Jan 2009', *Nuusbrief vir Militere Veterane*. 2009

Laubscher, Maj-Gen J.A.: Personal Notes & 'Operasie Savannah', Dagboek van Capt J.A. Laubscher; a publication prepared by Cmdt Sophia du Preez. 1986

Louw, Lt-Col F.J.: Personal notes

Lowes, Gnr M.: Personal notes

Mattushek, Bdr D.W.A.: Personal notes

McGimpsey, Maj R.G.: Personal notes

McKeen, M.: Personal notes

Monick, S.: *Where Destiny Leads—Transvaal Horse Artillery*

Nel, Col J.P.: Personal notes

Olivier, P.G.: Personal notes

Potgieter, Col J.H.: Personal notes

Steenkamp, Willem: *Borderstrike!* Butterworths. Durban. 1983

Swanepoel, Col G.H.F.: Personal notes

Trautmann, Lt-Col R.D.: Personal notes

Uys, Col P.D.: Personal notes

Uys, Ian: *Cross of Honour.* Uys Publishers. Germiston. 1992

van der Westhuizen, L.J. & Le Roux, J.H.: 'Armscor and the Birth of the G5 Artillery System', *Journal for Contemporary History.* University of the Orange Free State. 1997

van der Westhuizen, Lt-Gen C.P.: Personal notes

van Eeden, Lt-Col F.G.J.: Personal notes

van Heerden, Col J.J.: Personal notes

van Niekerk, Col H.: Personal notes

Wiid, Maj N.: Personal notes

Williams, Lt-Col P.S.: Personal notes

Wilsworth, Lt-Col C.S.: Personal notes

Zaayman, Lt O.: Personal notes

Zhdarkin, Igor: *We did not see it even in Afghanistan: Memoirs of a Participant of the Angolan War (1986–1988).* Memories Mockba. Moscow, 2008

Index